Never Leave on a Friday

Shirley J. Shepherd

This book is dedicated to my mother, Ruth (Witherell) Koch, who had unfailing faith in me. Her tenacity and determination, along with a little scolding, instilled perseverance in me that gave me staying power in more than a few difficult times. She believed I would someday write a book. Sorry it took so long, Mom.

Author's Note

The illustrations: For better or worse, I drew them. Some of the people who edited this book asked if I were going to include photographs. Unfortunately, most of the photos we took were degraded by time or by floating in a flooded cellar. I used to sketch a little, many years ago, so I decided to try to draw the pictures that were in my mind. As you will see, I'm not an artist, but I had fun doing them.

During this trip, I journaled constantly. Some scenes tickled me so much, I wrote them down within hours, or in some cases, within minutes. Thirty years later, with the help of my son Drew, I discovered a crate containing two three-ring binders, three spiral notebooks, two diaries, and several lined pads. My mother kept all the letters I wrote to her detailing our daily lives. I also found notes written on the backs of envelopes, receipts, and paper place mats. Dorin and Cory were aware I was writing down most of what they were saying and doing, so perhaps they were on their best behavior and were inspired to deliver a bunch of good one-liners.

In the thirty-plus years since we took our trip, I know many things have changed. I revisited a number of places by satellite photos and read other sailors' more recent accounts of the same areas. For instance, uninhabited islands now have hotels and casinos for tourists, which must be a boost to the local economy.

In 1988, the part of Prince Rupert Harbor in Dominica, where we had dropped anchor, appeared to be undeveloped. Or were we in the wrong place? We were the only boaters there. In photos from subsequent years, the harbor seemed to be teeming with cruisers and offered many things to do. However, Hurricanes Irma and María, in 2017, left horrific devastation in Dominica, Barbuda, the US and British Virgins, and Puerto Rico. These areas have not recovered, and my heart goes out to the wonderful, warm-hearted, and generous people who were so good to us.

In case you may wonder, I have changed the names of most, though not all, of the cruisers we met and the names of their boats. I did this to protect the innocent as well as the guilty. A few, though, are real names, such as *No Brass Ring* and the *Grace*.

You will notice we sailed with an astonishing lack of electronics, both for navigation and communication. That's because they hadn't been well developed yet and were not part of our daily lives. Hard to imagine, but we had to row ashore and find a public phone just to call home.

In an interview, the late Bruce Van Sant, author of *Passages South*, said when you sail against the trade winds from Florida to Venezuela and sail during the day..."you will be beaten to Hell." He recommended sailing each hop in the wee hours of the morning, perhaps at 4 a.m.

Too bad his funny and informative book was published in 1993, five years too late to save us from ourselves. I know Dorin would have treated Mr. Van Sant's book as a sailing bible. Certainly, our trip would have been much easier, but far less exciting and eventful, because there was a time or two when we were "beaten to Hell."

And so, I have a fun story to tell....

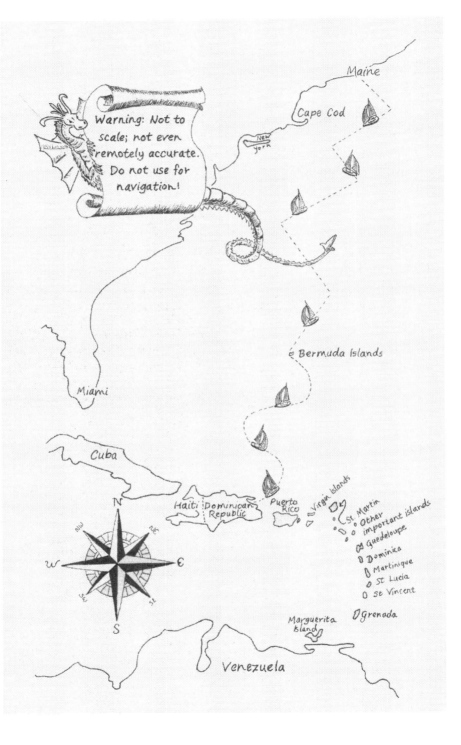

Map of the offshore attempt to get to Venezuela via Grenada, after which, without landfall, we turn around and hightail it back to Puerto Rico. We miss it by ~~a mile.~~ 70 miles...

A quick disclaimer: although this map may appear to be professionally rendered, it is not to scale and is not even a reasonable facsimile.

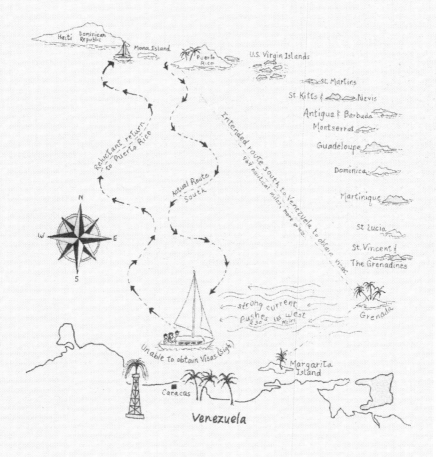

Haiti
Dominican Republic
Mona Island
Puerto Rico
U.S. Virgin Islands
St. Martins
St Kitts & Nevis
Antigua & Barbuda
Montserrat
Guadeloupe
Dominica
Martinique
St Lucia
St. Vincent & The Grenadines
Grenada

Reluctant return to Puerto Rico

Intended route south to Venezuela to obtain visas. 467 nautical miles, more or less.

Actual Route South

N
W   E
S

strong current pushes us west 230 miles

Unable to obtain Visas (Sigh)

Margarita Island

Caracas

Venezuela

Prologue

With butterflies in my stomach, I study the blackening sky.

"It may get a little rough for a few minutes," Dorin says as he and Cory come back to the cockpit. "How fast are we moving?"

"Six knots," replies Cory, glancing at the knot log.

The *Fandango's* maximum speed is six-and-a-half knots.

"Six?" Dorin frowns. "How much heel?"

"Fifteen degrees," I reply.

"Hmm. We may have to reduce sail a little more."

"Seven knots now," says Cory.

"Twenty degrees heel," I add as we lurch again.

White caps spit from the tops of three-foot waves. Rain begins to tattoo the boat.

"Okay," Dorin says. "Let's put another reef in. Shirl, you'll have to turn the boat into the wind." Hanging onto the lifelines, they go forward.

Historically, in winds over ten knots, this is not my best scene. True to form I turn the boat too far. "Look out!" I yell as the boom sweeps across with a bang. Now the stays'l is back winded, and the flapping main sounds like gunfire.

"Let her come around," Dorin yells.

In years past, I almost knocked him off the boat on three similar occasions, one time, twice in two minutes. Each time, in my horrified confusion, I forgot which way to turn to "bring her around."

Panicking, now, I pull the tiller toward me. When nothing happens, I rapidly push it away.

"Wrong way!" Cory and Dorin yell. But...which *way* is the wrong way?

Cory sprints toward me along the slick deck. He grabs the tiller, and the boat comes around. Dorin finishes reefing the flogging sail as the rain comes down in sheets.

Cory darts into the cabin and comes out a few seconds later with foul-weather jackets and safety harnesses. Struggling against a lurching boat, we pull on and fasten the gear.

White-tipped waves, now six feet high, smash into the lurching *Fandango*, throwing spray across the cabin top. I look at the inclinometer, and my stomach sinks. Twenty degrees.

A gust slams us. Thirty.

Something crashes to the floor of the cabin.

"Damn! The wind is still building," Dorin shouts. "We have to reef again. We have to reef the stays'l, too. I need your help, Cor."

No! The thought of both of them on the slippery deck with the wind screaming, while the boat drops out from under their feet every few seconds, terrifies me.

I look at the straining sails and the inclinometer. Thirty degrees. If we don't reduce sail now, we risk a knockdown.

Dorin catches sight of my face. "We have to. You have to bring it into the wind again."

"No. I can't. I'll knock you off. I can't do it."

"Yes, you can. We'll be okay. Let's go, Cor."

Cory and Dorin snap their safety harness tethers to the lifeline and grab the handrails as, crouching, they step out on deck, planting their feet in the angle between the toe rail and the deck. A wave crashes over the bow, and they're up to their ankles in foam.

As they near the mast, the boat slips sideways and down off a wave. Over the roar of the wind, Dorin yells something to Cory. I hold my breath while Cory unhitches his harness from the lifeline and, climbing up onto the cabin, refastens it to the mast.

A huge wave slams us, and the deck drops out from under their feet. I grit my teeth and force down a scream.

Chapter One
Departure

In 1987, before cell phones and before the blessings of GPS navigation, and way before radar could track storms, many people had successfully sailed on long voyages.

My significant other, Dorin, my 16-year-old son, Cory, and I had been planning an around-the-world trip on Dorin's 32-foot yacht, the *Fandango*, for more than three years. We had read a lot about the cruising life, we had a few years of sailing experience, mostly summers, and, Dorin, on his sabbatical from his teaching job, had made one trip down the intracoastal waterway and on to the Bahamas seven years before. We thought we were informed, knowledgeable and well prepared.

We spent the three summers leading up to the trip making major changes on the boat which were to accomplish two goals: to make the boat safer in offshore heavy weather and to keep it dry inside. Before the end of the trip, we were satisfied we had accomplished one of the two goals...because the boat was never dry.

Friends, family, and acquaintances asked about the dangers involved in such a long offshore voyage. We had gone through our own period of anxiety, the three of us discussing all of the known mishaps of offshore travel in small boats – hurricanes in the Atlantic, typhoons in the Pacific, partially submerged, floating containers (huge storage containers that sometimes fall off ships) anywhere, and modern day pirates within 100 miles of any land. The discussion of pirates included Dorin having to convince me there really are pirates in the Caribbean who prey on small boats.

Each night, after working all day on the *Fandango*, we read to each other from Seven Seas Cruising Association (SSCA) bulletins--stories of disasters that have befallen other cruising boaters at sea around the world. We discussed for hours the measures we would take to decrease the jeopardy. But then, by some unspoken agreement, we stopped talking about it – maybe stopped thinking about it. If anyone asked questions about the danger, we cracked a joke and changed the subject.

Realistically, we didn't expect any problems in the Atlantic this time of year. It would be a milk-run that allowed us to get our feet wet (not literally, of course) and give us some practice before taking on the rigors of the Pacific. I don't mind saying up front, we never made it to the Pacific.

After the final thirteen days of sprinting to prepare the *Fandango* for our trip--thirteen hectic days marked by multiple fast food meals and very few showers--Wednesday, July 10th arrives. Finally, this is the day we will begin our long-awaited adventure. Friends and family gather on the dock to say goodbye on this fresh, glorious, sunny morning. We are two months past our original departure date, and tension is high for Dorin and me. To get through the Atlantic before the hurricane season, to navigate the Panama Canal, and on into the South Pacific before typhoon season, we should have left two months ago, but here we are. We have not yet decided how we will handle this situation or what adjustments we might make.

People continue to arrive, and I wonder how they all manage to find us in this little, out-of-the-way port tucked thirteen miles up the Damariscotta River, in East Boothbay, Maine. A festive, party atmosphere has developed which chases away our fatigue. We're truly happy to see so many people who want to wish us well and see us on our way.

Still, Dorin and I have very mixed feelings about today's farewell gathering.

As we frantically worked on the boat over the past six months, we fantasized, each without the other's knowing it, of a romantic departure without fanfare: of working steadily on the boat until that magic moment when we realize there's nothing left to do. Then, on a dewy morning, we step onto the *Fandango*, untie the lines, and quietly slip out of the harbor. The early morning risers who come to watch the wisps of fog lift from the sea assume we are going for a day sail. Only we know a year will pass before we return.

We agreed it would be fun and satisfying to have a low-key departure with complete anonymity.

The daydream was threatened when a newspaper reporter called to say she wanted to cover the story of our trip, including the departure.

"But I don't want to be pinned down to a specific day and hour," Dorin said when I told him about the phone call. "You never know how many delays we are going to have. Besides, I don't want this to be a circus. I'd like to just slip away when we are ready with no one around who knows about the trip."

On the other hand, there were friends and family we hadn't been able to see while we focused all our time on preparations, and we wanted to say goodbye. My oldest son, Bill, his wife, Tina, and my parents intended to be present whether we wanted a farewell gathering or not.

Another fantasy also flitted around the corners of my mind as I had sweated in fiberglass resin and acetone fumes. Several years ago, before it ever occurred to me that I might sail away into the sunrise, a friend waved goodbye to me and other well-wishers gathered on the dock for a "champagne send off." Now it was I who would be sailing away, and this time I would wave from the deck instead of the dock.

After a lot of vacillating, we decided to have the group farewell. Throughout the last few months, while I retreated to the boatyard to work on the *Fandango*, Bill had handled countless and often unpleasant business details for me. With all I'd put him through, I couldn't help wondering if he was there to make sure I really was leaving.

"Hey, I've never seen your boat before," says Diane, a colleague of Dorin's, as she arrives. "Got time to give me a quick tour?"

I am not enthusiastic about this. The outside of the *Fandango* gleams and sparkles like a magazine ad. Inside it's crammed, chockablock full of stuff that has no stowage place. And besides, how do you give a "tour" of 18 feet of living space? The *Fandango* is technically 32-feet-long from stem to stern, but that is the length of the deck, not the space inside.

"I've seen bigger army cots," Diane says, as she leans in for a look at the tiny V-berth in the fo'c'sle of our sailboat. It is the bed that Dorin and I will be sharing in the coming year. It is piled with pillows, sleeping bags, books, a box of groceries, an extra sail and a guitar.

The only other thing I can think of to show her is the head. I wait for her to say, "I've seen bigger telephone booths," but she doesn't. Instead, she asks to use it. Our worst dread for today has been that someone would ask to use the bathroom. The head leaks furiously when you flush it, and we haven't fixed it yet.

As Diane leaves the boat, Bill swings onto the deck carrying his year-and-a-half-old daughter, Casey, in one arm, a pad of paper under the other and a pencil in his teeth.

He knows I'll ask him to take care of a few more loose ends for us: "Can you order this navigation software, and have it mailed to us in Panama? See if you can locate a Nicopress tool somewhere in one of these catalogs and have it shipped to Panama – unless it will take longer than three weeks. In that case, ship it to the Galapagos. Here's the address. This is Dorin's Visa number. Here's a signature card so you can handle Dorin's checking account. Can you leave this message off at the college? Send the check to the phone company? Pay this bill?" Bill listens, nods, asks questions, and makes notes. If he minds, he doesn't show it.

For the past two months, he's been our communication link with the rest of the world. This, of course, put him in the position of explaining to mutual acquaintances, "No, they haven't left yet." In our original plan, we'd leave by May 15th, at the latest, which we'd told everyone, including

Cory's high school. Because of this, they'd let him out early. It soon became clear that we wouldn't make that date, so when the local newspaper did a story, we gave them a new date – definitely May 25th. Memorial Day came and went, and we still worked day and night on the boat. A neighbor planted his garden, and before the boat mover arrived to haul us to the coast, the corn was knee high.

By the first week in June people said to Bill, "Hey, I saw your mother in Waterville the other day. I thought she left on a sailing trip." By the end of June, Bill avoided stopping in familiar places. In early July, he walked into his exercise club, where he hadn't been for weeks.

"Hey!" An old friend shouted from across the crowded room. "Where are they now?"

Bill groaned. "In Benton. In the boat yard." When Bill relayed this scene to me, he said, "I'm going to carry around a sign that says,

1. Not yet.

2. They are waiting for backordered supplies.

3. In about a week.

4. They can hardly wait."

Finally, as it became apparent we were really going on this trip, Bill contacted all the friends and relatives who wanted to be here today…twice. Once for July 8th, this past Monday, when we had been sure we'd be ready, and then to reschedule for today.

I had driven up from the coast to his house on Sunday to beg forgiveness and ask him to change the day from Monday to Wednesday, the 10th. We weren't going to be ready by the next morning. He winced, then stammered, "But, but, everyone is already planning…."

Then he sighed. "Are you sure Wednesday is going to give you enough time? Why don't you play it safe and say Thursday…or even Friday?"

"Well, you know we can't leave on a Friday. That old sailing superstition. Besides, I've got it all figured out. If we leave on Wednesday, we won't have to work up a sweat to be ready on time. I promise."

"Well, we better phone your mother and father right away. They already have a motel reservation. Susan asked for Monday off. I don't know if she'll be able to change it. Tina won't be able to make it for sure. She swapped her day off with someone else."

He shook his head in resignation. "Well, let's get busy." He ran one finger down the list of people to call and started dialing.

On Tuesday, I drove back to Bill's. A strange look came over his face when he saw me standing on his doorstep.

"I don't how to tell you this...." I began.

"No...!" He groaned.

"We can't change it again," he insisted a few minutes later over a cup of coffee. "Nick is going to be there with his bagpipes. Susan changed her day off twice. Your mother and father have already changed their reservations."

After half an hour of brainstorming, we hit on the only workable solution we could come up with.

"And don't ever tell anyone I knew about this," Bill warned.

I promised.

"Ya done good," I say to Bill now, though I feel a little sheepish. He shrugs as if to say, "Not a big deal." Casey sits on Bill's lap, looking around with a great deal of interest. She's never been on the boat before. I hold her hand while Bill and I talk. I have to look away when tears well in my eyes. She has been a constant part of my life since she was born. Now she holds her arms out to me, and I take her on my lap while Bill and I finish the "to do" list. She won't know me when I return.

"Hey, where's my daughter?" My father shouts. I look out of the companionway. Mom, with her twinkling eyes, her video camera on her shoulder, grins at me.

Sunday, when I phoned my parents, I'd explained we would be "out straight" and wouldn't have a lot of time to visit on the day before departure. When they arrived yesterday at 2:00 p.m. from Massachusetts, Mom said, "Is there anything we can do to help?" I felt guilty handing them a grocery shopping list since they had just driven five hours. Off they went, and when they returned, they had added as a treat a few extras they thought we'd enjoy, including a large bottle of Riunite. Little did I know then how much I'd appreciate that wine later on.

As I stashed these last-minute groceries on an already severely overloaded boat, Dad said, "If you don't have time to stop to eat supper, we'll get you some hamburgers from Burger King...or if you have time, we would like to take you to supper. We'd get you right back so you don't lose too much time."

Dorin, Cory, and I looked at each other and grinned. We'd been working almost around the clock for the last five days, and all meals had been Burger King meals.

"If you're serious, there's the Lobsterman's Wharf right there." I pointed to the restaurant on the next dock over.

What a luxury! Eating lobster stew out on the deck of the restaurant, every bite of my dinner reminded me of how we'd struggled to prepare meals, catch-as-catch can, on our boat's two-burner stove.

I listened to the cry of the seagulls and relaxed. As we chatted about details of the trip, the mast of the *Fandango* swayed gently with the incoming tide. After three years of planning and work, I could hardly believe it was about to happen.

On our way back to the boat, Dad pulled two battery-powered lamps out of his station wagon to lend us for the evening. Dorin had to crawl in and out of the sail lockers to tighten the stuffing box, connect the last of the plumbing for the water supply, and install the manual bilge pump which had just arrived late last week. The lamps were an enormous help. We connected the kerosene stove, bolted the radar antenna to the rear deck, and mounted the radar screen inside the cabin.

"I've got to crash for a few hours," Dorin said at one o'clock. Cory was still in the middle of a job and kept going until three. When Dorin and I awoke at four this morning he said, "You know we're not going to make it in time, don't you?"

"Yeah," I replied, "that means Plan Two." I felt so guilty.

In the gray light we moved the mountain of gear from the dock to whatever nooks and crannies the boat still offered, and there weren't many. Occasionally tempers flared, and we glared and snapped at each other.

"Where do you want me to stow this sail?"

"You can leave it here as far as I'm concerned."

"You can't put the tools in there. That's where the rest of the food is going."

"So you think we should go without the tools...."

Mercifully, Mom and Dad showed up at 8 a.m. with coffee and doughnuts and then disappeared for a while as we continued to work.

Now, here they are again, having enlisted Susan's help to blow up two dozen balloons. We tie them to the stern pulpit where they float and bob in the breeze.

I glance around the dock. My friend Emma, who is in her 80s, sits on an upturned dinghy, looking as comfortable as if she'd spent her life on the coast. She has a foil-covered package of homemade fudge in her hands. Her daughter Dorothy not only drove Emma to East Boothbay, a two-and-a-half-hour drive from her home, she also chauffeured Cory's friend Chris and my niece Kelli.

Three people from Dorin's department at the college make the trip. Nick attracts a lot of attention as he strolls down the dock in his kilt, carrying his bagpipes. There is also Diane, who commented on the size of our fo'c'sle bunk, and department chairman, Ed.

If only Lew were here, I think. He's another member of the department and helped Dorin bolt the new toe rails on the boat a couple of months ago. I smile, thinking that would've made five psychologists milling around on the dock among us normal people.

While everyone gets acquainted, I reach below and grab the bottle of champagne provided by my friend Carol. Over the last six weeks, Carol packed lunch for us and delivered it to the boatyard every day, so we wouldn't have to stop and fix a meal. She drove down on Monday to say a private goodbye and isn't here today.

"Shirley, dear," my mother says, "isn't it time for the champagne? Wait a minute! I have to get back further so I can get the whole picture." She steps back near the edge of the dock and looks through the viewfinder. "Okay, all set."

I hand Diane the bottle to open. The cork makes a satisfying "pow" and flies down the dock. I hold the paper cups, and she pours. Even Chris, Cory's sixteen-year-old friend, who put in countless hours working on the boat, takes a cup. Emma passes one to my mother who is torn between toasting us and putting the cup down so she can run the video camera. A group of curious onlookers a few yards away ask my mother what this is all about, and she tries to explain.

Diane lifts her cup. "May you have fair winds and following seas." Everyone lifts his cup for the first sip. Then Dad toasts: "Have a marvelous time, experience great things while you're gone, and may you return to us safely." There is a rumble of assent, and we all drink again. I drop my empty paper cup to the dock and stomp on it. "Mazel tov!"

From the dock, Dorin turns the boat around with the stern and bow lines while Cory and I start the rounds of hugs and kisses: Emma, my dear friend, Ed, Nick, who has to be hugged around the bagpipes, Diane, who says, "Take care of yourself," and Chris, who is shy about a hug. My mother lowers her camera, and I blink back tears as I look at her beautiful, smiling face. I turn to Dad. "Bye, bye, thank you both for everything." I turn to Kelli, my niece. For no reason, we grab each other and sob foolishly for a minute. Bill stands back, grinning and looking a little bashful. Niagara Falls streams down my face as I kiss and hug him and Casey goodbye.

Cory looks embarrassed. My nose is running.

The stays'l and jib are already up and flapping gently. Cory and I jump on the boat. Dorin hoists the main and lets out the sheet. The sails fill with a gentle breeze. He steps off to untie the lines.

"Aren't you going to start the motor?" someone asks.

"Nope, don't have to," Dorin replies as he pushes away from the dock and steps on the stern. All three sails catch the wind.

"Show off," laughs Diane, who is the only one who knows enough to appreciate the feat of taking off under sail from the backside of a T-shaped dock.

"What kind of song do you want?" calls Nick as we slowly round the end of the dock.

"Something upbeat," I yell back. Dorin lets out the sails some more, and we turn down the river. The red, yellow and green balloons pull and bob in the breeze, and we all smile and wave to each other as Scotland's sweet, melancholy notes drift across the water. The tears are still streaming down my face.

Dorin grins. "Boy, are you having a good time!" And then he nods toward the dock. "Do you think it was okay?"

Yeah, I think it was very okay.

"Show off," I add, blowing my nose, and he laughs.

"So. How far do we have to go before we turn back?" asks Cory.

"About two hours should do it," replies Dorin. "Don't you feel guilty?" he asks me.

"Yeah."

Chapter Two
A Second Start

It is now early in the afternoon, the farewell guests have long since departed, and we tie up to the fuel dock in East Boothbay.

A guy strolls out to help us. "That was a quick trip. World shrinking?"

Dorin, not wanting to explain our subterfuge, says that we had to return to correct some "rigging problems."

"But, ah, while we're here, we're just, ah, going to fill up our diesel tanks. Both of them."

The guy's eyebrows shoot up.

"And the water tanks. Here's our credit card."

"Sure," the guy says with a smirk.

"I think we've cast some doubt on our rigging story," Dorin says as the guy walks away with our credit card.

The fact that we have two diesel tanks is a matter of personal satisfaction because we created a new one under Cory's bunk. His bunk is located in the main cabin living space and is traditionally called the captain's bunk because it's the closest to the cockpit.

The legs of whoever occupies it tuck into a closed space we call the "toe" of the bunk. This helps keep the body from rolling out in heavy weather when the boat sharply heels (tips). It's a good design.

As in most boats, no space is wasted, so the designers also created a storage locker *underneath* this bunk. The outside wall of this locker is the hull. But, to access the locker, you have to take the mattress off the bed, put two fingers into holes of the wooden locker covers and pull up to get to the storage space below. It's dark inside, half the space is in under the toe of the bed, and sometimes it's wet. As we brainstormed about how to best use the space, Dorin came up with the idea of fiberglassing the insides of this cavity to create an additional fuel tank. I rather like fiberglassing jobs and Dorin doesn't, so, as soon as he taught me, years ago, all fiberglassing jobs became my jobs, and I became good at it.

Mostly.

This job was the most challenging I had done. The space was the size of a small sarcophagus, and half of it was under the toe, with no openings. Kneeling in front of the bunk, I sanded the inside of the hull and washed it down with acetone to prepare the surface. Bending and leaning into the toe, I laid down five layers of heavy fiberglass cloth. The difficult part was covering the "ceiling" of the space under the toe and getting into the pointy crevice at the very end of the space, which I had to do by feel since I couldn't see. I didn't use rubber gloves because I needed the information my fingertips could give me.

Dorin created two baffles made of plywood that fit against the shape of the hull. He put large holes in them to slow down the sloshing fuel while the boat bounced on the waves. I fiberglassed the baffles into place and finished by installing the metal fuel filler hole.

Then the moment of truth: with a hose, we filled the tank with water to check for leaks. I was tense, afraid that I had missed a spot—even a pin hole would be a disaster. When we were satisfied it was all good, we siphoned the water out, let the tank dry, and then I sealed the top with fiberglass. The only indication of a fuel tank was the filler screw cap.

Often, in those early days of trip preparation when I pulled my head out of the fumes, the hair on the top of my head was frosted with fiberglass resin which required me to "wash" my hair in acetone. The underside of my fingernails became packed with hardened fiberglass that was impossible to remove. It had to grow out with my nails. Each day I had to wash from armpit to fingertip with acetone to get the resin off. Yet, I couldn't get it all off, so slowly, black patches of resin tattooed my skin in random designs.

Today it all seems worthwhile. The diesel tank is full, and the extra fuel will help us get through those times when there will be very little wind, and we will have to depend on the motor to keep moving.

The rest of the afternoon we work quickly. The ham radio, our connection with the world, must be installed and connected to electricity, and the radar monitor needs to be attached to the antenna. We discovered at one o'clock this morning that we needed another fitting to finish the saltwater plumbing. We'll have to run into East Boothbay to pick it up, and we still have to get kerosene. We get to the parking lot and discover on our windshield a note from Bill, reminding us again that he has no knowledge of our fake departure and saying a last, gentle goodbye. And… "p.s. if you want to call Tina to say goodbye, she should be home tonight."

In the evening, I walk over to the public telephone at the Lobsterman's Wharf to phone Tina, but the line is busy for ten minutes. As I wait, it starts to pour. Tears mix with the rain as I walk slowly back to the boat. Lack of sleep must be getting to me.

I slip through the front hatch in the fo'c'sle without Dorin and Cory noticing, grab my toothbrush, and hoist myself back outside. I sit on the wet deck brushing my teeth and spitting in the dark water. Between sobs I try to figure out why the hell I am crying.

I spit one final time and look closer at the water and suck in my breath in shock. The dock light illuminates a rainbow sheen of oil. *It can't be us*, I think, but in truth I'm pretty sure it is. There is a $10,000 fine for polluting the ocean with an oil slick. Dorin has impressed this on me many times. Even as I try to deny it, I know what must be wrong. We filled the diesel tank for the first time today.

It leaks.

I call Dorin to the deck and point. He has the same reaction. "It can't be us." But immediately he says, "It must be the new tank."

"But how? We tested it with water."

"We filled it to within an inch of the top. We didn't want it to spill over on the floor. There's probably a pinhole at the top of the tank."

I recall how I worked on the toe of the tank mostly by feel, though several times I illuminated the area with a drop light. It looked okay, but I was uneasy with the spot where the tank came to a point from four directions. I gooped extra resin in that spot; yet, that is surely where the leak is.

My mind flails around for a solution that will make sense.

"Don't get alarmed, yet," Dorin says. "Let's think about this."

The three of us gaze at the circle of oil slick that reaches into the dark water beyond where we can see.

"Do we use Joy?" I ask.

"Yes, I think we'll have to. It's not like we can untie and sail away."

Before I can move, Cory goes below and brings out a large bottle of Joy dish detergent. He hands it to me, and I upend the squirt bottle and squeeze.

"No, too much. Let's see what it does," Dorin says. The penalty for trying to surreptitiously, by that I mean illegally, clean up an oil slick is something like three times greater.

I'm glad there are no other boats tied up here. I feel like a criminal and a scared one. We watch as the Joy breaks up the rainbow sheen, separating into smaller patches.

"Let me check the other tank." He opens the fuel filler on the floor of the cockpit and puts a measuring stick in. "There's a little room in this tank. I'll pump some across."

After Dorin pumps the fuel across, Cory squirts more Joy in the water, emptying half the bottle, and the oil slick dissipates.

"I'm so sorry." I can't stop saying it. I had gained confidence in my fiberglassing skills, but always in the back of my mind, I was concerned I would screw it up. This validates my every concern.

Dorin puts his arm around my shoulders. "I think we've stopped the leak."

"But what are we going to do about the tank?"

"No problem with that. As we use fuel from the main tank, I'll refill it by pumping the diesel from the fiberglass tank to the main one. Maybe with a lower level in the new tank, it won't leak any longer. We'll see in the morning."

Refusing to go below, I sit cross legged on the deck and watch the water for evidence of more diesel on the water, but it does seem to have stopped. An hour later I go to bed, miserable.

At dawn, Dorin and I quietly lift ourselves out of the front hatch, creep sternward and peer into the water. Not an oil slick in sight! He pulls my head into the crook of his neck. "Relieved?"

I nod, but I still feel guilty.

Cory joins us on deck.

"Good," he says, looking into the water beside the boat and then out into the bay. "So that's why you said our dish detergent had to be Joy."

"Yeah, it's kind of traditional among boaters because it's the great grease cutter the ads say it is."

The early morning sunshine turns the water into mounds of skipping diamonds. In a good mood, the guys tackle the radar first.

"The monitor was working before we installed the antenna," Dorin says. "Are you sure you matched the wires?"

Cory stiffens. "I'm *sure*."

"Have you guys read the directions?" I ask from below.

"Well, we'll just have to take the antenna apart and see what's wrong," grumbles Dorin.

"Have you read the card with the directions on it?" I ask from the galley.

"We had such trouble sealing it with that O-ring the last time," says Cory. "It isn't going to be easy."

Balancing on the stern pulpit rail, Cory unbolts the antenna while Dorin steadies it.

"Has anyone read the directions?" I ask as I search for them, opening drawers, doors, and plastic Ziplock packets bulging with "Important Papers."

"Yeah, that's a real design flaw, that O-ring," Dorin says. "Can't figure out why they would have designed it that way. Well, let's get this sucker opened up and see if we can figure out the problem."

They slowly lower the antenna to the deck and open it up with great care, trying not to disturb the giant O-ring. The O-ring rolls out.

They check the wires. "Well, Cor, you matched the colors right."

I glance out in time to see an "I told you so" glint in Cory's eyes.

"It doesn't make any sense," Dorin says. "It worked all right before we attached the antenna."

Returning to my search, I pull backrest cushions away in the dinette and frantically open each locker, looking through folders and notebooks. *Nada.*

"I'm looking for the directions!" I yell.

"Maybe the problem is where the cable attaches to the monitor," Cory suggests.

I climb onto the fo'c'sle bunk and yank open the storage units, knowing I wouldn't have stored the directions here. I go through the pages of our navigation and sailing books.

It takes them an hour more to painstakingly put the antenna back together. First, one tries to hold the two-foot diameter O-ring in place while the other attempts to close the cover. When their nerves shatter, they change places.

"Damn! Here! You try it!" They growl and sweat and eventually use contact cement to hold the O-ring in place. The cover finally goes on, they balance it back on the mini mast on the stern, and bolt it down.

"Hey, if anybody's interested, I found the directions!" I yell from the fo'c'sle.

"We'll have to check the monitor again," Dorin says, "but I can't imagine the problem being there." They come below and scoot into the dinette seat and behind the table so they can see the monitor mounted on the wall.

"Here's the directions," I offer. Neither of them acknowledges I'm there.

"Let's see, this is the 'on' switch," says Dorin as he pushes the button. "And this is the transmitting button." He pushes it. "So we should definitely have a picture now. I can't figure what the hell can be wrong!"

I look down at the directions in my hand.

1. Push the **on button** once.

2. Push the **transmitter button**.

3. Turn the **contrast knob** to the right until picture appears.

"Hey, wait, what's this knob for?" Dorin turns the contrast knob to the right and presto! A radar picture of the harbor appears on the screen.

They congratulate each other on their success.

I shake my head.

It's going to be a long trip.

The spreaders need adjusting, and the radar reflector still isn't up. We crank Cory, in his homemade, plywood-and-rope bosun's chair, up the mast and cleat the halyard off so he can be stable while he works halfway up the mast. While he is busy, we sit on the cabin top chatting with the young owner of a neighboring boat, *Trilogy*, about our coming trip. Suddenly the radar reflector bounces off Dorin's head, onto my shoulder and, before we can react, into the water. Dorin scrambles to the dock and reaches into the black water to grab it, but it zigzags downward inches away from his hand.

"It's deep here," the captain of the *Trilogy* says.

"Twenty-five feet," Dorin groans.

"Sorry," Cory says. "Can you get me down from here?"

The *Trilogy* captain gives up his own repair job and turns his efforts to retrieving our radar reflector. He and Cory drag the area with a small anchor, then a boat hook, to no avail.

Half an hour later they abandon the effort.

"We'll have to buy a new one at the chandlery. By the time we get and install it, it'll be too late to leave today. We still have a list of things to do."

"When *are* you leaving?" *Trilogy* asks.

"Well, probably tomorrow, if we get everything done today," replies Dorin.

"But tomorrow's Friday. Whatever you do," says our new friend emphatically, "don't leave on a Friday!"

We nod and smile. The precariousness of life on the high seas has caused those who chose this life or were forced into it, to develop dozens of superstitions, both good luck and bad luck, to give them a small feeling of control over their situations.

We've discussed this particular superstition among ourselves a number of times before. The fear of beginning a sailing voyage on Friday goes back at least hundreds of years, but probably thousands. There is no reliable source of its beginnings, although various historians have guessed that it has its roots in Christianity--Christ was crucified on Friday.

One story, though untrue, gets mentioned often: in the 1800s, when high seas travel had developed into an important means of transporting goods and supporting colonization, the Royal Navy attempted to finally disprove the bothersome superstition of severe misfortune befalling sailing ventures that begin on a Friday.

And so, on a Friday, they commissioned a ship which was named the *HMS Friday*. Her keel was laid on a Friday, she was launched on a Friday, and she set sail on her maiden voyage on a Friday. The last time she was ever seen was as she sailed into the horizon.

"You've got to be kidding." Cory shook his head a few months ago when the subject came up. "You mean to tell me if we were all ready to go on a Friday, you'd wait another day because of a ridiculous superstition?"

Today, I chuckle, but I feel a bit of tension when I think of breaking the old sea tradition....

"The search continues today for the bodies of three crew members of the sailing vessel Fandango, *which went down yesterday 300 miles off the coast of...."*

We assure our sailing friend from the *Trilogy* we will not leave on Friday.

At least one of us means it.

We finish everything that has to be done, and that night over supper Dorin says, "I don't know about you, but I'm getting antsy sitting here at the dock. What say we move down the river tomorrow and find a place to drop the anchor at the mouth of the Damariscotta? We don't have to actually start until Saturday."

We all feel the same way, tired of sitting at the dock and enthusiastic to go, but I still define the move. "It's not like we are *starting* the trip," I explain to no one. "We're just finding another place to start *from*. Then we'll leave Saturday morning."

"Fine," says Cory. "Just as long as we do *something*."

Friday, wispy morning fog rolls up the river. The weather report calls for patchy fog today and tomorrow. After breakfast, without fanfare, we untie the lines, step on the boat and quietly slip away from the dock. Anyone watching will think we are going for a day sail.

It's only thirty minutes to the mouth of the river. Before we are five minutes under way, the fog thickens to pea soup, and we turn on the radar. Cory and I crowd around the little screen in the galley while Dorin stays at the helm.

"I can see the shoreline on the right," I say.

"Here, change it to four-mile range and see what we get," says Cory. "Wow, we can see both sides of the river. Let's try the eight-mile range. This must be that bend in the river. This is great!"

"Can you see a boat behind us?" asks Dorin.

"Um, no, wait, yes. There's a couple of dots right behind us. That must be it." We feel so proud as we watch a small motorboat come out of the fog behind us. We've got radar, and we can "track boats in the fog."

I think of movies I've seen where the young ensign sits in front of the radar screen:

"Lieutenant," he says. "I think I've got something here." Everyone's attention focuses on the sweep of the green screen. "Good job," the Lieutenant says as he reaches for the phone. "Captain," he says quietly into the mouthpiece, "I think you'd better come up to the bridge."

"Have you picked up another boat?" asks Dorin. "More toward starboard this time."

"Yeah, got it!" says Cory, and we watch the boat's progress on the screen.

We feel powerful. Cory and Dorin exchange places, and he and I play with the ranges from half-mile to eight miles. We are impressed. We are invincible. On the screen we see we've reached the end of the river. Ahead lies the fog-blanketed Atlantic Ocean. I stand in the companionway stairs, and Dorin joins Cory in the cockpit.

"Well, whaddya say?" asks Dorin.

"Let's go for it," replies Cory.

"Okay with me if it's okay with you," I say. A butterfly that knows it's Friday does a double somersault in my stomach.

Dorin turns on the autopilot and adjusts the course. "We're off, crew."

I think back to our friends and family sendoff Wednesday, complete with bagpipes, and now to our unobtrusive departure today, and I realize we are lucky: we get to have our departure both ways.

Chapter Three
The Rising Cost
of a Life Raft

It's Friday afternoon, we're still afloat, and we're still in fog, but the three of us are in a great mood. It's exhilarating to actually be on our way. The wind is mild, about ten knots, and our speed is a lazy four knots. We are on a compass heading of 160 degrees. Our autopilot, a hydraulic ram attached to our tiller, steers the boat. We are on a beat, which means the wind is coming from almost straight in front of us, so the sails have to be hauled in close to squeeze as much speed as we can out of the boat. Close hauled sails cause boats to heel--to lean to the side. But it's a stable, fifteen-degree heel so we easily acclimate to it by grabbing the overhead handrails when we move from the front to the back of the cabin. We spontaneously grin at each other. We're sailing the Atlantic!

At the dinette, Dorin looks over the charts and reviews the celestial navigation books we brought. No one argued that we shouldn't bring those since they'd be our only means of navigation. We are hoping to be in Bermuda in ten to twelve days.

I sit in the cockpit and hand-make storage for wrenches we might need for engine repair. Since it requires sewing pockets onto the canvas, it's a job I regret I didn't get done when I had a sewing machine.

Cory has brought some fishing equipment, and because we are moving so slowly, he drops a line off the stern. We hope to reduce the drain on our food stores with fresh fish.

He gets a lot of action immediately, catching, but losing, two dogfish. In the process, he loses his best lure and one of the two weights he brought along. He tries again with another lure, and the line yanks almost immediately.

"Hey, I might need some help!" he yells. Dorin bolts up the stairs, and we jump to Cory's side in time to see a 30-pound shark struggling on the end of his line. He has the thrashing fish halfway out of the water, and we can see into its huge, gaping mouth, lined with knife-sharp teeth.

"Lemme help you, Cor." Dorin reaches across to grab the line but it breaks, and we watch the gray fish snap its tail and swim away.

Later, with a makeshift leader, he catches a five-pound dogfish, and it lands on the cockpit floor where it flips and flops around.

"We'll have to knock it out," Dorin says. He rummages in the toolbox and comes up with a 13/16 box end wrench, but the fish doesn't die easily. Cory grabs a 7/8 ratchet wrench and kills the fish with two blows.

I stand in the safety of the locker cover wondering what it would have taken to knock out the 30-pound shark if they had landed it. Could they have even done it without getting injured?

Dorin fixes supper, fried fish, and after I wash the dishes in the sea water Cory hauled in with a bucket, Cory stretches out on a cushion in the cockpit and reads a book. So, this is the sailing life, huh?

We sit around the cockpit keeping Cory company and reminisce about preparations.

We quickly fall on the topic of the *Tinker*.

The *Tinker*, a dinghy made to order in England, caused problems before we even got it. I had called England in February:

"We are leaving on an offshore trip in May. Will it arrive on time?"

"Oh, most certainly," replied a delightful British accent. "I would say it will be shipped so it will arrive in...um...Portland, Maine...is that near you?"

"Yes, just a couple of hours away...."

"...and it will arrive in Portland on April 28."

"What airline will you be using? I'll need to know so I can find out what flight...what time it will be arriving."

"I really couldn't say. I would imagine you could ring up the airport and ask them. Now how are you going to pay?"

"Can I send a check?"

"That would be difficult. Can you arrange to have it transferred to our bank today?"

"I don't know how to do that."

"Your bank should be able to take care of it. I'll give you our international bank number. Are you going to do it today?"

"Well, I could, I guess. Does it make any difference if I do it today or tomorrow?"

"Well, yes, actually. The price I will give you today is based on today's exchange rate. It changes rapidly, you know. Tomorrow, it could jump a bit, and it would cost you more."

"Okay, I'll do it today. How much will the whole thing come to?"

"Do you want the CO_2 inflation bottles to arrive full or empty? If it comes filled it will cost quite a bit more. It's considered a cargo risk, and there's an extra cost. $70 more, I believe. And the bottles will have to be shipped separately."

"Separate packages or separate flights?"

"Separate flights, different days."

"If they are shipped empty, can I get them filled here?"

"Oh, yes, I'm quite sure you can. If you have any problem, we have a representative in Maryland...is that near you?"

"No, that's quite far and...."

"...well, you can ring him up, and he'll help you, I'm sure. I'm certain there will be no difficulty."

"Okay, then ship them empty. Then I won't have to make two trips to the airport. How much will the whole thing cost?"

"With two sails and lifeboat canopy, the foot pump, hum...and shipping...hmm...at today's rate of exchange...do you want the amount in American dollars?"

"Please."

"It will be $3,427."

"What? The catalog said $2,200!"

"Well, unfortunately, we just had an increase in our prices. And of course the price in the brochure didn't include shipping. How old is the brochure?"

"We've had it for a year or more."

"Well, then, there it is. The exchange rate was much more favorable to you then. Do you still wish to order it?"

"Um, I guess so. I didn't...I don't...um, oh, okay, go ahead and order it, and I'll call you back later today if we want to cancel the order."

"What?!" exclaimed Dorin when I met him for lunch. "That's what? More than a 50% hike in price? That's ridiculous! That's gouging, that's what it is."

We talked through the alternatives, and Dorin decided to stick with the *Tinker*, given its stellar reviews. And he figured it would last us for many years.

After lunch, I went to our bank and found that the only person who knew how to do the transfer was at lunch. I went back at 2:00, and she said it would take several hours to do—it might not even go through today. I asked her to give me a bank check for $3427, and I took it to another bank. The transfer was made rapidly. "That'll be $40," the teller said. It hadn't occurred to me the service would cost. The *Tinker* now cost us $3467.

On April 27, I phoned four airlines in Portland to see when they had a flight coming in from England on the 28th. I got the same response from each one: "What's the flight number?"

"I don't know. I just know it's coming from England. How many flights do you have arriving from England?"

"None, directly," she said in an irritated voice. "I can't help you if you don't have a flight number."

When I explained the problem to another airline, the person suggested I just come to the airport and ask around at the various airline desks when I got there.

So at 6 a.m. I left Waterville, arrived in Portland at 8 and went from airline to airline asking about flights coming in from England. They kept brushing me off—directing me to other offices.

Finally, someone listened to me and sent me to the Airfreight Company, which wasn't part of the airport and was located a mile down the road.

The man at the airfreight company said I was at the right place, but my freight hadn't come in yet because it had been routed through the Baltimore airport and wouldn't be in until April 30! In addition to losing a full day of work, add $20 for gas, tolls and a hamburger--$3487!

When I arrived on the 30th—add another $20, now it added up to $3507—they said it was in Portland, but it hadn't cleared Customs yet. They were in the process of trying to find the name of a customs' broker who would handle it for me.

"Also, you'll have to go to the Customs' House in downtown Portland to pay the duty on it."

I hadn't even thought of duty. "Okay, if I go pay the duty myself, why do I need a customs' broker?"

"They have to take care of it. That's just the way it is. Here's the name of a broker." She handed me a scrap of paper with a name on it.

"Can't you phone him and make the arrangements for me?"

"Nope. You have to do that yourself."

"Can I use your phone?"

"They're all tied up now. We're using the modem...probably be tied up for an hour."

I didn't know my way around Portland very well except for the airport area, but I drove randomly around and found a mall where, after I bought toothpaste to get change, I used a pay phone.

"I understand you are a customs' broker. Can you tell me what you do?"

"I handle items coming into the country," he said in a rough, gravelly voice.

"Well, I have a small boat that just arrived from England that I want to pick up today. What do I do?"

"Go to Customs and pay the duty."

"Then what happens?"

"Nothing. It'll be released and the freight company will pick it up and you can take it."

"How much do you charge?"

"Ninety dollars."

"What?! Is that the duty?"

"Nope, lady, that's my charge...doesn't include the duty."

"But what do *you* do? If I go pay the duty and Airfreight picks up the package, what should I pay you $90 for?"

"This is the way it has to be done. Look, if you want to get somebody else, go ahead! I don't need your business. But I can tell you one thing. You won't get your boat until you pay a broker. Goodbye."

"No, wait, wait! Okay, how do I pay you?"

"Go pay it to Airfreight. Today."

"Then I can pick up the boat?"

'Yep, It's too late today, though. I can't take care of it until tomorrow."

"But it's only two o'clock. I drove all the way from Waterville today."

"Sorry, lady. You aren't satisfied, get someone else."

"Yours is the only name I have. Can you give me someone else's name?"

"Forget it!"

"Wait! Okay, all right. I'll go pay right now." I drove back to the airfreight people and gave them a check to cover the cost of the freight-- $120--and the customs' broker fee and went home. The cost of the *Tinker* was now $3597. This boat had better be a spectacular success!

The next day, May 1, Dorin had to work at his consulting job in Bath, which is halfway to Portland, so we figured we'd save gas. I'd leave him off at Bath, go pick up the *Tinker*, come back and get him. Cory agreed to go to give me moral support. Add $23 in gas and tolls plus three hamburgers-- $3830. Cory, exercising his new drivers' permit, drove from Bath to Portland, and we found the customs' office without too much trouble. The customs' men were super polite and pleasant. We paid them $173, bringing the cost of *Tinker* to $4003 — and drove back to the Airfreight Office.

"Hope you brought a truck," they said when they saw me. No, we hadn't brought a truck. We'd brought Dorin's hatchback Toyota. The brochure had said the *Tinker* could fold up so small, *you could carry it in the boot* of a car. We had figured if we folded down the back seats, there would be room to spare. It took two men fifteen minutes of twisting, turning and shoving to get the thing loaded. Still, the mast stuck out of the driver's window about four feet. When we got back to Bath, we scratched our heads...when Dorin got in the car, where could Cory sit? Finally, he climbed on top of one of the boxes and scrunched over with his chest on his knees. His head touched the roof. When he got tired, he alternated this position with laying on his side in a fetal position.

We had just picked Dorin up when it started to pour, but we couldn't close the windows because of the mast sticking out on one side and the oars extending out of the front window on the other side. I couldn't move my head, Dorin had trouble reaching the shift. Our tempers were precariously short long before we arrived home.

We opened the boxes when we got home and had to admit the *Tinker* was pretty. The mahogany seat and stern gleamed and even the oars were beautiful. Perhaps, we thought, after we had a chance to sail it, we'd decide it was worth the effort and money.

We tried to get the CO_2 cartridges filled at a local gas distributor, but the fitting on the tank was British (metric) so they couldn't fill it. Twice we phoned the representative in Maryland whose wife took the messages, but he never phoned back. $4.73 in phone calls.

"We'll just have to fill it in Bermuda," Dorin said. "Bermuda was a British colony until recently, but there is still a British influence. There's no doubt we can get it filled there. Meanwhile, we'll have to inflate it with the foot pump. As long as it's not an emergency, we should be okay."

We laugh now at his joke about a lifeboat being okay as long as there wasn't an emergency.

Dorin asks who wants to take the first watch, and Cory jumps at the four to eight p.m. watch. I volunteer for the eight to midnight stint which leaves Dorin with the twelve to four shift. Cory will pick up again with the 4 to 8 a.m. sunrise watch.

That's why Cory spoke up so quickly.

Going to bed at eight in the evening gives him eight hours of uninterrupted sleep. And if I go to bed right after my watch at midnight, I, likewise, will rack up eight hours before I have to begin my watch at 8 a.m. Dorin, on the other hand, will have to get a couple of hours sleep before he takes his watch at midnight, then go back to sleep at 4 a.m. Fortunately, he can fall asleep on a bed of logs ten seconds after becoming horizontal, so, it seems like a fair deal for me.

When Cory notices it's eight o'clock, he heads for bed. It is now my watch, and Dorin and I settle down to chat quietly in the darkening night.

An hour later Dorin says, "Well, it's nine o'clock. I think I'll get a few hours sleep before my watch. You'll be all right?"

A cold lump settles in my stomach. "Of course."

"Call me if you need me."

"Uh-huh." I pull my sweater tighter around my shoulders.

I stare at the dark, remembering seven years ago when I first sailed at night. Dorin had just bought the *Fandango*, and we sailed from Portsmouth, Rhode Island, to Mackerel Cove in Maine. It was the first time I'd ever been in anything larger than a rowboat. Most nights we dropped anchor, but the one time we sailed until dawn, I wasn't frightened, only because I didn't know enough to be.

A second time, three years ago, we again sailed all night. By then I knew enough. But before my watch even started, I became violently seasick in the choppy seas where the Kennebec River empties into the Atlantic, so Dorin stayed at the helm all night instead of taking turns as we had planned. While I alternately threw up in the sea water that sloshed on the cabin floor and moaned on the captain's bunk, I visualized the boat smashing against the rocks that I knew were just a few yards away.

We were two miles offshore.

He never again suggested we sail at night.

Until now.

Remembering this incident reminds me I have Scopolamine patches prescribed specifically for me for seasickness. I haven't put one on yet. But you are not supposed to wait until you are seasick. They are preventative, not curative. I check the radar and then dash below. I know right where they are. I tear open the box and pull out the clear plastic sheet the skin-colored, adhesive patches are stuck to. There are a number of places on your body you can place them, but I have already decided it will go behind my ear. I peel one off and carefully place it behind and just below my right ear. I put the package away and hurry back outside.

My radar shows we've cleared the last of the offshore islands.

Nothing to worry about.

Nothing except other boats.

In the cabin, I check the radar screen again. Not one blip. Settling back in the cockpit, I try to relax. Spontaneously, a fog scene from *THE SHIPKILLER*, a book we had all read, comes to mind:

> ...*She looked out at the sea, then behind them. Her body went rigid in his arms.*
>
> *"Oh, my God!"*
>
> *Hardin turned and stared.*
>
> *A black steel wall filled the horizon...*
>
> *He jammed the diesel wide open. It was too cold for sudden acceleration and it coughed and died. For a long moment the slack flutter of the sails was the only sound. The ship was a hundred feet away. Whatever powered it made no noise. Only the loudening of the cresting bow wave announced its coming.*
>
> *Hardin and Carolyn found each other's hands and backed toward the bow. They huddled there, clutching the forestay, watching in disbelief as the silent wall blacked out sky.*
>
> Siren *died with a loud crack of splintering fiberglass."*

I feel nauseated. I run down and check the radar again.

Nothing.

What would I do if a boat suddenly appeared out of the fog?

Hit the starter button and use power to get out of the way.

Rehearsing, I lean forward and put a finger on the starter button, then reach down and touch the accelerator. Flup, flup, flup, flup, the jib flutters. My elbows feel like "coffee-jitters" as I pull the winch handle out of the coaming locker and crank in the sail. I take a deep breath and relax...

...Hardin leaped. The water was violently cold. He broke the surface and pulled Carolyn to him. Something smashed his side. Pain coursed through his knee. Carolyn's hand was wrenched from his. He heard her scream once before the water buried him again.

I change position so that the starter button is less than arm's length away. I check the radar again. All clear. Back in the cockpit I move the tiller back and forth slightly. What if, in a panic, I forget which way to push the tiller? Pull it left, the bow will go right. Opposite... okay, I got it. A wave of nausea reaches up from my stomach and clutches my throat. It seems this watch will never end.

I check my watch.

It is 9:15.

Chapter Four
Thar' She Blows

"Why don't you go get some sleep," Dorin says when he reappears at 11:30. I gratefully climb into the dark fo'c'sle bunk. What is this thing in the way? Dorin's guitar and case that I insisted, over his objections, we bring along. We had moved it from the dinette to the fo'c'sle so we could sit down to eat. I try to push it aside, but it jams into the extra cushions and blankets stored there. How did Dorin fit in here?

Diane's army cot quip comes back to me. I wiggle and push until I find room to stretch out and close my eyes. The water rushes along the hull, inches from my ear...I'm below sea level. I hear the winch as Dorin begins to change tack, and then I roll against the hull as the boat heels over on the other side. The strangeness of this new life rumples and pulls like an ill-fitting suit.

I don't remember falling asleep, but at 4:00 a.m., I'm aware of Dorin moving the guitar. He climbs in on top of the mountains and valleys of blankets and sleeping bags and mushes to create his own space. I can hardly move. As we overlap our bodies, I close my eyes.

Suddenly, I snap awake. "Who's watching the boat?"

"Cory."

A sixteen-year-old child watching the boat with no one awake? In the dark?

"He's okay," Dorin reassures me. "He'll call if something goes wrong."

"But he doesn't have any experience. He might not *know* if something goes wrong!"

Dorin chuckles and puts his hand gently over my eyes. "Go back to sleep."

At dawn, I hear the flup, flup, flup of the stays'l followed by the whir of the winch. How, I wonder, did he learn so quickly what took me years to learn? I am suddenly proud of Cory's maturity and realize I have confidence in his sailing ability.

When Dorin gets up, he starts the motor to recharge the batteries because the autopilot has been on since we cleared the mouth of the river yesterday.

He asks me to check the compass setting on the control head for the autopilot. When I try to read it, the numbers are blurry—enough so I can't distinguish one from another. This is alarming. I could read the numbers yesterday. Dorin sticks his head around the companionway to read it himself.

I have really good eyesight. I know I do.

Disconcerted, I think this could be a liability.

The fog blankets us; there is very little wind. In the afternoon, the knot log, the instrument that tells us our speed, stops working. Dorin tinkers with it for a while. When it starts working again, it says 1.4 knots.

I could walk faster. And we've only gone 65 nautical miles.

We haven't been able to take a sun sight since we started, so we're plotting our course on the chart by dead reckoning, but it's guesswork at best. We keep track of our speed and direction, but there is no way to figure in any current and leeway drift. As we glide slowly in the long, shallow swells, I wonder how long fog can last.

Dorin thinks we may be nearing Georges Bank, a commercial fishing territory, so he's really tense about traffic. At 5 p.m., just minutes after Cory checks the radar, Dorin and I hear a motor running nearby. Cory dashes down the companion way to check the radar again.

"Do you have it?" asks Dorin.

"No, there is nothing on the screen," Cory yells back.

"It's getting louder," I call.

Dorin stares into the fog. "It sounds really close."

"I don't see anything." Cory's voice is strained. The noise sounds closer, and our tension vibrates with the loud throb of the unseen motor. Dorin peers into the fog in the direction of the sound, and Cory rapidly punches the radar ranges from half-a-mile to four miles trying to find the approaching ship.

"You should have it by now," yells Dorin, his finger poised over the starter button. "It's really close."

"Nothing! I'm on two miles...nothing, now one-mile, half-a-mile, nothing!"

"It sounds so close we should be able to see it!" I shout. "Aren't you going to start the motor?"

"Not yet. We won't be able to hear the other boat."

A 150-foot fishing trawler breaks through the curtain of fog fifty yards away on our starboard stern on a collision course. Dorin turns sharply to port; the trawler simultaneously veers to the right, and, we watch, weak-kneed, as it disappears into the fog.

"Why didn't it show up on the radar?" Dorin asks. "As big as it was, it should have presented a clear target."

"I've got it now," says Cory from below, "but it's just a couple of dots on the screen."

Looking over Cory's shoulder I realize I can't even see the two dots.

A minute later, as we start to relax, Dorin shouts, "I hear another one, and it's closing in."

"I've got it!" Cory yells. "The sea-clutter control button was turned too low! It's coming in at ten o'clock, less than half a mile, collision course." Pause. "You should see it by now."

Dorin loosens the sheets on the winches, turns sharply to starboard, rapidly hauls in the sails on the other tack, and we watch the second trawler within two minutes cross within yards of us. We listen intently as the motor dies away and continue listening in case there are more. Cory adjusts the screen and tracks our two "fishing friends" who are now almost six miles away.

The tension is down, but it's still lying there ready to spring again. What if it had happened during last night's watch when only one of us was awake? If it'd been my watch, what would I have done? Would I've been able to wake Dorin up in time to do any good? What if I had *dozed off?* What if it happens during my watch tonight--or Cory's?

My watch, a few hours later, turns out to be uneventful with Dorin waking up every hour to check. I take this time to ponder a bit more on the *Tinker* which is still tied to the cabin top.

Back in early May, we had taken it to the ocean for a trial run. On the beach, we inflated it with the foot pump, which is a bellows-type rig made of yellow rubber and wood. We had to take turns when our legs got tired of pumping air into the inner and outer tubes. It took 11 minutes to inflate it once we untied and unfolded it.

It's recommended that life rafts be able to be inflated and deployed in less than 60 seconds.

Once we'd inflated the *Tinker*, we stepped the mast, rigged the sails, and dragged it across the wet sand to the water. The wind was blowing hard, there was a chop, and it was cold. Cory and I sat on the rubber tubes that formed the structure of the boat. Dorin was at the tiller. As we bounced off the waves, cold water sprayed back and drenched us.

"Three people wouldn't be comfortable in here if this were a life raft," observed Dorin. "Only one person at a time could lie down. And, one of the other two would have to sit on a lap. And I don't like the way the bow scoops up water and drains it back."

We had not exactly bonded with the *Tinker* that day. Given our near brush with disaster earlier today, I hope we don't ever have to depend on it.

In the morning, Cory continues to fine tune the radar during his 4 a.m. watch and picks up a ship at four miles, tracking it until it passes at three-quarters of a mile. He gives us a quick lesson in radar tuning. When we had tuned out the "sea clutter," we had tuned out the trawlers, and we had not taken advantage of either the expanded target or the radar interference features.

"You know, I think I remember that Apelco suggests you don't rely on radar until you have done a trial run when you have visibility," Dorin says.

"You *read* the directions?" I ask in disbelief.

"Well, no. I heard it somewhere. Makes a certain kind of sense though, doesn't it?" I glance at him and see he's amused.

The reports we heard before leaving East Boothbay said the weather would improve by Sunday evening. Well, the improved weather had better hurry because it's noon, and there is no visibility and, therefore, no possibility of a sun sight. And, unfortunately, there's very little wind.

The tantalizing sun thins the fog so that it glistens, but minutes later it settles in a wet blanket. We have our radar on, but we find ourselves straining to see further than the few yards of visibility we have, and the vision of the huge trawler bearing down on us just beyond the gray curtain stays in the backs of our minds.

We run the radar and the autopilot around the clock, and, by last night, the batteries had drained twice in twelve hours. To conserve them, we don't use the electric lights at night except for the masthead light and depend on the flashlight to find things or check the instruments in the cabin.

This afternoon, Dorin connects the wires to the spare battery in order to start the motor in order to recharge the two main batteries. What will happen if we have to start the motor quickly and the main batteries are dead?

And that's not all. In the past two days we've been first alarmed, then annoyed, and now accepting about a head that continues to leak - the floor is always wet, ugh! - and a kerosene stove that starts with a flash and a bang and a puff of black smoke and is reluctant to keep going unless we pump the dickens out of the pressure valve every minute or so.

Yet the stowage problem causes the most grumbles. We can't even sit down without moving a pile of stuff from one flat surface, so to speak, to another.

During final preparations, we found we'd accumulated much more than would possibly fit on the boat as we weeded out the Do-We Really-Need-This? from the Absolutely-Must-Take! We also discovered vast differences of opinion on what we each considered necessary. With tempers frayed from months of hard work and frustration, we'd snapped at each other:

"Why are you taking two blankets *and* a sleeping bag? This is a thirty-two-foot sailboat, not a four-room apartment."

"Do we really need *two* replacement jibs?"

"Twenty sci-fi books? Where are we going to put sailing books? Or should we just leave them behind?"

"Why six pillows? We only have three heads."

"A cassette player and *how* many tapes?"

"A kerosene heater in the *tropics?*"

"What do you *mean*, it's either the guitar or the sextant?"

Though we eliminated almost half of what we originally intended to bring, we're still severely overloaded and overcrowded.

Cooking is a major ordeal, even discounting the stove difficulties. The margarine is under the pancake mix, which is under the Cup-of-Soup, which is under the spaghetti. It takes five minutes to dig out the mustard and replace everything. I question the value of each item I touch.

"Did we actually bring *cloth* napkins!?"

"Do we really need six mugs *and* six glasses?"

"Isn't a gallon of sweet pickles too much?"

"Didn't I tell you we were bringing too many pillows?"

In spite of the inconveniences and annoying clutter, we're happy to be on our way, and several times a day one of us beams and says, "We actually made it!"

On Monday, we sail comfortably on a reach at six knots on a calm sea and not much of a heel. Cory is doing his "homework." We received permission from the superintendent of his school district for him to skip his junior year if he made arrangements with his teachers to accomplish work while he was gone. One teacher has assigned him to collect and photograph seaweed, sea life, and birds and to keep a journal. Today he collects 13 different varieties of seaweed, lays them out on the cockpit seat, and photographs them.

Later in the day, Cory calls us to the cockpit to see a small pod of finback whales, but they are maybe 300 feet away and somewhat obscured by the fog. He estimates they are 60 to 70 feet long and tells us about the characteristics of the finback. Later he spots a large shark lolling close to the *Fandango*, barely moving. We wonder if it was injured when caught in a commercial fishnet and released. It drifts in our wake for an hour, and then slowly swims away.

On Tuesday, mid-morning, Dorin notices a school of dolphins keeping us company by swimming and diving playfully in our bow wave. Later, Cory spots a ten-foot shark swimming by.

So far, I have not been the first to spot sea life, but early in the afternoon, while I'm washing a few clothes on deck, I hear a whooshing snort that I remember from seven years ago on the Rhode Island to Maine trip.

Wow! Whales! I've never developed a fear of whales, and I'm so excited!

Cory comes running up on deck as soon as I yell, "Whales!", and we strain our eyes and ears in the direction of the "blow." Thirty feet away, a huge whale breaches. Magnificent flukes come out of the water and slowly, gracefully disappear back into the sea. I wait, hoping to see it again, but no luck. Dorin comes on the deck in time to hear one last blow beyond the fog.

While I don't fear whales, Dorin takes a less romantic, more practical, approach to them. He enjoys them a lot if they're a hundred or more yards away. We've read that whales won't attack unless provoked, but he's not convinced that one won't have a seizure as it passes, or perhaps think the *Fandango* is a long-lost lover.

I hope we see some more.

In early afternoon, Cory spots whales just ahead in the fog. We sail through a pod--twenty at best count. He and I stand on deck counting them as the waterspouts go up, sometimes as close as thirty feet away. "They're feeding," Cory reports. "Look, there's two more on this side! Four, five..."

"Great," says Dorin as I rush through the cabin to get the camera. "I've always wanted to sail through a pod of hungry whales."

I try to photograph the gray backs moving through the thinning fog. "Look! It's right by the boat! Wow! They're beautiful. Wow! There's another one. That makes ten? Boy, are they big. Look at the spout over there. Eleven. There's another one on the side. Two more. Wow!"

Dorin glances at Cory. "She's your mother."

"You brought her along."

A few hours later, Cory spots a whale he describes as "the biggest one yet." It breaches at twenty yards directly across the bow. He makes a note of our location: *41° 32' N Latitude, 68° 01' W Longitude.* And then it's gone.

Late in the afternoon, a couple dozen porpoise visit us, swimming and cavorting beside the boat. Ecstatic, we watch for a few minutes enjoying their playfulness. I'm afraid they won't stay long, and I'm torn between staying on deck to watch and sprinting below to get the camera again. I finally dash down and get it. "They're not leaping anymore," I say with my eye to the lens. "I'd like to get one good shot to show my mother."

As I lower the camera, the two closest porpoises leap several feet in the air. "They heard you," Dorin laughs. I push the button, but I know they are under the surface when the shutter opens and closes. A minute later, the pair turns ninety degrees from the boat, leaping and swimming rapidly in the direction in which their companions are disappearing. I feel like a kid whose friends have been called to supper in the middle of a game.

It's Wednesday. Since we started five days ago, the wind has always come in off our bow but never at a consistent speed. When we're not becalmed, we drift at a sleepy two knots, then the wind builds until we clip along at hull speed...six-and-a-half knots...just to die again in a couple of hours. The fickle fog tantalizes us in the same manner. The shimmering edges recede, giving the impression of a wide-open ocean, though never broader than about a mile. As we rejoice at our increasing vista, it closes back in, reducing our world to a tiny circle a few yards wide.

Cory's log entry for Tuesday afternoon is typical:

> *4 PM wind is up, we are storming along at almost 7 knots. Fog backing off, visibility at 1 mile.*
>
> *5 PM double reefed the main. Still 6 1/2 knots.*
>
> *6 PM fog closing in. Visibility half-mile and dropping.*
>
> *7 PM wind still dropping, shook out reefs. Visibility almost 0.*
>
> *8 PM becalmed.*

And so we move in fits and starts, beating southeast toward Bermuda. We're plagued by what proves to be a series of mechanical difficulties without end. Wednesday afternoon Cory writes in the log:

> *Motor off because of problem with main fuel tank. Engine died when Dorin switched to that tank. The prop shaft is making a noise, seems to be bent. Dorin said it probably happened when he got tangled in a lobster warp the last summer the boat was in the water. Almost no wind, but plenty of FOG!*

The next entry is also his, written in a very jiggly handwriting at four o'clock the next morning:

> *4:00 AM Flashliyht brokn. I am writiny in th dark. Becalmec, autopilot off. Liyht rain and mist, heauy fog, visb. maybe 100 yds.*

The rest is more difficult to read; lines and words overlap.

> *The toilet is on the blink (something) caught in the valve-- has to be taken aparl. Radar all cleor.*

5 AM Now I have some light, thank God. But nothing to write.

5:30 AM Large shark near boat, fin is six to seven inches above water. That makes it a six-foot shark!

7:00 AM Shark still circling.

The shark isn't the problem. The flashlight, however, is bad news. During the previous watch Dorin was holding it when it went out. We changed batteries but still no light, so it had to be the bulb. Because it was brand new, we hadn't brought extra bulbs. From that night on we depend on cigarette lighters after dark for inside stuff. Flick...check the knot log. Flick...check the inside compass. Flick...check the course on the autopilot...but it's difficult to make out the small numbers...let me see..."is that 130 or 150...ouch!" The lighter is hot. Because of the wind, the lighter is useless for checking the compass outside.

"Who would ever have believed that we'd be six days in fog?" Dorin asks when I get him up at midnight. He nods toward the radar screen. "Anything out there?" Every day since we almost got run down, we track two or three ships across the screen, sometimes altering our course to stay clear of them.

There were many times when, as a boat under sail, we had the right-of-way, but it doesn't make sense to expect a freighter to use fuel to change course to avoid us when we can easily change tack. We eventually realize that any other philosophy could make us very dead.

We are developing a great deal of affection for our radar.

We wouldn't have had the radar without the help of some friends. Dorin originally bought a used radar that turned out to be unfixable. For six months, the repair man assured us he'd have it done in time for us to leave. In the middle of June, he finally told us it couldn't be fixed because the schematic wasn't available. We were already so far over budget there was no question of purchasing another.

I felt very uncomfortable sailing without one. I'd sailed in fog before; it's a nightmare. My anxiety must have been transmitted to Bill. He phoned family and friends asking them if they'd like to donate toward a farewell present. A couple of weeks later, he presented us with $550, half the price of an Apelco radar.

"Even if we could swing the rest of the money," Dorin said after Bill left, "it'll take three weeks to get one in...if they don't back order it. Then we'd still have to install it. I don't think we can pull it off in time."

After he went back to work in the afternoon, I phoned the two marine supply houses we ordered from and asked them how fast they could ship a radar unit. Both of them said they were three weeks behind, and they couldn't guarantee even that. One of them didn't even have an Apelco in stock.

But we had no choice. Rummaging through Dorin's apartment, I found a Boat US catalog. The back cover advertised a recently opened outlet in Massachusetts. I phoned at 4:45 p.m., and the very helpful gentleman said they had two Apelcos left, but they were going fast.

"They'll probably be gone before the weekend is over," he said.

"Today's Friday. If I mail a check today and you get it tomorrow, will you hold the Apelco until someone can pick it up?"

"I'll put one of these aside until Monday. If your check comes in by then, you can leave it here for a couple of weeks, if necessary."

I wrote a check for $1052 out of an account that had only $43 in it and dashed to the post office, squeaking through the door with two minutes to spare. When I arrived back at the apartment, I called a friend and asked for a $500 loan to be repaid in six months. Done. Then I phoned my mother in Massachusetts. "Would you and Dad be able to drive to a store near Boston and pick up a radar?"

She took down the information and said they'd be glad to pick it up the first of the week. God bless my parents. I can always count on them. I was nervous that evening when I told Dorin what I had done. It's not our style for either of us to make a commitment without involving the other. He was not comfortable, but in the face of a *fait accompli*, what could be done? On Monday, I deposited the money that Bill gave us and the loan to cover the check I'd written.

My discomfort and guilt about buying the radar continued until tonight, six days into the trip, when he says, "It would have been a nightmare without the radar."

It sounds like "thank you" to me.

The next morning, the wind changes to a westerly, and the fog recedes steadily until the horizon becomes a distinct line between cloudless sky and rippling water. For the first time since leaving East Boothbay, the visibility is perfect. It's a shock to see we really are alone out here, as the radar has suggested much of the time. There's nothing to relieve the eye in the bland, duo shades of blue that present themselves wherever I look.

"I never had to go through anxiety watching the land disappear," chuckles Cory. "I never knew when it happened."

The wind dies entirely, and in the calm, we wallow for hours in the long, shallow swells. Perhaps the sensory deprivation makes us irritable because we snap at each other. I'm also feeling a touch of nausea. I brought twelve Scopolamine patches to put behind my ear, and two are already gone. I foolishly put one on for our two-hour "false departure." Since they only last for three days, I replaced it with a second one on Saturday. I certainly don't want to waste any, as I might not be able to buy more, so I hold off and try not to think about it.

Cory looks up from the log and reports we've traveled 398 nautical miles since leaving – 107 of which we accomplished in the past twenty-four hours. I think I remember Dorin saying it was 750 miles from New York to Bermuda. So, more than halfway there? All right! I guess we can stand one day of calms.

Today is our first opportunity to get a sun sight and find out exactly where we are. We don't have a Sat Nav, a satellite navigation system, so the sextant is our only means of navigating. I wonder if we'll be surprised when we find out where we really are. Dorin claims he's a little rusty at celestial navigation, but he doesn't anticipate any problem.

"Here's my watch," he says. "I just adjusted it by the radio so the time is accurate to the second." He also hands me paper and a pen. "You can sit in the cockpit. I'll sit on the cabin roof. Now when I say 'mark,' write down the time to the second. Then I'll give you the reading off the sextant. Write that down, also."

There's still no wind, but now the swells have deepened and are 4 to 6 feet, so he has to wait until the boat rises to the top of a swell to get a good view of the horizon

"Mark!" he yells.

I write 10:26 and 48 seconds.

He tilts the sextant and reads from the instrument, "Forty-three minutes, and 12, um, no, I mean 43 *degrees* and 12, um, minutes and eight, um...I mean 12.8 minutes."

"Got it."

"I'm going to do a few more. Ready?"

I adjust the watch on my wrist so I can see the face better. "Ready."

"Mark!"

I write down 10:28 and 11 seconds and wait for the reading off the sextant.

"Mark!" Dorin yells again.

I look up startled. "Wait a minute. You didn't give me the degrees."

"Oh, excuse me. Just ignore the previous one. The degrees for this one is...."

"But wait a minute. I didn't write down the time of this one."

"Oh. Okay, let's do it again. Ready?"

"Ready."

"Mark!"

I glance quickly at my watch, but before I can record the numbers, Dorin, in an effort to redeem himself, is rapidly reeling off the sextant reading: "43 degrees, 52.4 minutes."

Because I'm new to the process, I don't, for a second, realize it's not necessary to write down the sextant information the same instant he gives it to me. It will stay the same as long as nothing moves on the sextant. But, in an effort to write the degrees down as he says them, I have neglected to get the time again.

"I'm going to do one more," Dorin says.

"Um, I didn't get the last one."

"Why not?"

"Ah...never mind."

"Okay, one more will probably still be enough."

In a minute he yells, "Mark! 44 degrees..."

"Wait!" I yell as I write down the time, 10:31 and 14 seconds. "Okay, now...44 what?"

"Forty-four minutes and... I mean 44 *degrees* and 38.2 minutes."

Out of the corner of my eye, I see Cory suppress a smile and shake his head.

Dorin comes back into the cockpit and lays the sextant down on the cockpit seat and goes below. Cory dives for the precious, fragile instrument and puts it back in the box.

After twenty minutes with pencil and paper, Dorin says, "Well we can't possibly be where this says we are. I've checked it twice. Here, go through this with me."

I suspect this is a ploy to break me into the task of reducing the sight. He knows I've been apprehensive about it, and for months I've doubted my ability to catch on to celestial navigation.

"I really don't know anything about it," I say. "I don't think I would be any help to you if I looked at it. Why don't I wait until I have time to read the book? It would be a waste of your time. Really. I wouldn't know where to start. You know I have trouble with math."

He pats the seat beside him and motions me into it. He opens a book. "First you use the number of feet that my eyes were above the water when I took the sight and use it to look up the 'dip,' and then you subtract the dip from the sextant reading." He points to the "D" on the reduction forms he made up on the computer before we left.

"What's this?" I asked, pointing to a blank space beside an "IC."

"Oh...that's "IC" for index correction. Um, I didn't check the correction this time, but it wouldn't make that much difference, anyway. I'll do it on the next sight. After that you look up the refraction in this table and add it to the figure we just had."

"It says '*subtractive*' right here. Does that mean anything?"

"Oh, yes. Thanks, it's supposed to be subtracted not added. The table I used to use, told you to add it." He erases and reworks his way down the form making a correction to Greenwich time.

"This gives you the 'GMT,' Greenwich Mean Time," he says, "which you use to look up the 'GHA,' Greenwich Hour Angle, in this table. But it only gives it for hours. You have to look up the minutes in this table on page...right, here, 127."

"What's this?" I ask pointing to a column.

"Oh, that's to correct for the seconds. I guess I didn't do that. Okay, I'll subtract 2.0."

"Add."

"Oh, yes, pardon me, *add*."

"Mom," says Cory with an 'innocent' smile, "when you get done teaching Dorin will you teach me?"

We finish the form but still don't come up with an answer much different from his original.

"We can't possibly be where this says we are. Guess I really am rusty," says Dorin. "Let me spend some time with *Dutton's Navigation and Piloting* and see what I can find out." He scoops up the books and notepaper and heads for the fo'c'sle.

An hour later he reappears. "Well, I came up with a few things I'd forgotten, but it doesn't have anything to do with this problem."

He is worried and frustrated, but during the past seven years we've been sailing together, I've developed confidence in his ability to solve difficult problems, so I'm not concerned.

"Got it!" He says just after supper. "I don't believe I forgot this. Look, right here at the top of the page of the reduction table: for north latitude LHA *greater* than 180 degrees ZN equals Z. But LHA *less* than 180 degrees, ZN equals 360 minus Z. That's it! Now, I'll get to work on the sight."

Sure. Makes sense to me, I think.

Then my attention shifts. The boat rises subtly.

"There's finally some wind out of here," calls Cory. "We're starting to move."

I go up on deck to take advantage of the breeze. Within a few minutes the sails fill out nicely, and we finally move! The rolling motion we've experienced all day has stopped, and now, at 6:30 p.m., the *Fandango* slices neatly through the water at a very comfortable ten-degree heel. Sailing just doesn't get any better, any more comfortable than this. And we can see the horizon.

"I'll have a course change for you in a few minutes," Dorin calls from below. "We are almost in the Gulf Stream, by the way."

Yeah! Cory and I high-five. That invisible, moving "sea mark" that seemed so exotic when I studied the world map in seventh grade geography is close at hand. Now we're getting some place.

Chapter Five
'Twas a Dark
and Stormy Night

The sky is clear--it's a beautiful day. Yet, I notice gray clouds hugging the horizon.

"Look at that sky," I remark to Cory. "That's a line squall." I like being able to pass on bits of sailing knowledge to him. "Years ago, Dorin and I outran a line squall near Islesboro. They're something to stay away from if you're near land but nothing to worry about out here."

"Ah, yeah. We learned about line squalls in the Power Squadron course, Mom, remember?"

Dorin had signed Cory and me up for a course at a nearby high school the winter before we left. We learned a little bit about safety, navigation, knots and hitches...and weather.

"Oh, yeah."

As we watch, the small gray smudge grows to a large, dirty-yellow smudge, until it covers the whole southeast horizon.

The direction we're heading.

"Would you come look at the sky?" I ask Dorin.

"It's just a line squall," he says, poking his head out of the hatch a second. "It will only last fifteen minutes, or so. Nothing to worry about. I'll be up in just a minute." He disappears below.

A sudden gust of wind slaps the sails, and we snap over twenty degrees.

"We'll reduce the sails in a minute," Dorin yells up.

"I can see wind coming this way," yells Cory. "Up ahead the water is disturbed."

"White caps?" asks Dorin.

"Yeah."

Dorin comes bolting up the companionway steps. "Okay. Let's put a reef in the main." He looks at the sky again. "Let's take the jib down, too, until this goes by."

He and Cory work on the sails. I can't take my eyes off the sky. It's a strange charcoal yellow that's spreading rapidly.

In my mind's eye I see a wizened "old salt," a patch over one eye, a pipe in the corner of his mouth: *"Aye, Matey, t'was a dairty sky we saw that fiteful day. They was some of us aboard the Eagle who knew what was in store for us poor souls who rode her. T'was dairty weather, and we was headed stright into it."*

With butterflies in my stomach, I study the blackening sky.

"It may get a little rough for a few minutes," Dorin says as he and Cory come back into the cockpit. "How fast are we moving?"

"Six knots," replies Cory, glancing at the knot log in the cabin.

The boat's maximum speed is six and a half knots.

"Six?" Dorin frowns. "How much heel?"

"Fifteen degrees," I reply.

"Hmm. We may have to reduce sail a little more."

"Seven knots now," says Cory.

"Twenty-degree heel," I add as we lurch again.

White caps spit from the tops of three-foot waves. Rain begins to tattoo the boat.

"Okay, Let's put another reef in. Shirl, you'll have to turn the boat into the wind."

Hanging onto the lifelines, they go forward.

Historically, in winds over ten knots, this is not my best scene. True to form I turn the boat too far. "Look out!" I yell as the boom sweeps across with a bang. Now the stays'l is back winded, and the flapping main sounds like gunfire.

"Let her come around," Dorin yells.

In years past, I almost knocked him off the boat on three similar occasions--one time, twice in two minutes. Each time, in my horrified confusion, I forgot which way to turn to "bring her around."

Panicking, now, I pull the tiller toward me. When nothing happens, I rapidly push it away.

"Wrong way!" Dorin and Cory yell simultaneously. But which *way* is the wrong way?

Cory sprints toward me along the slick deck. He grabs the tiller, and the boat comes around. Dorin finishes reefing the flogging sail as the rain comes down in sheets.

A large wave smacks the side of the boat, flinging gallons of water on us. We stare at each other. It's warm, very warm water! New England's ocean waters warm up for two weeks in the middle of the summer, changing from frigid to merely numbing.

"Guess we're in the Gulf Stream," Dorin says with satisfaction.

Cory darts into the cabin and comes out a few seconds later with foul-weather jackets and safety harnesses. Struggling against a lurching boat, we pull on and fasten the gear.

White-tipped waves, five or six feet high, smash into the lurching *Fandango*, throwing spray across the cabin top. I look down at the inclinometer and my stomach sinks. Twenty degrees.

A gust slams us. Thirty.

Something crashes to the floor in the cabin.

"Damn! The wind is still building," Dorin shouts. "We'll have to reef again. We'll have to reef the stays'l, too. I need your help, Cor."

No! The thought of both of them on the slippery deck, with the wind screaming while the boat drops out from under their feet every few seconds, terrifies me.

I look at the straining sails and back at the inclinometer. Thirty degrees. If we don't reduce sail, we risk a knockdown.

Dorin catches sight of my face. "We have to. You have to bring it into the wind again."

"No, I can't. I'll knock you off. I can't do it."

"Yes, you can. We'll be okay. Let's go, Cor. Snap on before you step out of the cockpit,"

Cory and Dorin snap their safety harness tethers to the lifeline and grab the handrail as, crouching, they step out on the deck, planting their feet in the angle between the toe rail and the deck. A wave crashes over the bow, and they're up to their ankles in foam.

As they reach the mast, the boat slips sideways and down off a wave. Over the roar of the wind, Dorin yells something to Cory; I hold my breath while Cory unhitches his harness from the lifeline and, climbing up onto the cabin, refastens it to the mast.

A huge wave slams us, and the deck drops out from under their feet.

I grit my teeth and force down a scream.

Dorin turns toward the cockpit and yells something. I can't hear, but I know it must be to turn the boat into the wind. "Please, help me do it right," I pray. My teeth chatter. Our speed reduces as we change direction. I try desperately to feel the wind, watch the sail, and hold the boat so that it will lower tension on the sail. "Not too much, not too much," I caution myself. Dorin yells again, but the scream of the wind is too much, and I miss it. Is he saying, "That's enough?" Or, "Turn it more?" He pulls hard on the sail, but it doesn't budge.

I move the tiller a little more, and the sail luffs a little. A huge wave slams over the top of the cabin and douses Dorin and Cory to the waist. White foam blows horizontally off the tops of the ten-foot waves boiling around us. I try to remember from the photos in *Chapman's Piloting and Seamanship....* Is this a hurricane building?

Hanging onto the mast with one hand, Dorin and Cory pull on the sail with the other, and it comes down a yank at a time. Dorin braces his feet against the life raft tied to the cabin top, and, stretching out almost full length, he pulls on the reefing line.

Sometimes the third reefing line sticks, and I hold my breath, but this time it moves – in jerks, but it moves. He cleats off the line and yells to me again, but the wind whips away all words except "...sheet..." The main sheet. Release the main sheet while he tightens up the main halyard. The knot in my stomach tightens. I... CAN'T... DO...THIS. I stifle a sob.

Trying not to move the tiller, I lean way back and grab the sheet below the cam cleat and yank once, twice. Nothing happens. I know from past experience I can't pull the sheet out of the cleat unless I use two hands, but I mustn't let go of the tiller. Dorin and Cory are forward, risking life and limb, and I can't even do a simple thing like release the main sheet! A half-stifled scream of frustration comes out through clenched teeth as I yank again with all my strength. My knuckles jam into the top of the sail locker as the sheet releases, and the line plays out. Dorin cranks the main halyard tight. I pull in the sheet. Done.

Squinting into the rain, Dorin yells to Cory, who then unwinds the halyard for the stays'l. I've forgotten they still have to reef the remaining headsail! One of them has to undo his safety harness, work his way up to the stays'l boom and reattach. In a crouch, with one hand on the rail and the other on the lifeline, Dorin works his way up the lurching deck. He attaches the six-foot safety harness tether to the stay and braces his feet against the toe rail, shoulder against the stay. It takes two hands to reef the stays'l. At that moment a tremendous wave strikes with such force, the boat stands still and shudders from mast to keel. Below, objects crash to the floor, but I don't take my eyes from the men on the deck. The water sweeps around Dorin, waist high, and then rushes down both sides of the deck. Before it backs around the coamings and empties into the cockpit, Dorin has the sail down and ties the first reefing point. Hanging onto the stays'l boom, he creeps to the back of the sail, ties the remaining point, and works back to unsnap his harness. Meanwhile, as the boat lurches and slams into the waves, Cory braces his body against the mast, quickly tightens the halyard, and cleats it off.

They still have to get back to the cockpit, unhitching and reattaching every time they get to a stanchion. Dorin gets as far as the mast and nods for Cory to go ahead of him. Cory slides carefully off the cabin top and then realizes he can't reach back far enough to unclip his tether. My nerves are so on end, I growl a scream. On his knees, on the cabin top, he un-clips, his grasp moves from mast to handrail as he slides on his back until his feet touch the deck, his face averted to avoid the driving rain. Behind him, Dorin extends his arms forward, providing some protection for Cory in case he slips.

Trembling, I hold my breath as they unclip and reclip their harnesses to each section of the lifeline. It's almost dark, the wind screams furiously, water rushes along the deck above their shoe tops. The rain beats against their backs so hard it bounces off.

Cory steps into the cockpit and reaches back to unhitch from the lifeline and reattach to the brass eye bolted to the cabin. Dorin steps into the cockpit behind him.

"Whew!" he laughs, wiping his face on the towel Cory hands him. "I thought this was just a little line squall. It shouldn't last much longer, though. The autopilot seems to be holding okay. No use staying out here. Let's go below and wait it out."

We're still a twenty-degree tilt to starboard, and the stairs are drenched. Handhold to handhold we make our way down the stairs and across the jerking cabin floor, picking up and shaking off dripping objects, for we now have six inches of water on the low side. A teakettle, a couple of plastic cups, a medical box, two pillows, five or six books, and several pads of white lined paper float on the floor. We stack what we can in the sink and tuck the rest into crannies for now.

"Damn," exclaims Dorin softly, after he flips the bilge pump switch. "It's plugged again."

"Do you want me to use the manual?" Cory asks. The manual pump is in the cockpit.

"No! This will be over soon. We aren't taking on any more water. No use you sitting out there now."

Wave after wave slams us. Sometimes we come to a shuddering stop, and other times we snap sharply over, then back.

We are taking a beating.

Cory lies back on his bunk on the starboard side. There are cushions and blankets piled high on the dinette seat. When I push them back, they form a backrest that allows me to lean back in a semi-reclining position. I brace my feet against the cabinet on the other side of the passageway to keep from sliding off the seat. Beside me, Dorin hoists himself onto the ice box next to the open hatch. It's totally black outside.

"We must be getting hit with one squall after another," he says. "Should quiet down in less than an hour...."

Bam! A wave knocks us over further, and I gasp in surprise, bracing myself until we slowly swing back up to thirty degrees. We hurtle and bash along at seven knots. Again we slam sideways, and the boat goes so far over it feels like it can't possibly come back up, but in a couple of heartbeats it does.

The next time it happens, I lean forward and look out into the darkness.

For Cor's sake I don't react to what I see. Nearly on its side, the boat slides diagonally down a huge wall of black water. I stiffen my knees and push hard against the cabinet to keep from being thrown up out of my seat. Again, I feel that we tip beyond what the boat can take. Just when I think we are going over, it swings back up to what is already too much of a heel. My legs shake, and I can't stop them.

I don't look outside again.

I remember the conversation I overheard at Goudy and Stevens boatyard just before we left. Dorin was talking to another boater. "It's a funny feeling," the man said, "when you see your spreaders hit the water."

"That probably qualifies as a knockdown," Dorin had replied.

The shaking in my legs becomes an all-over body tremble that I can't control. One thought repeatedly demands attention. Why have I allowed Cory to be in a situation with the potential for such danger? In past scrapes on the boat I haven't been frightened, but it was Dorin and I alone. Cory is only sixteen and full of hopes for the future.

I put him out here.

I have to fix this. I have to protect him.

Then I am overwhelmed by the thought that I am powerless to do so.

Bam! We are going over, I know it. At the last second, we come back up. I slide my hand along the rail that separates the ice box from the dinette and touch Dorin's hand. He covers my hand and gives it a squeeze.

"Ya okay?" He asks in a normal voice. I'm glad the trembling hasn't reached my hand. He's always been impressed with my disinclination to whimper. I don't want to spoil it now.

"Yeah, fine," I reply, grateful the trembling hasn't also reached my voice.

Ka... bam! It sounds like a ton of water pounds the top of the boat.

From the dark corner of Cory's bunk comes a soft warble:

> "The mate was a mighty sailor man,
> The skipper brave and sure.
> Five passengers set sail that day
> On a three-hour tour,
> On a three-hour tour.
> The weather started getting rough,
> The tiny ship was tossed.
> If not for the courage of the fearless crew,
> The Minnow would be lost,
> The Minnow would be lost."

When Dorin and I stop laughing, Cory says, "Well, I've got the four o'clock watch in the morning. Time for little Cory to go to sleep." He turns over...and falls asleep! I'm still chuckling and reflecting on his knack for breaking tension with humor when we are hit so hard, I do come up out of my seat.

"There's no use being this uncomfortable or letting the boat take the strain," Dorin says, patting my hand. "We could heave-to until morning."

I ask him to explain.

"You back-wind the stays'l and lash the tiller to the lee side. The boat will just mush along without heeling much, and we can wait this thing out. My guess is that before morning it'll be over, but meanwhile we can get some rest."

I catch my breath. "You have to leave the cockpit?"

"No, I don't. There's no danger to this at all. I'll be right back. Go on up and climb into bed."

We're still lurching sharply, which causes me to whack my head on the radar as I pull myself to a standing position. I grab the rail, now the table, now the heater. I reach the fo'c'sle, turn around, and hoist myself into the bed. As I push the guitar aside and scoot across to leave room for Dorin, I realize I'm still wearing my wet foul-weather jacket, safety harness, and wet sneakers. I don't care a whole lot.

I hear the ratcheting sound of the winch, and a minute later the boat comes smoothly upright to a comfortable fifteen-degree heel.

We still roll, but not as much. The waves still hit us, but not as hard. The companionway boards fall into place, and the hatch cover squeaks shut.

"How's that?" Dorin asks as he slides in beside me. We lay there for a while listening to the water rush over the decks. Sometimes a wave slams the foredeck, and spray rushes over the cabin top, but we are relatively comfortable.

"How are you feeling?" Dorin asks with a yawn. There's a cavernous distance between his relaxed yawn and my tension.

"Fine," I say. "I seem to have a stomachache though."

"It's probably the tension," he mumbles, moving my head to his shoulder. "It's going to be all right." He falls asleep immediately.

I make an effort to relax. By now I should be used to the water rushing inches away from my head. Bam! A quart of water squirts under the closed hatch cover directly above our bunk and lands across our stomachs. Without a word Dorin sits up, screws the hatch down tighter, and goes back to sleep.

I visualize the kitchen of my old farmhouse. I am making supper. My kids, watching the black and white TV screen, sing... "If not for the courage of the fearless crew the *Minnow* would be lost..."

I smile and eventually fall asleep.

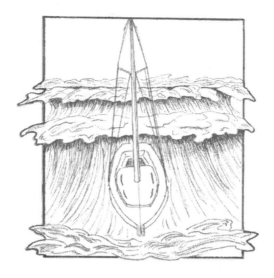

Chapter Six
Sea's Got a
Little Chop to It

The catch that secures the fo'c'sle door is broken. With every toss of the boat, the door bang, bang, bangs against the lavatory cabinet. In the galley, the dish cupboard doors don't have their fasteners attached yet, a job we intended to do underway, so the double doors open like a cuckoo clock when the boat slopes left. They snap shut hard when it rocks to the right. Attached to the fronts of the doors are wooden holders for knives and forks. The metallic tattoo of the silverware emphasizes the cuckoo clock rhythm – rattle snap, rattle snap. In the sink something--the tea kettle?-- goes tick tack, tick tack. The noises are nerve-racking, then bang! A wave thunders across the boat.

Dorin wakes up every fifteen minutes to look outside. Shortly after daylight he heads for the cockpit. I hear him snap his tether to the eye bolt. A minute later the boat tips sharply to the side and heaves and bucks once again. I roll over on my stomach and look out of the fo'c'sle toward the stern. Dorin is at the tiller; behind him a wall of blue-black water, so high I can't see the top of it, bears down on the boat.

"Good mornin'!" Dorin says cheerfully. I catch my breath, but, miraculously, the wall doesn't break over the boat. We slide down it.

"Nice weather out here. Sea's got a little chop to it, though."

He calls to Cory, who rolls out of his bunk and is on his feet and moving along the pitching floor before he's fully awake.

"Still got your safety harness on? Good."

Cory reaches for a handrail that lurches away from his grasp. He uses the table to catch his balance.

"I need you to take the tiller for a while. I have to work on the motor, and the autopilot can't handle this stuff."

As Dorin gives instructions to Cory on how to handle the boat, I roll over on my back and struggle to sit up. I have to turn 180 degrees so I can swing my legs over the side of the bed. My feet are twelve inches shy of being able to touch the floor. I wiggle forward an inch. I've got to go help. Another wall of water behind us blocks out the sky, and we slide down it at an alarming angle. The "loopy" roller coaster feeling finds a place in my stomach.

"What course should we be holding?" asks Cory.

"The conditions aren't giving us a choice right now. We just have to keep the wind and seas behind us until this is over. We're heading in approximately the right direction, though. This will be over soon. By the way, we lost the mooring ball last night and the anchor roller off the bowsprit. Looks like that's all the damage we took."

I inch my fanny forward, ignoring the queasiness. I need to get to the cockpit to help Cory. With one foot finally on the wet floor, I lean against the door jam, trying to control the rising nausea. I ease the other foot to the floor. I hate throwing up.

Dorin glances down. "How are you feeling?"

The boat rolls sharply. I don't dare open my mouth. I shake my head.

"Better lay down for a while," he says. "Can I get you anything?"

Slowly I nod and carefully hoist myself up onto the bed. I lean backwards until I'm on my back. My legs still dangle over the side. Good enough.

"What can I get for you?" Dorin leans into the fo'c'sle.

"Pills. Medical box. Foot of Cory's bunk." We stored boxes of medical supplies in three different places.

Dorin rummages around for a few minutes. "Nope, this has bandages in it."

"Galley locker."

The galley locker is a cavernous hole, housing everything from electrical supplies to pots and pans, as well as two of the medical boxes. Dorin digs his way to the bottom. The motion relief pills are in the second box.

"Be right out, Cor," he says in response to something Cory asks. "Hold on for just a minute."

"I thought you were using Scopolamine patches," Dorin says.

"Yeah, I did when we first started. They only last three days. But I didn't get seasick."

"But we didn't have any motion," he says with a half grin.

"Right." I grab the bottle and frantically work on the seal. Dorin hands me a glass of water, and I gulp down a pill.

"Try to relax." He helps me swing my legs around into the bed. "We're getting these swells and waves because of the wind last night, but they should be calming down soon. I've got to look at the motor. Tried to run it to charge the batteries, but it won't keep running. Knot log is broken, too."

"Bilge pump?"

"Yeah, I'll get to that as soon as I get the motor going."

In fifteen minutes, I slip gratefully toward sleep. As I wander in and out of consciousness, I'm aware that Dorin is moving around in the salon.

"Whasa matter?" I ask groggily.

"I'm fixing the bilge pump. It's clogged. Both of them." I hear him pry up the floorboards to get at the bilge.

"Neesum hep?"

"No," he chuckles. "I've got it under control. Cor, reach in and hit that switch, would you?"

Later I hear them talking outside. "We're still picking up speed, and we're going to start burying the bow into the waves. Let's try running under bare poles and see if it helps."

I listen to Dorin's footsteps overhead as he walks along the deck. The boat lurches, and his feet leave the deck. Before they land again the bow dips and scoops up hundreds of gallons of water. Is Cory keeping an eye on Dorin? Is he dangling over the side of the boat on the end of his harness tether? I roll over to shout to Cory, then I hear Dorin moving on the foredeck. He later tells me the wave rolled over him waist high. I continue to listen for every scrap of evidence that he is still on the boat.

Then I hear him back in the cockpit talking to Cory. "How's that?" he asks.

"Better, I think," Cory replies. I drift back into the welcome fog and then out of it.

"Is it getting difficult to steer? Okay, we're still going faster than we should. I'm going to put 600 feet of anchor line with the big anchor out behind us to see if that will slow us down a little. This should be calming down soon."

It seems like forever he is on the foredeck pulling the anchor line out of the locker and attaching it to another anchor. The bowsprit scoops up water each time we reach the bottom of a wave.

I awaken suddenly, my heart pounding. I fell asleep before he was back in the cockpit! How long did I sleep? What's happening? I roll over to see Dorin, a pile of line at his feet, lowering the anchor off the stern.

"Four knots under bare poles, trailing six-hundred feet of warp!" He says. "Would you believe it? Is it steering a little better? Want me to take over for a while? Why don't you get some rest."

Cory plows down the stairs and falls in his bunk. The next time I wake up, the shadows and fog are gone and so is the nausea, but I'm thirsty. Handhold to handhold, I move to the galley. The boat still bucks and slides on a stiff heel, but I make it to the cockpit.

The sky is clear and the sun sparkles on the ocean waves. Cory mans the tiller again, bareheaded and sunburned. His eyes are bloodshot from too much sun, but he's grinning. Both feet are braced against the opposite side of the cockpit as he leans back, pulling hard on the tiller. We're still "sluicing" diagonally down 25-foot waves.

"Have you eaten?" I ask, hanging onto the handrails.

Cory shakes his head. "I'm more thirsty than anything." He carefully watches the steep wave approaching from behind. It appears, as it lifts us, that it will crest and dump on us, but at the last second Cory gives an extra tug on the tiller, we slide over a bit, and the wave passes. We're back in a valley looking at the next wall of black water, pierced in its center by the anchor line trailing from our stern.

The sail locker lid in the cockpit is propped up. Dorin's arm and shoulder, gleaming with sweat, are visible in the opening.

"He's fixing the bilge pump," says Cory, following my gaze. "It wasn't plugged. Something wrong with the cable, I think."

Intending to get them each a drink of water, I grab what appears to be semi-clean cups from the clutter in the sink. Air and a few drops of water squirt convulsively out of the tap. As I pump faster, air just keeps whooshing out.

"We are out of water in the big tank," Cory says mildly.

To change to the second tank, I have to turn off the empty tank first. I pull a sleeping bag, a blanket, four hardcover books, a cushion, and the medical box out from under the foot cavity of Cory's bed--where does he put his feet?--and feel for the valve under the bed cushion. The queasiness begins again as I close off the valve of the empty tank and stuff everything back. To get to the saddle tank valve on the other side of the boat, I push back the pillows, cushions, blankets, and foul weather gear that form a mound that nearly obscures the dinette table.

The boat tilts and rolls while I turn the valve. Back to the sink: pump, pump, splat, pump, pump, pump...water!

Both of them seem grateful for the glasses of lukewarm water.

I ask the time and Cory replies that it's noon. I rummage around in the cupboard and find a can of tuna. Feeling around the drawer, I locate the can opener and hand it outside with the tuna.

"Yum, my favorite," Dorin says as he steps back up into the cockpit. Dorin doesn't have many dislikes, but canned tuna is one of them.

I shrug. "Better than squash," I say, since this is his other dislike. As he attaches the can opener to the can, the bow slams into the bottom of the wave and the bowsprit goes out of sight. We watch until the bow lifts like the front of a hobby horse, scooping up water that runs down both sides of the cabin more than four inches high. We know this because some of the water spills over the four-inch toe rails and back into the ocean. When a higher river of brine spills into the cockpit, Cory rises off the seat in time to keep his shorts from getting wet. Dorin gets wet because he's focused on holding the can of tuna high enough to keep it dry.

"Sorry," says Cory. "I was focused on food."

Dorin hands the open can to me. "Here, it's good," he says and grins.

I shake my head. Canned tuna is okay, but not on a queasy stomach. I turn back, grab the forks out of the drawer and hand them to Dorin.

"*Bon appétit*," I say, and slowly make my way back toward the fo'c'sle.

"Your loss," he says. "Yum, so good." I glance back, but he isn't eating the tuna. He hands the can to Cory. "Why don't you start? I'll take the helm for a while."

I kneel in front of the can cupboard and find a can of corned beef. I hand it outside.

"That was the fish course," I say. "This is the meat course."

I climb back into the hot and stuffy fo'c'sle. I'd like to open the hatch cover to get a breeze, but every once in a while, water sloshes over the lid, and so I leave it closed.

Dorin leans in a few minutes later. "The bilge pump's fixed. Something is still wrong with the motor, though. We'll need it to charge the batteries."

"Is it serious?"

"How could it be serious with our run of good luck?"

A few minutes later I realize I didn't get a drink of water for myself. Cory is at the helm, and Dorin is elbow deep in the engine compartment.

Even if I were to get up, I wouldn't be able to get close enough to the sink to pump water.

"I think that's got it. It was the fuel filter," Dorin says as he slips the engine cover in place. "It's two o'clock. I'll take over in a minute, Cor, so you can get out of the sun."

"Didn't you say the height of the waves would drop?"

"They built up because of the wind. I think the wind has dropped a little. This should be over by night."

"Are we on a course that will take us any closer to where we are supposed to be?" Cory asks.

"No, I'd have to say no. Until this subsides, we are unlikely to be on a course that will put Bermuda in our sights. At least we're heading south. Ish." He grins at Cory. "That's something right there."

When I awake again, I'm still a little queasy, but thirsty, so I slip out of bed. The boat is heeling so much I go down on my knees and crawl to the galley. Sitting on the floor in front of the cupboard, I find the ham I'm looking for. Using the winding key, I open the can and grab two forks and stick them into the ham. I hand the can outside onto the bridge deck and head back to bed. The dizziness and nausea are back, but I don't want to take a pill and continue to be drowsy. I fling my arms and legs out to keep the rolling motion of my body to a minimum, when I realize I didn't get a drink yet. I try to go to sleep.

"Turn the masthead light on," Dorin tells Cory. I roll over and look out. It's almost dark.

"It won't go on," he replies. Dorin swears. "Take the helm, Cor, I'll have to tear into the wiring in the head. We must have a short."

"We have a lot of water in the corner," I tell him.

"The electric bilge pump is on the blink again. I think it's the electrical connections this time. When I get the masthead light to work, I'll pump the water out with the manual pump."

Half-an-hour later another oath. "I'll have to pull up the floorboards. The filter for the bilge pump is plugged again."

I'll have to wait for a glass of water until the floorboards are back in place, so I try to relax and ignore the bing bang, rattle snap, tick tack, gurgle sounds that reminds me I am many miles, light-years even, from my home and familiar surroundings.

"It was a matchstick plugging the filter," Dorin mutters. "Now how did that get in there?"

The boards go down, Dorin flips the bilge switch, and I make my way to the sink and grab a glass. Pump, pump, pump. I glance in the glass as I lift it to my mouth. There are floaties in it. Little chips of stuff, floating lazily toward the bottom of the glass,

"Yeah," Cory says, smiling as he watches me. "It's got junk in it. You have to strain it through a towel."

Leaning hard against the sink, hanging on with one hand, I strain the water.

Water is the best liquid in the world. It's great...until I stop.

"Yuk. It takes like swamp water."

"Yeah," says Cory, still grinning. "We noticed."

"Let's heave-to again," says Dorin. "I don't want to put the strain on the autopilot, the compass light isn't working, and it's clouding over, so we won't be able to steer by the stars. Looks like some more squalls building up over there so we might as well sit tight and take it easy. I've got to put up some sails though, so I can bring her around. Go lay down, Cor. I can do it."

I listen to the taps and thonks of lines rapping against the deck overhead, and, as usual, when anyone leaves the safety of the cockpit, I'm tense. The winch whirs, the boat drops and lifts, and I hear airborne feet slam back to the deck.

"Get out the boards," Dorin yells to Cory as he reaches the cockpit. They lash the tiller over and pile down the stairs. Just as the last board slides into place and the companionway lid slams shut, it starts to pour.

"Whew! That was close," laughs Dorin. "There are some line squalls that are going to give us a little discomfort for a few minutes, but it shouldn't last long."

For a few minutes? Shouldn't last long? My eyes lock with Cory's, and he grins and shrugs.

Lightning flashes through the little portholes, brightly lighting the cabin. A crash of thunder follows.

"Better unhitch the radio," Dorin says, diving toward it. Cory flicks a lighter and holds it near the radio so they can see. The lightning and thunder come so close together there isn't time to count between the flash and the clap.

We find places in the salon to settle back in the dark and wait out the storm.

"If this doesn't stop in half an hour, we might as well just get some rest until it clears up," Dorin says.

"My bed is soaked," Cory snaps irritably. "There's water dripping in my face!" He pulls a wet blanket over his head and turns over.

The electric storm seems to be hovering over us," Dorin says. "We should be sailing out of this any time now."

I look at him in the glare of a triple flash of lightning. Anytime now. Yet, rather than decreasing, the waves seem to be getting higher. They crash across the bow and slam the boat around. The wind builds, and the rigging shudders. The whole boat shakes.

As we lay in the fo'c'sle listening to the storm, our hands touching, I realize we are in bed for the second night in a row fully dressed with our safety harnesses on. Dorin still has his foul weather jacket on and his jeans are wet.

"I have to try to call Glenn on the ham radio at 11 o'clock. I hope the storm is over so I can reconnect the radio." Dorin spent months learning Morse code and studying for his radio license so we could get national and world news and the high seas weather reports on a ham radio. We also needed a contact person to keep us in touch with the world--someone who would know where we were. Glenn is a ham radio operator who volunteered to be our contact. They have an agreement that they will attempt to communicate at 11 in the evening. So far, they've talked a couple of times, but talking on the radio is something Dorin is not comfortable with.

Suddenly, it's quiet.

We still mush along on a heel of fifteen degrees, but the electrical storm dissipates, and the silence is beautiful. Twenty minutes later, just as Dorin is about to reconnect the radio, thunder rumbles...another storm.

All night long, one squall after another beats on the boat. Sometimes the waves break so hard that it's difficult to believe the boat holds together. The howling wind strains the rigging; the shivering spreads to the whole boat. Lightning strikes so close that we hear the crash of thunder at the moment the cabin lights up. It sounds like explosions beside the boat. I don't sleep, and at 4 o'clock I am close to the breaking point.

"I...can't...stand this...anymore!" I gasp. An unreasoning, frightened part of my mind says we must be able to stop it somehow.

"We are just getting one squall after another. It can't go on forever," Dorin explains. "The boat's all right."

"But our mast is the tallest thing around here. Doesn't lightning strike the tallest thing?"

"Don't worry about it," he whispers pulling me closer. "It's not going to happen. We grounded the shrouds, remember?"

"What happens when lightning hits a boat and it isn't grounded?"

"Could blow a hole in the bottom."

"Really?"

"But it's not going to happen."

Crash! A wave breaks over the entire boat. Water rushes down the decks to drain off. The explosions go off in rapid succession. My heart races, my legs tremble again. How much more can the boat take? Flashing rapidly, almost like a strobe light, the lightning keeps the front cabin almost perpetually lit. Like a Fourth of July finale, the thunder crashes in overlapping volleys again and again. Another wave punishes the boat, and I choke back a scream of frustration and fear. Dorin tightens his arm around my shoulders.

I don't dare speak.

So gradually that I barely notice the change at first, the storm moves from directly over us until it rumbles in the distance, moving ever further away, like a departing train.

It's 4:20 a.m., thirty-two hours after the storm began.

"I told you it wouldn't last long," Dorin says. He pats my hand. "You okay?"

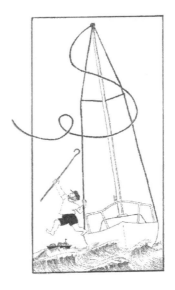

Chapter Seven
Where in the World is Bermuda?

When we awake at 6 a.m., we hear Cory moving around in the galley. "I'm making pancakes. They'll be ready in five minutes."

"He's been on watch since 4:30," Dorin says. "I watched him go."

We decide to stay heaved to until the pancake breakfast is done. I'm so hungry I barely notice the bad taste caused by the water. That's what maple syrup is for.

Dorin and I pick up after breakfast while Cory takes the helm.

"Hand me the binoculars," yells Cory. "How far south you think we are?"

"What do you see?" Dorin pops his head outside.

"Well, it could be a lighthouse. Could we have been blown far enough to be sighting Bermuda?"

"I guess it's possible. Let me take a look." Dorin climbs into the cockpit.

I slip out of the bunk and move rapidly, and overhand, through the cabin and outside before the nausea has a chance to start again.

In only a few minutes, we realize the spot on the horizon is growing rapidly larger. In ten minutes, we identify it as a US Navy destroyer.

"Let's try to hail them on the VHF and get a position fix," Dorin suggests. VHF (Very High Frequency) is the other radio on board. It's used for short distances, and we will only use it in an emergency or to hail other vessels.

"I imagine they monitor Channel 16. All commercial boats are required to. Let's put up some sail and get a little closer first."

The wind is only about 15 knots so Dorin and Cory crank up all three sails so we can close the gap a little between the paths of the *Fandango* and the destroyer. I watch the gray boat grow larger and feel relief to see some other life out here. And, it would be nice to know exactly where we are.

"So. Who wants to use the radio?" asks Dorin when we go below.

"You're the captain," laughs Cory, lying down on his bunk.

"No, I have to watch what's going on outside."

"Looks like it's up to you, Mom."

"No way!" I reply. "I don't how to use that thing."

"Yeah, well, I'll show you," offers Dorin.

"No thanks, I don't even know what you're supposed to say."

"Just say 'calling the Navy destroyer.' Wait a minute. I'll be able to give you the numbers from their bow. Then, just say, 'this is the sailing vessel *Fandango'* and wait for an answer," Dorin explains as he goes outside.

I recognize avoidance when I see it. I can hardly believe these guys, who've been fearless in a raging storm, are afraid to use the radio.

"Why don't you give it a try, Cor?" I ask, as I follow Dorin into the cockpit.

"Why don't we just forget it?" asks Cory. "We can figure out where we are later."

"We might not get a sun sight today. The sky is still clouded over," says Dorin. "Somebody get on the radio."

"Mom?"

"I'm in the cockpit. Cleaning."

Cory heaves a sigh and climbs out of the bunk. "Okay, what am I supposed to say?"

For five minutes, Cory repeatedly tries to hail the Navy ship, which by now is so close we can read its identification numbers without binoculars. No answer. The wind stiffens and then suddenly gusts 25 to 30 knots, and we heel sharply.

"I'm taking the sails down!" Dorin yells, as he works his way forward. He uncleats the halyard and pulls on the jib, but it's stuck and won't move. We're heeling hard, and I hear the teakettle crash across the cabin below. "Bring her more into the wind."

He has the jib in one hand and the halyard in the other, trying to "see saw" them and free the sail. Before the boat comes fully into the wind, it lurches. Dorin grabs for the stay to steady himself, and the halyard flies out of his hand. The wind carries it out around the shrouds. Meanwhile, the jib starts to flap, sounding like firecrackers.

"Christ!" yells Dorin. I have never heard him utter this oath in all the years I've known him. The halyard blows almost horizontally. With difficulty, he makes his way toward the shrouds and, with the boat hook, tries to catch the flailing halyard.

Cory comes flying into the cockpit. If Dorin swears, he knows it's a crisis.

"Turn it more into the wind!" Dorin yells to me again. Cory and Dorin lean out over the lifelines, trying to catch the whipping, flying halyard. I glance at the huge destroyer. It glides silently by, heaving slowly in the heavy seas. As the *Fandango* comes into the wind and straightens up, the halyard swings close enough for Dorin to snag it with the pole. Cory takes it back to the mast, and Dorin makes his way back to the bow where the jib still flogs. He yanks hard on the sail, and, after a couple of minutes, it finally slides to the bottom of the forestay. The destroyer moves rapidly away from us as the sun breaks through the clouds.

"Damn! We've lost the battens out of the stays'l," mutters Dorin. "Never mind now. Let's get the rest of the sails down. This wind doesn't seem to be dying!"

While they work on the sails, I steer the boat and watch the Navy ship, the symbol of security and hope, move rapidly away and out of radio distance. (We were later told that it's Navy policy not to answer hails from yachts unless it's a mayday situation.)

"I've got to get a sun sight, if I can, today. Looks like the clouds are breaking up. It would be nice to know where we are. Can you handle the helm for a few hours, Cor? It's going to be rough for a while until these seas calm down."

Cory takes the tiller, and we're off and running, literally – the wind and water at our stern. The waves are higher than yesterday. Bracing his feet on the opposite side of the cockpit, Cory stretches out almost full-length to hold the tiller to him.

I want to pull my weight today. I stay in the cockpit so the nausea doesn't have a chance to get started. The sun is already warm. I dive back for a minute to get the suntan lotion and sunglasses. Across from Cory, on the "downside" of the cockpit, I watch carefully as he surfs down the waves. I'm going to have trouble handling it when my turn comes, I think. Cory is cheerful and grinning as he steers the *Fandango* through the valleys and mountains of the Atlantic Gulf Stream. I think he's enjoying this! He sees it as a challenge. *Jeesh!* I grouse to myself.

"Can you take it for a minute, while I put lotion on?" he asks. I grab the tiller from where I am and have to push forward. There's nothing to use for leverage, and I bend over double trying to hold the tiller away from me. I don't know how to do this, I think, as the boat rises to the top of the wave. The wave moves past, dumping us into a deep trough. Pushing against the tiller, I watch the trailing anchor line. At the top of another wave, I realize water is going to break into the cockpit. I give an extra yank on the tiller, as I saw Cory do. The stern scoots over a bit, and the wave breaks harmlessly beside us. Cory offers to take the tiller, and I refuse. I'm nervous, but I need to do my share. He changes sides with me so I can brace my feet against the seat on the other side and lean back.

The tension reduces minute by minute. By the time half an hour passes, manning the helm is a challenge that has an element of fun.

It's strenuous work, and we trade off hour by hour. The sun turns the sky blue and the water bluer – there are splashes of deep lavender and bright turquoise in the broiling waves. The sea waters I've known all my life have been black or gray. In spite of lingering fear, the colors of this ocean, more southern than I've ever seen it, enchant me.

Even with sunscreen, the sun takes its toll. While I turn pink, Cory deepens yesterday's burn. We're reluctant to go below and get hats and a second pair of sunglasses – the boat is at such a heel that it's difficult to get to a standing position, much less climb out of the cockpit. Because a locker had to be emptied to make a repair, the cockpit floor is full of things to climb over – the six-gallon kerosene can, a plastic bucket, hoses, and a toolbox. In the cabin below, things are so strewn around it would take forever to find sunglasses and hats. So, we sit and burn and trade one pair of sunglasses back and forth.

Each time we rise to the top of the 20-foot wave, we see we're alone in this vast, tumbling area. The horizon is a leaping, undulating line which makes it difficult to get an accurate sun sight at noon. Cory writes down Dorin's "mark" several times. I'm amazed that he can get any sight at all.

Dorin climbs into the fo'c'sle bunk with paper and pencil to reduce the sight. I glance in an hour later with the intention of asking him for a glass of water.

He's sound asleep.

No wonder. He has been up almost around the clock.

When it's my turn at the tiller, I tell Cory to go below and rest, but he refuses, and I'm grateful. As the day wears on, the effects of the sun and physical strain, as we pull and tug over every wave, are grueling. There is also the strain of wondering what the night will bring. I realize, except for the destroyer, we haven't seen a boat during the day or by radar at night since the storm began. In fact, it's the first time since we started that we hadn't picked up other boats, at least on radar, two or three times a day. Is there something we don't know?

To break the boredom, we play "trivia" games. Name four of the five Marx Brothers. List five of the seven dwarfs. Give the names of King Henry

VIII's wives in order. List cities or states whose names begin and end with "A."

We change places at the tiller. Think of five songs with colors in their titles. List six books that have become movies. Name twelve pro football teams.

We change places at the tiller. We're thirsty and roasted by the sun. In our fatigue we make mistakes, and the tips of waves wash into the cockpit, leaving us ankle-deep in brine, which drains slowly out of the scuppers. Each time, without thinking, I brace for the shock of cold water and am surprised instead by its warmth.

Dorin wakes up, strains us a glass of water, finds my hat and sunglasses buried under the mountain in the salon, and goes back to reducing the sight. Within five minutes he's asleep again. He awakens an hour later to the sound of sloshing bilge water and wearily heaves himself out of bed to tear up the floor once more. The filter on the bilge pump is clogged again. We're not taking on an alarming amount of water, just enough to be annoying.

The long day wears on, and the waves continue to drop in height. Under bare poles at four or five knots, we ride the rushing waves, keeping the wind and waves more or less at our backs.

Dorin comes out and joins us in the cockpit. He watches the wall of water behind us thoughtfully. He catches me watching him and grins. "Sure are big suckers, aren't they?"

"Is this what Diane meant by 'following seas?'"

"I didn't know she had this much influence!"

As the light starts to fail, I become tense again. Will we have another night like last night? What is the possibility it could get worse?

"I think the wind is starting to abate," says Dorin. "If it does, you're going to notice a significant reduction in the height of these waves by tomorrow." We've heard this before. Do we dare believe?

We heave-to and, before it gets too dark to see, Cory cooks supper – spaghetti with white clam sauce. We load our servings down with Parmesan cheese to kill the swamp taste, and, in the dimming light, we eat a hearty meal, the first in forty-eight hours. The wind dies to ten knots, yet the height of the waves decreases only slightly.

Just after dark we see lights on the horizon; it is a real spirit booster. It's nice to have company in this great expanse, and it gives us something different to look at. We pick it up on radar eight miles away, but we've already identified it as a cruise ship because of the brilliance of the spot in the darkness.

We start the motor, switching the cables to the emergency battery, in order to change course – but not too much. We want to get a good look, but not too close. Standing in the cockpit, the three of us watch the diamond glitter separate into hundreds of individual lights as the ship closes the distance. I've never seen a cruise ship before so I want to see what it looks like. Dorin answers our questions about life on a cruise ship. He's made two Atlantic crossings. One thing is clear: they have showers and fabulous food on that ship.

"I bet they don't eat Spam," Cory says.

The ship doesn't alter its course in the slightest, which makes us think that they haven't picked us up on radar and our masthead light isn't working. The mammoth boat crosses our bow at less than half a mile away. We can see some people on the deck, but very few. We guess that even in a boat as large as a cruise ship, rolling in fifteen-foot waves must be uncomfortable. We don't try to contact them, assuming, because the destroyer didn't respond, there is something wrong with our VHF radio. We watch as the sparkling boat glides silently away, becomes a dot, and finally disappears.

Tonight we sleep without our safety harnesses. The bed is still wet, which used to be my pet peeve in boating. Tonight, I don't care. Dorin keeps watch by himself by sticking his head out the front hatch every twenty minutes. I sleep soundly until morning.

On our tenth day at sea, the waves are down to ten feet and dropping. Dorin gets a decent sun sight and reduces it.

"We can't possibly be where this thing says we are," he says – but we are. The wind brought us southwest – a couple of hundred miles too far to the west and still 140 to 190 miles to the north. We change our course toward southeast at almost the precise moment the wind begins blowing from the south, putting us on a continual beat. We also adjust our expectations – two more days to Bermuda, at least.

By the end of the day the waves are down to four feet, and I'm ecstatic. I have learned that I'm not likely to get seasick if I stay in the cockpit or stay lying flat when I'm below. In the salon I pick up the box of Scopolamine patches to put it away.

"Did you read the directions on those?" Dorin asks.

"What, these? You just peel and stick."

Dorin laughs. "Earlier, I was going to put the box somewhere safe, and I saw there were directions."

Cory and I do a double take. "You read directions?" I ask.

"Did this time. It says, 'to avoid blurred vision, wash your hands before and after applying.' Did you?"

"No, not even. Not at all. Well, now, that's a relief. I thought I might have a severe vision problem."

"Always good to read directions," he says, but he can't keep a straight face.

Cory says until we get to Bermuda he doesn't mind doing most of the cooking if I do the dishes. It's a great deal, and I grab it.

The major problem with meals now is that it's impossible to disguise the taste of the water in pancakes, pasta, instant mashed potatoes, and rice. Dorin and Cory try to ignore it, but my appetite decreases with every meal. I wash the dishes out on deck in a plastic pail with ocean water and hand them back down to Cory to put away when they dry.

The next two days become increasingly terrific and mostly uneventful sailing days. Each day the oceans smooths a little more until it's like a lake. It's usually calm at sunrise, but by nine o'clock a steady breeze pushes the *Fandango* along at four knots. The wind increases slowly, and most nights we reach a steady six knots that last until dawn.

During these days we settle into a comfortable routine. Dorin cooks pancakes for breakfast, I wash dishes, Cory puts them away.

Dorin takes the day's first sun sight, and he teaches me how to reduce it. He and Cory take turns at the tiller.

I realized, just before the storm hit, we accumulated so much laundry that I have to wash our clothes by hand in saltwater. During the storm all our clothes got wet, both dirty and clean, and they have to be washed and dried to prevent mildew.

I can fit three articles of clothing in the plastic pail at one time. With a canvas bucket, I haul enough water up over the side to fill the pail – four buckets – add detergent, and then slosh and scrub the clothes. After wringing them out, I dump the water overboard and haul more in to repeat the process with the same three articles of clothing. It usually takes four changes of water before they are clean enough to begin the rinse, which usually requires two changes of water. I calculate that it takes twenty-four canvas buckets of water to wash two shirts and a pair of shorts.

I wash clothes the better part of each day, but I never seem to catch up. Cory cooks lunch; I do laundry until mid-afternoon -- the point when I know I'll scream if I have to face another pail. I hang the laundry along the lifelines and fasten it with clothespins, and when I run out, I tie the items with string. I always hope it will rain for a few minutes and rinse the clothes with freshwater. Articles washed in saltwater never dry thoroughly and feel uncomfortably damp when you wear them. Most often the rain comes when the clothes are almost dry, and I have nine more pieces ready to hang up, but I leave the nearly dry ones on the line, so they get the benefit of the shower.

When the waves drop to normal, the autopilot again becomes our best friend, and without the need for manual steering, I stand watch all day, from eight in the morning until four in the afternoon, since I'm outside doing laundry anyway. Cory takes over in the afternoon until it's time for him to cook supper. He is creative in varying our menu, given the limitations of no refrigeration or fresh produce.

After supper I wash the lunch and supper dishes, check the laundry, fold and put away whatever is dry, and hang up more from the damp pile I have ready.

I think, during this time, about how much I hate housework and cooking when I'm on land. I'd rather be sanding or fiberglassing than stuffing clothes into a washing machine. In fact, I'd rather milk cows or pump gas for a living--I've done both--than any kind of housework. In the past few years, I managed to convince my kids that, since I'm the breadwinner, they should do all the cooking and laundry. I haven't had wrinkled fingertips in eight years. I look at the huge stack of yet-to-do-laundry and sigh.

My romantic fantasies of "roughing it" on the boat never included this.

Dorin is apt to get only four to six hours of sleep at night, so he tries to nap during the day. He also takes care of whatever repair jobs come up--there are always several--and he works on navigation. The celestial navigation is coming along pretty nicely, but there are many places for error, and occasionally a mistake gets by undiscovered for a while.

Every day we wait for Dorin to announce our new position after the noon sun sight so we can compare the number of miles traveled, according to the knot log, to the number of miles that we are closer to our destination. We find we cover, according to the knot log, between 80 and 120 miles in twenty-four hours.

On the evening of the eleventh day, Dorin asks for the binoculars. "I'm not sure, but I think there's a glow in the sky over there." He scans the dark horizon, and we squint in that direction.

"Yeah, I can't tell for sure, but it looks like it might be," says Cory.

We strain our eyes and agree there is indeed a glow. What else can be out there but Bermuda? Hooray! At last! We change our course somewhat to the west and aim at the glow all night. But it never gets any closer. Just before daylight we decide it must have been a trick played on our eyes by our wishful minds.

Later that day, July 22, Dorin announces that if the wind holds, we may sight Bermuda by tomorrow. Our spirits soar again. We are ready for landfall.

The next day is bright and sunny, and the three of us stay out on deck and squint at the horizon all day. We expect Bermuda, that little dot in a large ocean, to show up on the bow.

At noon we spot a welcome guest...a strange and beautiful bird circles our boat. Land can't be far away.

"Birds are known to fly hundreds of miles from land, though," Dorin says.

It's a large bird with a long, split tail. It appears to want to land on the rigging but doesn't quite dare. Soon there are several, and we keep straining our eyes for a sign of land on the horizon.

At 3 p.m. Dorin finishes reducing the sun sight he took earlier in the day and says, "We can't possibly be where this says we are. According to this, we are still 200 miles north of Bermuda and 50 miles further west than we want to be."

West!? West because we adjusted our course to follow the "ghost glow" on the horizon.

He reworks the sun sight, takes another, and works and reworks it. He asks me to go over the figures. We can't find any mistakes.

Disheartened, Cory flops on his bunk. Thirteen days on the ocean. The food we make with foul-tasting water is unpleasant, and a number of foods like canned fruit and canned ham have dwindled to almost nothing. We are all sick of drinking lukewarm water.

"Okay," says Cory with resignation, "show me where we are in the chart." He calculates, for maybe the twelfth time since we left, how many days we still have to go. Two more, minimum.

That night we run out of swamp water and have to switch to the rubber tank that we had installed in a locker to give us extra water for the longer offshore legs. We already know from trying it a few days earlier that the water tastes like rubber, in spite of rinsing the tank out several times before we installed it.

Again, Dorin and Cory endure the experience stoically. Not me. I've been limiting both water and food, in the first week because of nausea, and lately because the taste is objectionable.

I'm very happy with the resulting weight loss. At 5'2" tall, my 175 pounds made me very overweight. Dorin told me I'd lose weight quickly once I got on the boat, and I looked forward to ridding myself of at least the 30 pounds I had gained in the last four years. The day before we left, I bought a pair of white painters' pants in the chandlery at the Goudy and Stevens boatyard, size 18, and they were very tight when I put them on.

Now they won't stay up unless I tighten the drawstring and make gathers around my waist!

In spite of being pleased with the weight loss, I feel desperate about the drinking water. I sense that Dorin is irritated with my steadfast objection to the water, so I tell him about the time, years ago, when I made a strawberry shake in my blender. I was very thirsty and chug-a-lugged the entire thing without pausing for breath. As I finished, I looked into the bottom of the glass and saw *half* the rubber gasket that had apparently been put *inside* the blender rather than outside. At the same moment a burp told me where the other half was. For three days, the taste of rubber rolled up from my digestive system and punctuated my meals.

"I didn't know you'd been traumatized," he laughs. "I wish there was something I could do to help the present situation."

It's not only the drinking water, of course, but the food cooked with it. Since I've eaten very little and been very tense, a dormant ulcer has been bothering me for the past week. I pop Rolaids several times a day, which helped at first, but the pain has increased in the past couple of days. I have to lie down in the cockpit between loads of laundry to quiet the burning in my throat and the gnawing pain that goes from my belly to my backbone. I also feel quite weak.

Tonight, after almost two weeks at sea, I can't sit up at all without a lot of pain, so Dorin takes both of our watches. I wake Cory at 4 a.m. and he says dreamily, "I was just about to eat a French fry! You woke me up too soon. It was one of those French fries, you know, the real kind that don't need any ketchup. Not the little ones, but the fat ones that are crisp on the outside and soft on the inside."

Crispy French fries. I need to upgrade my dreams.

The next morning, I remember there is Maalox in one of the medical boxes. Dorin tears through the galley locker again and finds it. I swig it straight from the bottle before getting up. I feel relief in a few minutes. Cory has been keeping close tabs on the canned fruit, particularly the peaches. We were under the impression they were all gone, but Cory works his way to the bottom can in the last row and pulls out the cling peaches in heavy syrup. He opens them for me for breakfast, knowing I can't handle the Goodyear pancakes. After breakfast, more Maalox.

By mid-morning I'm up on watch again, feeling much better, but so thirsty. Cory finds a little instant pineapple drink mix, artificial flavor. We mix it with a quart of water, and the two of us share it. Dorin declines, since he disguises his water with coffee. At lunch they have macaroni, I have the last can of tuna.

After lunch, on our ham radio, we pick up Radio Bermuda on the boat's stereo FM! The three of us sit around the dinette and listen to the homey, small-town format of church suppers and fundraising efforts in a British accent, and drool over grocery store commercials advertising fresh produce and Popsicles made with real juice.

For supper, Dorin and Cory eat mashed potatoes, green beans and Spam. I eat the green beans and Spam. After each meal, I tip the bottle of Maalox and thank my mother for thinking of it.

During my watch tonight, the autopilot arm comes loose again from the tiller post, as it has several times a day for the past few days. After Dorin gets up twice to reattach it, we decide to steer manually, using the stars to hold the course. We still don't have a compass light. It's partly cloudy, so I have to find another star as the clouds pass over. I think it's fun for the first hour, but keeping my head tilted up and steering at the same time causes a stiff neck and aches in my shoulders. At the end of my watch, I'm very glad to turn it over to Dorin. We're on an easy beat with a steady wind, so he ties the tiller and lets the boat sail itself while he dozes off and on! I ask him why he didn't do that for me. "Didn't think of it," he replies.

When I wake Cory at four, he says, as he stumbles to his feet, "What I really want is a thick piece of French bread with butter on it. Really crispy crust, soft in the middle so it will hold a lot of chili when you scoop it up. You know the kind I mean?"

He heads into the cockpit and immediately picks out a boat on the horizon. It's a pleasant night so we sit outside with him for a while to help keep track of the ship. Cory nods toward the boat. "I bet that is a cargo ship full of ice cream. Seventeen flavors. They wouldn't miss a couple of gallons, would they? Why don't we radio them and say, 'Hey, send five gallons of ice cream over here, and we won't fire on your boat.'"

"No," I say, "I can tell that tanker is carrying Pepsi. Thousands of gallons of Pepsi. Cold enough you don't need ice."

"If they just had enough ice on board to make a very cold martini...so cold it would chip my teeth...." says Dorin.

Immersed in our own private food fantasies, we sigh.

It becomes a fine, sunny sailing day again, and Cory produces the last can of fruit for my breakfast – a can of pears. I can't remember anything ever tasting quite so good. I have half the can for breakfast and half for lunch. I try to sip water, but I immediately become nauseated. I'm willing to accept that it may be psychological, but that doesn't change the end result. Then I remember the Riunite wine my mother and father gave us for the trip.

We had agreed to open it on the first full moon, and they, in Massachusetts, would toast us. But, the first full moon had come and gone in the fog or the storm, and we hadn't known when it was. So here was the wine, unopened. I take a mouthful, and it seems to quench my thirst.

We tune in Radio Bermuda for a while and frequently ask whoever is close to the instruments, "What's the knot log say? How fast are we going?"

"We've gone two miles since the last time you' asked. Two-and-a-half knots."

In the hot afternoon, I sip from the bottle several times, holding each sip in my mouth before swallowing, and again, it seems to satisfy my thirst.

For supper, Cory prepares mashed potatoes, lima beans and whole kernel corn. I have the corn. And several sips of the wine. And Maalox. The three of us sit outside for a while in the dusk.

"When I get home," Cory says, "I'm going to go visit Aunt Peg for a week. She has five kinds of homemade muffins at a time. She makes the most food for each meal I have ever seen. Turkey. I remember having turkey at her house one time with five vegetables and seven pies. It wasn't Thanksgiving either.

"Then, while I'm right there in Townsend," he continues, "I'm going to go stay with Mom and Grampy for a week. ("Mom" is what he calls my mother.) Remember the Finnish pancakes they make for breakfast with as many strips of bacon as you want? And a huge boiled dinner at night? And Eggs Oscar for breakfast? Remember the shrimp cocktail Grampy made for us last time we were there?

"When I get home to Maine," he continues, "I'm going to stay with Dad and Fran for a week. She makes piles of real mashed potatoes, the kind that don't need any gravy, but you make a hole in the middle of the potatoes and fill it with gravy anyway because it's so good."

"What I'd like to have," I say, "is pork ribs and sauerkraut the way my mother makes it."

"I don't eat beef much," says Dorin, "but I could go for a steak, two inches thick, so rare I have to hold it on my plate."

Cory finally heads for bed, and as he reaches his bunk, he calls back, "I can beat all of that...I wish I had a fifteen-inch pizza."

Dorin's sun sights seem to be right on the button. As he does a running fix, we keep coming out where we think we should be. The autopilot continues to disconnect several times a day and finally refuses to stay on at all. So, we have to man the tiller around the clock.

But, if the weather continues as it has and we have good winds at night, we should sight Bermuda tomorrow. Remembering a couple of past disappointments, Cory tries to stay skeptical. There is very little canned food left, but I pick a can of black olives that I split between breakfast and lunch. The guys have pancakes for breakfast and rice for lunch. I sip the wine for my liquid and take Maalox between meals. I feel weak but much better than in many days.

That afternoon Cory says, "Pizza."

"What about it?" I asked.

"What I want is a pepperoni pizza from Boles Market. You know the kind where the little pepperonis curl up on the edges? And there's a pool of grease in the middle of each one? That's what I want for supper. And ice cream. I want three kinds of ice cream in the freezer when we get home. I want to be able to spend two days just trying to decide what kind I'm going to have."

"I'd love to have a sixteen-ounce Pepsi," I reply.

"You're repressed," he says, grinning.

The three of us lounge in the cockpit tonight and talk about what food we most want to order when we get to Bermuda. Cory wonders if we can phone in an order and have pizza delivered to the dock before we even clear Customs.

The sailing conditions the next day are absolutely perfect. This is the day we're supposed to see Bermuda, maybe by 10 o'clock in the morning, though we'd still be 25 miles or six hours away. Our spirits soar.

I have a can of artichoke hearts to nibble during the morning…and, of course, alternate Maalox and warm Riunite. We don't see Bermuda by 10, and Dorin's noon sun sight suggests we may be 70 miles or more further away than we had hoped. That would mean another full day of sailing. Cory's disappointment is evident. It's the first time I've seen him look like he might cry. He doesn't listen to the rest of the discussion but goes out and lies on the shady side of the deck and closes his eyes. Dorin takes another sight, and this one varies from the first. An hour later, I scooch down beside Cory.

"Okay," he says, staring up at the sails, "tell me where we *think* we are."

I explain the best and the worst estimates. "That means probably one more day," he says, his voice struggling between bitterness and acceptance.

"I don't think so," I reply. "I believe the sight we got yesterday, and we've gone 80 miles since then. I still think we'll see it today. So does Dorin."

Cory goes back to the cockpit. I carry my bottle of wine on the foredeck with me, take a few sips and settle down to watch for Bermuda. Hand on the tiller, Cory stands watching from the cockpit, eyes scanning ahead. At three o'clock there's no land in sight, and noticing the red skin on my midriff, I realize I've had too much sun, so I slip into the fo'c'sle through the hatch and lie down. We all want to be the person who sights Bermuda first. I know it won't be me.

Sounding very downhearted, Cory asks Dorin if he'll take the helm for a while. He goes below and reads on his bunk. I feel badly for him.

At 3:15, I hear Dorin say, "Crap!"

"What?" I ask, sitting up.

"Nothing. Not to worry."

Assuming it's a minor problem, I lie back down.

At 3:30, Dorin says quietly and calmly, "Come out here and look through the binoculars, if you would, Cory."

"Land?" asks Cory, tumbling out of bed.

"Well," replies Dorin casually, "there's something out there."

We race to the cockpit, and Dorin hands Cory the binoculars.

He looks for a couple of seconds and then nods at Dorin. "And dead off the bow," he says with a smile.

"That's the good news," Dorin says.

"What's the bad?" Cory asks.

"The approach chart to Bermuda blew overboard. It sank almost immediately."

"How did *that* happen?" Cory asks. "What was it *doing* out here?"

"Damned if I know," says Dorin, who is suddenly busy trimming the mainsail. "We still have the large-scale chart. We can make do. Not as much detail, though."

"Hey," I say, "land is in sight, the weather is great, and the visibility is excellent. After all we've been through, how difficult can it be?"

"I like your optimism, Shirl Jean. But would you sail up the Damariscotta River without a detailed chart?"

"No."

"Well, Bermuda will be just a touch trickier."

"Hey, hey, stop this talk. We're not turning back, people!" Cory says.

And because nobody has said it yet, he adds weakly, "Lay-und ho."

Chapter Eight
Bermuda on the Rocks

The outline of Bermuda gradually becomes clear and distinct in the bright afternoon light. The white dot Dorin first saw has expanded into a row of gleaming, half-inch-high, multistory buildings.

"That must be it, huh? Bermuda?" I ask.

"Well, if it's not, I don't know where the hell we are," Dorin says with a chuckle. "Didn't think I'd find it, did you?"

"Didn't think we'd live that long," Cory says.

"But you're sure it's Bermuda?" I ask.

"Let's put it this way," Cory calls back from the bow. "If they ask for our passports in Spanish, I will not be surprised."

"I wonder how they're treating Americans in Cuba these days," I muse.

"And all this time I thought you guys had total faith in my expertise!"

Our eyes strain ahead, and, amazingly, new thin ribbons of land pop out of the horizon. "Look! There are more over there on the right," Cory says.

"Oh, yeah. Wow! Oh, look...no, over on that side! There's more stretching out over on the left. See it?"

Dorin looks through the binoculars. "Yup...take a look."

Through the binoculars I watch as these new bands of land appear to grow their own buildings.

"Here, Cor, come take a look. There is more out there than you can see."

"I don't need binoculars," he jokes as he walks back to the cockpit. "Only old people need binoculars." But he takes them anyway. "Hey, there's more land over there!"

"Do I have time to change?" I ask. "I've been saving an outfit to wear on my first day in Bermuda."

"You've got all the time in the world. We're still a couple of hours away."

In the cabin below, I wash up with handy wipes, change from the shorts I've worn for three days into my white culottes and pink blouse, and hurry back to the cockpit.

Now this twenty-mile-long, twelve-mile-wide island appears to stretch in front of us across the whole horizon.

"I can smell something sweet...flowers? Is that possible?" I ask.

"People who have been out to sea claim they can smell land before they can see it," Dorin replies.

"Boy, I wish we had enough water so I could wash my hair. I haven't washed it in a week. It must be sticking up all over the place!"

Squinting his eyes, Cory looks at me appraisingly. "Yeah, just a minute." Grinning, he spits in his palm then rubs his hand across the top of my head and down the side. "There, that's better."

"It's probably time to think about putting up the quarantine flag. You want to do the honors, Cor?"

From the fo'c'sle Cory retrieves the yellow flag required, internationally, for all foreign boats entering a port.

"Do you think they sell pizza here?" Cory asks as he runs the flag up the line to the spreaders.

"Well, Bermuda has a couple of cities like St. George's Harbor and Hamilton, and apparently Hamilton is fairly large, so I suspect they do."

Dorin nods toward Bermuda. "Look at 'er now."

Layered between a deep-blue sky and a sparkling turquoise ocean, the white skyline begins to take on the coloration of individual buildings...of trees.

"You sure are having a good time," Dorin says, watching me. "This is Shirley-Jean-Koch-from-Dudley-Road's first foreign country, isn't it?"

"Except for a couple of times I chaperoned school trips to Québec, it is, yes."

I scan the horizon again through binoculars. "I can see windows in the hotels!"

"That's nothing," Cory grins. "I can see them without binoculars. I can even..." He glances at me out of the corner of his eye. "I can even see a pizza store. Hmmm, I can even read the sign on the door..." He squints. "Yup, they're open till 10 o'clock."

"Izzat so? Well," I say, "I can even see a house...there's a family having a barbeque in the backyard."

"I can see that," Cory responds. "And there are Pringles on the table."

What's on the grill?" asks Dorin.

"I can see that," I say. "Hamburgers with onions and green peppers...and cheese...and tomatoes. And Pepsi!"

"And ice cream," adds Cory. "Four kinds of ice cream."

"What's for me?" Dorin asks.

Cory responds, "And a martini for you."

Sitting back, Cory puts his feet up on the locker. "That's it. I'm not eating again until we're on land. And I'm having pizza."

"You haven't even had lunch yet, Cor," says Dorin, "and I don't think we'll be there until after dark. Customs may be closed by then, and we'll be stuck on the boat till morning."

"Maybe they'll come out after hours. Maybe they'll deliver pizza to our boat if we tell them we haven't eaten in three days. Anyway, my next meal is going to be deep-fat-fried something, dripping with grease, and pizza, even if I have to wait till tomorrow."

I'm with Cory. We have found Bermuda at last, and, with land in sight, there's no food on board that appeals to any of us.

The autopilot works great, leaving the three of us free to lounge around. We know very little about the country, and we each become preoccupied with our individual fantasies of what it might be like. Anticipation mingles with fear of the unknown as the *Fandango* slowly draws closer to the island.

At five o'clock, Dorin picks out the first buoy with binoculars. There are no visible identification marks on it. He and Cory go over the chart.

"If this one is C5, then C6 should be visible momentarily, just to the left." And moments later a buoy becomes visible.

"It doesn't look right, though. Check the depth meter, will you?" Dorin asks.

I duck my head and look down into the cabin. "Three hundred and fifty-four feet."

"Well, at least we have plenty of water under us. As long as that holds, we can get this figured out. Cor, take a look at this and see if you can make any sense out of it."

Cory studies the chart and then compares it to the sketch and the directions in the *Yachtsman Guide to Bermuda*.

"I'm not sure. It doesn't look right. Well, this could be C6, I suppose, and there's a third buoy further on," he points in the distance, "which would be this one here on the chart… but it doesn't fit with that strip of land over there."

"Yeah, that's what I thought. How's the depth?"

I look down into the cabin at the blinking red numerals again. "It's three hundred and forty-six feet."

Soon a red, white and blue ship becomes visible near a seawall, and we realize, in a couple of minutes, it's sitting at anchor. Above the waterline is a wide band of rust, giving the impression it has been there a long time. There is no one visible on deck.

"I don't suppose that's a temporary navigation marker," Dorin says. "You know, to mark number C7 buoy?" Dorin asks. "Lightships have been used as temporary navigation markers for a long time. Could they have moved that boat in for that sort of thing, maybe while replacing a buoy? The position kind of fits with the other buoy. I wish they were marked. Then we'd know for sure."

"Um, two hundred and seventy-five," I call out. We've lost seventy feet of depth in three or four minutes?

As we draw closer to the "lightship," a powerboat comes alongside the small ship, a man appears on deck, and the two parties appear to engage in a brief conversation. Then the powerboat heads toward the city.

"If we're looking at this chart right, he is heading into shallow water," Cory remarks.

"Well, here on the chart there is a shallow-draft channel that says, 'local knowledge' right in the direction he's going. I'd say that's the channel, and he has local knowledge."

"Now it's two hundred and six," I call out. If we were approaching the wrong way, I think, the powerboat would have come by and warned us.

"Did you say two hundred and sixty?" Dorin asks.

"No, two hundred and *six*. Now it's one eighty-two, one sixty-five...."

"It's dropping that fast?!"

"One hundred thirty-one...yes!"

We're almost within hailing distance of the ship at anchor, but no one is on deck now, so we continue toward welcoming Bermuda. Tree-covered cliffs on the right and green sloping hills on the left frame the attractive city directly ahead.

A dark squall is forming at the right tip of the island, stealing a small portion of the island from the sunshine. We watch the black smudge as it moves quickly over the countryside, dumping its load of rain. Right behind it, the sun dries the freshly washed green and gold trees.

The cloud is now almost over the city. Daydreaming, I wonder if the people there know what's in store for them in the next few minutes. Does the radio station report the movement of such small storms?

"It is raining on Palm and Mangrove Streets at the moment, but we have reported clearing on Coconut and Hibiscus Avenues. Rain is forecast for Royal Street in five minutes."

I can tell by the direction the squall moves it's not going to hit us.

"Take another look with the binoculars, Cor," says Dorin. "See if there are any markings on that buoy farthest away."

"Can't see any."

"Eighty-seven!" I call, breaking out of my reverie.

"Damn! We're going to have to take down the jib, quick, and slow this thing down. Gimme a hand, Cor."

They dash forward and, in less than twenty seconds, the jib wilts to the deck. Cory bolts ahead to stuff it into the bow pulpit.

"What is it now?" Dorin yells jumping back into the cockpit.

"Fifty-two. Forty-eight."

"Let's hope it's getting shallow because we are in a channel. I'm not going to take a chance, though. As long as we remain outside the buoys, we'll be all right. The guide indicates deep water outside. We're not going in any farther until we get a positive identification on one of those things."

"Why don't we start the motor?" Cory asks.

"We'll have to, though the depth meter won't give us an accurate reading with the motor running. The way it's hitched up, the alternator causes a problem...."

"Thirty. Twenty-four, nineteen, seventeen, fourteen...." I scramble down the steps into the cabin so I can see the depth meter better.

"What the hell...? It can't be that shallow. We're still outside the buoys!"

"Twelve, ten, eight...."

"We've got to get the other sails down...."

"Five!"

Dorin reaches for the starter with one hand and with the other lifts the locker cover and grabs toward the autopilot arm. He wants to steer by hand. "Quick, Cor, drop the stays'l...."

"Three!" I yell.

Bang! We're only moving two knots, but the boat jars so hard we're thrown off balance. Dorin flips the autopilot off the rudder post and pushes the tiller hard to the side, and the boat swings toward the open sea. Crash! I feel another blow vibrate through the cabin floor to my feet and legs. Is water pouring in? I scan frantically, picturing it seeping rapidly up around the floorboards.

No water.

"Five, six, seven, ten, twelve, eleven, twelve, thirteen! We must be out of it!" I yell, relieved.

Dorin pulls on his beard. "I think we wiped out the autopilot. The rudder jammed the arm when we hit. Let's leave the sails for a minute, Cor. We can use the extra power to get out of here. Of course there's very little wind at this point, so it's not going to help a whole hell of a lot."

"Twelve, fourteen, fifteen, seventeen, twenty-one...." My voice trails off with relief.

"Whew! That was too close." Dorin grins wiping his forehead. "If the wind doesn't pick up in a minute, we'll get the sails down and just motor on out. What do you think? Heave to and come in in the morning when we've got plenty of light?"

"Sounds good to me." I climb back into the cockpit. "We were just hitting on the keel, weren't we?" There is a big difference between a 3500-pound steel keel and the thin fiberglass hull.

"Oh, yeah. I'm sure it didn't touch the hull."

"Boy, what excitement! Bouncing off the reefs in Bermuda. We're not going to tell my mother about this."

"Look, it's no big deal. We just hit a couple of rocks. I'm going to start the motor so we can get out of here."

Finally, I relax, gazing back at the magic wrought by the slanting, end-of-the-day sun's rays. Cory, his tan golden in the sun, is halfway down the deck, leaning against the shrouds, watching the city as we pull slowly away.

"Look at the contrast of the dark squall in the sunshine out over the water. Isn't it dramatic?" I ask.

"Mm-m-m," murmurs Dorin. "Very pretty. How's the depth?"

I look down into the cabin and for half a minute large red digits blink 020 every half second without changing. "It's holding at twenty."

That's not entirely accurate. Let me idle the motor a minute and see what we get."

My heart lurches for a beat when, in the silence, the depth meter blinks to 019 for half a second and then 018, 017, 018, 016. The numbers change rapidly.

"Sixteen, sixteen, fifteen, twelve, ten!" No, not again....

"What the hell...?" Dorin shifts into reverse, churning the water as the boat slows down.

"Ten, eight, seven, DAMN! Six, six, seven, six, five, five--four!"

Bam! I'm thrown against the hatch cover as we bash into a reef. Cory grabs the shrouds for balance. Dorin nudges the tiller to one side to get away from the reef. Bang! With a screeching, grinding sound we smash again.

"That felt like rock!" Dorin shouts. "Not soft coral."

"Maybe brain coral," Cory shouts. "I think that's hard."

Dorin swings the tiller the other way and accelerates a little.

"Twenty-two, twenty-three, twenty, twenty-six," I shout out with relief.

"No, that's not accurate. I don't think we're going to be able to run the engine." Dorin cuts the power. With a crawling feeling in my stomach, I watch the numbers blink back to 07, 08, 07, 07, 05.

With a crunching noise we come to a sudden jarring halt. Dorin swears as he swings the tiller back and forth.

"What's the matter?!" Our eyes are glued to him. "What's wrong?!"

"We're stuck on the rocks. We can't move."

"The keel or the bottom of the hull?"

"Just the keel. I think."

Dorin starts the motor in reverse and continues to push the tiller back and forth.

With a grinding noise, the boat wobbles side to side on its keel. Then, with a sickening screech, it slides off the reef. My eyes dart around the cabin floor again, looking for signs of water.

Our sails luff a little in the wind, giving us enough speed to steer.

"Seven, six, three!" Ka-bang!

"We seem to be boxed in," Dorin yells.

"I see some dark places in the water," says Cory. "Are those the reefs? I can go up on the bow and try to tell you where they are."

"Yeah, go ahead, Cor."

I continue to read off the depths. Cory leans over the bow pulpit and shouts back, "Over this way, more! Okay, straight ahead, port, port, quick! Okay straight ahead, keep going...a little more to starboard. Okay. Good. Now port, more...more!" Bang! Cory lurches forward, catching the stay.

"To port a little more, okay straight, ah...no, starboard. No, try port...damn! There's no way out!"

Crash! Another bone jarring slam into the reefs.

I call out the depths while Cory scouts paths through the black shadows in the water. In spite of our efforts, every few minutes the jagged, iron-hard reefs snare our keel, sending a ringing sound through the hull and bringing us to a standstill. I wonder how much of the fiberglass that Cory and Chris covered the keel with is still intact. How strong are the keel bolts? They haven't been seen since the boat was built twenty years ago.

A sudden chill sweeps by and the sails fill out. The three of us look up at the black sky the moment the rain starts. Absorbed with the reefs, we hadn't noticed the squall change direction. Now it's on top of us, pushing the boat much faster. The first drops dimple the wind-riffled bay.

"I can't see into the water!" Cory shouts.

Dorin hits the ignition button. "Take the helm!" he yells, as he jumps out of the cockpit. "Let's get the sails down!" I scramble to grab the tiller as the clouds open up. The rain comes down in sheets, bouncing off my legs. I look at my crisp white culottes; in a few seconds they're soaked and sagging.

Dorin and Cory, their figures blurred in the driving rain, fight with the straining sails. This can't be happening, I think, as I try to turn into the wind--we are so close to our destination.

The boat picks up more speed, and the keel slams hard against the reef, throwing the men off balance. As I swing the tiller the other way, the stays'l slithers toward the deck. The mainsail jams partway down and continues to catch the wind, forcing the boat forward too fast. Dorin yanks on it with all his strength. Cory jumps to the cabin top, and together they pull on the flogging sail. The nearby city is no longer visible. I've even lost track of which side it's on. The yellow-gray water beside us is alive with whitecaps and splattering rain. Bang! The boat shudders from a tremendous jolt, and the sail comes down. They work frantically to tie it to the boom. Even without the sail, the wind drives us forward.

I remember stories of boats whose bottoms were torn away by reefs. If the hull cracks, we might have time to inflate the raft...which locker is the foot pump in? If we get a hole in the hull, we'll have to abandon within minutes. Assuming we all survive and can swim the couple of miles to the shore...the boat will be gone.

I recall stories of heroic efforts to stop up holes in hulls to keep boats afloat until they could get into a harbor. If we suddenly see water on the cabin floor, will we be able to find out where it's coming from? I imagine pulling up floorboards, peering frantically into lockers, while the water rises rapidly around our ankles.

The tropical air is not cold, but my teeth chatter. The rain comes down in torrents as Dorin and Cory jump back into the cockpit. Water streams off the end of Cory's nose, off Dorin's beard. Grabbing opposite ends of the soaked towel, they try to dry their eyes.

"Get the life jackets out?" I ask. Dorin tips his head up giving me a quizzical, amused look, but Cory tears into the locker and tosses three jackets onto the cockpit floor.

"Read the depths to me," Dorin says, taking the tiller. "Hey, whatsa matter? You cold? Your teeth are chattering."

"No, just nervous, I guess."

The rain and wind stop suddenly, and we look up to see Bermuda appearing through the mist, sparkling once more in the golden late afternoon sun.

Cory dashes back to the bow to spot reefs, and I stand on the bottom step of the galley watching the three red digits blink rapid changes. The motor is running so the readings aren't accurate, but at least it gives us an idea of how much water there is under us. For the next half hour, Dorin cautiously slips the motor in and out of gear, carefully picking his way around the black patches that Cory calls out in the gathering dusk. Sometimes we only graze the reef, and he gently nudges the boat on. Once more the *Fandango* gets stuck on a reef, and he has to back it off.

"It's too dark. I can't see anymore," Cory yells.

"We'll have to do the best we can. I think we may be out of the woods, at this point, anyway." He cuts the motor and glances down at the depth meter before starting it again. "We have twenty-five feet of water under us right now."

Sweet relief. Through the porthole I see the glittering night lights of Bermuda and yearn for the security they represent. At this moment people are sitting down to dinner…safe…dry.

Then I realize I have to pee. That will mean sliding my wet culottes and my wet panties down…and back up again. Oh, yuk! On the way to the fo'c'sle, I fumble for a cigarette lighter so I can find some dry clothes to put on, reading the numbers as I pass by the depth meter.

"Twenty-one, nineteen, fifteen, twelve…." Bang! The lighter flies out of my hand as I land on my hands and knees on the cabin sole. "Ouch!"

"Twelve?!" asks Dorin, idling back.

"That's what it said!" I pick myself up off the floor, my heart thumping against my ribs. Not again! In the dark, I won't be able to see if any water is coming in. He turns the boat the other way. Bang! He eases the motor into reverse, cautiously backs out of the cul-de-sac, and tries another route.

I no longer have the urge to go to the bathroom. Standing in the dark, focusing on the red numbers, holding onto the grab rail overhead, I am exhausted and irritated…my rain-drenched culottes slap around my legs. My excitement, my exuberance, my anticipation about reaching Bermuda have been washed away by the storm, and with each crunching lurch against the coral, they have completely left me. My needs have regressed to survival. And dry clothes.

I grab another lighter and check my watch. It's 9:35.

We hit less frequently now, and a gentle wind comes up. Cory puts up the small jib sail, and we move along slowly without the motor. Still clutching the overhead handrail, I call of the changing numbers. My voice cracks with fatigue. "Fourteen, fifteen, fourteen, sixteen...."

"Fifteen, fifteen, sixteen, seventeen..." Cory's voice is behind me, and he takes up the rhythm of the numbers.

"Sit down," he says and goes on reading. I gratefully sink down on the galley step, leaning my head against the icebox. The depth fluctuates in the low twenties and stays there. Cory says he'll call out the depth only when the number goes below nineteen. When I notice his reactions slowing after a while, I take over. When I'm tired, he steps in again. The depth gradually levels off in the high twenties and then thirties.

Dorin sits in the cockpit steering the *Fandango*, listening to the numbers. He closely watches the slowly changing landmarks, lights from shore, anything that will help guide us out.

When the depth stays in the forties for five minutes, Dorin calls us outside. "I want to pick your brains for a minute. Look at those lights and at the ship. If we head over that way, does it look like we'll be going out the way we came in?"

We are heading toward the "lightship," which is now lit up like a birthday cake. We agree we're going to pass it at the same angle we came by it in the afternoon.

"I always thought this hull was as strong as steel," Dorin says, settling back contentedly in the dark. "They made this boat before they knew for sure how strong fiberglass was. It's really thick." He chuckles. "Hey, we made it through, gang! We sure could have done without this little complication, though, huh?"

"Little complication," I laugh. "What would you consider a big complication?"

"Oh, a big complication is having gin on board and no vermouth."

"Or..." offers Cory, "running out of toilet paper four hundred miles offshore."

"Or," I say, "a bottle of wine without a corkscrew."

"For that to be a complication, you have to have wine with a cork instead of a screw cap," teases Dorin.

In the black night, the glitter of Bermuda grows dimmer. We relax as a feeling of exhilarated well-being settles over us.

Dorin and Cory exchange thoughts about where we had actually been compared to where we had thought we were. I glance occasionally into the cabin and watch the numbers only go up.

"We're heading way out for tonight," Dorin says, "and we'll heave-to until morning. We'll figure out what we're going to do then.

"I'm going to try calling Bermuda Harbor Radio. The VHF probably still won't work, but I think we should try. Bermuda Radio uses radar to scan the surrounding area, and they may be sending a rescue party. We don't want anyone out looking for us. Be as embarrassing as hell. Bermuda Radio has a reputation of being super polite and helpful."

"Maybe they can tell us where we are, so we know where to go tomorrow," Cory says.

"Good point, Cor. I'm sure they can."

Cory takes the tiller, and Dorin goes below. Miraculously, the VHF microphone works. To identify our boat, Dorin gives our vessel documentation number 513671.

"This is Bermuda Radio," says a veddy British voice. "I read you, American boat number 513671." There seems to be sarcasm dripping from his clipped syllables. "What can I do for you?"

Taken aback, Dorin pauses a moment and then goes on. "My VHF is only working sporadically. I'm, ah, having trouble with the microphone switch, so I may not be able to continue transmitting once I release it. I'm calling to tell you we seem to have misread our charts this afternoon and found ourselves among the reefs. We, um, we thought we were approaching the northeast entrance to Bermuda, but that's apparently not where we were. We are all right now. We're just going past the lightship, and I just wanted to let you know we're not in trouble. We're heading offshore to heave-to for the night. We'll contact you in the morning for information before we come in." He releases the transmitting switch.

The British voice comes back, sounding disdainfully arrogant. "For your information, there is *no* northeast entrance to Bermuda, vessel number 513671. Repeat, there is no northeast entrance to Bermuda."

"Yes, pardon me, I meant east."

"Do you have a British Admiralty chart *on board*?" The sarcastic voice continues.

Including the chart that blew overboard, we actually have DMA, Defense Mapping Agency, charts which are usually identical to the BAC, British Admiralty charts, but rather than complicate the discussion, Dorin clicks the switch several times until he gets it to work again and says, "Yes, we do. Over."

"Well, if you had *studied* the charts you *say* you have, you would know that there is no lightship in Bermuda. Repeat, there is not and never has been a lightship in Bermuda."

I look outside as we cruise slowly past the brightly lit, rusty boat with no visible crew that looks like it could be a navigation marker.

Click, click, click, Dorin works the switch until the "go" light comes on again. "Well, whatever it is," he says, "we are going by it and will soon be out to sea. We'll heave to until morning, and I don't expect we'll have any further problems tonight. Over."

"Tell me, American vessel number 513671, does your boat have a *name*?" I gasp at the continued sarcasm.

Dorin pauses, controls his temper, clicks the switch until it works and says, "Yes, it's the *Fandango*." He spells it out.

"Well, *Fandango*...since this is a distress call, I'll need your name and some information."

Dorin gives the requested information and tries unsuccessfully to sign off.

"*Fandango*," the voice comes back. "I suggest you try to *study* the charts you *say* you have on board. Do you have British Admiralty chart number...?"

"This is the *Fandango*, over and out," Dorin says and snaps off the VHF button. Standing there in wet clothes, Dorin and I stare at each other. I want to reach through the airwaves and strangle the guy. Exhausted from the effort of surviving the past few hours and exhilarated because we had succeeded, the last thing we expected was this.

"That's the last time I have contact with Bermuda radio," says Dorin. "I was just trying to be helpful, in case they were concerned."

I realize that the discomfort Dorin has when using pubic airways has just been multiplied, and I continue to seethe while we motor steadily away from Bermuda. If this is the attitude of Bermuda people, I don't want any part of it. If we weren't nearly out of fresh water, we could just keep going. Maybe we'll just get some supplies and pull right out again. But then, hmmm, but then...we'll be on the open seas again.

"Do we have to stay in Bermuda as long as we planned?" I asked.

"No, we can just get some food and water, get the CO_2 cartridges filled, and pull right out again, if you want to. Unless the autopilot arm is gone. Is that what you want to do?"

"Yeah, I don't know that I'm going to like Bermuda very much. What happens if the autopilot arm is broken?"

"Well, we'll have to order a new one to be shipped from the United States. I don't think we want to steer this boat around-the-clock, do we? It will only take a few days for it to come in. Then, we'll just install it and take off. How's that sound?"

"Sounds good to me."

"As long as I get my pizza," says Cory.

"What time is it? And what's the depth?"

Cory pushes the light button on his watch. "Eleven-thirty."

"Four hundred and sixty-four feet," I say.

"Let's go a little more. I'd like to be off soundings before we stop."

At midnight we go about the quick business of heaving to.

"We'll have to keep watch tonight." Dorin gathers me into a hug.

"Can we make it two-hour watches?" I ask, collapsing against him. "We're all exhausted."

"Good idea. I'll take the first watch. I have so much adrenaline going I won't be able to sleep for a while anyway."

He stays on for three hours, as the lights of Bermuda become dimmer and almost disappear as we drift slowly away. He wakes me and shows me the tiny pinpoint of light he'd like us to keep in sight until morning. But he sits with me for a while, and we talk about this afternoon.

"What *is* a lightship?" I finally ask. "I've never heard of it."

"I thought you'd never ask," he mumbles over a big yawn. "The one I've heard the most about is the Nantucket Lightship. You don't know about it? You grew up in Massachusetts."

"Nope. My knowledge of coastal stuff is limited to Gloucester."

"Well, lightships were used in other ports, too, and were like floating lighthouses so approaching ships knew where they were. Off Nantucket Island, south of Cape Cod, there are treacherous shoals, so there's been a series of lightships moored there for over a hundred years. Just a few years ago, the last lightship was replaced by a large nav buoy."

"But that's offshore, right? The ship we saw today was near land."

"Yeah, somewhere, I read that when a buoy was ripped loose from its mooring in a storm, they used an old rust-bucket fishing boat as a temporary marker for locals until they could reinstall the buoy. So..." he yawns again. "When I was trying to make sense out of what I was seeing today, I jumped to a conclusion. It's easy to do in stressful situations. Can be dangerous. This time it was also embarrassing...had to announce it over the airwaves, didn't I? Are you disenchanted?"

"No! After what we've been through, you're my hero."

"Like I just said, be careful about jumping to conclusions," he says with a chuckle as he stands up. "You okay to take your watch? You don't have to sit out here as long as you check every half hour or so. Our position lights are on, and boats will pick us up on radar."

"Yes, I'm wide awake, but maybe I'll sit at the dinette."

"Okay, I'm going to get a little rest." He kisses the top of my head.

Laying my head on my arms at the dinette table, I sit and doze. Every ten or fifteen minutes, I wake and stick my head up out of the companionway to look around for the tiny light that marks Bermuda. Sometimes it takes a few minutes to find it, and I have to watch to be sure it's not a boat moving slowly across the horizon.

At five, I wake Cory and crawl into bed. At seven, I hear him starting the stove for coffee. I fall asleep again and wake up when I hear him getting the sails ready to hoist. I roll over and peek out of the fo'c'sle.

"Ready for breakfast?" Dorin asks, stirring up pancake batter. "You know we haven't eaten since yesterday morning?" he asks, flipping pancakes onto Cory's plate. "Cor, yours are ready."

Cory swings down the companionway without touching a stair. "I've been looking at the big chart and the sketch in the book since it got light, and I think I know where we are. And where we have to go. It's going to take a while," he says.

While Cory downs a record fourteen pancakes, Dorin listens to his explanation.

"You're right, Cor." They agree on a course, and Cory hoists the sails.

I eat one rubber-flavored pancake liberally syruped, but I can't stand the thought of drinking the water...the wine is gone. I feel physically weak and shaky, but in good spirits. Today we get real food and clean water.

We take turns at the tiller, and by ten o'clock we identify beyond doubt where we are. With the land on our starboard, we head toward the east approach to Bermuda--St. George's Harbor. Cory takes the tiller for the next three hours. He keeps lining up with the buoys, but as soon as we come off soundings and the depth reads less than two hundred feet, I panic and ask him to skirt the buoys farther out from land. He is impatient with my caution, and even I know I'm being unreasonable, but Dorin, seeing my tension, asks Cory to stay out farther.

We watch huge, black clouds pile up in the sky over Bermuda, and as dark squalls skitter across the horizon on our port side, Dorin and Cory bet on whether or not the *Fandango* will outrun them. We keep track of the black, ferocious one in the bay on our starboard side. As it moves toward us, obliterating the buoys, we know this one won't miss us, but it's still fifteen minutes away, we guess. I check the depth meter. We have over three hundred feet of water under us.

A large, graceful sloop with a tall mast that had first appeared out of the horizon almost dead ahead of us captures our attention. It's still a mile away when it turns toward the land, and we realize it must be headed to Hamilton. It continues in that direction...toward the squall. We become apprehensive as we watch it approach the worst looking squall we've seen. We wonder when they're going to drop their sails, but they don't. We watch with distress as it heels sharply when the wind hits, and it disappears into the black cloud. Did we look like that yesterday?

I steer while Dorin and Cory take the sails down and close the hatches. Dorin and I go below. I throw a foul weather jacket to Cory just as the first raindrops hit. We smile at him from below.

"No use all of us getting wet," Dorin chuckles.

"Isn't that why you brought me?" Cory grins back and steers by compass in the pelting rain. I'm grateful they agreed to stay out in deep water. In five minutes, the sun is out. Dorin spots a cruise ship on the horizon, heading for Bermuda.

"They'll probably reach the channel before we do. We can watch and see where they turn in." The large ship moves rapidly and enters Bermuda before we are close enough to tell for sure which buoy marks the entrance.

The men discuss a particular buoy that isn't marked, but before they have to make the decision of whether or not to turn there, Cory spots another one farther ahead that turns out to be C17, the one we've been waiting for.

As we approach the buoy where we have to enter, the water becomes very shallow. At seventy-five feet I start to panic again.

"It's supposed to," Cory explains. "See, right here in the chart, it says forty feet. It's going to go down to twenty before we get into the channel."

It doesn't help. Sitting on the stairs, my stomach in knots, I watch the depth meter. The yawing ulcer pain comes back. Every time the depth drops five feet, I yell out the numbers. I feel like a fool.

I listen to Dorin and Cory discuss the identity of a particular buoy. Don't they *know*? There's only fifty feet of water below us, and they don't *know* for sure which buoy this *is*? I'm not cut out to be a sailor. How can I continue the trip after Bermuda? I can't, I decide. I just can't take this kind of tension anymore.

My heart is in my throat. I pull my knees up more, to ease the pain in my stomach. What are we doing so close to land?

"Come on out and see what's going on," Dorin calls.

"You won't believe it," says Cory, still at the helm.

I reluctantly stagger on shaky legs to the fo'c'sle. I stand up on the bunk and open the front hatch. There, only a few hundred yards away is emerald green land dotted with graceful, pastel houses. There are trees and flowering bushes everywhere. The lay of the land, with cliffs and hills, is exquisite. The bright, lush, green vegetation is startling between the blue sky and the turquoise water. I thrill with the changing colors of the water: lavender, blue, and green chase around the edges of the most brilliant turquoise I've ever seen. And, the air smells so good.

We're already in the channel. Cory is still at the helm. He and Dorin discuss the buoys--which ones lead off toward Hamilton, which ones will guide us through the cliffs into St. George's Harbor. A beautiful, large, white bird similar to a seagull, except its tail is a long point instead of a fan, soars above us.

Finally, I can appreciate what I see.

We are close enough now to see details, and the tiny, narrow opening to St. George's appears. I resonate to the sights and fragrances that are so close. An arrestingly beautiful black woman stands on the high, stony point just outside of the harbor opening. I wave enthusiastically to her. She looks amused and waves back. A run-about scoots by us, and I wave to them. They laugh as they wave back. I'm elated. I'm ecstatic. I'm enchanted.

Bermuda up close is even more gorgeous than Bermuda at a distance. There are people fishing off the rocks in the tiny channel that is the entrance to St. George's. I wave to them. Smiling, they wave back. There are charming, beautiful, pastel houses; there are flowers everywhere; there are palm trees. Palm trees!

I look back and Cory is handing the tiller over to Dorin.

"You sure, Cor? You brought it this far. You can handle it."

Cory shakes his head. We're now inside the exquisite harbor, dotted with many anchored boats.

I keep calling out, "Look at that building! Look at the flowers! Isn't it beautiful?"

Over us, several of the long-tailed birds swoop and wheel on the breeze. They are bigger and so different from the seagulls I adore. It adds to the exotic feeling of this incredible moment.

Cory and Dorin seem to enjoy the scenery but keep their minds on the chart and try to orient themselves in the harbor. I am more than content to let them so I can enjoy the extraordinary beauty of St. George's Harbor from the water.

"I'm trying to figure out where the customs' dock is from this sketch," says Dorin. "What do you think, Cor? Over there?"

"Let me check the chart."

In the past few days, as we listened to the Bermuda radio station, I studied the *Yachtsman's Guide*, memorizing the drawing of this harbor. I point to a tiny island and yell back, "It's over there on that island."

On the front side of the island a large, distinctive stone house stands out; from it, a long line of colorful laundry hangs drying in the breeze.

We chug by the island and take another turn around the harbor.

"I can't quite get oriented, Cor. You think it's over there?" Dorin points to a place further into the harbor.

We go by the island a second time, and I yell back, "It's right over there...on the island. Where the building is." No response, but I'm having too much fun to care.

After another turn around the harbor, Dorin comes up beside a huge, beautiful, wooden yacht named *No Brass Ring*. Dorin yells to the man on deck, "Where is the customs' dock?"

The boater points toward the stone house. "It's on that island," he shouts. "Just radio them on channel 16, and they'll come right down." I don't look back at Dorin and Cory, but I'm stifling a guffaw.

As we slip around the corner of a seawall and pull up to the dock, I'm nearly delirious with delight. I can see people across the canal. I'm actually in a foreign country! We're going to have water and food soon! We're safe!

Our VHF mic will not work to call Customs. We hope our yellow quarantine flag will be seen by someone. We race around the cabin, picking up and stowing last minute stuff in crannies, so we'll be a little bit presentable.

I nervously get out our passports and the boat documentation. I have never been through Customs before, but I've read stories, especially in Seven Seas Cruising, about the difficulties.

We sit quietly in the humid, sweltering cabin, lost in our own thoughts. Now that the boat has stopped moving, the afternoon heat is blistering. We hear a voice outside. "Permission to come aboard?"

A handsome black gentleman dressed in a crisp tropical uniform is standing on the dock several feet above us holding a briefcase.

"Come aboard," Dorin says. The man grabs a shroud six feet above the deck and swings down onto our deck with ease. When his hand leaves the shroud, he examines it and wipes it off. The shrouds are caked with salt six feet above the deck!

"Whew, it's hot today," he says as he bends his height down into the cabin. He examines our passports and our documentation and asks for our port of departure.

When Dorin says, "East Boothbay, Maine, USA," he raises his eyebrows.

"Ah, Maine," he says and looks impressed. "You have come a long way." I remember, then, Dorin's having told me that most boaters work their way down the Intra-Coastal Waterway and then depart from Florida for the island chain, thereby missing Bermuda altogether.

As the customs' official fills out a form, he is a model of courtesy and efficiency. Though he is reserved and professional, he responds to our questions and comments regarding Bermuda.

Dorin mentions our contact with Harbor Radio last night, but we don't push our luck by giving our opinion of the radio operator. The officer says he had been made aware of our call and comments dryly that an experience among the reefs can be "quite unpleasant."

He does an almost imperceptible double take when he looks at my passport photo. I admire his self-control. In the picture my hair is curly and shoulder length, and I'm wearing makeup and earrings. Now my hair is only three inches long, straight, and flat. I figure I've lost 15 pounds or so, and, with no eye makeup, my face looks bald.

"I've suffered a bit of damage since that was taken," I say. He nods, and I think he's trying to suppress a smile.

He responds to our questions about water and food, including where he thinks we might be able to buy pizza. He tells us where we can tie up for a couple of days before we move out to an anchorage. We tell him we are out of water, and he says we can leave the boat at the customs' dock for a short time to go ashore and get something to drink. He wishes us well and leaves, as crisp and pressed as when he arrived.

His courtesy and consideration forever changes our bad impression of Bermuda that we had formed the night before.

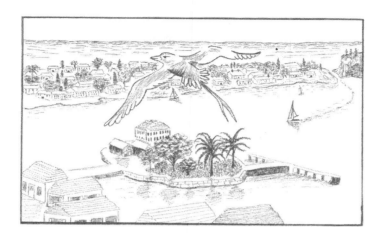

Chapter Nine

St. George's, Bermuda

"That went better than I thought it would," I say.

Dorin nods. "Yeah, he was very professional. And nice. Bermuda could be okay if he is more representative of the people who live here than that guy last night."

"That jerk, you mean," I say.

"So. Ah, does that mean I get more than one pizza?" Cory asks.

"As many as you want." Dorin says. He turns to me. "Do you want to go get a drink of water before we move?"

I couldn't see any quick place to get a drink within walking distance. "We'll be filling the tank in a few minutes," I say. "I'd like to wait and get a drink then."

"I'm good, too," Cory says.

He and I untie from the dock while Dorin starts the motor. We grab shrouds and swing over the lifelines onto the deck. Dorin motors away from the dock. Five minutes later we come to a soft but sudden stop. We had read that this harbor is laced with sand bars, and sure enough, we are stuck on one. Dorin shifts the transmission from forward to reverse and back again, moving the tiller and wiggling us ahead by inches. There is nothing Cory and I can do but watch and try to will us off the sandbar. With a dozen anchored cruising boats in the bay, this is embarrassing and for none so much as Dorin, yet he looks unperturbed as he works the shift, throttle and tiller. Of course, he's done this a time or two in Maine.

A few minutes later, an open fishing boat comes along side and asks for our stern line. Cory tosses it to him, and the fisherman pulls us off quickly. Dorin thanks him, and I know he wants to ask, "How much do I owe you?" But the boat owner gives a little salute and pushes the throttle forward. He's off to the harbor entrance and open water.

"Well, that was really nice of him! But, getting stuck was embarrassing," Dorin says with a shake of his head. "Okay guys, we're heading to Dowlings Marine, right over there. Let's get ready to tie up at the fuel dock." He points, but Cory is already below, pulling up the cushions so he can open the three water tanks in preparation for filling them. I tie the fenders to the lifelines to cushion the boat from the dock. As we come to a soft stop, Dorin puts the transmission in neutral; I step onto the dock and tie the bow line to a dock cleat. While I cleat off the stern line, Dorin turns off the motor and steps off. He picks up the water hose lying on the dock and hands it down to Cory.

"Ready?" Dorin calls.

"Ready," Cory yells back and Dorin turns on the spigot. A few seconds later, the sweet sound of fresh drinking water soothes my soul.

Cory pinches the hose over to slow the flow as he moves from tank to tank. As soon as all three are full, Dorin turns off the water and then tells the dock attendant we need fuel. He jumps onto the boat, and, with the pronged tool, unscrews the bronze diesel cap in the floor of the cockpit. When the tank is full, he hands the nozzle back to the attendant, along with a credit card. While the guy leaves to run our card, Cory fills two cups of water from the galley sink and hands them out to Dorin and me. Then he fills one for himself.

Fueled and watered up, we head to our temporary "berth," the stonewall the customs' official had indicated. All other boats in the harbor are at a moorings or anchored, but we are pleased we have been given this space at the seawall for a couple of days, which will make it easy for us to leave the boat and return—no rowing the *Tinker* or sailing it into a dock for each excursion. The tide is high so Dorin leaves extra line when he cleats off the boat to allow for the tide's going out.

In anticipation of going into town, we have spiffed up as much as we can, but among the smartly groomed, local people and the fashionable tourists, we are still a motley crew.

Dorin is in salt stained khaki shorts, t-shirt and sandals. His extra-long hair is topped off with his captain's cap; his beard is long and scraggly.

Except for his Greek fisherman's cap, Cory could almost pass as a tourist because he is wearing full-length, immaculate, white deck pants and a proper polo shirt. He hasn't shaved in weeks, though, so, amidst all of the close-shaved people, he does stand out. Though I haven't worn a skirt in two years, I follow the counsel of other boaters and wear the only skirt I have. But, in the two hours since the customs' official looked at my passport photo, I haven't made any further improvements.

But what sets us apart from everyone else is our staggering gait. After weeks at sea on a constantly moving boat, we had gained our sea legs, but it now feels like the land is shifting under me. I wobble between the guys, and then notice they are wobbling too. "Illusory motion," Dorin explains. "We've got to get our land legs under us."

I laugh as I try to walk straight on rubbery legs. Cory says, loudly, "Mom, it's all that wine you drank." My bark of laughter is accompanied by a nicely timed hiccup.

As we walk down a narrow sidewalk, stepping aside for people coming from the opposite direction, I look at lush pink and purple flowers cascading from balcony railings. I can't take my eyes off the gorgeous flora, so Dorin puts a guiding hand on my back to keep me from walking into people.

In a couple of blocks, we begin to adjust a little to the stable land. Then, I gasp when a sudden movement jumps me. Inches from my shoulder, a small lizard scurries down the white wall of a house to the sidewalk and dashes around the building. No one else reacts. Maybe this is commonplace. While I am nearly phobic about some reptiles, I am not afraid of lizards—small ones anyway--but sudden movement can make me jump. I want to be sophisticated enough to take wall-climbing lizards in stride.

We soon find ourselves in a town plaza called King's Square. Like an oasis, a restaurant calls us forward, and without consulting each other, we head toward it. A hostess leads us to a second-story porch overlooking the bay and seats us next to the rail.

Oh, bliss.

We are dry, comfortable, and back in civilization! A waitress with a British accent gives us our menus and takes our orders, but we start with drinks: two glasses of cold water each, all of which we down in ten minutes. Then I order pineapple juice, Cory orders milk and Dorin a dry martini. When Cory's milk arrives, it has a straw and ice cubes floating in it. We look at each other, not knowing what to make of this. Doesn't the milk start out cold? Doesn't it become watered down as the ice melts? The paper on the straw has been removed except for the top inch and a half— something we have never seen before.

Cory pretends he is going to blow the paper cap off the straw.

"No! We're in a foreign country. And look how clean everything is," I say.

Indeed, there is not a scrap of paper anywhere in the square below us. Impishly, he blows it onto the red and white checked tablecloth, and then, without the straw, he downs the milk in seconds, reminding me he is still a sixteen-year-old, though lately, especially during our harrowing journey, I have been thinking of him as a man.

When the waitress who has been hovering comes to the table, he orders another one.

"That one was a little warm," he says. "I'll go slower on the next one."

Dorin sips his martini appreciatively and says he's having another.

As we become hydrated and cooled by the onshore breeze, we relax and talk about our experiences. I feel tension drain from my body, but in the back of my mind, I think, *you still have to go back out there.*

Enjoying the British influence, Dorin orders steak and kidney pie. I have broiled fish, and since they don't have pizza, Cory has spaghetti. The waitress asks us if we want any dessert, but we order more liquid. I consume two Cokes, and Dorin drinks two more waters and tops it off with a second martini. "Cold?" I ask him. He smiles. "It's chipping my teeth," he says with satisfaction.

When we leave the restaurant, we are not ready to return to the boat, so we wander around the square. There is a grocery store that is closed, but I peer into the windows and see oranges. Oh, be still my heart: oranges!

"We have to go shopping in the morning," I say. "We need produce."

"We need everything," says Cory. "Unless you want to finish off the spam first?"

"Let's save that good stuff for later. Since you are the chief cook, you had better shop with us tomorrow," I tell him.

In the square, there is a replica of an old sailing ship. The *Deliverance* is the ship that Sir George Somers built when shipwrecked on the island back in 1610. While the replica is usually open for tours, it is closed now for repairs.

We find another tourist attraction, a twenty-minute film that gives an interesting presentation on the history of Bermuda. In the process, we discover that many ships carrying goods and treasures have sunk on Bermuda's perilous reefs. A few hundred wrecks make it a popular dive sight.

Soon, a steel drum band sets up in the square and people gather. Those flocking to the area appear to be as much locals as tourists. People are dressed in business suits, shorts and t-shirts and colorful sarongs. The mood is upbeat, and the crowd joyfully rocks out the rhythm of the metal drums. We stay for half an hour until fatigue makes us retrace the path back to the boat.

A man dressed like a cruising boater is pacing back and forth on the rock wall we are tied to.

"Is this your boat?" he brusquely asks. Dorin acknowledges it with a nod. "What's the problem?"

"Your bow line is chafing! Look, it's almost cut through. I've been waiting. I didn't want to touch your boat, but I was afraid it would drift into the harbor." He is obviously agitated. We realize immediately the tide has gone out during our absence, much more than we had thought it would. The deck of our boat is now substantially below the level of the seawall. The lines that hold the *Fandango* in place are taut and straining, and indeed, the bow line is badly chafed. Dorin thanks him for his concern, but the gentleman is not in a talking mood. He stalks away.

I'm too short to manage the seven-foot drop down to the boat, so Dorin and Cory each grab a wrist and lower me down until my feet touch the deck. With ease, Cory leaps down and finds a spare line in the locker and hands one end to Dorin. Between them, they loosen the stern line and replace the bow line.

"A bit larger tide than I had anticipated," remarks Dorin dryly.

We sleep on level beds without the sound of water rushing by the hull, just a very gentle rocking. Heavenly. We all get a good night's sleep, all at the same time.

The next day, I wash my hair in the sink using water from the tank. Though I had been using seawater to wash my hair, the shampoo wouldn't lather, and my hair dried stiff. Knowing we'll top off the water tanks before we leave, I use the water and shampoo liberally.

Dorin makes pancakes with maple syrup and we eat our fill. I can't believe how good they taste made with fresh water.

"I'm thinking about inflating the *Tinker* and sailing over to that beautiful wooden boat and introducing ourselves," Dorin says of a large cruising yacht.

"Okay, that's great, but we have to go grocery shopping," I say. "Aren't you guys looking forward to fresh produce? We can make salads."

"Yeah, and steak," Dorin says.

"How about twenty pounds of hamburger?" Cory asks.

We decide Dorin and I will go grocery shopping, and Cory will inflate the dinghy. That raises the discussion of the CO_2 cartridges. "We'll have to go into Hamilton to a marina where we can get them filled. Maybe we can do that today," Dorin says.

"I'm still going to inflate the *Tinker* with the foot pump," says Cory. "I can do that while you're shopping. I want to sail it around the harbor when you get back."

"Don't you want to come shopping with us? Pick out some stuff?"

"I trust you." He pats me on top of the head. "You'll do fine."

At the same small store we peeked into last night, Dorin and I learn the cold truth. Because everything is imported, the prices, compared to US prices, are exorbitant. A four-ounce jar of jelly costs five times what I pay for it at home. I only buy a few things—enough for a couple of meals. Three oranges are among the items.

I find the walk back to the boat less arduous than the night before. While I'm still weak from little food for so long, my walking muscles are doing much better. On the way, I spot a small shop that sells clothing and we stop in. I buy a second skirt that falls in line with our budget better than the food does. It's a large instead of an extra-large.

When we return to the boat, the yellow *Tinker* is tied to a cleat, floating and bobbing off the stern. Dorin and Cory step the mast and rig the sail.

"You want to take her out for a spin?" Dorin asks Cory. I had, myself, failed the first few times I tried to sail a fiberglass dinghy when Dorin was trying to teach me. I wonder if Cory really wants to begin in such a public place among experienced, watching sailors.

In a second, Cory swings over the lifelines and down into the dinghy. I watch, amazed, as he takes a long-distance turn around the bay, darting among the boats moored further out and using the sail like an expert. "Wow, where'd he learn that?" I ask.

Dorin raises an eyebrow and cocks his head as if to ask, "Really?"

"What? Oh, yeah. I see what you mean." He's been sailing a much more difficult boat with, not one, but three sails, for three weeks.

When Cory returns, he leaps up to the *Fandango's* toe rail and over the lifeline. With his and Dorin's help, I awkwardly lower myself into the dinghy—not an easy feat-- and settle myself on the inflated tube that forms the sidewall of the little boat. Dorin swings down with ease and takes the seat by the tiller.

"You coming, Cor?" Dorin asks.

"No, I want to walk around the town for a while."

I open my mouth to object, but with a gesture from Dorin, I close it. Cory jumps onto the retaining wall, and with a wave, strides purposefully away.

"He's earned the right," says Dorin. "He'll be fine."

Dorin seems so happy sailing the *Tinker*. He maneuvers over to the large and exquisite wooden, two-masted ketch, *No Brass Ring*. The hull is finished in "bright work" --varnished rather than painted.

"Don't you wish we had a pilot house like that?" Dorin asks.

Instead of the traditional open cockpit, their pilot house would allow them to be protected from wind, waves, and rain. And sun.

"But wouldn't that be...cheating or something?"

Dorin laughs out loud. "I like the way you think."

It is our intention to knock on their hull and introduce ourselves, but they see us coming and invite us on board.

Dorin hands the man our line, and he ties us off to his boat. With Dorin giving me a boost, we climb aboard. The owners, Bill and Mary, introduce themselves and make us welcome, handing us lemonade with ice cubes clinking against the glass. Ice cubes? "Where do you buy ice cubes?" I ask.

Dorin looks taken aback by my question and seems a little embarrassed.

Mary smiles and says, "We make them on board."

I am stunned.

"Come look at our fridge. See? We have a freezer."

I miss some of the ensuing conversation as I process the idea of a boat's having not just a refrigerator, which I knew fancy boats could have...but a freezer? Think of what you could do for meals if you had a freezer. Then, I tune into the conversation and hear that they built this boat themselves.

"So, you're nicely set up for running the motor to keep the refrigerator going," Dorin remarks.

The men talk about the details of refrigeration management while I think about pork chops. Surely, I had seen several packages of pork chops in the freezer.

"So," I finally say to Mary, "you pretty much cook normal, land-based meals?"

"Yes, tonight, for instance, we are having fried snapper, a salad, and some vegetable. I haven't decided what yet."

I tune back into the men's conversation. Dorin is giving a short, mild version of our trip so far, characteristically leaving out the trauma. He outlines our itinerary for going through the Panama Canal into the Pacific and on to the Galapagos. Bill appears concerned.

"I don't think you have enough time to do that," he says. "It's a good goal, but by the time you get into the Pacific, it will be the height of typhoon season. I wouldn't do it."

"What do you suggest?" asks Dorin.

"Well, we've been to the Dominican Republic. Haiti and the Dominican Republic share the island of Hispaniola. Though nobody calls it that. It's mostly referred to as the D.R. We went to Samaná in the D.R., and we liked it. From there you can always continue to Puerto Rico and then on down the Leeward and Windward Islands to Venezuela. A lot of good places to stop. And, cruisers we've talked to like Venezuela. Rate of exchange is great."

"Can I get charts here for the Dominican Republic?"

"No, there are very few charts available here. You can check it out in Hamilton, but I already did. Mostly they just have charts of Bermuda and a few of the US southeast coast."

While they talk details of the Dominican Republic, Mary offers to show me around the boat and there is, it turns out, a lot of boat to show. When I see the main cabin with a bed made up with sheets and pillows, I blurt out, "So it probably doesn't ever get wet in here?"

She treats my question with kind seriousness and explains they have a large bilge, so any water they take on has plenty of room and never comes above the floor. Also, she tells me, it's a tight boat so there are very few places the water can come in.

Then she asks questions about the trip we've just had. I find myself blurting out the details of the storm. She is sympathetic, and it sounds like she'd been there, done that.

"We got through it, but I feel like I just can't go back out there. I was pretty scared most of the time. It's different for Dorin. He's not afraid."

Mary laughs. "Of course he was afraid. Maybe more than you because he knew more about what was happening. He just didn't show it. That's the mark of courage. And leadership. He knew he had to keep his crew calm so they could function and do what had to be done. He probably didn't want you to experience any more fear than you already were, either."

I am stunned.

"Listen, he's a very competent sailor. Your son, too. I can tell by listening to Dorin. You have an excellent crew to take care of you."

She tells me that experiencing storms like that are rare, and as long as we don't go into the Pacific this time of year, it's unlikely we'll ever go through that again.

When we return to the salon, Dorin and Bill are looking over a chart spread out on the table.

"I've been talking to Bill, and I think we should change our plan. You okay with that?"

When I nod he says, "We probably can't reliably get charts here, but Bill has a twenty-year-old chart for the Dominican Republic. Could you copy it?" he asks. He knows I can. I've copied other charts, patterns, drawings.

"You can take it with you and bring it back when you're done," Bill says.

"Thanks for everything," Dorin says. "We'll be back with the chart." They shake hands.

Dorin helps me into the *Tinker*, which is a long step down from the wooden boat, and I settle on the side tube. He hands me the rolled-up chart and unties the *Tinker's* rope from the *No Brass Ring* cleat.

With one hand, I hold the chart on my lap and grab the rope looped along the outside of the tube with the other. We skim across the sparkling water, and I gaze at the *Fandango* many yards away.

"You know, even if we change our plans," Dorin says, "maybe we could get to Venezuela, then Colombia, and work our way into the Pacific, just long enough to get to the Galapagos...."

He looks closely at me. "You are being uncharacteristically quiet, lady. Kind of hard thinking about living on our garbage scow after seeing how the other half lives, huh?"

"No! No, that's not it. Actually, I like roughing it."

He raises his eyebrows.

"No, really. I lived in a tent for several months when my kids were small. With no plumbing, just a chair with a hole in the seat positioned over a hole in the ground...a tarp on three sides. Just like the bathroom I made at the boatyard. I like challenges. Their boat is nice, but I think something would be missing if cruising were all that easy. Like camping in an Airstream instead of a tent."

"Hmmn. You sure?"

"Well, all right, ice cubes would be nice. Or a dry bed. Okay, if I could pick just one, I'd pick a dry bed."

He smiles. "Okay, then. Why so pensive? Watch out, I'm changing tack." He pushes the tiller to the side and allows the sail to move smoothly across the boat.

"Well, I'm not sure I'm cut out for the kind of cruising that scares me to death. And I am always too sick to be any help. I'm the kind of crew you wish you had left behind."

He lifts my chin and looks into my eyes. "Hey, you're doing great."

"No, I'm not. I was so terrified out there. I didn't realize it was going to be that...that dangerous."

He turns the tiller to center which brings us into the wind. The *Tinker* stops dead. The limp sail flaps in the light breeze, and we rock gently on the tiny waves. He looks at me with a penetrating gaze.

"Shirl Jean. When we changed out our huge port lights for smaller ones so large waves wouldn't punch out the windows, when we beefed up the sides of the cabin with three-quarter-inch plywood so giant waves couldn't sweep the cabin off the boat, when we put on higher toe rails, and when we installed eye bolts to hook our harnesses onto, what did you think we were doing that for?"

I catch my breath. He doesn't wait for me to reply.

"Remember when we talked about large, dangerous storms, and I read passages from Joshua Slocum's book, and we talked about waves that could crash over the boat—that boats even capsize? What did you think?"

A small fishing dinghy slows as it goes by. At first, I think he is wondering if we need help, and then I realize he is just letting his bow wake lower so it doesn't toss us around. Dorin nods his appreciation to the boater, who tips his hat, and then speeds up as he heads toward the harbor entrance.

What did I think? Good question.

I mull it over for a minute.

"I guess, I guess I thought it would be exciting, daring, adventurous...but not...not real. I didn't get it." I shake my head. "No, I didn't really get it."

"So, where do we stand now?"

"I keep telling myself, I shouldn't have endangered Cory's life. What was I thinking?"

"And so?"

"Well, I have asked myself if I can go back out again. Even if I can, should I allow Cory to go? His father would buy him a plane ticket home in a heartbeat."

"How does Cor feel about it?"

"I haven't talked to him." I think back over the past days and how Cory handled challenges with humor, how he took on extra responsibility when I was sick. The way he took discomfort in stride and cracked jokes about it. And then it dawns on me. He *did* get it when Dorin explained about the risks involved. He expected it to be difficult and daunting.

Dorin waits while I ponder. "Okay, now that I'm thinking about it, I would guess he's hooked on adventure. He wants to test himself." I remember him striding confidently away from the *Fandango* this morning. "He wants to explore."

"Look, Shirl, I don't want you to do anything you don't feel comfortable with. If you want out, I won't think less of you. If you want to go home and take Cor with you, I will buy the tickets. I have single-handed before...I can do it again."

At that second, I realize I don't want this adventure to go on without me. I don't want to go home to a boring life and be left out of the excitement. I love challenges. I love facing the unknown.

"No, I don't want to go back."

"Are you sure?"

"Yes. But I wish I weren't so useless. Instead of helping, I'm a burden that you guys have to take care of."

"Okay, Shirl Jean. Listen to me. Haven't I always said there is no woman I have ever met that I would sail with for more than three hours, except you?"

"Yes. But...."

"Still true."

"How am I any better than other women you have sailed with?"

"Well, for starters, you don't whine."

I shrug.

"Until now, of course." But he smiles. "Look. I won't promise it won't happen again, but I promise it will get better, a lot better, sometimes. I know *you* will get better. You'll get over the seasickness...it's just a matter of time. And you will develop some confidence in the boat. And you will contribute equally, and I don't mean by doing laundry. And, one last thing. I'm getting better at celestial navigation."

"Okay," I laugh. "You got my attention about not doing laundry."

"Oh, I didn't mean you won't have to do laundry. I just meant you can also do your share of sailing and navigating."

"Do I have to cook?"

"Are you kidding? I'm not pushing my luck."

A movement catches my eye, and I see Cory leaning against the *Fandango's* shrouds. He waves at us and then raises his hands as if to ask, "What's up?"

"I guess we better get back," I say. "By the way, you are the bravest man I know. How come you don't get scared?"

"Are you kidding? I'm scared all the time. Look at the captain we have." Then he pulls on the sail as he turns the tiller, and the *Tinker* gently bucks us back to the boat.

Chapter Ten
Tourists in Bermuda

"So, are we going somewhere, or are we just sitting here all day?" Cory asks. "I think we should go into Hamilton today."

"Yup, it's time." Dorin puts a hand on my shoulder. "So, co-captain, do you think we are ready to put our energies into being tourists?"

I know, for sure, the bestowal of the co-captain title is something he hopes will make me feel better. I lift my brow and cock my head as if to say, "really?"

"Not going to work, huh?"

"No."

"I was just clutching at straws. Sorry." He looks sheepish.

Cory watches us, looking perplexed and then annoyed.

"If you guys have whatever it is all straightened out, let's get going. Or, I'll leave without you."

There is standing room only on the bus, so we grab handrails, but immediately a gentleman stands up and offers me his seat. I think about saying, "I'm all set," but it seems like more than passing courtesy on his part, not merely a gesture. I decide it would be rude to refuse, so I accept. Long before the fifty-minute ride is over, I am truly grateful.

There is more window space than I have ever seen in a vehicle—huge panes of glass with almost no interruption. As soon as we move, I flinch and look at Dorin because we are traveling on the left side of the road. We knew this would happen. It's the British system, and we expected it, but that doesn't keep us from gasping in alarm when the bus careens around corners on the wrong side. Dorin shrugs nonchalantly and smiles, but I know him. He is the most sensory motoric person I know. When he watches football on TV, he goes through muscle contractions and body movements, as he lives through the moment, trying to make the play successful. Now he throws a smile in my direction each time we successfully negotiate a curve, but then he is immediately back in "driver mode," leaning as if he could get that bus back onto the correct side of the road.

I continue to suck in my breath as we wind around the island, buses passing us, going in the opposite direction. It feels like there are only inches to spare between the vehicles.

This anxiety doesn't keep me from loving the view. The immaculate landscaping is vivid, green and beautiful. Houses are white or tropical colors and are set off with lush, but well planned, trimmed vegetation, and everything, everywhere is impeccable. Not a scrap of paper, not a discarded...anything. We get a close-by glimpse of an inlet with anchored, spic-and-span sailboats. The water is crystal clear, and the boats look orderly and scrubbed, as if they are prepared for a photo shoot.

Dorin bends to my ear. "Just like our garbage scow. Minus the scuz."

Frequently, mopeds, usually with two helmeted people aboard, zip by us. There seem to be many more mopeds and scooters than cars.

As we near Hamilton, the buildings are single and two-story, many painted in pink, yellow, or turquoise and looking quite modern.

We get off at the bus terminal on Church Street and follow other passengers downhill to Front Street, near the water. Not sure where to go, we wander a little on the busy street and stop to watch a smartly uniformed policeman ensconced in a protective "cage" in the middle of the street. His arms never cease moving as he beckons and windmills the traffic in precise movements that seem beautifully choreographed. Other tourists are also intrigued. Cameras click and movie cameras whir. This is great entertainment.

"It's after lunch time. I'm getting hungry," Cory finally says. "Where's this place you guys said you wanted to go for lunch?"

Mark, Diane's husband, had volunteered a day to help us get the *Fandango* ready. He told us about a "do not miss" restaurant he loved when he visited Bermuda.

"Yeah, it's the Pig something Tavern," I offer. "I should have written it down."

"The Hog Penny Pub?" asks a man strolling by. He is dressed in a white shirt, tie and lightweight sports coat. However, he is wearing Bermuda shorts and knee socks and carrying a briefcase.

"Yes, I think that's it!"

In that appealing British accent he says, "One block in that direction and turn left onto Barnaby Street. It's just around the corner on your right. Splendid choice."

We hurry along the sidewalk, and I realize I am sweating profusely. On the boat there is always a sea breeze. We are near the water here, but maybe the sun reflecting off the pavement makes it hotter.

Or maybe I just sweat a lot.

Because of the time I spent in the sun approaching Bermuda, my midriff is a giant blister. My damp shirt is now stuck to my belly, and I gently pull it away. I feel the blister break, and liquid runs into the waistband of my new skirt. Yuck.

We turn the corner onto Barnaby Street and there is the restaurant. Cory pulls open the door and signals us to go through. We step inside the cool, dimly lit dining room. We pause and take it in.

"Oh, my," I say.

Dorin takes my hand and says, "So I brought you to the right place, huh?" Then he whispers, "Will it do me any good?" and gives me an exaggerated leer.

"You'll have to play your cards right," I say.

"Righter than this?" he asks incredulously.

The wooden tables are inviting, the brass is polished, glasses sparkle, and the decor is interesting. The lighting is cozy and soothing. Though it's past lunch and the place is nearly empty, we are seated and given menus. Dorin and I look around in admiration.

"They sure do got ambience," he says.

"It's expensive," Cory points out. "But look at this stuff!"

"Cor, don't look at the prices. Just order whatever you want," Dorin says.

We order beverages: a tall Coke for Cory, iced tea for me and, of course, a martini with a twist for Dorin. We kick back and sip, except Cory, who chug-a-lugs his, while we try to narrow down our menu choices. It is astonishing to think that days before we had been living on lima beans and spam.

"Bangers and mash," Dorin says. "I always wondered what that would be like. I'm going to try it."

Cory orders the five-ounce Hog Penny Burger with mushrooms and onions. I order fish and chips. We share bites of our food with each other, eat slowly and enjoy.

Dorin signals for the bill. "After lunch, let's just find the Yacht Club and get our mail, if there is any. I'll come back another day and find a marina where we can get the CO_2 cartridges filled."

We stop another businessman to ask for directions to the Bermuda Royal Yacht Club. He is courteous and helpful, directing us farther along Front Street.

Two blocks later, we find the grand, pink, very impressive building.

We had read in cruising guides that women are not allowed in the Royal Bermuda Yacht Club, so I had already decided I was going in.

I lead our little party into the lobby and ask the clerk for our mail. He seems confused, and I wonder if it's because I have breached protocol, or if we have misinformation about being able to give the yacht club as a temporary address, or most likely, we don't look remotely like their usual patrons. While we tried to "slick up" for this occasion, we still look like cruising bums. After taking stock, he finally nods politely and looks for the mail in another room. Appearing somewhat surprised, he comes back with a thick manila packet for us, secured with a large elastic band.

I thank him, and he nods dismissively.

As we head to the door, Dorin whispers in my ear, "Are you disappointed he didn't try to throw you out?"

"Yeah. I would have stood my ground just to see what would happen, but I think he disapproved of the three of us equally."

"Well, except for me," Cory says. And sure enough, he still could pass for a yachting guy.

"Wow, looks like people remembered our existence," Dorin says, nodding at the fat envelope. "But let's save it until we get back to the boat. Looks like there's a lot."

On the way to the bus terminal, dark clouds approach, and suddenly rain comes down in torrents, just as it did when we approached Bermuda. People dash for doorways or step into stores. We find shelter under an overhang outside a store and watch as the water rushes down the street and comes up to the level of the sidewalks. There is not a single piece of refuse in the water. In ten minutes, the squall passes, and the sun comes out. The water level drops quickly, and emerging from their shelters, men, women, and children resume going about their business.

On the return bus ride, curiosity overcomes me, and I open the mail from home. The envelope contains the first section of our hometown newspaper. There, taking up half the front page of the *Waterville Morning Sentinel*, is a large photo of the *Fandango* and a story of our trip.

I squeal loudly, and all passengers turn to look at me. Dorin and Cory, embarrassed, say, "Shh."

"But, look!" I say, "it's about us."

Dorin is sitting beside me, and we read the story together. Cory is standing, but he also leans in to look at the newspaper. The story talks about the fact that we'd survived bad storms at sea and that the crew had experienced sea sickness.

"Great!" says Dorin, exasperated. "See? That's why I didn't want publicity."

"Seasick?" says Cory indignantly. "*I* haven't been seasick."

"But how did they get this?" I ask.

"I'd guess the reporter must have contacted Glenn. This is all stuff I told him. I certainly didn't mean it for publication."

"Well, Cory," I say, "since we've been front page news, you'd better call your father when we get back to St. George's and let him know you're okay."

There are also letters from my mother and several other people and some mail forwarded to us by Bill. I am impressed that the mail system recommended by Seven Seas Cruising Association worked so well. Then another thought occurs. We had asked my mother to buy and mail to the Galapagos a swaging tool in case we need to replace any cables. Has Mom already sent things on to the Galapagos? We had given both her and Bill that contact address, but now our plans have changed. We won't see the Galapagos.

How do I feel about this change? I had done a lot of research on the Galapagos and have been looking forward, for instance, to seeing large iguanas roaming in their natural habitat. But as I think of it now, I have to admit our scaled back plan, with little or no time in the stormy Pacific, appeals to me.

A lot.

When we arrive back at our boat, we are struck by how scuzzy and disorganized it is. There are lines running all over the deck and cockpit floor, everything is dirty, and there are things lying about that should be stowed. The contrast between our boat and all other boats that we've seen since we've been here is stunning. Maybe this is why the man who hovered over our boat to watch the chaffing line was so disgusted. There is nothing shipshape about the *Fandango*. Ship shabby is more like it.

Dorin cooks supper, and while we eat dinner on the boat, we make lists. We realize that many things that we brought, we don't actually need.

It seems ridiculous that we thought we'd need a stove for heat. Or sleeping bags. Or coats, sweatshirts. We decide to box up the excess stuff and mail it home.

Dorin contacts Glenn by ham radio, and they discuss the newspaper article. We can tell from Dorin's end of the conversation that Glenn thought we'd be happy about the exposure in the paper. Dorin doesn't disabuse him of this idea, but after they sign off, Dorin says he will not be giving Glenn any more colorful information. "Just our location and that we are doing fine."

At bedtime, I don't have the nerve to pull my shirt away from my body because it's stuck. I put a damp towel over my midriff. One time during the night, Dorin turns and starts to lay his arm across my belly, and, feeling the wet towel, pulls back.

"Sorry, sorry," he mumbles and rolls the other way.

The next day, while Dorin goes into Hamilton again on CO_2 business, Cory goes into town to find boxes. I gently peel off the shirt and dead skin comes with it. The eight by four-inch area is oozing and disgusting. I put on the halter top that led to the sunburn in the first place so the blistered area will be open to the air.

It's time now to cull the extraneous items that have been making life difficult. I pile up all the things that have been driving us crazy as we shoved them from place to place: sleeping bags, thick jackets and coats, blankets, extra pillows. The purge is deeply satisfying.

"Oh. Wow. That looks bad," Cory says when gets back with flattened boxes. He points to my midriff.

"It doesn't really hurt much, though. It looks worse than it is."

"That's good. Hey, we are sending the furnace back, right?"

"Yes, Dorin said last night we can send it back." Though it's small, we find the stove inconvenient to get around. While Cory unbolts it from the bulkhead wall, I tape the six large boxes, and we fold, pack and cram in everything we can do without. We seal and address all the boxes to Bill. Lucky him.

I am getting stoked. Now that we have space, I can see it's time to reorganize and make better use of it. But, first things first.

We attack the exterior next, stowing gear, securing the lines, and tucking things out of sight. When we had lowered the sails outside of Bermuda, for the sake of expediency, we had hastily secured the lowered mainsail onto the boom with ratty lengths of short rope that hung down from the droopy sail in various lengths at uneven intervals. Until now, I hadn't even noticed how bad it looked. In fact, I'm used to this. When Dorin and I sailed Maine waters in the summers, this was our usual MO. Why bother to tuck away the mainsail when we are in a small cove and are just going to take off the next morning anyway? I can see this philosophy needs adjusting now.

After we fold, neaten and refasten the sail, Cory locates the green sail cover from the bowels of the locker, and we lace it on. Then we scrub the boat from bow to stern with scrub brushes and a mop, using buckets of sea water to wash over it. Since everything was painted and varnished before we left, it looks great when we're done.

"Still," Cory says, "we have to keep putting on layers of varnish. The sun and water will keep breaking it down."

"Whoa! What did you do with the mess?" Dorin remarks when he appears at the top of the retaining wall.

"We made good use of our time. So, how'd it go?"

"Would you believe the marina did not have the right fittings for these particular CO_2 cartridges? They sent me to Bermuda Industrial Gas, and they didn't have them either. The guy there said he'd go to a hardware store to buy a tool that would allow him to fill the cartridges. If that didn't work, he'd phone around and see if anyone in Bermuda has a way to fill them. I told him I'd check back tomorrow. I don't understand it. The *Tinker* is British made. This is a British territory. Why wouldn't they carry the fittings? They do have fittings but not for these. I'm beginning to wonder if we made a mistake buying the *Tinker*.

"Oh, on a different subject," he says with a smile, "I picked up a newspaper. A cargo ship ran aground yesterday about where we were on our first approach. Apparently, it isn't all that unusual. No one was hurt, but there was damage, and they'll have to pull it off the rocks. I feel better now."

"Vindicated?"

"Massively."

In the afternoon, Dorin and Cory do some repairs while I go into "reorganization mode." I look at what we need frequently, as well as what can be put in less accessible places. The storage compartment at the top of the stairs, created for this trip, and which we have named the Bridge Deck Locker, is critical because of its proximity to the cockpit. At the same time, it's probably the most protected storage on the boat. Bone dry. Along with navigation aids, small tools, and first aid stuff, I place matches and flashlights in it.

The guys are just climbing out of the sail lockers when a gentleman stops by our boat. I duck quickly below, slip into a shirt that covers my gross midriff and pop up onto the companionway stairs.

"Hello, there!" Dorin says to the guy. "I didn't think I'd see you here."

He introduces us to the man he had talked to at the Industrial Gas place that morning. Like many residents we have seen, he is black and speaks with an elegant British accent.

"I'm afraid I have bad news," he says. "There is no fitting like the one you need to fill your bottles anywhere in Bermuda. I telephoned all marinas." He hands the cartridges to Dorin. "I am very sorry."

"Thank you for trying. That was very nice of you to do that for us. I was going to go in tomorrow. You didn't need to come out here. Can I reimburse you for your time and expenses?"

"No, no, it is not necessary. I live in St. George's, so I came here on my way home from work. I wanted to see your boat." He smiles admiringly. "I can see you have it outfitted for offshore travel. Please, have a good evening."

They shake hands, he nods an acknowledgment to Cory and me and starts to leave. Then he turns and adds, "Perhaps you will have better luck finding the fitting in your next port. Have a safe voyage." As he walks away, I think of how this gentleman is one more example of the politeness and friendliness of Bermudians. I am glad we cleaned up the boat before he arrived.

After a supper of spaghetti with clam sauce and Parmesan prepared by Cory, I clear the table and spread out the chart I need to copy. In a couple of hours, I have an approximation of the chart of the east coast of the Dominican Republic and an enlargement of the insert of Samaná Bay.

"Ya done good," Dorin says. "This will work!"

Cory, who's been in the cockpit studying, leans into the salon. "Someone's coming," he says. We go up the stairs just as a runabout full of people comes alongside.

"Hi, there," Dorin says.

It's quickly apparent this is a family--a dad, a mom and four kids.

"We want to welcome you to Bermuda," says the father.

"Why don't you tie up and come aboard," Dorin says.

Cory cleats off their line on the *Fandango* and then leans out to take the hand of the mother so she can step up onto our deck. They introduce themselves as the Brown family, Robert and Polly and their kids, whose names I can't keep track of. They live here and tell us they are the owners of a yacht in the bay called *The Oliver North,* which we had noticed soon after we arrived. We try to make ourselves comfortable. Dorin perches on the hatch cover, and Cory balances on the stern pulpit. The rest of us take up all of the seating in the cockpit and are nearly knee to knee.

They are a delightful family with a great sense of humor. We ask many questions about Bermuda. When Dorin comments on how clean the country is, Robert tells us that there is a littering law that is very strict. For instance, he says there is a $500 fine for litter coming from an automobile, and the driver of the vehicle is responsible for infractions. Dorin comments that all the cars are spotless, and Robert tells us that people wash their cars every week, usually on Sunday, including taking the wheels off to wash behind them and under the car. We are surprised to learn that, by law, each family unit is allowed only one car. He tells us most people use motorbikes and scooters.

They are a high-spirited, fun-loving family, and we enjoy their visit. As they are departing, Dorin asks, "So, if you don't mind my asking, why did you name your boat *The Oliver North*?"

Robert swings over our lifelines and down into his runabout. He shrugs and says, "He's a great American hero." There's a pause. "Right?"

There's another second of silence, and it occurs to us that he's joking again. But it appears he's seriously waiting for an answer.

"Well, it depends on whom you ask, I guess," says Dorin. "Good of you to come. Feel free to stop by again. We enjoyed meeting you."

"We will be back here in a couple of weeks," Robert says. "If you're here, we will invite you to our boat."

In the morning, I'm happy to see that a crusty scab has formed where the blister used to be. I opt for a shirt that covers the ugly mess. I am not in much discomfort, but when Dorin and Cory take an early morning dip in the bay, I can only watch.

Our big tasks of the day are to phone Auto Helm of America to order the replacement arm for the autopilot and to mail the boxes to Bill. While Cory and I bring the boxes up and stack them on deck, Dorin walks a few blocks to use a pay phone and comes back in a taxi.

"I got a hold of them. They said they'd ship out the part immediately. It's under warranty. They are sending it general delivery to Bermuda. I just have to ship back the old one. So, now let's get these boxes loaded."

The driver helps Dorin and Cory load the boxes in the back seat and trunk, and they take off for the post office. What a relief to have the boxes and their contents out of our cruising lives.

To celebrate, when they come back we have lunch at a nearby restaurant. When we return to our boat, we are surprised to see a cruise ship docked close behind us, its bow rising majestically above us.

"It's documented out of Panama," Dorin says.

As we stand in awe, our necks craning, our eyes rolling upwards toward the bridge of the huge ship, he adds, "You don't ever want to see this view from our boat when we're at sea." I reflect for a moment on the book, *The Shipkiller*, and say, "Amen to that!"

Hundreds of people stream down the gangplank on their way, Cory predicts, to the t-shirt shops. He follows the crowd and later tells us that he was right. The gift and t-shirt shops were mobbed.

When Cory returns, Dorin is standing on the side deck, hands on hips, looking thoughtfully up at the hulk of the monster hull. "Well, crew," he says. "I think we've pushed our luck on this temporary berth as far as we can. What say we move out to an anchorage today?"

I resist emotionally. It's so convenient here, and, big surprise, I've developed an emotional attachment to the land. But he is right. Better to move before we are told to. And we won't have to coordinate our onshore excursions with the tide so that I can climb off the boat and onto land. And back.

We do a minimum of prep to untie and motor out into the bay. As soon as the "umbilical cord" is broken, I have a positive reaction. I love the independence, privacy and the vacationey feeling of "camping out" on the water. Dorin finds a place near *No Brass Ring* but far enough away to allow us to swing wide on the anchor rode as the tide goes in and out. From now on, we will row or sail the *Tinker* into the dock. As we set and test the anchor, to be sure it doesn't drag on the bottom, our spirits lift.

"This is the life," says Cory, as he stretches out on the cockpit seat. He puts his feet up on the opposite seats and laces his hands behind his head.

Later in the day, the cruise ship leaves. We watch, unable to take our eyes off this monster-sized ship, which, now that we think of it, can't possibly fit through the town cut to get out to sea. The closer it gets, the more impossible it seems.

"Looks like it will scrape the sides as it goes by," I say.

"But it got in here. It's got to be able to go out," Cory observes.

Hard to say from our angle how close the ship comes, but it does slip through smoothly and is quickly out of sight as it heads for open water.

Over the next few days, I tackle the laundry, using the usual method with saltwater. But, since it rains here once a day or more, I hang them on the lifelines so they will get rinsed in fresh water. If I am lucky, they get rinsed twice.

The first day, while the laundry is drying, I spray bleach to kill mold in the interior of the fo'c'sle and the mattress, both sides.

I have to keep track of the fast-changing weather. When the laundry is nearly dry and I see a shower coming, I whisk them off the lines and toss them down the front hatch into the fo'c'sle. In twenty minutes, they are dry. When I wash our sheets and pillowcases in saltwater, I use the last of the water in the rubber tank, laced generously with baking soda, to rinse out the saltwater. I throw the sheets over the boom to dry, and pillowcases join the rest of the laundry on the lifelines. The sheets come out smelling April fresh. We finally have the most comfortable sleep since the beginning the trip with clean, fresh smelling, dry sheets and pillowcases.

I continue to reorganize, and the guys continue maintenance, including wiring, checking and tightening fastenings, and the bilge pump. Dorin redesigns rigging to better control the foresails.

"It's a lot easier to repair stuff while we're sitting here in the harbor," Cory observes. I catch my breath, plunging deep into a flashback of Dorin fixing the bilge pump as we sluice down gigantic waves on a slippery, thirty-degree heel.

In the afternoons, we sightsee, sometimes the three of us, and sometimes Dorin and I go by ourselves while Cory does his own exploring. On one trip into Hamilton, Cory goes to the library for four hours to study biology while we have lunch and wander around the water looking at sailboats. When we meet him back at the library, he says he's got 20 pages of biology notes. Dorin has heard that the library has charts, so he checks. There are chests with dozens of labeled drawers, very wide, side to side, but only inches deep. Dorin checks the labels and pulls several drawers open and quickly confirms Bill is right. There are no useful charts here for us.

Cory has been picking up a British accent that he tries on us. It sounds convincing to me, and I tell him so, with the warning I might not have a good ear for this. That evening he tells us that for fun he used the accent while shopping in town. He was startled when a British clerk asked him what part of England he was from.

One day Dorin and I walk, hand in hand, to the White Horse Inn next to the water for lunch. We sit outside enjoying the weather, the smell of saltwater and flowers.

"You are from the United States," our waiter says. "What state do you live in?"

"Maine," I say.

"Oh, I know Maine," he replies. "I have been there. Where, in Maine do you live?"

I assume he's been to the coast where a lot of tourists go.

"We live in a little city called Waterville," Dorin says.

"I have been in Waterville!" he says with surprise. "I know your city."

"What brought you to Waterville?" Dorin asks.

"My son goes to Thomas College."

"He's a soccer player!" Dorin and I say together.

Thomas has an outstanding soccer team, and they recruit outside of the states to build their team.

"Yes!" he says, animatedly. "A full scholarship. I hope he does well. Thomas College is a good school, correct?" We assure him it is.

"How does your son like winter?" Dorin asks.

"Winter? You people are going to have to do something about that!" He shakes a finger at us, but he's smiling.

"We did," Dorin replies. "That's why we're here."

Then we exchange addresses and phone numbers, and we invite him to call us next year when we are home and he is in Waterville, so we can get together.

"What are the odds that we'd come to this restaurant and get this particular waiter?" Dorin asks.

After lunch, the three of us take the bus into Hamilton, as we've been meaning to tour the Botanical Gardens. From Hamilton we take another bus to the Gardens.

There are no tours that day, so we walk around on our own, captivated by exotic plants we've never seen before. The flowers, in such great variety, are incredible in color and form. There are formal gardens, natural gardens, and cactus gardens. We are astounded by our first look at a banyan tree. There are many "trunks" supporting the same tree. A passerby tells us that the tree sends down "newbie" trunks—shoots that grow down from above until they touch the ground, where they establish new roots. We wander among the many slender trunks that are part of this huge spreading tree.

"You enjoying this?" Dorin asks, putting his arm around my shoulders.

"Oh, man, yes. See, this is what travel is all about. You get to see things you didn't even know existed!"

"You're welcome," he says, happily.

"Good news," Dorin says the next day. "The autopilot arm came in. We will be able to leave soon."

"Yay," I reply. "That *is* good news." My heart is racing, and I discover a knot in my stomach.

We haven't talked about departure since the day we had the heart-to-heart while floating in the dinghy twelve days before. While we've been tourists and while I reorganized the boat to make offshore cruising easier, I've allowed myself to turn firmly away from that reality. Denial, I think they call it.

Installing the autopilot arm is quick, and the guys talk about taking off soon.

"We have to re-provision food supplies," I say. "We'll have to fill the tanks. And, we are going to take some gallons of bottled water, too. Oh, yeah, we have to get caught up on laundry." I ramble on, trying to come up with a long list of things to do before we leave. We need to approach this departure business slowly. It could take days, giving me time to adjust to the idea, I think.

"We have to sail over to *No Brass Ring* and bring back their chart," Dorin says. "Maybe we can take a taxi to the laundromat. Then we'll grocery shop and fuel up, fill the tanks. We could leave by tomorrow!"

He reads my face. "Or the next day."

I nod but don't dare speak. When we get back from doing the laundry in the afternoon, we do sail the *Tinker* over to *No Brass Ring*. We talk to Bill and Mary about a possible departure very soon.

"Yes, I think you guys had better get going," Bill says. "I've been listening to NOAA[1], and there are tropical depressions heading this way. We're going to stay put, but if we were leaving, we'd get out now."

---

[1] NOAA Weather Radio is created by The National Weather Service (NWS) to provide weather, hydrologic, and climate forecasts and warnings for the United States, its territories, adjacent waters and ocean areas, for the protection of life and property and the enhancement of the national economy.

Dorin flashes a sympathetic glance at me and then tells them it sounds like a good idea. We confirm that we are going to the Dominican Republic, and they give us a crash course of life for boaters in the Dominican Republic—the D.R., Bill reminds us, is what it's called. "And the port town of Samaná, I understand, is officially called Sta. Bárbara de Samaná, but I've only heard it called Samaná."

He gives Dorin a list of radio frequencies for weather, and we promise to stay in touch by ham radio.

"You have an English/Spanish dictionary on board, right?" asks Mary.

I'm embarrassed to say we don't. With all of the planning we did for a year, how did I not think of this?

"You'll be fine," Mary says, and I realize I must be as easy to read as a first-grade primer.

"Yes, I'm sure," I say. "We appreciate all your help."

Dorin squeezes my hand as we prepare to get into the dinghy. Then, it's down over the side, and we are bouncing over an unusual chop in the bay. "You okay?" he asks.

I nod but can't talk. Almost can't breathe.

Before returning to the boat, Dorin and I go to the grocery store and bring back our supplies by taxi. We load them into the dinghy and sail out to the *Fandango*.

When we get to the boat, Cory says, "Don't touch anything that is wood outside or in the companionway. I just finished re-varnishing. And supper will be ready in five minutes. I still have difficulties with rice on this stove, but I think it'll be okay. It's curried rice and chicken."

To avoid the cockpit while the varnish dries, we eat a delicious supper in the cabin, while Cory tells us about trees, birds and lizards of Bermuda.

"Let's get the water tanks topped off and fill the diesel tank," Dorin says. "We'll motor over there and then anchor out in the bay tonight and leave first thing in the morning."

"And, hey, it's not a Friday," Cory says.

"Yeah, um, how are you feeling about heading out?" I ask him.

"I'm glad to get going. I mean, I like it here. It's been fun. But I want to get back out there. We have a lot more to see, right? We only have a year."

In the morning, the guys take the sail cover off and stow it. They let some air out of the *Tinker* so that it's only partially inflated and haul it up on deck. Below, I put away anything that could become airborne. I make tuna sandwiches for an early lunch, and we eat in the cockpit not saying much, lost in our thoughts. While I clean the galley, Dorin tries to notify Glenn on the ham radio to let him know we are leaving, but he doesn't get through. I think he's relieved.

Finally, Dorin starts the motor, and Cory hauls the anchor and fastens it to the bowsprit. At 1:30, Dorin shifts into forward gear and turns the *Fandango* toward the opening to the sea. Bill and Mary are out on deck to wave goodbye. We motor through the town cut, and Cory notes in the log: *2:15 cleared spit buoy, knot log reset at 0000, speed under power 3 knots.*

At 2:30, Dorin and Cory hoist the three sails, and Dorin tells me to turn off the motor; we heel slightly as the sails fill, and we pick up speed. At these times, I always feel a touch of anxiety when we are no longer under power—power means control, right? But there is always an immediate release from tension when the dominant sound is near silence, followed by an awareness of water singing around the hull and sweet bird calls.

Cory's next log entry gives a hint of his mood. *Running free and clear on a reach under all full sail! Still on soundings, 50 feet, heading 115 degrees magnetic. Perfect weather hope the wind picks up.*

At 3:30, having worked out the course we will be sailing on for days, Dorin turns the *Fandango* on a beat causing us to heel to fifteen degrees as he close-hauls the sails.

"Sorry about that," he says. "When the wind shifts, we can go on a reach, and it'll be a lot more comfortable."

"Not *when*," I say to Cory. "*If.*"

"Could happen." He shrugs. "Or not."

Chapter Eleven
The Passage
and the Passenger

It's Sunday, August 9, and our first day on this second leg of our trip. Once we are underway, we easily slip into the familiar routine, and I'm surprised to realize it feels good to be back out on the water. I know the butterflies will resurface if I think about *storms of cruising past* or *storms of sailing future,* so I concentrate on the present which, so far, is not stormy. Not a cloud in sight and the ocean reflects the blue of the sky, but adds, in the gentle waves, its own textures of turquoise and lavender.

"We're off soundings," Cory reports at 3:30 p.m. That means our depth sounder, which measures down a maximum of 500 feet, is no longer reading the ocean floor and has stopped sending signals to our boat. The red digital numbers that were so crucial near Bermuda are no longer showing.

Dorin nods. "Good."

"Good?" I say. "Fabulous!" Seven years ago, on my very first sailing adventure, we were bringing a newly purchased *Fandango* from Rhode Island to Maine. I was nervous when the depth was more than fifty feet back then. Dorin had chuckled and asked, "Can you swim to land from here?"

"No, of course not."

"Why would it make any difference, then, if there were fifty feet below you or 500?"

I laughed. "Yeah, I see what you mean. It's not like I could stand up and touch bottom in either case."

As we sailed in subsequent summers along the rugged coast of Maine with its hidden rocky hazards, I learned not to be a shore-hugger. Our recent adventurous approach among the reefs of Bermuda reinforced this opinion. I feel much more secure knowing the depth beneath our boat is measuring in the hundreds of feet.

We are on a compass heading of 200 to 210 degrees. As long as we stay close-hauled on a beat, we can maintain this.

"What's our speed?" Dorin asks.

"Four knots," Cory replies.

Dorin fusses with the sails and we heel a little more.

"Now?"

"Six!"

"All right!" Dorin says with satisfaction. "If we can keep this up, we'll be in the D.R. in ten days, two weeks tops. But don't worry. Soon the prevailing winds will change to easterlies—that's what we can expect at this time of year, and we can maintain this course on a reach. It'll be much more comfortable."

"I don't think I know what a reach feels like," Cory jokes. "Could be boring."

Through the night, we continue on a beat, taking four-hour watches. On this Monday morning, Dorin reports that he had trouble with the autopilot during his watch, and I groan. "No! Really? You just fixed it!

Damn!" I have reached the firm conclusion that the quality of our lives depends on the autopilot.

"Not a big deal," he says, irritably. "I fixed it already. Again." I don't know if it's because of my reaction, or because he, himself, is disappointed, once more, in our self-steering device.

"Assuming the winds stay like this, we could put up the awning," he says.

I am stunned. I have completely forgotten about the awning. During the winter before we left, my mother and I, at Dorin's suggestion, made an awning from Sunbrella marine cloth. The idea was to protect us from sun and rain in the cockpit, but it could also collect rainwater if need be, via a fitting in the center to which a small tube could be attached. I had completely forgotten we had it—didn't even know where it was.

It doesn't take Cory long to climb into the sail locker and find it underneath fenders, life jackets and hanks of old, grimy line. He tosses it out into the cockpit and climbs out after it.

Other than being a little dirty and smelling musty, it's none the worse for wear. We tie the gray rectangle to stays and shrouds; it more than covers the cockpit, and we are ecstatic when we find immediate relief in the shade underneath.

Dorin grins from the galley where he's making coffee. "Think it might work out?"

"It's a whole other living space! Like another room. With fresh air!" I exclaim. "Whew, it will be so much more comfortable out here. I can't believe we didn't think of it before!"

"Well, we either didn't need it because of fog or couldn't use it because of high winds," he says. "Could have used it in Bermuda, I guess. Not very yachty though. We'd have stood out as cruising bums."

Cory is lounging in the shade. He adjusts his cap, folds his arms, and nods. "But that's what we *are*," he says with satisfaction.

I look around our new, shady space and think how much we would have enjoyed the awning while at anchor in the bay in St. George's, no matter what the yachting neighbors thought.

"And you know what else? It also feels more private," I say. "Not like we're on view, sitting in the cockpit. I love this thing."

"Keep in mind, if we get a lot of wind, we'll have to take it down. But we can put it up anytime we're in port."

I feel like our lives have just gotten a whole lot better.

On Tuesday morning, the direction of the wind is still unfavorable, so, in order to stay as close as possible to the compass heading we need, we are still on a beat. But the heel isn't bad, maybe ten degrees, and it's not uncomfortable.

"Sorry, you guys," he says. "I checked the Pilot Chart, and the wind should be favorable this time of year. It should switch around to easterly any time now."

Cory laughs. "Yeah, this is tough sailing," he says, leaning casually against a taut main sheet. "Should we break out the life jackets?"

Later, Dorin listens to NOAA, with its mechanical "robot" voice, on the ham radio.

"There are tropical depressions moving into the region. I'll have to keep an eye on them."

"Depressions? Like in pre-storms? Plural?" I ask.

"Yeah, three of them to be exact, spread out in different locations."

"Do we actually know if this Samaná place is a port of entry?" Cory asks.

"I would guess so," Dorin answers. "Bill would have told us if it weren't, I think."

"Just wondering. There are a couple of bigger cities in the Dominican Republic."

"Oh? Bill didn't say anything about that."

"How do you know, Cor?" I ask.

"I looked up the D.R. when I was at the library in Hamilton. There's Puerto Plata on the north coast and Santo Domingo, that's the capital, on the south coast. They're bigger cities, and both are ports of entry."

"Well, it's likely Samaná will be, also," Dorin says, though he doesn't sound entirely convinced.

On Wednesday, our fourth day at sea, Dorin has the "chart" that I made spread out in front of him on the dining table.

He listens to NOAA at noon and tells us Bermuda could be in the path of tropical storm Arlene. I'm sure alarm shows on my face because he adds quickly, "But we shouldn't get any of that stuff."

"But the tropical depressions...."

"I will be monitoring and charting them." He points to where he has already penciled in notations. "We'll change course to avoid them as much as we can."

He glances up at me. "That is, if it's important to you," he says with a twinkle in his eye.

My chore for today is sewing repairs. While we were trying to make the most of limited storage before we left, I designed hanging storage—a series of pockets stitched to a four-foot by twenty-inch piece of light canvas that would be screwed to the back of the head door. My sewing machine is really tough, so I was able to stitch elastic across the tops of the pockets to keep stuff in. Because they have been stuffed to bulging and used often, several of them are wearing out and have holes in them. Luckily, I brought some light duck canvas material for patching.

I get out my sewing kit, which is primarily large needles for sail repair, waxed twine, pliers and a leather palm. The palm, a necessary item for sail repair, is a piece of leather that slides over the hand and has a large and effective metal thimble built into the palm for pushing needles through the resisting, thick sailcloth. Cory unscrews the whole rig from the door, and I settle in the cockpit with my project.

"As long as you're in the mood for domestic chores," Dorin jokes, "let's think about how to replace the battens we lost in the storm. You can remove the batten pockets and make more. I brought a piece of sail cloth."

"Sure, no problem. Just get some battens. Maybe at the batten store?"

"We could order them."

"Shipped to where?"

"Hmm. Yeah, it could be getting tricky to figure out where we will be. Maybe battens are overrated."

Since sail sewing is tedious and time consuming, I am satisfied we have come to a good solution on the battens.

The next day, Thursday, Dorin talks to Bill of the *No Brass Ring* via ham radio. Bill tells him that tropical storm Arlene will be passing just a little north of Bermuda, and they are already getting slammed by high winds. He is preparing to move the boat to a more protected part of the harbor and says he has his hands full. Dorin wishes him well and signs off.

"Looks like we're lucky we moved when we did," I remark. Remembering my reluctance to leave Bermuda, I feel almost weak-kneed with gratitude that we will not have to deal with this storm. Meanwhile, our sailing conditions are nearly perfect, with only occasional white, puffy, cumulus clouds lazing across the sky.

Cory trails a fishing line from the stern. We get a few nibbles that relieve the hook of bait, but "no cigar" on hooking anything.

We are taking on a small amount of water, not enough to be alarming, just enough so the floor is always wet. While the bilge pump is automatic, Dorin wants to conserve batteries, so we flip the switch when we want it to pump. In the afternoon, the bilge pump gets plugged again. Dorin lifts the floorboards and removes a tiny piece of cardboard.

"Now how did that get in there?" he asks. "And damn this shallow bilge anyway. If the bilge were deeper, the pump would be at the bottom and not where it could try to filter every bit of flotsam that goes by."

Cory volunteers to cook supper. As usual, with noodles and a variety of canned stuff, he comes up with a delicious meal.

On Friday morning, Dorin says, "If it's all right with you guys, I'm going to change the heading a little. There's a tropical depression that's developed in the Windward Islands and coming through, south of us. If we head more easterly for a while, it should pass below us. We won't be heading directly toward the D.R., so we'll add a day to the passage. Whaddya say?"

"I guess," Cory says. He doesn't sound convinced.

"Yes," I say. "I'm for it."

Dorin smiles. "I thought it would break down that way. I'm going to add my vote for dodging the depression."

We'll take a hit in terms of arrival time, but I'm okay with being on the ocean longer if we can avoid a storm. The autopilot is working fine, so we go about the business of housekeeping, cooking, laundry, boat maintenance, navigating, and reading. We have four novels we agreed to bring on the trip. We've only had a few minutes, so far, to devote to reading.

As on most days, Cory is on watch all day because he is in the cockpit doing homework. He hauls in samples of seaweed and photographs or draws and labels them in his field journal, using a biology book and a few others he brought as references.

Late morning, he calls us to the cockpit and points to something just a few yards off our starboard side.

"Look at that floaty thing."

I see an inflated plastic bag bobbing on the calm surface. "Yeah, it's disgusting how much stuff boaters throw into the ocean." We have been seeing floating debris like empty ketchup and shampoo bottles ever since we left Bermuda.

"Look again." He flips through pages of a textbook.

We slowly gain on the plastic bag and will be alongside it shortly. As we near, I see it has translucent colors, purple and turquoise, like a bubble.

Dorin joins us, and we are only four feet from the floating object.

"I think it's a...." Cory is still flicking pages, one at a time, now. "Yes! Here it is. It's a...."

"Portuguese man-of-war!" Dorin says.

"How did you know?" asks Cory. "Have you seen one?"

"No, I was just reading over your shoulder. You wouldn't want to get near that thing. Most jellyfish can sting, but they say the man-of-war's sting is especially painful and can be dangerous to your health, like shock or heart attack."

"Here it says they aren't even jellyfish."

"What!?" Dorin glances back at the book.

"It says, 'This stinging marine animal is jelly-like but is not a jellyfish. The float that looks like a bag can be blue to pink in color and anywhere from three to 12 inches in diameter.'

"The bag thing is how it moves. The wind blows it," Cory says. "What do you think? Twelve inches across?"

"Oh yeah, no doubt about that," Dorin says.

I climb out of the cockpit, squat on the deck, and look over the lifelines to get a closer view.

"Look at those tentacles. They are such beautiful colors!" The graceful, ribbon-like, and sometimes ruffly tentacles are unbelievably brilliant shades of deep purple, lavender and pink.

"Those are *long* suckers, too," says Dorin.

In the clear water we can see the tentacles for many feet until they disappear in the depths.

"How long do they get?" I ask Cory.

"Up to 65 feet!"

We are moving slowly away from this enchantingly beautiful creature, so I hop into the cockpit and then back to the stern, so I can watch it as we go our separate ways.

Cory notes the event, adding our longitude and latitude position as close as we know it to be, and then draws the Portuguese man-o-war with colored pencils.

During the night, a week into this leg of our trip, part of our electrical system fails, so we don't have cabin lights, position lights on the mast, or autopilot. Or compass light. It fails on Cory's 4:00 a.m. watch, so he steers by hand until daylight, checking his heading on the compass with a flashlight.

At daylight, Dorin troubleshoots the electric system, removing the cover of the electric panel which has dozens of bundled wires attached to many switches. Since he wired the boat himself, he is in his element.

At noon he says, "So, Shirl Jean, let's take some sun sights. Then, while I'm working on the electrical system, you can reduce them and tell us where we are."

I would like to refuse, but he is right. I probably can do this, and I sure as hell can't repair the electricity.

I take the notes from the sun sight to the chart table, and using the form and the manual, I reduce the sight. When I am done, he logs our position at 25 degrees and 53 minutes north, 62 degrees and 51 minutes west: 420 miles from Bermuda and 525 miles northeast of Cape Samaná. Almost halfway!

By the time we know where we are, Dorin has fixed the electrical problem so we can use the bilge pumps and listen to the radio for news and weather.

"So, we are still on schedule for a ten-day passage?" asks Cory. We have maintained a speed of five to six knots without much discomfort.

"More like two weeks, but no more than that."

After supper, we are all sitting in the cockpit when Dorin spots a small, grayish brown bird circling our boat. It's smaller than a seagull, and a lot larger than a sparrow or robin, with longer legs and a wider wingspan. Its head is white with black patches around its eyes. The long beak is also black. We are an estimated 400 miles from land, so we are amazed.

"How the heck would a small bird make it this far from land?" I ask. "It must be so tired."

"They can ride the thermals for long distances," Dorin offers.

"Maybe it hitched a ride on other boats. Maybe a freighter," Cory says.

When it lands on the forward most part of the awning, we can see only its tail from inside the cockpit. The bird takes flight a few minutes later and circles again before landing on the *Tinker*. Dorin has grabbed the camera from below and hands it to me. I move slowly, not wanting to scare it off, and am able to get a shot.

"It must need to rest," Cory says. "Maybe it'll stay for a few minutes."

Then the little guy takes off and circles the boat, landing back on the edge of the awning. Minutes later it's airborne again, perhaps deciding the sagging, rippling edge of the awning isn't stable enough.

The three of us are focused on our new friend and barely talk as we watch it fly away from the boat and then back. Suddenly, it darts down to the starboard cleat between the cockpit winches and appears to settle. A few minutes later the little fellow hops down onto the sail locker cover and is perched next to me, facing the same direction I am and standing perfectly still. Cory brings tiny pieces of bread and gently tosses them. I try not to move, and finally our avian visitor starts to pick at the bread.

In a few minutes, the bird makes side to side stepping motions and then squats a bit and appears to be resting. I sit without moving as long as I can so I won't disturb it, but eventually I have to use the head. When I reappear, the bird is still there and continues with us through the night, even during shift changes.

"Come quick," Cory calls to us at six a.m.

We dash to the galley.

Cory holds up his hand for us to stop.

"It's down in the foot well," he says softly. "It's too small a space for it to fly out."

He slowly reaches down and picks up the bird. As soon as it clears the foot well, the bird spreads its wings and flies out of Cory's hand. We watch it circle once then head north until it's quickly out of sight. It was inevitable, we know, but we agree it was fun while it lasted. I don't mention to Dorin and Cory that the little guy had been a symbol of land that must exist beyond the "endless" sea.

On Monday, we are becalmed in bright sunshine. While it's irritating, at least we have the awning. We wallow all morning, but none of us mentions how much more time we will be at sea if we are stalled in calms for long.

At noon Dorin says, "I challenge you guys to a bowline tying competition."

"Hah!" I laugh. "Yeah, like it isn't obvious the odds are stacked in your favor."

He has tried on numerous occasions to teach me how to tie a bowline (pronounced **boe**lin), but I am knot-challenged. He talks me through it each time. "The rope goes 'out of the rabbit hole and around the tree and back into the rabbit hole.' No, the rope, the loop is the other way." He flips it over in my hand. "Okay, now try it. No, from under the loop for the rabbit to come out of the hole." Eventually, I get it, but there is then no way for me to use this knowledge regularly. Usually a year goes by before I try it again. It has a specific purpose, like to attach the sheet to the jib, let's say. But the jib sheets are already attached. I do know knots that I actually *use,* like a square knot, learned in Girl Scouts, and my favorite, the clove hitch that I learned during my first sail with Dorin.

In the week we spent bringing the *Fandango* from Rhode Island to Maine, we stopped in several ports. It was my job to tie fenders (rubber bumpers) to the side of the boat when we docked. Sometimes I got the knot backwards, but it still worked.

Now that I'm no longer a novice, I use the clove hitch to secure the dinghy to a dock. I always walk away feeling cocky and confident when I nonchalantly toss off a clove hitch.

But a bowline has me tied up in knots. However, during the winter before we left, Cory and Dorin spent some time in his living room speed-tying the bowline. I couldn't see the point. When do you ever have to rush to tie a bowline?

But it was fun for Cory. Sometimes he beat Dorin.

"Sure. Let's go," Cor says enthusiastically.

Dorin pulls some short lengths of line out of a sail locker and hands one to Cory.

"Okay, Shirl, tell us when to go."

We spend a fun fifteen minutes, and by the end, Cory wins every time. Dorin looks both chagrined and amused. "I don't know, Shirl. It's getting harder every day to maintain a position of superiority over the younger generation. I can't even figure out a way to cheat!"

"Give it time," I say.

"So, gang, if we had wind today, I was planning to change course again to avoid a depression, but we're not going anywhere very fast, so it should pass us before we get there." In the afternoon, he reads the American Practical Navigator, and, on the foredeck, I do laundry. It's definitely easier to do on a level, stable deck.

"Hey, come here," Cory yells. "You won't believe this."

I hurry along the deck, duck under the canopy and step into the cockpit. Dorin is already standing on the rear deck.

Not fifteen feet astern is a giant sea turtle, using really large, paddle-like flippers to effortlessly push its way through the water. It has exquisitely beautiful, intricate patterns on its back.

"Yikes! I didn't know they got that big," I say.

"Yeah, it's gotta be, what? Five feet long?" Dorin asks.

Cory has already found the chapter on sea turtles. "Um, well, if it's a Green turtle, yeah, it can get that big."

I try to process the fact that, if I could stretch out beside it, it would be almost as long as I am tall. Even though I can see how big it is, I can't quite believe it.

"It could weigh 700 pounds. Look at these pictures. Does it mostly look like this one? That would make it a Green." We look over the pictures and agree that the grayish green turtle looks like the one labeled in the book.

"It says, '*Sea turtles are our planet's most ancient creatures and have been on the earth for about 150 million years.*' Hey, that means they were actually here during the dinosaur time."

"Yeah, I read that somewhere," Dorin says. "Keep reading." Dorin leans over the lifelines to watch the turtle.

"'*Like other species of turtles, green turtle females crawl out of the water and onto beaches, dig nests and lay eggs, 100 to 200 at a time, and then return to the ocean. Eight weeks later, hatchlings emerge and scramble into the ocean to avoid a multitude of predators, including birds and crabs. Only a few hatchlings survive.*'"

I watch the turtle move so gracefully and easily through the water and realize it's catching up to us. "How fast can they swim?" I ask.

"Um, let me see." Cory turns the page. "Okay, it says one mile an hour when it's migrating."

"Well, that's an indicator of how fast we're not moving," Dorin says.

"Yeah, it's gaining on us." I kneel on the deck and admire the colors and pattern of its shell and the texture of its front flipper legs.

"Listen to this," Cory says. "'*Like all species of sea turtles, Green turtles are an endangered species. They are hunted and their eggs are collected by humans, a legal practice in some countries, though many countries have laws and ordinances to protect turtles and their nesting areas.*'"

Dorin walks forward on the deck to keep pace with the turtle.

"Hey, look, he's outrunning us. We'd better catch up, if we want turtle soup for supper!" Cory says.

The giant turtle reaches our bow and continues for ten more yards and then dives deeper into the water and is quickly out of sight.

"Maybe it will come back up," I say. "It needs air, right?"

"Nope. It can stay down for half an hour or even more in cold water." Cory closes the book and joins Dorin and me on the foredeck where we watch the surrounding water, hoping it will reemerge.

"That was awesome!" Cory says. "So this is what sailing in the Bermuda Triangle is like," he says while he begins his sketch of the turtle.

"At least some of the time," Dorin replies.

"We aren't in the Bermuda Triangle," I say. "Right? I mean I don't really believe in it, but we aren't in it, right?"

Dorin laughs and Cory looks amused. "Where did you think it was?" Cory asks.

"Somewhere out in the middle of the ocean," I reply, trying to visualize a Western Hemisphere map.

"Ahem," Dorin says.

"We've been in the Triangle since we left Bermuda," Cory says. "Right?" He looks at Dorin.

"Yes. But we don't believe in the mysteries of the Triangle. I guess boats have really disappeared, but it's much more likely that isolated violent storms have been the culprit. Or pirates. Or both."

I nod. We'd talked about the Bermuda Triangle when a story hit the news, and Dorin had given me this explanation. But a little tension surfaces now, as it did then. I remember sitting in front of our console radio when I was a child, listening to the news. I asked my mother what the Bermuda Triangle was, and she gave me the prevailing popular belief that it was a mysterious place out in the ocean that, when boats and planes go into it, they don't come out. But I'd never have to worry about it, she reassured me...it was way out in the middle of the ocean. I chuckle thinking I would mention the Bermuda Triangle in my next letter to Mom. Or maybe not, on second thought.

At three a.m. on Tuesday, we are still becalmed, when I see a ship crossing our bow. Radar tells me it's three miles away and not on a collision course. This is the first boat we've seen since we left. In spite of the presence of the ship, I doze off. At 5:00 a.m. Dorin wakes me up to take over the watch and realizes we are off course.

"The autopilot isn't working," he says and scrambles down the stairs. He pulls open the motor cover and says, "It's because the batteries are dead."

"Oh, no!" I say, alarmed. "What'll we do?" As usual I'm thinking of the things we need electricity for: interior lights, exterior position lights, bilge pumps, the motor, the ham radio, the autopilot!

He gives me a quizzical look. "Why do you think we have the reserve battery?"

"Oh." Yeah, the reserve battery.

The motor starts easily, and the autopilot arm cranks the tiller post, and, after a couple of seeking yaws, the boat swings back on course.

"We'll have to motor all day to recharge the batteries," he says. "Just as well. Still no wind."

At night, we turn off the motor and there is enough wind to move at three or four knots. It's a relief when the sound of the motor stops, and all we hear is the slight rushing of the water by the hull. The sky is clear, and we are amazed that the night sky is thick with stars from horizon to horizon. It reminds me of the skies of my childhood in the country.

"But look," Dorin says. "This is not the sky you are used to. Look over there," he points to the horizon on our port side.

"That's the Big Dipper, just above the water."

And, yes, it's true. I can see it. "That's so...unreal," I say.

"And look over there, to the north, low in the sky. It's the North Star. It will get lower every day we travel south. That's why I like night sailing," Dorin says. "It's one of the few places where you can really see the stars."

We continue to star gaze long into the mellow night.

At 7:30 a.m., on Wednesday, Dorin yells down to Cory, "We've got a wind springing up. We're doing six knots." The wind gusts, and we heel sharply to twenty degrees.

"Take down the awning," Dorin yells. "Let's reef the main and take down the jib."

Cory and I untie the awning, and I fold it while they reduce sail. We are jubilant to be moving at hull speed again. We start estimating a new arrival date in the D.R.

Then an hour later, the wind dies. The guys put up the jib and shake out the reef in the main. Cory and I put up the awning again, and we ghost along all day, barely moving.

Dorin looks in the Pilot Chart. "It says there is a 1% chance of calms this time of year. Sorry, guys. We should really be moving at this point."

"It's okay. But good thing we brought a lot of food and water," I say.

This is our eleventh day at sea, and all our fresh produce is gone, but we have plenty of canned and boxed food. We are still working on the water in the main tank.

We are barely moving at two knots, just enough to maintain steering. Cory does homework, Biology, all day. I read old issues of SSCA, *Seven Seas Cruising Association*, and Dorin reads *Dutton's Navigation and Piloting*.

"If, I mean, *when* the wind picks up, at least it should be from a favorable direction," Dorin says. "The Pilot chart says there's 71% chance of easterlies here at this time of year."

Dorin makes lentil soup for supper and it's delicious. After supper, he contacts Glenn briefly to let him know our position.

During the early evening, wind develops, shifting, finally, to easterly.

"Yes! About time!" Dorin says punching the air with his fist. "Now we can change tack and head straight for Hispaniola. Should be an easy reach all the way."

"Can we maintain five to six knots?" Cory asks.

"We should. I'm going to let the sails out as far as I can and still keep them full. Let's take down the awning for tonight."

We are elated. At 11:00 p.m. my watch starts and there's a heavy cloud cover. Night sailing with no heavenly bodies to provide light can be freaky, at least for me. When stars or, even better, the moon glitters off the water, you can see your immediate future ahead of you. Now, I stare into the dark as hard as I can to see what's in front of us, but I can barely see the bowsprit and am looking at a wall of black beyond, which makes me imagine there is a partially submerged shipping container right in our path. Hitting a container, and they are bigger than a bus, can sink a yacht. Gradually, I grow more uneasy because the wind has picked up, and we are screaming along into the blackness at a little over six knots. The boat feels funny, like it's shivering. I call Dorin who, like always, instantly arouses from a dead sleep and comes up into the companionway.

"What's up?"

"Should we reef?"

"What's the speed?"

"Between six and seven. Mostly seven. And it feels funny. Like the boat is...I don't know...stressed, maybe? And the autopilot seems to be struggling. Maybe it's my imagination."

Dorin pauses for five seconds while he looks at the sails, and then steps into the cockpit calling Cory as he moves. Looking like he's still asleep, Cory comes up the stairs.

"We've got more wind than we want with this much sail. Let's take some down."

By now, we don't need to communicate. I turn into the wind enough to take pressure off the sails. At the mast, Dorin uncleats the jib halyard and lowers it. As it comes down, Cory, reaching over the bow pulpit, hauls in the sail. He unfastens the shackle from the top of the sail, passes it under the bow pulpit and refastens it to the top of the sail. We learned in the early days, that if he just tucked the sail away temporarily, the wind would catch it and try to raise it back up the stay.

He heads back to the mast where Dorin is lowering the mainsail, and standing on the house, he helps tie the reefing points. I notice neither are wearing safety harnesses, but then, it's not slippery, since we are not taking water over the deck, and we are not heeling a lot. Cory is quickly back in the cockpit.

"Turn back on course." Dorin is still at the mast.

I watch the mainsail fill and begin to pull again, and we pick up speed quickly.

"How fast?" Dorin asks.

"Six. A little under. Back to six," I reply.

"Okay, how does it feel now?"

"Much, much better."

Cory two-steps down the stairs and climbs into his bunk. I wonder if he will remember this in the morning.

Back in the cockpit, Dorin stares at the sail, adjusts it with the cockpit winch just a tad, and then watches again.

"You were right. There was too much stress on the rigging and mast. How does it feel now?" he asks.

"Really good. Easy. And still six knots."

"Okay, here's the new plan. The first time you think of reefing, Shirl Jean, is when we'll reef. You obviously have a better feel for the stresses on the boat than I do. And we shouldn't be barreling along beyond hull speed. So, don't be afraid to tell us when it occurs to you."

And just like that, he goes back to bed, saying to call him if there are any further problems.

I ponder that information for a while. I'm flattered that he thinks I have a feel for the boat. I don't know if it's true or not but nice that he thinks so. I also realize he has just given me an enormous amount of power. It gives me a feeling of security that I can make the call, but he trusts me not to let unreasonable fears dictate when to reef. Then I realize there is the risk that I will overcompensate and wait too long. I decide to take on this new responsibility, but to...well, be responsible.

In the early hours on Thursday, the autopilot stops working during Dorin's watch, at 2:30 a.m. He steers for two hours and then gets Cory up. Cory takes the tiller and steers for two hours. Dorin checks on him, and they decide to heave to until daylight since the wind has died, anyway.

Cory and I take turns steering by hand in light easterly winds during the day while Dorin re-rigs the autopilot so that the arm is on the outside of the locker instead of under the cover, and it's attached directly to the tiller. He drills a hole in the end of the tiller and uses a stainless-steel cylindrical pin, that we had tossed in our random fix-it supply box, to hold it to the autopilot arm.

The new attachment point, with the stainless-steel pin, seems like a winner. Because it's outside, we can see it. But several times during the day, the autopilot droops a little and becomes disconnected from the tiller.

The inch-long pin is still press-fit into the little hole in the bottom of the tiller, so Dorin joins them together again and it works for a while.

That night it is dark, cloudy and windy again. We've already reefed at my suggestion and are still flying along at 6.5 knots--hull speed--when the autopilot droops, but this time we hear a loud plunk as the pin falls out of the tiller and onto the cockpit floor.

There's a little water sloshing around in the bottom of the cockpit, and we can hear the pin roll around, but it's too dark to see. Cory bolts down the companionway stairs, comes up with the flashlight, and just as he hands it to Dorin, we hear the pin drop through the scupper. The brass scupper fitting has slots in it to allow the water to drain and to keep other stuff from going down the drain, but the slots are pretty big. Dorin shines the light on the floor, but we aren't surprised that we don't see the pin.

"Oh, crap. Oh, damn," I say, alarmed. Without this piece we have to man the tiller around-the-clock, which is so tedious and tiring.

"That's the only pin we have, right? Can anything else go wrong?" I ask.

Dorin's head snaps up, and though I can't see his eyes, I know he's looking at me.

"Let's not get upset yet." His voice is steely, his words clipped.

I think, if not now, when? The magic piece that allows the autopilot to steer is gone. The hose attached to the scupper empties directly into the ocean, and I visualize the vital pin, right at this moment, making a rapid descent to the bottom of the sea.

"Cor, take the tiller, if you would." Dorin goes below and removes the stairs in front of the motor. "I'm going to take the scupper hose off."

I suck in my breath, audibly, thinking the ocean will immediately pour in through the hole in the hull.

But, *first*," he says pointedly to us both, "I'm going to turn the sea cock off."

Cory chuckles as if this is something he already assumed. "Good move," he says.

"It's a survival skill, Cor," Dorin jokes.

Just under the cockpit floor, a hose is attached to the brass scupper. The hose leads to the fitting, the sea cock, in the side of the hull, which is below the water line and allows water from the cockpit to drain. Where the hose is fitted to the sea cock there are two clamps that we had tightened down to hold the hose on. What I had forgotten was the lever on the sea cock that allows you to close it. After he moves the lever to the off position, Dorin finds the nut drivers we have in our toolbox to loosen the clamps.

"Okay, now, Shirl, I need you to find a pan and put it under the hose when I pull it off."

I'm thinking this is an exercise in futility. The piece is already three quarters of the way to the bottom of the ocean having had a head start on us.

"There will be a lot of debris in the hose that's been slipping through, and it must be built up by now. That's why the scupper has been draining so slowly."

I get a pan and get ready to slip it under the hose as soon as it comes off. Some sea water empties into the pan, but not much. He fishes up into the hose, pulling out all kinds of junk, mostly seaweed.

When the hose appears to be empty, he carefully fingers the debris in the pan. In half a minute, he uncovers the part and gives a grunt of satisfaction. He's not looking at me, but I can feel his "I told you" radiating from him as he re-clamps the hose, opens the sea cock and puts the stairs into place. Back in the cockpit, he reattaches the bottom edge of the tiller to the top curve of the autopilot ram. But my tension doesn't go down because I can envision this happening ten minutes later—the autopilot ram will droop, and the pin, left in the bottom of the tiller, will fall out. The scupper hose is now clean.

The next time we will not be so lucky. As if reading my mind, Dorin asks if I know where the waxed twine is. I dig out the canvas bag from a locker in the head. He wraps a length of twine tightly around the tiller and the ram several times so that the autopilot cannot droop. He cuts the ends with his rigging knife.

"If you're all set to finish your watch, Cory and I can get some more sleep."

Cory heads for bed. Dorin lingers for a couple of minutes, watching the sails, tweaking them with the winch.

Then he looks in my direction. "Shirl, you need to stop panicking so soon. It's not good for anybody." His voice is low, and I know he doesn't want Cory to hear.

I replay my words in my head and hear the strident tone. I feel a creeping blush coming on. "I'm sorry. You're right. I will do better. But I have a question. Weren't you a little bit worried?"

"Me *worry*? Never happen."

"What I should have thought of is, even if the piece were lost, you would have whittled another piece out of duct tape or something."

He chuckles. "Thanks for the vote of confidence." He heads to the fo'c'sle.

The rest of my watch is wonderfully uneventful, and it gives me time to think about the many times in the seven years we've been summer sailing when something has gone wrong mechanically, and he has found a creative way to solve the problem.

Friday, we continue at hull speed. Sun sights confirm we are nearing the coast of the Dominican Republic, and we see in the distance large, passing ships, several a day. Now there are birds soaring, riding high on thermals; we know we are getting close to land. Tomorrow we will have been out here for two mostly comfortable weeks.

At 8:30, Saturday morning, while Cor cooks breakfast, Dorin and I are in the cockpit drinking coffee. He points out small boats traveling from west to east.

"They are running parallel to the coast," he says. "So, we should see land soon."

At 10:30 Cory notices mountains rising out of the mist ahead of us, and I realize that landfall, after sixteen days at sea, had become something of a theoretical concept.

We watch, entranced, as the land becomes more distinct in the emerging sunlight.

Soon, we are headed directly toward shore and realize the land is a sandy beach stretching to the right and left as far as we can see. Close behind is thick jungle growth, but not a sign of habitation on this land. While terra firma should be a comforting sight, I'm on edge: where are the people? Why are such pristine beaches deserted? This feels so mysterious.

Dorin takes a sun sight and reduces it quickly.

"I think, extrapolating from my sun sight yesterday and the one today, I'm pretty sure we are approximately twenty-five miles to the east of Samaná Bay."

Twenty-five miles is not a big deal at this point, nor are we desperate for water and food like we were when we approached Bermuda.

Steering by hand, we change course to a westerly direction and sail until five o'clock. We eat in the cockpit, as usual, while we scan the landmass and see no sign of life.

After supper, Dorin stands in the companionway, looking around. Mountains that appear close to the shore are lined with rows of palm trees that stand like individual sentinels silhouetted against the darkening sky. "Looks like a beautiful country," he says. "I am really taken by it.

"I've been watching the coast and looking at your chart, and I'm sure we are still well east of Samaná Bay. I'm not comfortable this close to shore so let's get some sea room. I'm changing tack so we can head away from land while still moving parallel to the coast. We're going to be on a run when we change tack. The awning would act like another sail, and we don't want to stress it. Let's take it down."

Cory takes the tiller while Dorin and I take down the awning.

Changing tack puts us on a run with a good fifteen knots of wind at our backs. I think of Diane's farewell toast: "may you have fair winds and following seas." We finally get it right.

Cory has not experienced a run before, and with all sails up and 15 knots of wind at our backs, he is having a blast at the tiller. This is the trickiest point of sail, but he gets the hang of it right away, keeping the sails full and pulling.

I look at Dorin with surprise. He nods, grinning, and I can see he is proud of Cory.

As it continues to get darker, I know we will not be entering Samaná Bay because, in all the time I've sailed with him, Dorin has never entered a harbor at night unless he knows it like the back of his hand.

He goes below, turns on the radar, studies it, and looks at the chart on the table. When he comes out on deck he says, "Let's head in."

He catches my surprised look. "We have some daylight left, and we won't go all the way into Santa Bárbara. I don't think we want to heave-to out here tonight, do we? We can drop anchor part way into the bay and motor in at first light."

My eyebrows are up as I look at him.

"Look, right here," he says pointing to the "chart" I have made. "See, plenty of depth just inside the channel."

"That's a drawing," I say.

"Right. And you did a good job."

"It's not real," I reply. "It's a reasonable facsimile."

"Yeah, I know. I trust you."

I am wide-eyed as he steers into the opening of the bay, which I'm comforted to see is very wide. We do not run aground, and as night closes in, we move to the side of the channel and drop anchor, satisfied we had a good passage.

"Not so bad, this time, huh?" he asks me.

"Not so bad. I can deal with, no...let me go further! I can *enjoy* this kind of sailing."

We decide that, because we are fairly close to the channel, we will turn on our position light and keep watch through the night. Dorin goes to bed right after supper, so Cory and I sit in the cockpit and talk about what difficulties we might have with the language. He reminds me he took a year of Spanish last year and might be able to remember a few words. "I can say 'hello, how are you?'"

Around eleven o'clock, as I'm starting my watch, I see, many yards from our boat, a small green glow from beneath the water. And it moves a little, getting nearer, then further away and smaller. I am shocked to my center.

"Cor!" I whisper loudly. "Come here." He hasn't fallen asleep yet so he is immediately in the cockpit.

"What?"

"Look!" I point to the green glow.

"What is it?" he asks, uneasily.

What comes to mind at that moment is the article with photographs in a magazine that we read in Bermuda about never-before-seen, ugly, ferocious sea life found at great depths.

I ask Cory, in a hushed voiced, if he remembers the article.

"Yes. Viperfish."

"Right. It said something about these deep-sea animals staying very deep during the day but going to shallower depths at night. I think they lure their prey with a chemical process called bio...something, right? They create a white light with their organs, photo...something, to lure other sea life, and then they attack with their hinged jaws and needle teeth!" I almost whisper.

"Bioluminescence is the process," he says. "They have photophores."

"Yeah, that's it."

"But this is a *green* light and the water isn't deep here," he says.

As we watch, the green glow, that's sort of like a basketball, slowly gets closer and larger. My tension goes sky-high.

"Go get Dorin," I tell Cory.

In thirty seconds, Dorin is leaning over the stern pulpit looking into the water. "I don't know," he says. "I have never seen anything like it."

"Maybe it's a luminous fish?" I ask. "But why would it keep changing size? Sometimes it seems as big as a Volkswagen."

"I don't know. But it does seem like some sort of sea life." Dorin's voice is strained. He steps back down into the cockpit beside Cory and me and hitches his pants, something he does just before taking action. But what action? We don't know what to do, but we are united in our tension as we watch the thing come really close to our boat, maybe only fifteen feet away. My heart pounds. Suddenly, the green glow becomes very tiny and then disappears.

"*¿Necesitan gasolina?*" a deep male voice comes to us out of the dark. We are momentarily shocked. And we don't understand.

"Helloo, there," Dorin says.

There's a silence, but we can feel the presence, feel the tension.

"*¿Son americanos?*"

"Yes! Yes, we are American. We just came in from Bermuda. We dropped anchor for the night. We tried not to anchor in the middle of the channel. Are we okay to stay here tonight? Or do you need us to move?"

Another long silence and then finally, "*¿Necesitan gasolina?*"

Cory jumps up on the rear locker, grabs the tightened main sheet and leans toward where the voice is coming from.

"*Sí, somos norteamericanos. No necesitamos gasolina, pero muchas gracias.*"

"Okay. *Buenas noches.*"

"*Buenas noches.*"

Then a small boat motor starts up, the sound quickly diminishing toward the direction we know to be Santa Bárbara de Samaná.

Dorin raises his eyebrows and looks at Cory. My mouth is hanging open. Cory gives a sheepish shrug. "Well, I told you I took a Spanish class. It was year before last, actually. I barely remember anything."

"Sure," says Dorin.

"What was the green glow?" I ask.

"Look." Dorin is pointing across the black water, and I see half a dozen more green lights of different sizes further away from our boat.

"He was using an underwater light for night fishing. I read about it, but I never saw it in practice before. I should have figured it out before *you* guys got so scared."

"Scared?" Cory and I say in unison.

"Well, good night," Dorin says. "Call me if you see any more *mysterious* sea life."

Chapter Twelve
¿Cómo Se Dice...?

On Sunday morning, we're all up by six, excited and nervous about how this day will go. I prepare ham, eggs, and coffee while Dorin and Cory cover the mainsail, neaten up the cockpit, and put away extraneous stuff that has accumulated here, there, and everywhere.

"Don't forget to get out the quarantine flag, Cor. I think it's in the cabinet behind the table," Dorn says.

I hand plates of hot food out to them, and we eat breakfast in the cockpit, as usual, while we tease each other about our foolish fears of last night.

"So, Members of the Fearless Crew," Dorin says to us. "What approximately did you think the creature was?"

"A viperfish?" asks Cory.

"Okay, you guys," I say. "Don't tell me you weren't a little nervous. Remember, we'd just seen a giant sea turtle and a Portuguese man-of-war with tentacles long enough to wrap around the boat. So, yeah, once I thought of the viperfish, my innermost scaredy cat was wondering if this were another creature, not yet known to man, that could surface from the deep."

While they are laughing, I add, "With green tentacles. Long ones. That can reach up into the cockpit."

"But at least we know Cory can rescue us from any situation that involves Spanish," Dorin says.

"No! That's why I didn't tell you guys. I don't really know more than a few words."

"Yeah, we probably will need more than a few words," Dorin says.

Mary had told us that very few people speak English--only the elderly and young children. She said that in the Samaná Peninsula, English had been a second language from the time that former African American slaves arrived on the peninsula, right after the Civil War, and they passed the language down. But more recently, she said, a law was passed that English could not be spoken and would not be taught in schools. A generation passed before it was decided to teach English in schools again. So the children know a little English, but if you find elderly people, they can translate for you.

"A quick way to learn is to say, '¿Cómo se dice...?' That means, 'How do you say...?' And they are happy to tell you," Mary says smiling. "But," she holds up a cautionary finger, "then they think you speak Spanish, so they are likely to give you more information than you can use. In high speed."

Now Dorin says, "Maybe more people will speak English than we think. Let's get going."

Cory hauls anchor, Dorin starts the motor, and we chug into the channel of the bay on the way to Santa Bárbara, *Samaná Bay de la República Dominicana*.

"That must be Levantado," Dorin says as we approach a large island on our portside.

A few minutes later, an inflatable dinghy with three local teenagers comes from the direction we are headed, turns sharply around in our wake, and overtakes us. The young man at the tiller waves to get our attention.

Dorin puts the motor in neutral, and we slow to a drift.

"Captain, you go wrong in the bay," he says. "I can help you. I can be your pilot."

Cory says to Dorin, "We are in the channel. There are no hazards on the chart. I say we just go in on our own."

"It's not a chart!" I say.

"You can buy Dominican flag," the young man says. "I sell you flag. My sister make. Only five dollar. You need flag, Captain."

He has a point. We will have to get a Dominican flag.

"Let's not get off on the wrong foot," Dorin says. "We don't know the customs yet. Let's just go along with this."

Cory shakes his head in disapproval.

"Okay," Dorin says. He has a few ones and fives in his shirt pocket, as Bill from *No Brass Ring* had suggested. Dorin leans over the lifelines and gives the guy a five. The flag does look like it's skillfully homemade and plenty sturdy enough.

"I can change money for you," the kid says. "I can give you special good rate. Better than bank."

We had been warned by Bill and Mary not to let locals change money for us as they will fudge the rate of exchange in their favor.

"We'll wait until we get there," Dorin says.

"Okay, follow me, Captain," he says. He revs the motor, slips it into gear, zips his rubber dinghy in front of us, and signals us to follow. He continues on in the exact direction we had been going.

"See?" Cory says.

As we approach the harbor area of Samaná, we are surprised to see a tall, multi-arched, exquisitely designed bridge that spans a long distance from the mainland to an uninhabited island.

"I wonder what it's for?" I say.

"I'm sure we'll find out," Dorin says.

As we chug deeper into the harbor, we see it's dotted with a dozen cruising boats at anchor. To the right are the docks, and there is a small, white military ship, with mounted guns, tied alongside the dock. Behind is a small town with colorful buildings that begin at the shore and climb up the hillside. Farther up the hill the buildings, covered with rusting tin roofs, become more crowded, almost seeming to touch each other.

The dinghy slows and circles back near our cockpit. "You have to back in, Captain. There is place behind that boat. You back in. I will tell *aduaneros*, Customs, you are here."

"He wants a tip," Cory says. "He didn't earn it."

The young man maneuvers his rubber boat against our hull. He stands and grabs the stanchions. "I help you, Captain, yes? I pilot for you."

Dorin digs another five-dollar bill out and hands it to the guy.

"Thank you, Captain. I will tell Customs you are here. Back up to the dock." Then he motors away among the boats, and we lose sight of him.

Because of the pivot point of the rudder at the stern, backing up is tricky, but Dorin is now in his element. On one occasion, a few years ago, the *Fandango* was part of a Fourth of July water parade down the Kennebec River in Augusta, Maine, and he rigged it to *sail* backwards all the way just for fun. Now, with the benefit of the motor, he maneuvers into position, slips the boat into reverse, and between two other yachts, neatly backs up to the dock.

Cory steps off with the stern line and takes a turn around a cleat, making the boat temporarily fast. Dorin grabs an extra line and winds it around a rear cleat. Then he steps up on the dock and ties off that line as Cory fastens his side. Done.

"Let's get this place cleaned up," Dorin says as they come back aboard. We race through the boat, straightening up the mess. I fold and stack the blankets and pillows in the fo'c'sle and stash today's laundry. Cory neatens his bunk, puts away the books, and sweeps the floor. Dorin washes the pans and dishes and wipes the countertop while I get out the documentation we will need for the *aduaneros*.

We are about to sit when Dorin notices the broom standing against the wall. Grabbing it, he looks around frantically for a place to stow it and finally slips it under the thin mattress on Cory's bunk.

The three of us sweat in the sweltering cabin, looking out of the companionway, watching the activity on the dock. We wonder if our helper really contacted Customs, or has he abandoned us?

Twenty minutes later, two dark-skinned Customs and Immigration men, dressed in sharply pressed khaki uniforms, arrive on the dock.

Dorin goes up two steps in the companionway.

"*¿Permiso?*" asks one of the men.

"Yes, yes. Come aboard," Dorin says. The dock is a little higher than our deck, so they easily step, one at a time, over the stern pulpit and onto the rear of the *Fandango*.

"Do you speak English?" Dorin asks.

One man quickly shakes his head no.

"A little." The other guy smiles tentatively.

Then he demonstrates his bilingual ability. "Whew, hot!" he says as he wipes his forehead with a handkerchief and starts down the galley stairs. Both government men appear a little uncertain as they look around our tiny cabin.

"Yeah," says Dorin. "Is this seasonally normal, or is it particularly hot today? Have a seat."

I wince, wondering how these words sound to someone with a tenuous grasp of English. In the past, I have teased Dorin about his complex syntax and vocabulary, which becomes increasingly complicated when he is tense.

"I'm not that bad," he'd said. "Right, Cor?"

Cory smiled and shrugged. "Well, let's just say your verbosity really blossoms when you are nervous."

"When you talk to anyone who doesn't know English well, just use simple sentences and small words," I had suggested.

"I know, I know," he'd snapped. "I remember when I was learning Dutch. Don't you guys think I know how to keep it simple?"

Seasonally normal? Simple?

The English-speaking official clears his throat and says, "*Sí,* Yes...uh...hot. Today." He slides behind the dinette table and sits down. The other official sits beside me on Cory's bunk. Dorin hoists himself up on the icebox.

The man sitting at the table folds his hands and smiles nervously at each of us. He seems to be waiting.

We all glance around at each other. The officials nod and smile again; we smile back.

I take a deep breath. "You, ah, want to see our papers?" I finally ask.

"Papers! *Sí,* papers," he says, looking relieved.

I open the plastic packet on the table and hand him our passports and ship's papers.

"Ah, *gracias. Pasaportes.* Thank you."

He pulls a used envelope out of his shirt pocket and with a stubby pencil carefully copies down our names on the back of it. When he's done, he smiles up at Dorin and asks, "Where you come from?"

"Well," says Dorin, nervously clearing his throat, "we started out from Maine, actually. Boothbay Harbor. Pardon me, *East* Boothbay...."

I stare at Dorin. Has he forgotten, from our experience in Bermuda, the man simply wants to know our last port of departure?

"...unless, of course, you want our residential addresses...we live in Waterville, at least I do. The crew comes from Fairfield, Maine. But we actually left from East Boothbay. Then we sailed off-shore...."

The man's eyebrows shoot up in alarm. He knows he's in trouble. "Puerto Plata?" he breaks in. Beside me, his fellow officer nods his head vigorously, as if Puerto Plata in the D.R. is a good answer.

"Well, no, we had considered going to Puerto Plata, but we weren't able to obtain any appropriate approach charts for that particular city."

Sitting on the companionway stairs, Cory leans his mouth into his fist to hide a smile.

"Santo Domingo?" the official tries hopefully. Santo Domingo is, as Cory has told us, the capital, located on the southern shore of the D.R.

"St. George's, Bermuda," I say.

"*Ah. Sí.* Bermuda. *Gracias.*" He smiles gratefully and writes on the envelope.

"*¿Documento?*"

"Document? Clearance papers?" I ask.

"*Sí,* yes. Papers, please."

I get out the clearance paper from Bermuda.

"Where you go from here?" he asks as he looks over the paper.

"Well," replies Dorin, "originally we intended to go through the Windward Passage and then on into the Panama Canal..."

The official looks worried until he recognizes Panama Canal. "*Sí, Panama Canal.*" He puts his pencil to the envelope in front of him. I notice his knee jiggles nervously under the table.

"...then we changed our minds because of dodging the tropical depressions..."

The man glances furtively at the other official then frowns with concentration as Dorin continues.

"...so we thought we might try Hispaniola. Now, is the whole island called Hispaniola, and is it divided up into Haiti on the west and this country—the Dominican Republic, on the east?"

The man's smile freezes. His eyes dart rapidly from face to face. "*Sí, Dominican Republic...*" he says tentatively.

"...and anyways, we had thought we might try to sail into Puerto Plata..."

"Ah! Puerto Plata!" He starts to write.

"...but, as I said, we didn't have the appropriate charts, so we decided to come here to reprovision." Dorin's speech is becoming increasingly manicky. He runs a hand down the back of his neck and wipes his palm on his thigh.

"From here we anticipate going to Puerto Rico for a few days and then probably head down the Mona Passage to Venezuela in the foreseeable future."

Cory scrunches his smile closed with his hands, but his ribs are shaking.

There is a long silence. The man smiles thinly, but there is panic in his eyes.

"Where...?" A bead of sweat runs down his cheek. He catches it with his handkerchief before it reaches his chin.

"Where...you...go...from...here?"

"Puerto Rico," I say.

"Ah, Puerto Rico!" He mops his brow and writes on the envelope.

"How long your boat?" His eyes flick hopefully to me, but perhaps he thinks it's not appropriate to address me directly when the captain is sitting right there. So he looks at Dorin.

"Do you want the length on the waterline or the length overall?"

"Um..." The man's eyes twitch from side to side.

"Thirty-two feet," Cory jumps in. The official smiles warmly at Cory.

"Firearms?" He carefully looks past Dorin and directs the question at Cory.

"All we have on board is the flare gun," says Dorin, "but that's stowed away securely in the emergency pack in the sail locker. Do you want to see it?"

"Flare gun?"

"Yes."

The official looks over at me and says slowly, "You...have *firearms*...on boat?'

"No," I reply.

He starts to write on the envelope, but the man sitting beside me clears his throat and speaks to him in a low voice in rapid Spanish. He is kneading the thin mattress we are sitting on, and I remember we are sitting directly on the broomstick. Does he think it's a rifle?

There is a brief, staccato exchange between the men. The one in charge appears to have the final word, shaking his head as he slides out of the dinette seat. He folds the envelope and tucks it into his shirt pocket.

"We finish," he says with evident relief.

"What should we do when it is time for us to depart?" asks Dorin. "Do you suggest we find your office, or should we simply phone you on VHF?"

"¿Sí?" the gentleman says hopefully and glances rapidly from face to face to see if that response will fly.

"Don't you want to search the boat?" asks Dorin.

"No search," he says and shakes his head vigorously.

"What do I owe you?" Dorin asks.

The Official looks uncomfortable. He speaks to his companion in Spanish, and they shift from foot to foot as they look at each other.

"It is Sunday," says the leader apologetically.

"Oh, absolutely. I have every intention of paying you for coming out on your day off. How much do I owe you?"

They look embarrassed. "What you think?" he asks the man who had been sitting beside me, and who I thought understood no English. He shrugs his shoulders. The leader shrugs.

"Um, what you think?" He looks at the floor self-consciously and glances at his colleague again. "...um, twenty?"

"Twenty sounds fine!' says Dorin, relieved. He hands them two ten-dollar bills in American money. They both look at the money and then at each other.

"Thank you, thank you!" says the customs' official. He shakes Dorin's hand and nods a small, formal bow to me. His colleague grabs Dorin's hand and pumps it. "¡Gracias! ¡Gracias, Señor!"

Cory moves out of the way, and they rapidly climb the stairs, jump off the boat, and head down the dock, looking at the money and talking to each other with gestures. They look happy.

"Well, that went well, don't you think?" asks Dorin.

We later discover the unofficial going rate for weekends is twenty pesos. The exchange rate is three-and-a-quarter pesos to a dollar. In this case, they deserved it in American dollars.

"Cory, how about you take down the quarantine flag and put up the Dominican Republic flag? I'll get out our American flag," Dorin says.

In ten minutes, we are "flagged out."

I go below to change into a skirt while the guys move the boat out into the bay and cruise around while Dorin looks for a place to anchor far enough from other boats.

As I come out into the cockpit, Cory drops the anchor, the chain rattling as it plays out. Dorin watches for a few minutes until we swing on the anchor, and he is convinced we are set.

We are excited and a little nervous to go ashore and explore. Everything looks so different and exotic from anything else we've seen. Cory pulls the dinghy alongside, and we clamber down in.

We're not far from the docks, and we have not yet stepped the *Tinker's* mast, so Dorin rows us in. To the left side of the docks, there is a short seawall and a hard-packed beach. There are children on it waving to us and shouting, "Here! Over here!" In minutes we are close, and a boy, about eleven or twelve, in rolled up pants, wades out into the water. "Give me line," he says. "I take care of your boat."

Cory hands the older boy our line, and two younger children grab the end of the line behind him and tug on it to help. He pulls us up on shore as much as he can. Dorin, slipping off his boat shoes, steps into the shallow water and helps pull the *Tinker* high enough so I can step out without getting my shoes wet. Nice.

"I watch your boat," the boy says. The younger boys, maybe six or seven, nod vigorously.

"Okay! Thank you!" Dorin says.

"You think it'll be okay?" I ask in a whisper. Having read bunches of warnings about foreign ports, I'm a little anxious.

"Sure!" Dorin says.

I notice Cory looks back at our dinghy a couple of times as we walk away.

We wander in the direction of a row of beautifully proportioned European-style buildings painted in attractive colors and fronted by picket fences.

As we stand around asking ourselves where do we go, a rickshaw-like conveyance with local people in it, hauled by a motorbike, zips down the road. We watch in amazement, still wondering what to do, when another comes along and stops in front of us. The driver asks something in rapid Spanish. We look at Cory, and he shrugs his shoulders at us as if to say, don't look at me…I don't know what he said.

"Well, let's get in," I say.

"And go where?" Dorin asks.

But Cory is already climbing in and sliding over so we can fit. And, the three of us side against side, barely do.

The driver turns to look at us.

"*Heladería*," Cory tries. The guy looks puzzled. "*La tienda de helado,*" Cory tries again. The driver's face lights up. He nods, and we are off. I look at Dorin, and he shrugs looking relaxed and delighted, happy to have Cory take over. I am still a little tense. Where are we going? How will we find food? Should we have learned some Spanish before we started? *Of course* we should have. I remind myself that the Dominican Republic was not in our sailing sights when we started this trip. But Panama was.

Stores and open stalls line the street and women, dressed very conservatively in shirtwaist dresses, walk along the street holding umbrellas in one hand and market baskets in the other. The umbrellas look exactly like the ones we use for rain, but these are used for shade. I can see why. It's blistering hot, even under the vehicle awning. We pass an artist on the sidewalk who has his paintings, bold and colorful, on display. I point this out to Dorin, and he nods in appreciation. "Aren't they neat?" he asks. "Would you like to look them over another time?"

In our early days, Dorin and I used to comb the coastal galleries in Maine and Massachusetts, enjoying seascapes and nautical artwork that spoke to us. This powerful Dominican artwork speaks to me.

The vehicle stops a minute later and Cory climbs out. Not knowing how much to pay, Dorin gives the driver a one-dollar bill. From the guy's reaction, he is very pleased. (We later found out we could have had 12 rides for that one-dollar American.)

Cory opens the door to a store and motions us in.

"Wow, Cor, way to go!' Dorin says. We find ourselves in an ice cream parlor much like the ones we experienced in our youths—wrought-iron tall stools at a chrome and Formica bar. There are also Formica tables and wrought iron chairs. A ceiling fan turns slowly to cool the parlor, and even without it, it would be much cooler in here than outside. The ice cream flavors are in English, as well as Spanish, and there are a dozen. We spend a happy half hour eating the best, creamiest ice cream we have ever had. We are still working on our American currency of one-dollar bills, since we haven't changed our money yet. Dorin offers three dollars, and again, it seems like this is adequate. The woman who served us tries to give us change, but Dorin waves her off. She says, *"Muchas gracias,"* with a big smile, and Cory responds with *"De nada."*

"What did you say?" I whisper to him.

"It's like 'you're welcome.' Only it's literally 'of nothing.' Kind of like saying, 'Don't worry about it. It was nothing.'"

That doesn't seem like it expresses much gratitude. Once we are out of the oatBut maybe something is added in the translation.

We step outside into the heat and see that our driver and vehicle are waiting across the street. He waves to us. Cory nods, and the guy starts the motor scooter.

I wonder where we are going next, but in the face of the success we've just had, I am now perfectly content to see how this unfolds.

"¿Mercado?" Cory says to the driver, his voice rising as if in a question. The driver nods, and we have barely squeezed ourselves into the seat, when he takes off with a roar.

"We need food, right?" Cory asks. "How much money do we have?"

"A pocket full of ones and fives," Dorin says.

The pedestrian traffic has increased in variety, as well as numbers, along the sides of the streets. A few women carry baskets on their heads, but most carry baskets or string bags on their arms. Children run and chatter to each other and break up in laughter. I am amazed to see donkeys carry loads of what appears to be long sticks.

"Sugar cane, I'm pretty sure," Dorin says.

There is an increasing number of vehicles of the kind we are riding in, but all are over-filled with Dominicans, sometimes five or six, including children on laps and teenagers or adults standing up, hanging on  behind. A bicycle goes by in the opposite direction, and there are three cheerful passengers in addition to the driver: one on the cross bar, one on the handlebars and one sitting behind. Then, I notice, among these complexions of many shades, we are the only white faces in this scene, but no one appears to give us a second glance.

There are more stores with signs in Spanish and flowers, flowers everywhere. Suddenly, we stop in front of an open-air market. The driver nods to Cory and asks, "*¿Aquí?*"

"*Sí.*" Cory swings out of the tiny vehicle and looks around. Dorin hands the driver a one-dollar bill.

Vendors, displaying their goods in baskets, crates and sometimes on a cloth on the ground, are packed in as close as their displays allow, leaving narrow paths for shoppers. I'm trying to absorb what I see: many of the vegetables and fruits spread out in front of us are a mystery to me. There are fly-covered sides of beef and skinned chickens hanging up in the noonday sun. I don't want to offend by sounding critical, but Dorin and I look at each other and don't say anything.

Business is lively as vendors call out to shoppers; money exchanges hands, and market baskets get filled.

I feel Dorin's hand on the small of my back encouraging me to move forward. "Whaddayasay?" he whispers in my ear. "Should we shop?"

I am bewildered and overwhelmed. I don't know what I want from this array of produce and don't even know how to begin shopping.

Cory steps around me and starts to browse but then quickly moves to a vendor who has a wooden stand that looks permanent.

"*¿Cómo se dice....?*" Cory asks as he picks up a lime. I recognize this phrase that Mary has taught us.

I edge closer, hoping maybe I can learn some Spanish.

"*Limas,*" the vendor says. Even I can understand this. Maybe Spanish will not be so difficult. Then he says something that sounds like "bendy sink oh." These words can't possibly mean anything.

The slim woman with dark, straight hair tied back at the nape of her neck and an apron over her conservative dress rattles off rapid-fire Spanish, and then she puts three limes in a little bag and holds out her hand for money.

"No, veinte y cinco..." he says, pointing at the limes.

She looks startled. *"¿Veinte y cinco limas?"*

He nods. *"Sí."*

Looking unconvinced, she gets a bigger bag and counts out the limes. Cor asks Dorin for money and hands her four dollars. We still don't know the rate of exchange, but she takes the money and seems quite pleased.

Close by, a chubby woman, maybe in her fifties, whose wares are spread out on a cloth on the ground, has been watching the transaction. From her seat on a crate, she speaks sternly to the woman who sold us the limes. A brief argument ensues, and the lime seller folds her arms and turns her back to the woman. She appears to have won the argument. The older woman turns to Cory and says, *"Lo siento."*

"She says she's sorry," Cory translates.

The woman continues in Spanish and Cory nods. "I think she said we paid too much."

I look at her offerings which are meager compared to some others but do include a couple of charming homemade dolls.

The woman on the crate motions us closer and indicates her produce. "What you want?" she asks.

"I want to buy something from her," I say to Dorin and Cory.

"By all means, do," Dorin says.

While she doesn't have much, she does have carrots, cabbage, coconuts, and some unripe bananas. I point and she puts them in bag that she hands to me with a smile. Dorin is holding a five and a couple of ones. He offers her the five, but she shakes her head and takes the ones from him.

"Gracias," Cory says.

"No!" the woman replies. "Wait. Your money." She holds out a handful of coins.

Dorin shakes his head and says, "No," and then adds his first Spanish word, *"Gracias."*

"Be careful," she says. "She charge you too much. Too much."

"I want to think about getting back to the boat," I say.

"Yeah, me too. Let's start walking back the way we came."

We walk barely a minute, when our chauffeur comes putt-putting up from behind and stops beside us. He says something in Spanish and gestures for us to get in, which we are very happy to do. He stops near the seawall to let us out, and while Dorin fishes out another one-dollar bill, I look to see if our dinghy is still there, and it is--still being guarded by the children.

"*Muchas gracias, Capitán,*" the driver says.

"*¿Dónde está el banco?*" says Cory. The driver points to a one-story building nearby.

Inside the bank, the clerk looks at the two twenty-dollar travelers checks Dorin has slid toward her. "Today," she says and slides forward a paper with the rate of exchange on it.

"Three-and-a-quarter!" Dorin tells us. "That's great!

She asks for identification in English and is soon counting out a lot of fancy, colorful bills. She adds some coins to the pile and pushes them forward.

"*Gracias,*" Cory says as we leave.

"How much do we give our helpers?" Dorin asks.

"Well, we've been overpaying since we got here," Cory says. "They probably depend on newcomers not knowing the rate of exchange or what's reasonable. So, let's offer one peso and see what they say."

"One for each," Dorin says firmly.

As we approach the sea wall, the kids yell and gesture to us. "Here! Your boat safe. I take care of it." We walk down the steps to the gravelly bit of beach.

The leader of the boat guards taps his chest and says, "Eduardo." He points at Dorin. "You name?"

"Dorin."

Eduardo nods thoughtfully and then says, "Okay, Captain."

He points at Cory and listens attentively to Cory pronouncing his own name.

"Cory," repeats Eduardo, but with the Spanish accent, he rolls the "r." It sounds very cool. Cory then points to me and says, "Shirley."

Eduardo shakes his head and shrugs his shoulders. "Okay, Miss," he says to me. "You get in boat." The boat has been turned around so the bow faces the bay. I step from dry land into the boat and settle on the forward seat. "Okay, Captain, you and Cory push boat and then you get in."

Eduardo wades out into the water, pulling hard on the bow line. Dorin and Cory grab the line that runs around the outside of the inflated tubes and lift and tug. The little boys push on the wooden stern.

Eduardo yells, "Okay, Cory, you get in now."

Cory steps over the side and pulls the oars out from under the seat and puts them in the oarlocks. Dorin pushes the boat a few more feet. As the stern of the *Tinker* begins to float free, he jumps in and sits on the seat.

He hands the three boys, who are standing in the water, a peso each, and they yelp for joy.

"Told you," Cory says.

"*Adiós, Capitán,*" Eduardo shouts. "See you tomorrow. I help you."

As Dorin rows us back to the boat, he says with delight, "Wasn't that neat?"

"They will be waiting for us every day," Cory says.

"They might go to school during the week," Dorin says. "I hope we see them again. That Eduardo is an ambitious kid. With a great attitude. He's probably adding to the family income."

I feel happy, euphoric even. We are afloat, we are heading to our boat that I realize I think of as home, and we have successfully made a trip to shore in this exotic, beautiful country.

On the rear deck, beside the unripe bananas, Cory puts the limes on the cover of the lazaret locker—all twenty-five of them. He gets a knife from the galley, and sitting on the rear locker, rapidly cuts the limes in half, turns them inside out, and eats them. He piles the empty, inverted peels beside him, and before long, there is a mound of lime peels. We watch him in amazement. "Aren't they sour?" I ask.

"Kinda," he says but barely pauses as he sucks on a lime and then grabs another one.

"Knocking out a case of scurvy?" Dorin asks.

"Can't be too careful," he replies, tearing into yet another lime. When he is done, the empty rinds of all twenty-five limes are stacked on the stern of the boat, and Cory looks happy. The bananas are so hard I can't peel one, so we leave them on the lazaret locker to ripen.

We spot a boater in a small dinghy motoring toward us, and Dorin greets him at the shrouds.

"Welcome to Samaná," the guy says. He grabs our toe rail to hold his boat dinghy still and introduces himself as Jim. He points out his boat.

"We get together on shore every afternoon to socialize at a little outdoor bar. It's really comfortable, with thatched shades over the tables and great martinis. Please come join us tomorrow."

"We certainly will," Dorin says. "You are talking my language."

The conversation continues as Jim fills us in about the harbor, the country, and the cruisers who are anchored in this harbor.

"What's with the bridge?" I ask him.

"Beautiful, isn't it? It's for walking only, and we're still trying to figure out what it's for. No one seems to have an answer."

Then Jim pushes off and motors back to his boat.

For supper, I cook the carrots and cabbage and open a can of corned beef.

"I wonder what we'll do for fresh meat?" I ask.

"I don't know. We'll have to ask other cruisers," he says.

As the sky fades into darkness, pinpoints of light twinkle from the shore and soft salsa music wafts across the water, creating a vacation atmosphere. I could so get used to this place. I drift off to sleep, contently listening to the music.

Chapter Thirteen
Bridging the Gap

The next afternoon we row ashore and again leave our boat with the kids, who appear to have been waiting for us to head their way. This time one of the younger kids is holding a paper cone filled with peanuts in the shell for sale. Once we are out of the boat, Dorin holds out some D.R. coins and Eduardo picks from among them and says, *"Gracias, Capitán.* I watch your boat."

We stroll around town enjoying the sights, while trying to find the bar. I point to an electricity pole that has dozens of tangled and knotted wires attached and not running through insulators. Just wired together—jury-rigged. In some cases, the wires run directly into small cinder block homes through a window or a small hole in the wall.

I get a little start when I notice a practitioner has hung a shingle outside of his combination residence and office. It says, Rx and Voodoo. I am curious about this mixture of medical philosophies and decide that it might work quite well with the patient really believing in the power of the medicine.

Soon after, we find the outdoor bar, which is appealing because of the thatched roof "umbrellas" over the tables. Other Americans have gathered, all couples except for one gentleman sporting a nicely trimmed gray beard. Jim waves us to join him and his wife Helen at their table. He introduces us to the couple at their table, Mac and Cindy. The man with the beard is Sebastian.

"Mac, here, is our sailing-community communications guy," Jim says. "His real name is Colin MacDonald."

Mac extends a hand. "Catch you on VHF," he says. "Unless you have a ham."

"Uh, yeah, um, actually, I do," Dorin says. He is reluctant to throw this information around, as he doesn't like what he calls "mindless chatter" on the airwaves.

I notice with relief the women are wearing pants or Bermuda shorts, not skirts. Since I only own two skirts, this is good news. We order our drinks, and after downing a Coke, Cory excuses himself to go exploring.

Dorin and I spend the afternoon getting acquainted with the boating people and asking them questions. They are all early retirees who have elected to cruise, mostly for an indefinite period of time. Chuck and Dottie of the yacht *Seahaven* are the couple with the most experience, having been at this for over five years, while Janice and Jake of the yacht *Kermit D*, only for about a year.

All of them have a lot on us newbies who've only been cruising for a couple of months. We gain a lot of information about the local restaurants, and I find out there is a market where they sell imported frozen meat. There is a book exchange inside the bar, but the boaters also trade back and forth among themselves. Then Janice tells me something that makes my heart sing. "We bring our laundry to the dock on Thursday mornings. A woman or sometimes her husband will take it away and bring it back two days later, clean and folded. Everything comes back immaculately clean.

They dry the clothes on bushes, so they smell amazing," she says. "And it's expertly folded. None of us do our own laundry in this port."

I'm thinking life can't get any better.

I ask about the electrical wires that do not look exactly legal or safe.

Sebastian laughs. "Well, the story seems to be, anybody who needs electricity, usually for a fan or a TV, just taps into the wires at the pole and essentially gets free electricity. The government provides the electricity, and they don't like not getting paid, so frequently they shut the electricity off in the evening for a few hours."

I must look shocked because Sebastian says, "They do just fine. You'll see. It hardly slows them down."

Dorin asks dozens of other questions and, as usual, absorbs information like a sponge. They are eager to help and, I can tell, are enjoying their position of knowledgeable, superior travelers-by-yacht.

Then the subject comes up about how each of us got here. We find they all came down the Intracoastal Waterway and then hopped along the island chain through the Bahamas, the Turks and Caicos, and then on to the Dominican Republic. From time to time they bumped into each other, so they were acquainted by the time they arrived and decided to stay for a while. Their next stop is Puerto Rico, but they are in no hurry to leave. They will have to sail across the Mona Passage, and everyone knows, they say, that it is extremely dangerous.

When they ask about our experiences, Dorin tells them we sailed offshore from Maine to Bermuda and then, again, offshore to the Dominican Republic. There is a long, awkward silence during which nobody moves.

"Must have been an adventure," says Sebastian finally.

Dorin nodded. "When having drinks with friends, adventure is what you call something that was sheer terror at the time."

Everyone laughs, and the tension diminishes. Dorin regales them with stories about our travels, relating them as if we were blundering blindly around, just barely escaping from our countless, ignorant mistakes. They chuckle and then laugh out loud. Someone buys a round, and they toast the "fearless crew" of the *Fandango*. It appears we are in.

That night, we decide to try one of the restaurants the group recommended that is a long hike up a steep hill. Dorin and I find our walking muscles have deteriorated once again during the sixteen days at sea. Cory jogs ahead then turns around and jogs backwards, motioning us to catch up. "Come on, people. Mungryscweet." Cory talk for "I'm hungry, let's go eat."

The restaurant, like many of the buildings here, is cinder block, but large and airy, with cloth napkins and tablecloths and flowers on each table. Sitting by a large open window we can see the whole harbor.

"Okay, I'm loving this place," I say.

At that moment, a chicken jumps onto the windowsill not three feet from me, and I notice there is no glass or bars in any of the windows. The restaurant is open to the air. A waiter approaches and shoos the chicken. It flaps its wings and hops back out to the ground.

The waiter gives us menus in Spanish.

"*Pollo* is chicken," says Cory. "That would be safe to order because I know what that is."

Dorin and I both look out of the window where several chickens scratch and peck at the ground. "Do you suppose...?" I ask.

"Undoubtedly," says Dorin. "But they probably have whatever they serve tonight all prepped."

"And, maybe this, *Bistec*, might be beefsteak," Cory continues, "but I'm thinking that's *vaca*. No, maybe *vaca* is cow, not beef or meat."

A handsome young man in a white dress shirt and black pants is our waiter. I order chicken by pointing to the menu. I'm not ready to say *pollo*, the word that Cory pronounces *poe yo*, no "ls". Dorin orders the *bistec*, as does Cory.

While we are waiting for our meal, the lights go out.

"Uh oh," says Dorin.

But within thirty seconds, the grinning waiters come walking out of the kitchen with lit lanterns and put them on each occupied table. It gives the restaurant a romantic glow.

"I wonder how they'll cook the food?" I ask.

"I bet they cook with gas, given the tenuous situation with the electricity."

Very soon our waiter appears with our food. Mine is, indeed, half a roasted chicken. The guys do get steaks that look wonderful. The dishes come with rice and a variety of vegetables that are well-seasoned and delicious.

After dinner, Dorin asks Cory how to order coffee.

"*Café negro,*" he says. "That would mean black coffee."

"Are you sure?" Dorin asks, clearly uncomfortable. All residents here are black. What if this is an insult?

"It's not 'negro' as people would say, meaning the race. The word *negro* means black. Just say, 'naay grow,' but, like, snap the 'r,' roll it a little. Mom, you want *café con crema,* but I forget what sugar is."

The waiter comes back, and Dorin, still looking skeptical, says, "Café...naaygrow."

"*Sí,*" the waiter nods and repeats Dorin's order. We relax a little.

The waiter looks at me. "Um, *café*...." I look at Cory for help.

"*Con leche o crema,*" he says. Then he pantomimes stirring coffee and the waiter says, "*Ah, azúcar.*"

Cory nods as he looks at the menu.

"*Y usted?*" And you? the waiter says to him.

"*Batido de vainilla.*"

"*Con helado?*"

"*Sí,*" Cory says, grinning at him. He turns to us. "Vanilla milkshake with ice cream."

Dorin and I look at Cory in amazement. Who is this kid?

"Don't get excited," Cory says. "These are just a few basic words. I can order food but only a few items. Oh, yeah, I just remembered, *sopa* is soup. Salad is *ensalada.* 'Cause, you know, they sound sort of alike."

"Well, then, we won't starve," Dorin chuckles.

"They are open for breakfast," I say. "Let's come back for breakfast tomorrow morning."

"Okay, eggs are *huevos.*" It sounds like he is saying "way bohz."

The waiter catches on we are trying to learn Spanish. He holds up a fork he is clearing from our table.

"*Tenedor,*" he says, smiling.

We repeat it back to him. He nods and smiles his approval.

He takes the spoon beside Dorin's cup and holds it up. "*Cuchara.*"

This is an easy word to say, and when Dorin and I repeat it, he nods again.

Then he indicates the cloth napkin beside my plate. "*Servilleta.*" It's obvious he is enjoying being a tutor.

"Sorbetta," I try.

He smiles and shakes his head no. He repeats the word, and it sounds something like "sayr be **yay** tah." I try again. He shrugs and waggles his hand, as if to say, so-so. Then he smiles and says, "Okay. *Bien.*"

"Good enough," Cory says. "And that concludes tonight's portion of Speaking a Language in a Foreign Country when you don't know the language."

We pay and leave a tip. We love this place and the waiter, not much older than Cory, is great. As we head down the hill and into town, there are lanterns inside and outside of the houses. We can't tell where the salsa music is coming from, but I love it.

"I bet they have gasoline generators for nights like this," Dorin says.

I am aware of a feeling of well-being and contentment. "No wonder people don't leave here. I could stay for a long time, if we could eat in this restaurant every day."

"Well, it's inexpensive enough. Why don't we?"

And so we do, at least for breakfast and dinner. They have a breakfast omelet to die for, which I order every day. And every day, Cory, who is still as skinny as a rail, orders a *batido con helado*, milkshake with ice cream, and, when he quickly downs the large, creamy drink, he orders a second one. Our waiter and his fellow waiter watch this event every day, chatting about it and chuckling. They obviously get a kick out it. After a couple of days, the second *batido* is ready and delivered to our table as Cory finishes the first. The only meal we ever eat on the boat is a cold lunch. Not having to fight with the kerosene stove which, by now, has blackened the ceiling over the stove with sooty smoke, is such a relief to all of us.

Three days after our first afternoon social with the other cruisers, Dorin and I deliver a bag of laundry to the dock and meet the shy man who takes it away. He says, "Two day," and holds up two fingers. "*Sábado*. Saturday."

We come back on Saturday in the morning, and the gentleman materializes out of nowhere, it seems. He tells us how much we owe, which is such a bargain. Our laundry is crisply folded, and back at the boat when I unload it, I find it is cleaner than it has been since we started our trip, including the one time I used the laundromat in Bermuda.

Meanwhile, the bananas that were supposed to ripen on the rear of the boat seem to have gone from hard-as-a-rock unripe, to rotten. So, feeling a little guilty, I drop them off the boat at night. When I mention it at our daily martini social, they laugh and say what we had was plantains. A cousin of bananas—not sweet and not eaten without cooking.

On the recommendation of the yachters, we also try a Chinese and an Austrian restaurant. Both serve wonderful food, so we put them in rotation.

One day, Dorin goes headfirst into the lazaret locker and pulls out his mask, snorkel and fins.

"Going diving?" I ask. He has been a scuba diver for years.

"No, you are," he says. "You can use my stuff. And it's called snorkeling. No tanks. You just use this tube to breathe with."

I look at the murky water. It doesn't look inviting.

"Go get into your swim stuff. We'll go way out into the bay in the dinghy, where it's bound to be clearer."

That actually sounds appealing. It's hot and the water will be cool. Yes, I think, it's time to try this. After I change into cut-off jean shorts and a t-shirt, Dorin is already standing in the dinghy, holding it against the hull. He rows far away from the cluster of yachts, stops and drops the tiny *Tinker* anchor. I am a little nervous but kind of excited. Maybe this is the beginning of steps that will enable me to do the serious diving with tanks.

He helps me fit the mask to my head, making sure my hair isn't stuck underneath it. My eyes and nose are inside and the strap is tight around my head. Once the snorkel is attached to the mask, he has me put the end in my mouth and breathe.

"Okay, now one way to get into the water is sit on the tube, hold the mask against your face and fall backwards."

"And the other way?"

"Well, you can just slip over the side feet first, as if you were going swimming."

I choose option two, which is quite pleasant. The water feels wonderful, cool but not shocking like Maine water.

"So, now, just put your face in the water and practice breathing through the snorkel."

With one arm looped over the rubber dinghy tube, I tentatively put my face in the water. The first impression, which lasts three seconds, is that I can see seaweed swaying, and, alarmingly, there are long, very thin fish swimming lazily below me. The second impression is that there is water pouring into my mask. I jerk my head up, and in the process, inhale through my nose, which brings on choking and coughing. I pull off the mask and continue to cough until my windpipe is clear.

"Don't worry," says Dorin. "That can happen."

I'm thinking, then why didn't you tell me?

"The strap probably isn't tight enough. Here, let me adjust it."

I slide the mask and dangling snorkel off my head and hand it to him.

"It's always a little alarming when you start. Don't worry, you'll get used to it."

"Used to what? Water going up my nose?"

"No, you shouldn't get any water in your nose. Look, sometimes a little might leak in. Happens to me. So, what you do is, you push against the mask at the top here and then take a breath through your snorkel, you know, your mouth, and then blow hard out of your nose. That will clear the water out of the mask. Here, try it with your head above water. A dry run, so to speak." He chuckles.

I put the mask back on, which is much tighter now, and follow his instructions. Nothing happens.

"Bigger breath, blow harder!"

I do and my ears snap like they do when they adjust to airplane pressure. Simultaneously, I feel the mask lift slightly near my eyes. Okay, that must be air going out. So the water will do the same thing.

"Just blow hard," he says and pats me on top of my head as I prepare to try again. I put my head in the water and this time I don't notice anything visually—just concentrating on what I feel. And what I feel, immediately, is water pouring into the mask. Big breath in, I blow hard through my nose, but before I can even get air in, the water is up to my nostrils. I blow as hard as I can, and it seems like I have forced a bubble of air into the mask. But the water just keeps coming in.

Dorin leans over the dinghy, his face close to the water. "You're doin' good, Shirl Jean."

I whip my head up out of the water and look at him. The water in the mask is just up to my nostrils. I glare at him and pull off the mask, this time not inhaling. The water from the mask pours down my face.

"See, that was better! You didn't even choke. Let me look at the mask. Put it on. Let me see. That was good."

"You think so?" I ask, but the sarcasm is lost on him. He's in his teaching mode.

"Yes, you're doing fine. You just need to practice a little more."

His fingers examine the mask, smoothing hair away from my face. "There's obviously a leak somewhere here. Let me tighten the strap again."

I pull off the mask and hand it to him. He adjusts it, but it's so tight I have trouble getting it back into place. He examines it closely. "There, good. It should be fine now. All divers occasionally get a little water in their masks. This is just a technique they learn. Just…big breath in—through your mouth and blow hard…through your nose."

"Yeah, I get the sequence," I say.

"Why don't you stretch out, float on top of the water and then put your face in. Maybe it will make a difference."

I stretch out in the "dead man's float" position that I learned in swimming lessons when I was eight. I take a breath through the snorkel, hold it, and lower my face in the water. Immediately, water pours, faster than before, into the mask. I jerk my head up and look at him. The water is up to my eyeballs.

"Oh, that didn't quite work out," he says. "Maybe what you should do is…."

I pull off the mask and toss it into the dinghy.

"I'm done."

"Yeah, well, I'm not sure what's going wrong. Maybe we can try tomorrow. For some people, it just takes patience and practice."

"Don't count on it." I say. I'm a little annoyed at his patronizing words, but I'm also disappointed. Just the one, quick glance at what was in the water below us had sparked an interest. I think I would love this activity. But maybe I'm not cut out for this.

Dorin rows us back to the *Fandango*, where Cory lounges against the shrouds, watching. "How'd it go?" he asks as we approach. I can see, by his carefully studied posture, and hear, from the tone of his voice, he knows it didn't go well.

"She did well," Dorin says. "Just a little more practice. She'll get used to it."

I can tell even he's not convinced.

"Whoa, what happened to your face?" Cory asks.

"Why? What's the matter?" I ask.

"Well, um, she, I think I had the straps too tight," Dorin says. "So, you want to give it a try, Cor?"

Cory shakes his head. "Ah, no, maybe some other time."

Cory is a marginal swimmer, which causes me some guilt and concern. Six months ago, my sister, her kids, and another niece came to visit us in Maine. We went to the local indoor pool for a family party. As I watched the teenagers horsing around, I noticed Cory stood about halfway down the pool in water up to his chest. While his cousins swam to the deep end and back, he didn't join them. Afterwards I asked him why.

"I can't swim," he said. I was thoroughly shocked. All of my five sons could swim. Right? When Cory was under a year old, I took him to Baby Class swimming at this same pool. And, of course, just like all the babies, he could swim under water.

His brothers, all of whom are older than he, had taken swimming lessons and could swim very well. And! During the summer, they all went to their Dad's on weekends. He has a camp on the lake, with a dock. They all went swimming there. Right? Wrong.

"I just stayed where I could stand when I was at the camp," he'd said.

"And nobody noticed you weren't swimming?"

"Guess not."

I contacted the Girls' and Boys' Club and was able to sign him up for a few private lessons. He worked hard at it, and by the time we were ready to sail, he could do a decent crawl and swim the length of the pool under water.

Now Dorin nods, as if he had expected Cory's answer, and looks sad. He feels like he's failed us, I think. "Okay, some other time," he says.

Though we travel mostly by *motoconcho*, we also want to explore by walking. One morning, Dorin and I decide to explore roads we haven't been on yet. After an hour, the sun is overhead, and we are sweating profusely.

"I think we bit off more than we can chew," Dorin says.

"Yeah, I need to sit a minute," I say. I find a rock to sit on, but the sun still beats down, and there is no shade in sight.

We start to walk again, and a large farm truck comes by. In the back of the truck there are half a dozen adults and a couple of children, standing up. The truck suddenly brakes and pulls over to the side. As we approach, the driver leans out of the window.

"Get in. You ride."

The truck is traveling in the direction we are going. I look at Dorin.

"What do you want to do?" he asks.

"I want to ride!" I say. "But how will I get up into the truck?"

"I'll give you a boost," he says.

I nod to the driver. "*¡Muchas gracias!*" He nods back.

At the back of the truck, which has a very high bed, Dorin kneels and makes a step with his clasped hands. I'm uncertain how this will work out. I feel like I'll be off balance. I tentatively put my foot into his hands, and then, when an arm comes into my vision, I grasp the hand of the man who is trying to help me. With his aid, I swing easily into the bed of the truck. Dorin places his hands on the bed of the truck and hoists himself up without aid. *"Gracias,"* I say to the man who has helped me.

"De nada," he says and then walks back to the other passengers who now seem to be huddled close together at the front of the truck bed. We stay where we are near the back and hang onto the side. The truck shifts into gear, and we are off, bumping along the road.

I notice a little boy of maybe six looking at us, his eyes filled with fear. He slides further into the crowd and, peeking from behind his mother, watches us with big eyes. I wonder if we are the first white people he has seen this close up. Or, does he have reason to fear us because we are white?

The driver of the truck stops for us to get off about two blocks from the docks. Dorin jumps down and reaches both hands up. I lean forward, and he grabs me by the waist and swings me down. We say our thanks in Spanish. Dorin reaches for his wallet, but before he can even get it out of his pocket, the driver waves and departs.

"I continue to be in awe of the people here," Dorin says. 'Wasn't that neat?"

Every day we work a little on Spanish. Cory talks us through some phrases, and we pick some up from vendors and other boaters. *Mercado* gets us to the open-air market—the best place to shop, and *marina* gets us back to the docks. We ask, *¿ Cuántos pesos?* or *¿Cuánto cuesta? –* how much does it cost, and, astonishingly, are understood. If the answer is *veinte y cinco,* twenty-five; *medio,* fifty; or *setenta y cinco,* seventy-five, we usually understand. If we look confused, the vendor writes the price on her hand with a ballpoint pen and then presents her palm.

We also know *agua,* water, as well as *pollo,* chicken, and *tortilla con vegetales,* omelet with vegetables. At first, I think tortilla is wrong. I know what a tortilla is, and it's not an omelet. Nevertheless, when I order it, a delicious omelet appears.

I know *mañana* is tomorrow, and I can count from one to ten. Dorin has mastered the days of the week. We both can greet people with *buenos días, buenas tardes,* and *buenas noches*: good morning, good afternoon and good evening. And, of course, the most important, *muchas gracias*, for which there are many, many opportunities.

My curiosity about the bridge continues because it's such a dominant and lovely feature in the bay. There are actually three bridges, all connected. The first part is a short piece that begins at a small peninsula, where a tourist hotel is located, which goes over the beach to a spit of land that looks like an island. The second part of the bridge spans a short space of ocean to another tiny island. And that's where the third section takes off. There are fifteen arches supporting the high bridge that ends at a larger, uninhabited island. The water appears to be shallow in this space, and we never see a local boat go under the bridge.

I have seen a few people walk part way across it. They stop and look down, and it's a long way to the water. Then they turn and go back to the hotel.

Cory brings a sketch to our restaurant and asks the waiter about the bridge. In reply, he just shrugs his shoulders. Other cruisers who know a little Spanish have asked, but the only answer they get is, *"No lo sé."* I don't know.

I name the bridge the Mystery Bridge. Dorin calls it the Bridge to Nowhere. Cory comes up with what we accept as the winner: The Island Connection.

When two weeks have passed, we decide it's time to check in at the post office to see if a part that we ordered through Glenn has arrived. We assumed it would take a fairly long time.

We approach who we think is a policeman, though we're not sure if it's the military or if the police and military are one in the same. They wear military-style uniforms and carry very big side arms. They seem friendly enough but very serious and official.

Dorin clears his throat and says, *"¿Dónde está....?"* Which means, we've been taught, "Where is...."

The official who has the confident bearing of a general, politely turns his attention to Dorin.

"¿Sí...?"

"Ah, *¿Dónde está* the post office?"

"Ah, ¿qué, what?" The officer leans toward Dorin slightly, in concentration.

"Post...*office!*"

The officer shakes his head in puzzlement.

"Mail," Dorin says. "Letter? Post...*office!*" He repeats it louder, "Post *office!*"

The gentleman shakes his head again.

I dig out a postcard from the fanny pack I've taken to wearing and show him.

"Aa-a-ah!" the officer says. "*Post* office!" with the emphasis on the first word, where it belongs.

"Yes, *sí*, post office!" I say. Dorin's head nods vigorously.

The office snaps his fingers, motions to a young soldier and speaks to him in Spanish. The young man motions us to follow him three blocks to the post office. We thank him profusely.

When we enter the post office, there is a nun in a street-length habit at the counter talking to the clerk. I take this time to look around. We've heard a story from cruisers that may or may not be true: when the regime changes in this country, the outgoing regime, or the employees (depending on who's telling the story) strip their government places of employment of anything that isn't nailed down. The new government has to start anew. In this very post office, the story goes, all the mail was dumped in a pile so the pigeonhole cabinet could be carted away. The current cabinet is six feet tall, I estimate, and possibly ten feet long. I'm not sure why anyone would want this item, so maybe the story is false. Even if true, maybe it only happens in Samaná, certainly not in the big cities where the new leadership would be able to protect the government's property.

While I've been musing, I have been half listening to the conversation between the clerk and the nun. I pick up that she is speaking with a Castilian accent—using the "th" *lisp*, where in Central and South America they would use the "s." I assume she is a missionary from Spain. As the dialogue continues, the woman seems confident and assertive and appears to be arguing with the clerk. It appears he is annoyed. His face gradually closes; finally, he just looks at her without responding. Then, his face a mask, he just shakes his head "no."

Looking angry, she storms out of the building. The clerk turns toward us, sees we are Americans, and comes close to rolling his eyes. He is not expecting this to go well either.

Dorin, apparently having had enough of a verbal exchange with a local, gently pushes me forward.

"*Buenos días,*" I say.

"*Buenos días,*" he replies cautiously and nods.

From my fanny pack I pull out a piece of paper with our names on it that also says, "General Delivery, Sta. Bárbara de Samaná, República Dominicana." Mary of *No Brass Ring* in Bermuda had given this to me. We passed this information to Glenn via ham radio, asking him to pass it on to Bill, who by now, I hope, has passed it onto my mother.

The clerk looks at it and nods. He goes to the wall of wooden pigeonholes and sorts through an inch-thick stack of envelopes, comparing them to the paper I have given him. He finds one, smiles, and gives it to me. It's from Mom. I am ecstatic! "*¡Gracias! ¡Muchas gracias!*" I say. He seems pleased at my reaction.

"*También, un paquete?*" I use the words I memorized. Also a package? I am nervous, thinking I must be saying it wrong. But the clerk, though he looks like he understands, shakes his head no.

I have a letter to mail to my parents, which I have already addressed. The clerk nods, puts a stamp on it, and tells me how much. I still don't know money, so I fan out a few peso bills. He takes one and gives me change in coins. Whew! We have completed the transaction and have not annoyed the clerk.

"*¡Buenos días!*" I say.

The clerk smiles and nods. "*Buenos días.*"

I am now emboldened enough in the following days to row the dinghy to the dock by myself to leave off laundry or go to the market. I love the feeling of being an independent stranger in a strange land.

"I think we should go to Puerto Rico," Dorin says one afternoon as we row into shore. We've been here over two weeks.

"Gee, I don't think I'm ready to leave here."

"Me neither," he replies. "But I'm getting antsy. I want to get charts for the next part of the trip. And I think I can get parts there, in Mayagüez. They have an auto parts place. I want to at least get some fuel filters. We can zip over, stay a few days, and then zip back. Maybe by the time we get back the part will be here."

"Sure, that sounds good."

I want to hear what our yachting friends think of this, though. And hear, we do.

"You don't have any charts!"

"It's dangerous, that crossing."

"Mona is treacherous."

"Unpredictable."

"We know someone who got the shit kicked out of him," Jim says. "He came back here, sold his boat for next to nothing, and flew home. That was the end of sailing for him."

I look at Dorin, who nods. He appears to be listening and processing, but his eyes narrow, and I can see a stubborn tilt to his chin.

Sebastian says, "On the other hand, you survived a stormy Atlantic. This won't be any worse, and there's a good chance you won't have any trouble at all."

There is squirming in the group, but no one else says anything.

"If you're still into chart making," Sebastian says to me, "I have a chart of the west coast of Puerto Rico you can copy."

Already I have butterflies, but I nod and say thank you. This has come so suddenly and their warnings of danger have my heart racing a little.

The next day I tape together four pieces of paper from Cory's notebook and spend three hours reducing the chart to fit on them. This time I pay a lot of attention to the depth lines around the coast...now that I fully understand this will *be* our approach chart. When I copied the chart for the Dominican Republic, in the back of my mind, I thought Dorin would pull some kind of backup plan out of thin air, something more substantial than my drawing.

Sebastian has also sent along another chart showing the whole of Mona Passage, including Mona Island, halfway between the D.R. and Puerto Rico.

Meanwhile, the guys have gone for some fresh produce and eggs. When they get back, we haul the anchor and motor to the dock, backing the *Fandango* up to fill the water tanks.

"Okay for departure tomorrow morning?" Dorin asks us.

"I'm ready," Cory says. "We could leave right now as far as I'm concerned."

"I'm good to go tomorrow morning," I say. This gives me time to get my courage up.

At 9:00 a.m. the next day, Dorin says he will find out where to check out with immigration. Everyone has told us it's not necessary—you just go.

"But I want another stamp on our passports," Dorin says. "It won't take long." I give him our passports in a plastic bag, and he rows ashore.

In two hours, he is back, triumphant, with stamped passports.

"You remember that story about the local people cleaning out government buildings right after an election when the opposing candidate wins? Well, maybe it's true. I asked for directions, and finally found the immigration place. In a huge room, maybe big enough to play basketball in, there was this tiny desk, like a student desk, in the middle of the room. One guy sat in a chair, and there was no other furniture."

"Oh, wow. And how did it go with the officer?" I ask. I'm curious to know how Dorin communicated.

"Fine. The guy was nice, but he seemed puzzled or confused. I explained I wanted a stamp and gave him our passports. I put two bottles of beer on his desk in appreciation. He didn't look at the beer but looked the passports over and asked me something in Spanish. I pointed to his stamp pad and stamp.

The guy said, *"No, no es necesario,"* and I know what that means. So I said, *"Por favor,"* and pantomimed stamping the passports.

"He shrugged his shoulders and said, 'Okay.' And there you go."

"There I go what?"

"'Okay' is a vocabulary word in every language."

It's now 10:30, and Cory and I have finished getting the boat ready to move. We motor out of the bay, waving to Jim and Helen, Chuck and Dottie, and Janice and Jake, who are lounging in their cockpits. Chuck and Dottie stand up and wave back to us. Sebastian steps into his cockpit and gives one blast of his air horn. Before we are out of sight, Mac calls us on the VHF. Dorin tells Cory to answer and Cory reluctantly does. "This is Mac of the *Fancy Dancer*. This is Mac of the *Fancy Dancer*. Over?"

"Uh, this is the *Fandango*," Cory says. "Um, over?"

"Have a good crossing, *Fandango*. Have a good crossing. Over and out."

"Hey, you think maybe they like us?" Dorin asks.

"Yeah, probably because you are so humble," I reply.

"I did my best," he says with a smile. "Difficult, though."

Chapter Fourteen
For Want of a Cotter Pin

As soon as we are into the open ocean and discover a nice wind, the sails go up and Dorin cuts the motor. The sun is out, the sky is a cloudless, brilliant blue, and the water throws its million-dollar diamond sparkle across the surface. I feel the wind on my face and arms, and it ruffles my hair. As we glide over shallow swells, it's impossible not to be happy to be out on the water again.

Once in a while we glance back and see the *República Dominicana* gradually shrinking and then disappearing. The breezes are light—just enough to keep the sails full and pulling at five knots. We tack a couple of times and are satisfied with our progress.

That evening I'm on watch, and the sky is full of stars. I sit back and enjoy the nighttime spectacle from horizon to horizon. Suddenly, the wind picks up, and we're moving at six plus knots and heeling at fifteen degrees. I stand up to get Dorin to reef, when I hear a loud snap. Suddenly the boom slams across the cockpit taking with it the mainsheet tackle—a heavy, multi-pulley system—which is now no longer attached to the traveler, which is attached to the boat. I try to understand what I am looking at as the boat dips sharply in a wave, and the mainsheet tackle, swinging and jerking wildly, hits me in the forehead.

"Dorin!" I scream. I try to grab the mainsheet where it attaches to the boom, but it yanks around unpredictably.

Suddenly Dorin is there. "What's...." But then he sees what's up and lunges at the flailing tackle and main sheet, but the boat wallows and bucks, and he misses.

"You're bleeding!" he yells as he swipes at it again. Then he jumps up on the rear deck behind the traveler and, using both arms, captures the errant tackle.

"You okay?" he shouts. The boom with full sail still yanks back and forth, threatening to shake him loose. "Get the mainsail down!"

I jump up on the house and undo the halyard, but the sail, still full of wind, doesn't budge. Then Cory is there pulling on the sail, hand over hand, and slowly it comes down.

"What the hell happened?" Dorin asks. "Cory, your mother is bleeding. Get the first aid kit."

"No, it's nothing. I don't feel it anymore. Yeah, what the hell happened?"

With a flashlight, we examine the traveler and see that the stainless-steel cotter pin, which holds the shackle pin that holds the mainsheet tackle to the traveler, has broken. We find a piece of it on the cockpit floor. Rusted.

"Get me something so I can reattach it," Dorin says.

"What?"

"I don't know. Anything!" He is hanging onto the boom, which is still yanking him around as we wallow in swells. "It'll only be temporary."

I frantically rummage around in one of the fix-it boxes, hoping I can find some flexible wire, but the only thing I see is a jumbo safety pin. I grab it and run back to the cockpit.

"Will this work?"

"Let me see. Maybe we can make it work just to get us through the night."

He tries to immobilize the boom and mainsheet tackle while Cory inserts the shackle pin and tries to fasten the safety pin. Dorin lets more line through the pulley, and with the tackle much closer to the traveler, Cory is able to fasten the safety pin.

"That's not going to hold," he predicts.

"Well, let's try it," Dorin says.

So, carefully, they gradually put pressure on the mainsheet tackle by tightening the mainsheet. And it holds.

"Let's take down the sails and motor until morning, so we can keep an eye on it during daylight."

In the morning, we hoist the sail, and it pulls well. Our unusual tackle fastener seems to be holding nicely and the day is uneventful. The cut on my forehead is barely visible, though I have a bruise to show for the excitement during my watch.

We continue to tack every couple of hours to maintain our course, but it's no big deal. That night during my watch I hope to see a glow in the sky that will be Puerto Rico, but I don't. Before morning, on Dorin's watch, we lower the sails and run the motor so we can turn southward into the Passage toward Mona Island and maintain our course. We sight the lighthouse on Mona just before first light and hang a left toward what we hope is Boquerón Bay, near the lower west corner of Puerto Rico. We continue to motor until we finally see land, and when we do, we put up the sails and turn off the motor. I smile, realizing it's important to Dorin and probably to Cory to enter Puerto Rico under sail.

I'm below making coffee when Cory yells for me to come up. I move the hot tea kettle from the stove into the sink and dash up the stairs.

"Look, there's a squall coming!" Dorin shouts because, just that quickly, the wind is screaming. The sky is black behind us. I take the tiller while the guys wrestle down the sails and fasten them.

"Look!" Dorin points to our starboard side. In the not very far distance, I see what looks like two tornadoes on the ocean.

"Waterspouts," Dorin says. I relax a little because waterspouts sound a lot better than tornadoes.

"They are tornadoes on the ocean," he says. "And two of them!"

"But they won't come closer?" I ask.

"Hard to say. They could. They're unpredictable."

Suddenly a third waterspout forms and the wind howls. The weather has closed in so that we can no longer see the land.

"I've never heard of three at a time!" Dorin shouts. "Get below. Close the boat. Close the hatches!"

"Four!" he says. I look as I start down into the galley, and sure enough, a fourth waterspout has formed. But at that moment, one of the first spouts dissipates and drops to nothing.

"Get going!" Dorin yells. Though we have no sail up, the boat pitches and jerks wildly. "I'm going to point back toward the ocean! We need to get away from land."

I toss him his safety harness, and he shrugs into it. Below, Cory is already closing the port lights and snugging them down. I go forward and close the front hatch. By the time I'm done, Cory has pulled out the companionway boards and is sliding them into the slots. As the *Fandango* snaps over, the teakettle flies out of the sink and hits him in the back. If the water is hot, he doesn't react. He pulls the hatch cover shut with us below and Dorin outside. Cory sits on the ice box and hangs on to the handrail to keep from being thrown off. I sit on the settee. We look at each other. He can see I'm scared.

"Well, maybe those chicken sailors in Samaná did know something," he says with a smile. I smile back. Like Dorin, he has a knack for breaking the tension with humor.

We can hear rain rapping on the house and decks, thunderously loud, as we toss around.

Cory jumps off the icebox and pulls back the hatch cover enough to pull out the top board, then he slides the cover closed again.

We can see Dorin standing at the tiller, holding onto the boom overhead.

"Hey, what are you doing?" he yells.

Cory and I stand so we can see out into the cockpit through the five inches where the top board would be. The rain streams off the bill of Dorin's cap and runs off his beard. He runs his hand over his eyes to clear the water. He looks back down at us and laughs out loud.

"You two look funny, your faces peering through the gap."

I can see that he has fastened his safety harness to the bulkhead hasp, so I relax. We continue to watch him. He glances at us once in a while and shakes his head and smiles.

"Looks like your safety pin is holding," Cory teases. Then he shakes his head like he still can't believe it.

I realize if the cotter pin had let go during this melee and the boom had been slamming around out of control, it could have been much worse.

Suddenly, I see the ocean sparkling behind Dorin. The sun is out. Cory pulls the boards out, and we bound up into the cockpit. The waves are enormous, and we are still tossing around, but the wind has died.

"How strong was the wind?" Cory asks.

"Sixty, I think," Dorin says. "By far the strongest wind I've ever been in. Well, crew, that was interesting. Just a little squall. See? Mona Passage isn't so bad."

Gradually the waves dissipate, though the water is still very choppy.

"We're now closer to Mayagüez than Boquerón, I'm sure," Dorin says. "Let's go in there. That's the port of entry for us anyway."

We motor toward Puerto Rico and land is soon in sight. We drop anchor in the broad harbor of Mayagüez in the early afternoon. There are very few sailing yachts here. Beyond a long stretch of beach, modern city buildings rise above the palm trees.

"I'm not going to like this bay," says Dorin. "It's too open and shallow, and we're going to get swells. We won't be staying here long."

Dorin rows into shore while Cory and I deal with the usual mess that happens during even a short cruise, even when there's no storm. We are below when, three hours later, Dorin shouts, "Ahoy! Hey, I'm back." Cory goes out to tie the dinghy to the stern cleat while I pump a big glass of water and bring it to the cockpit. Dorin chugalugs it and then pats the seat beside him. "Sit down. You won't believe this. I asked a Puerto Rican guy where Customs and Immigration is. I figured he wouldn't speak English, but, you know, worth a try. He said he would drive me there!

"I really lucked out. His English was excellent, so we could talk. I asked him where he learned it, and he said he had spent three years in the states—New York City, a long time ago. When we got to immigration, he went in with me. There were people ahead of us, so we sat down and talked for an hour or more.

"He asked me a lot of questions about our trip...said his grandfather had been a fisherman here in Puerto Rico. When he was a boy, he went out on fishing trips with him. He had some really interesting stories to tell. Man, oh man, we had a great time!

"On the way back, we stopped at a bank. I wanted to cash some Traveler's checks. When we got back to the shore, I wanted to get my wallet out, but I stifled, Shirl Jean. You'd have been proud of me. We shook hands, and he wished me good luck with the rest of our trip. How's that for hospitality? I think we are going to love this country.

"But hey, I want you to see something," he continues and motions us toward the *Tinker*, tied at the stern of the *Fandango*.

We climb into the dinghy. He unties and rows us to shore. There, near the water, a huge dead shark is being carved up by a fisherman. There is a small crowd of onlookers, but when they see us, they part to make room. I am surprised at how big the shark is, but most amazed and alarmed that its huge mouth is gaping open, the upper jaw unhinged. It has a double row of long teeth, both upper and lowers, that look as sharp as knives. The fisherman looks pleased that he has drawn a crowd and chats with them. It appears he is answering their questions, and I wish I could understand.

While I'm fascinated, I'm also grossed out.

"Just think," Dorin says to me. "Some of those teeth will end up on chains around women's necks."

"Yeah, or as earrings. Yuck."

"Seen enough?"

"Yep."

"Me too," Cory says.

We eat supper aboard that night and find that the *Fandango* rises and falls in the swells coming in from the ocean as Dorin predicted. He checks the anchor every hour through the night to be sure it has not pulled loose.

The next day we take a taxi into the city. After our time offshore, in Bermuda, and the D.R., it's something of a culture shock to see familiar chain stores like Sears and fast food restaurants like McDonalds in the mall. Though I hadn't noticed the heat of the day, the air conditioning is a welcome relief.

We stroll through and linger momentarily in front of the glitzy, storefront displays.

But after a little more browsing, we realize there is no place to buy charts here, which was our primary reason for coming to Puerto Rico. In fact, there is nothing we can use or even want at these stores. Yet, it's comforting to me to see price tags in American dollars.

We finally find a couple of stores of interest--a dive shop and a bookstore. In the dive shop, Dorin has Cory try on a mask and snorkel, and it seems to fit.

"If it turns out you like snorkeling, Cor, we'll pick up some fins for you."

I try on a couple of masks, but Dorin is not satisfied they will fit right. Finally, as a last resort, he buys a kid-sized snorkel and mask for me.

"You think this'll work?" I ask. It's in a bubble pack, so I can't try it on.

"Worth a try," he says.

In the bookstore, I ask if they have any Spanish-English dictionaries.

"I think we have one," the clerk says. "Nobody asks for them too much." She finds it and rings it up. I am so happy to have this key that could open a few locks.

Near the mall there is an auto parts place. Cory and I find an ice cream shop and eat our cones while Dorin goes inside to buy fuel filters and a bagful of other automotive stuff.

At McDonald's we pig out on French fries, hamburgers, and chocolate shakes, Cory scarfing down five quarter-pounders, two large French fries and a large vanilla shake.

"Mm, mm, mm," Dorin says, wiping his mouth with a napkin. "I'd forgotten what gourmet food tastes like."

We all agree it's fun exploring cuisine from different places and different cultures, but it's really comforting to be able to wallow in our very own American fast food.

It's a taxi ride back to the beach and then a long row against an onshore breeze back to the boat.

The next morning, over breakfast, Dorin says to Cory, "We're headed to Boquerón today. How about you take over?"

Cory looks surprised. "Me?"

Dorin drains his coffee cup and nods.

"Yeah. Be the captain. Tell us what to do. Can you handle it?"

Cory shrugs casually. "Sure," he says. "Now?"

"Whenever you're ready."

"Okay, you guys," Cory says. "Clean up below and get shaped up so we can haul anchor." Standing on the locker, he starts undoing the sail ties.

Dorin roars with laughter. "Hm. Guess he was ready."

"Do you think he's been thinking of this for a while?"

"He's been thinking of this since he was ten."

On summer weekends, Dorin and I used to take Cory and his older brother Andrew on sailing trips. Cory was so short he had to stand on a plastic crate to see over the house when it was his turn to steer.

"Dorin, get ready to haul anchor," Cory says. Dorin nods and goes forward.

"We're leaving under sail, Mom. Get ready to hoist the main."

"Under sail?"

"Yeah, of course. Easy harbor to get out of and just enough wind. Get ready to hoist the main. We'll put up the jib when we're out of the harbor."

Cory detaches the tiller from the autopilot and grins at me. "Don't worry, Shirl. It'll be an easy day-sail."

I chuckle as I climb on the house, grab the winch handle, and start unwinding the halyard from the cleat.

"Hoist it just a little. I'll tell you when to stop."

I slowly raise the sail until it starts to flutter.

"Enough!" he yells. Then he lets the boom out, and as the sail starts to fill, the boat swings a little.

"Haul the anchor!" he yells to Dorin, and Dorin swings the lever on the windlass as fast as he can. The anchor chain clanks as it takes up the slack.

"Get ready," Cory says to me.

"It's clear!" Dorin yells to Cory, meaning it is free of the bottom. He continues to winch it up.

"Hoist!" Cory yells to me, and I crank as fast as I can, looking up, watching the sail move steadily up the mast. Cory pulls the boom in close, and the boat moves forward on a beat in the gentle wind.

"Yahoo!" Dorin yells from the bow as he pulls the anchor on board and fastens it down.

Cory hand steers down the coast to Boquerón, adjusting the sails from time to time. Dorin doesn't say a word and looks quite satisfied with the situation.

"I'm going to motor into the bay," Cory says as he consults my 'chart,' spread out on the cockpit seat. Dorin nods and waits. Cory starts the motor and asks Dorin to lower the jib and me to lower the mainsail.

As we motor slowly in, getting an idea of the lay of the bay, we see a long, curved sandy beach ahead lined with a fringe of palm trees. Straight ahead and quite far into the bay, there are half a dozen boats anchored. Dorin and Cory discuss where to anchor near the cluster. Once they decide, Cory throttles back and drifts to a stop. Dorin drops the anchor and Cory, using the motor, backs and sets the anchor in what we believe is a sandy bottom.

"Well done, Cory," Dorin says. "We'll have to have you solo someday. You, too, Shirl Jean."

"Not a chance," I say, and I mean it.

We go ashore for supper, and after a short walk, we find a little restaurant. The menu is in Spanish, and we order what we recognize. Cory orders spaghetti, Dorin the chicken, and I get brave and order the *pescado*—fish, a word I recently learned. The service is super, but the food is just okay compared to the wonderful meals we had been eating at our favorite restaurants in the D.R. At the end of the meal, I say to the waiter, *"La cuenta, por favor."* It's my new phrase, and the first time I've used it, so we watch his reaction. I'm sure what I've just said is probably unintelligible because it sure sounds that way to me. He nods and bows and brings our bill. Whew!

"Put a check mark in the plus column," Dorin says.

The next morning, we watch as a man from a nearby yacht lowers himself into his dinghy and rows toward us.

Dorin, always hospitable, invites him onboard. I, on the other hand, am always conscious of how small and messy our boat is and hope potential guests decline. And he does.

"I'm Bob. That's our boat," he says and points to the yacht. "The *Grace*. My wife and I would like to invite you to lunch on our boat."

We accept and while Bob rows back to his boat, we quickly do some sprucing up, which means a change of clothes. We row over to their impressive yacht and meet Bob's wife Binney, who is gracious and who, we discover with delight, has a lot of information about everything. Their boat is roomy and so very comfy. Snuggling back in the cushions, I think, 'now this is the way to live.' We had brought a bottle of wine, which Binney opens, and while we eat lunch, they tell us about the stores in the neighboring town of Cabo Rojo, which is not to be confused, they say, with Cabo Rojo, the cape on the coast south of us.

It's a long, leisurely afternoon while we trade stories, and they give us a beginners' course on how to make living easy in Puerto Rico.

When Bob finds out we made landfall in Samaná without a proper chart, he motions Dorin over to his chart table and spreads out the chart for the Dominican Republic. Dorin takes one look and throws his head back, expelling a big belly laugh. He motions for me to join him. He is still laughing out loud when he signals Cory to join us at the table.

"Look at this," he says. "I can't believe it."

My jaw drops. "Say *what*?"

"Sure puts a different light on things, doesn't it? Come here, Cor. Take a look."

Cory looks over the chart and then does a double take. "Samaná is here?" He puts his finger on the chart. "Well, look, then. This must be where we dropped anchor the first night. And Samaná is just a little way into the bay, in this teeny, tiny inlet. I thought we were at the end of the bay. The whole of Samaná Bay."

Dorin is still laughing. "Yeah, me too. And, look, here's your Island Connection bridge, Cor."

"That didn't show on the chart I copied," I say.

"No, it didn't. But it was an old chart. No telling when the bridge was built, but I bet it was after that chart was made."

"The bay is huge compared to the little portion of it we'd been anchored in," I say. "It must be a hundred times larger than we thought."

"Oh, at least," Dorin says. He is still chuckling. I'm trying to adjust my perception of the town of Samaná and its relative size, compared to the vastness of Samaná Bay.

Bob shakes his head. He is incredulous that we used a hand drawn, inaccurate chart.

"But it got us into the anchorage," Dorin says. "I guess that's all that counts."

We tell them we are interested in snorkeling, but this bay looks very muddy.

"It's seasonal," says Bob. "We've been having some heavy rains. The dirt runs down the mountains and makes the bay muddy. It gets much better."

We learn about how the local taxi system works.

"It's called the *público*," Binney says. "Just walk to the park, and the taxi will be waiting, curbside. Or, if one isn't there, it will be within an hour."

"Be prepared," says Bob. "You get in and sit there and wait until the taxi is full because the driver won't budge an inch until it is. He expects to take one passenger in the front and four in the back. Not the most comfortable way to travel but very reliable."

When we try this the next day, in five minutes we are packed in like sardines. No one seems comfortable with the necessary sweaty, shoulder-to-elbow, bare-skin contact, but stoically everyone accepts it. This is a real trial for me, and it's all I can do to stay still and not pull my arm out and lean forward.

The town of Cabo Rojo is beautiful, with a central park rimmed with palm trees and flowers. There is a charming old church nearby and many one-story shops around the square.

A card table is set up in the park, and a game of dominoes is in progress. Two men face each other; a crowd has gathered to watch. As each man takes his turn, he slaps a tile down with emphasis. The crowd reacts with ahhs, ohs and gasps. Both men are intense, and at the end, when the final tile goes down with gusto, there is applause and cheering as the two men rise and shake hands with each other and then with their admirers in the crowd, who slap them on their backs or hug them. They are replaced by two other men who begin a new game. The dominoes tournament spectators, who are standing, resume watching.

We stroll around and check out some stores. In one, Dorin buys a set of dominoes, saying he'd like to learn. We also pick up a deck of cards that displays the Puerto Rican flag. We eat lunch in a café that has a menu only in Spanish, but we figure it out. After a very pleasant afternoon, we take the *público* back to Boquerón.

We hang out with Bob and Binney for a couple of days because their company is so pleasant. They tell us of sailing couples who sold their boats and happily settled in Puerto Rico. The only downside they experienced was that it took weeks to get electricity in their new homes. I find myself yearning a bit for such a life. If one could only learn Spanish....

They tell us about a bar in town called María's. "María kind of befriends yachters," Bob says. "We meet there most afternoons or sometimes after dinner. She's got a good menu of appetizers. Great margaritas. She also has a small library for boaters. Leave a book, take a book. If you have any books you're done with, bring them."

We check in that evening, and I leave the one book we have all read, a Stephen King, and take away a Tom Clancy. We are delighted by this bar with its covered patio for outdoor dining. Out of curiosity, I order plantains. María tells me I will love them. "*Plátanos,* they are so good."

When they are delivered to the table, the plate has four long slices of what looks like large bananas cut in half the long way and grilled. My first bite tells me this will not become a favorite. They are dry and tasteless.

"Try a little salt," says a woman from the next table. I shake salt on and try again.

"Helps if you put syrup on them," says another person from the same table. She hands me a small pitcher of syrup. I try again.

"Course it never helped me," she adds dryly.

I take a salted, mapled bite. Ugh. "Nope," I say and push the plate away. "Dry, dry and the texture is...dry."

"What?" says María, who has come back to check on me. "You don't like it?" She is obviously disappointed. "Why boat people no like? They are *deliciosos.*"

"Sorry," I say. "I'll just eat Cory's fried mozzarella sticks." I steal the batter-fried stick of cheese from Cory's plate and dip it into a marinara sauce, and it *is* delicious. "Can you bring more?" I ask María. "I can eat a plate of my own." María is pleased at this.

"Yes, I get more for you. You like it."

We enjoy a long evening of libations and snacks and good conversation with the boaters who are anchored in the harbor. We listen to amusing and hair-raising cruising stories from them. In the past, I would surely have wondered if these were tall tales that had been told again and again, embellished and embroidered each time. But now I'm willing to take these stories at face value. From my experience with cruising so far, they could all be true. The company is so pleasant we decide to stay for a few more days.

On the weekend, the beach becomes a recreation spot for Puerto Ricans and vacationers from away. You can tell the locals because they range from many shades of light bronze to black. You can tell the visitors by their extremely vulnerable, pasty-white skin. I think of my belly burn in Bermuda and hope they are wearing plenty of sunscreen.

On Sunday, the bay is alive with locals on roaring jet-skis that criss-cross each other's paths so they can jump each other's wakes. The driver of one of them looks back to check on his companion trailing him and almost hits the *Grace* dead center, turning just a second before impact and upending his jet-ski. The *Grace* rocks gently from the wave kicked up by the machine. When the driver of the jet-ski surfaces, he is laughing. He rights the jet-ski, climbs back on and roars off to join this buddy.

September 30th, a week after arriving, Dorin tells Bob he is thinking of having the boat hauled so he can check a few things...maybe clean the bottom of barnacles and other sea life that might be hitching a ride.

Bob tells us of a small fishing village between Boquerón and Mayagüez called Puerto Real. There is a fishing co-op that has the room and the hydraulic lift to haul boats for repair.

"It's pronounced pw-**air**-toe rey-**ahl**," Bob says.

Since this was not a place we had planned for a landfall, I didn't spend much time on this on the chart. In fact, on my drawing, it appears to be a dimple on the coastline, reminiscent of the tiny inlet that is Samaná, which does not even show on the chart I drew.

"It's a nice little bay and tricky to get into. There are reefs and a sand bar at the mouth. You have to stay as far south as possible when you enter. It's a narrow opening."

The three of us take the *público* to Cabo Rojo and from there another *público* to Puerto Real. We ask a couple of girls, maybe ten years old, one wearing a school uniform, where the *Villa Pesquera* is. They point, and then look shyly at Cory who, as usual, looks his finest.

"We show you," one of them says. They lead us farther down the small street in the direction we are already going. The houses on the ocean side are built on land but extend out into the water on stilts. I am immediately envious.

At the end of this short street, we find the fishing co-op called *Villa Pesquera,* Fishing Village. By now the girls are giggling and looking shyly over their shoulders at Cory. He is either oblivious or ignoring them.

"What you name?" they ask him as we arrive at the gates of the fishing co-op.

He politely tells them but walks a little faster and passes Dorin and me. The girls stop at the gate but continue to watch him.

We find the office in the back of a combination café and bar. Dorin introduces himself to Félix, the manager. He tells Félix we have to sail back to Samaná because we are expecting mail to come in, and then we will return to Puerto Rico. Félix and Dorin come up with a date that we can be hauled. He asks Dorin if we have a chart of the opening to Puerto Real Bay, and he says no, just the one I copied from another boater in the D.R. Félix shakes his head in disgust. I sense he is thinking, "North Americans...!"

He goes into an office and comes back with a chart that he unrolls on the bar. Dorin and Cory sit side by side at the bar while Félix points out the features of the opening of the bay.

On the way back to the *público* stand—not a stand actually, just a sidewalk where the taxi will stop, the girls follow us at a distance, still giggling.

In the *público*, Dorin says, "I like that little village. I'd like to see a little more of it." Having been charmed myself, we are in agreement.

In Boquerón, we row out to the boat, haul anchor and sail to Puerto Real, Dorin having no problem getting into the narrow harbor opening.

"This is the best of the harbors on the west coast," he says. "Much more protected."

The smaller bay seems so cozy to me. We drop anchor near a few boats and relax in the cockpit while we discuss what to do about supper.

"I think I saw a restaurant down the street when we were here this morning," Dorin says. We row into *Villa Pesquera* and walk down the cobblestone street, quickly finding *Brisas del Mar*, Sea Breezes, which, we discover when we enter, has a screened veranda reaching out into the bay. Extending from this is a long dock that has a couple of dinghies tied to it. We talk about how much fun it would be to row directly into the restaurant when at anchor in the harbor.

We order what we know: *pollo, arroz y habichuelas*—deep-fat fried chicken with rice and beans. We each get half a chicken that has not been breaded, and the crispy skin is intact. It's delicious, and we are getting used to rice and beans. Sipping his martini, Dorin says, "I'm telling you Shirl Jean, I am already bonding with this place."

"Yeah, I think I could live here. I love the harbor, the quiet town. I'd love to live in a house that extends over the water. The weather is so pleasant, not too hot. The people are really nice."

"So, could this be your new retirement destination?" Dorin asks, smiling. "I was thinking it was the D.R."

"Hmm. Tough choice. I need a little more experience in both places," I say. "Good to explore options."

We hear a loud water ka-plop in the direction of a nearby dock where a few sailing and fishing boats are tied up.

"Look!" Cory says. "Pelicans! They're diving for food."

A half dozen pelicans circle high above the dock. Suddenly one dives headfirst, wings out at a ninety-degree angle, and enters the water aerodynamically, its wings now close to its body. Seconds later it surfaces and gulps the huge fish down its gullet. They continue to soar and dive into small spaces between the boats. I hold my breath, thinking they will miss and land headfirst on the deck of a boat, but they don't. Sometimes three or four pelicans hit the water within seconds of each other.

Cory reaches for the camera on the table. "I want to go over to that dock and see if I can get some pictures, close up," he says. We wish him good luck.

"See? If I lived here, I could relax every evening and watch the pelicans dive."

"Doesn't get any better," Dorin says, watching me with amusement. "What about your family? Your parents?"

"We'd have to have a place big enough for company."

"We? So you're including me in this retirement plan?"

"Yeah, of course. Wouldn't be any fun without you."

He leans his chair back on two legs, laces his hands behind his head and nods. "Yeah, I could take a lot of living in this place. I'm sure there are many appealing towns in Puerto Rico, but I have to tell you, I really, really like it here."

Our waiter comes by and suggests we try the flan for dessert. We linger over rich custard, which I decide is my new favorite dessert, and glasses of wine until dusk.

Cory is waiting at the dock where the *Tinker* is tied up. "I've been wandering around looking things over, and I've found some places to shop. I'll surprise you tomorrow."

When we awake after an incredibly good night's sleep, interrupted only by the crow of a rooster at four a.m., Cory is gone with the *Tinker*. Dorin makes some coffee, and as we settle in the cockpit, we see Cory sailing the dinghy toward us.

Cory stands up and ties the dinghy to the base of a stanchion, hands me a box, and then swings up on the boat.

"I grabbed some money," he says. "Wait 'til you see this."

We open the white box, and nestled inside are six fabulous, fragrant pastries. "I saw this place last night. It's a bakery. They have fresh bread, cakes, pastries...."

"That settles it," I say. "We're moving to Puerto Real when we retire."

"I'm in, too," says Cory.

There are a variety of cream-filled, chocolate-covered, lemon-rich flaky pastries, and we take our time choosing which we want.

"Go ahead, Cor," I say. "You brought them home, so you choose first."

"Are you kidding? I picked them out. I'll love them all."

"And there's always tomorrow," Dorin says. We pile into the pastries, and Dorin makes more coffee. "I actually and *finally* feel like I'm on vacation!" he says.

"There's also a mom and pop store down on the corner, in case you need groceries."

"When you check things out, you really check 'em out," I say.

"So, we going to stay here awhile?" Cory asks.

Dorin and I glance at each other. "We like it, too," I say. "It's just exotic enough to feel like we are in the tropics, but the living is easy because there is enough stuff that is familiar. The best of both worlds."

"We have to head back to Samaná, but we'll come back here and stay for a bit. At least until we get the boat hauled and in shape."

Cory nods, satisfied.

Later, we sail ashore in the dinghy and explore the little town, discovering, close by *Brisas del Mar*, a small yellow building next to the bay. The sign says: *Efectos de pesca, Ferretería*. Below it says *Se vende Hielo*. "Fishing effects and hardware," Cory translates. "And they sell ice!"

"We gotta check this out," Dorin says as he opens the door.

He is delighted. "What a find! A hardware store for boats. This will be a great resource when we haul the boat, and it's so close to the *Villa Pesquera!*"

Across the street, we stop in at the mom and pop store, which has a little bit of everything. We buy jars of mango and guava jelly. Dorin and Cory grab a Coke, and I try a soft drink called Malta Goya.

The friendly proprietor opens our bottles for us. I tentatively sip the Malta Goya. "Okay, my new favorite beverage," I say.

"Yeah, and it makes you look tough," Cory says. "Like you're drinking beer out of a bottle."

"Good if you have sick stomach," the woman proprietor says. She rubs her stomach. "We give to babies who are sick."

After a couple of days lying around, reading, doing a few boat upkeep chores and walking around town, Dorin says it's time to head for *Samaná* so we can be back here in time to be hauled.

As we are busy taking on water and fuel, the two little girls suddenly appear on the dock with their bicycles. "Hello, Cory!" they say.

"Hi," he says, but he is preoccupied with his tasks. We pay for the gas and water, and Dorin tells Cory he should take the helm to motor out of the bay.

As we pull away from the dock, the girls yell in unison, "Cory, we love you!"

Dorin and I laugh, but Cory just rolls his eyes and shakes his head. We leave the harbor the same way we came in, and then we are headed back to the D.R., all of us looking forward to spending a little more time there.

Though the trip is mostly uneventful, weather wise, during the thirty hours that give us comfortable and steady fifteen-knot winds, the radar stops working. The speed knot log dies, the bilge pump works sporadically, and the VHF that tends to be temperamental, stops altogether. Most worrisome is the prop shaft, which bangs so much we can't run the motor.

"Good thing we are going to be hauling the boat," Dorin says.

This is a reminder we have to cross Mona Passage once again, which gives me a few butterflies. How many times will we defy Mona and remain unscathed?

When land comes into sight, it's the easternmost part of the Dominican Republic, which we now know, from Bob's chart, is Cape Engaño. We follow the coastline just as we did when we first approached the D.R., enjoying the familiar beach, the palm trees and jungle foliage, until we know we are at the wide opening of the *Bahia de Samaná,* or Samaná Bay. Near the entrance, the wind shifts enough we can let out the boom and sail in on a close reach.

Because of Bob's chart, we now understand the land mass to our starboard is a peninsula that extends far into the Atlantic Ocean from the north coast of the D.R. called, appropriately, Samaná Peninsula. We are also clear that the anchorage we thought of as the end of the bay is only a tiny tuck along the inner side of the peninsula.

"Hey, can I take the helm?" Cory asks. "I haven't had much—or any—practice with a reach."

"Help yourself, Cor!" Dorin steps aside and joins me, perched on the rail of the stern pulpit, holding onto the back stay.

"*Punta Balandra,*" Dorin indicates with a nod at the stone-faced cliff that rises out of the water. Along the top of the point, the palm trees stand silhouetted against the brilliant blue sky.

I laugh. "I'm kind of in awe about how much we didn't know."

Cory turns from the helm. "Remember when I thought it was ridiculous that that guy offered to lead us in? Now that we know, it seems like it was a good idea."

We keep the familiar Levantado Island to our port and head on in toward Sta. Bárbara, Samaná, enjoying the view of the beaches and jungle foliage on our starboard.

Then the familiar Island Connection bridge appears, and I am deliriously happy because it feels like we are coming home.

Wait! Wasn't I just in love with Puerto Rico?

Dorin notices my mood. He shakes his head and chuckles, "Fickle, Shirl. You're a fickle-hearted woman."

Chapter Fifteen
Trouble in Paradise

The *Fandango* sails smoothly into the harbor toward the cluster of cruising yachts ahead.

"I'm done," Cory says, and turns the tiller over to Dorin.

"So we're going to do the old anchoring under sail trick, huh?" I ask.

"Our choices are limited."

"To?"

"Anchoring under sail," Dorin says and grins.

My face must give me away because he chuckles and says, "I thought you liked a little tension when entering a harbor. That's why I always do this. Sometimes it's hard to pull off. I have to come up with some manufactured crisis to satisfy your insatiable need for excitement."

I laugh, but I'm a little tense nevertheless.

"Look," he says, "we've done this dozens of times. Have a little faith. Have a little fun."

He is right. One time, we even picked up a mooring in a crowded harbor at two in the morning without a working motor. It was a one-shot deal but involved Dorin's sprinting from the cockpit to the bow, grabbing the boat hook from my hands, and sprinting back to catch the mooring ball as it slipped by the stern. Needless to say, I had missed picking up the mooring ball. His comment as we came to a stop was, "See, that wasn't so bad."

And it wasn't. I have to admit we always experience exhilaration upon success in a crisis that has the adrenaline pumping for an hour.

Today we know that there may be more boats anchored here than when we left. Without the motor, we don't have the luxury of making a few passes while we figure out the best place to attach ourselves to the bottom of the bay.

We keep the mainsail up to have enough speed so we don't stop dead while we still need maneuvering room. The jib is also pulling, and we chug right along. I know Dorin is concerned about too much speed because the anchor won't set if we aren't at near a dead stop.

I am standing on the house beside the mast, and Cory is on the bow ready to release the anchor. Dorin scans the harbor, which does have half a dozen more boats in it than when we left.

"Okay, guys. This will be a little dicey," he yells. "I'm aiming for that spot over there beyond the ketch and the yawl. Shirl, lower the main now. The jib should pull enough to keep us moving."

I uncleat the halyard and the main slowly comes down. Our speed diminishes, but momentum and the wind in the jib keep us moving.

"Good! When I tell you, lower the jib, Shirl. Cor, get the anchor ready. I'm going to turn to port the last minute to slow us down. As soon as we are three-quarters around, drop the anchor."

As usual, when we are doing you-gotta-get-it-right-the-first-time maneuvers, my heart is pounding. I begin to unwind the jib halyard so there are only two turns around the winch, making it quick to drop the jib.

"Now, Shirl!" I unwind and the halyard plays out a little, but the wind keeps the jib, attached to the forestay, up and filled. Cory, crouched in the bow, reaches up and pulls it down the stay, hand over hand. We slow down, but I'm not sure if it's enough. The wind on the boat keeps us moving. But we are nearly out of room. There is shallow water and mud flats not far away.

"Get ready, Cor." Dorin turns the tiller hard to starboard, and the *Fandango* turns to port and slips sideways but comes nearly to a stop.

"Now!" he yells, but Cory has simultaneously released the anchor, and with the chain rattling out of the hawse pipe, it's well on the way to the muddy bottom.

We wait, not speaking, to see what will happen. The boat is still. But is the anchor holding? Then slowly the boat begins to swing an arc on the anchor line, and we know it's secure.

Cory laughs and pumps his fist.

"Whew! Way to go, Zohner!" I say. "Ya done good. Again!"

He hitches up his pants and shrugs his shoulders. "Aw, it ain't nothing, Ma'am." But he grins from ear to ear.

"Okay, Cor, take care of the flag thing, will you?" he says. "Quarantine flag first. I'll have to row in to find Customs and Immigration and ask them to come out, since we can't back into the dock."

While he's gone, we neaten up the cockpit, tossing stuff into the sail lockers, and then declutter the main cabin.

An hour later, Dorin rows back, followed by a fiberglass dinghy with four crisply uniformed customs' officials in it. None are the original guys who checked us in the first time. These guys seem kind of put out, and rightfully so. They usually step from the dock to the deck; now they've had to row to the yacht and climb aboard. All four men pull themselves up and over the lifelines and step into the cockpit. I figure four of them came out because two would be at risk climbing aboard an unknown yacht. Two of the officers stay outside, and the other two come below.

I have the documents out, and they make quick work of copying information and, like their predecessors, do not want to search the boat. They are back in their boat and heading to the dock in ten minutes. In the pocket of the head guy are eighty pesos, quadruple the rate because of the inconvenience of four of them coming out to us.

"Gotta show our appreciation," says Dorin. "They really had to go out of their way."

Cory and I roll the sagging mainsail into itself and fasten it around the boom with sail ties. We tuck the whole thing into the sail cover and fasten it with the ties that are attached to the cover. Then we put up the awning we are so fond of. We learned from the last time we were here that the awning is the most stable and taut when we use the boom, raised up a little with the topping lift, as a "tent ridgepole."

Dorin has been rummaging in the port sail locker.

"Cor, I want to try a smaller jib. Why don't you start taking that one off?"

Cory lifts the billowing sail out of his way so he can kneel at the stay, but it still envelops him to the waist. He pulls back the spring-loaded fastener and slips it off the stay. Then he feels along the edge of the sail, pushing yards of sail cloth out of the way, to find the next one. He has six undone when Dorin calls to him.

"Never mind, Cor. This sail isn't in as good a condition as I remembered. We'll keep that one. What do you say we head for shore? You guys must be hungry."

Cory stands up to shake out the sail, so he can start re-attaching it.

"Never mind that now. Just hank it on any old way, temporarily, to keep it from blowing off the boat." In a minute, the sail is secure enough that we can leave for lunch.

We climb the hill to our favorite restaurant, figuring they probably think, since we've been gone for ten days, we aren't coming back.

We barely get seated when two waiters sashay out of the kitchen, each smiling broadly, each carrying a tall *leche batida*. They saw us coming. We laugh as they set the glasses down in front of Cory. They are also laughing, enjoying their joke of anticipating Cory's ordering two milkshakes.

There is the ever-present salsa music playing, and one of the waiters says, *"Anoche, bailamos."* And he dances with his hand on his belly, gracefully demonstrating the typical hip movement.

"Fiesta?" asks Cory.

"Sí, era el cumpleaños de mi madre."

"They danced at his mother's birthday," Cory translates. "Last night."

Smiling, the waiters nod in approval and applaud. *"Sí, tú hablas español. Bueno."*

Then I realize they understand some English.

We order and enjoy the meal because it's the best we've had since we left here.

"How'd you guys like to go on a motorcycle tour of the area?" Dorin asks.

"Yeah," Cory responds. "Like rent a motorcycle?"

"Sure. The rental place has a guide who will take us around."

"Okay, when?" Cory pushes his empty plate aside.

"How about we see if we can do it after lunch?"

Cory raises his hand for the check. "I'm ready."

"I can ride with you, right?" I ask Dorin. I have no interest in learning to solo on a motorcycle today.

Dorin owns a 1972 Yamaha motorcycle that he enjoys during the summer, and I have ridden behind him. My opportunities were limited though because I usually had a job during the summer. However, he did take his bike to the coast one time. I had Bill leave me off at the Belfast boatyard with the idea that, after a day sail, Dorin and I would use the bike to get back to Waterville. It was one of those times when we had motor problems on the *Fandango* and didn't get back to the dock until well after dark. By then it was raining and fog had settled in. We put on our helmets. I tucked in behind him and wrapped my arms around his waist. It's a long, narrow and winding road from Belfast. I couldn't see anything partly because of the fog and rain and partly because the visor of my helmet kept fogging over from my breath. I was aware that Dorin kept running his hand over the face of his mask to wipe off the rain. Several prayers and an hour and a half later, we pulled into Bill's driveway where my car was parked. When we went inside to get my keys, Bill propelled me to a full-length mirror and turned me around. There was a broad streak of mud from my butt to my neck.

"Yeah, I've been meaning to get new mud flaps," Dorin said.

Now, years later, Dorin, reading my mind, grins at me from across the table. "This might not be that much fun for you. I don't think there's any mud here."

I laugh and nod but voice my real concern. "I'm worried about the fact that Cory doesn't know how to ride a motorcycle."

"Sure I do," he says. "I've been riding friends' motorbikes."

"*So* not the same," I say.

"We'll talk him through it," Dorin replies.

I sit looking at them thinking, "*Okay, this is the difference between boys and girls. Guys just jump into any activity and learn by doing. Most girls want instructions and a lot of practice before soloing.*"

"Let's get going." Cory pushes back from the table while Dorin pays the bill.

Ten minutes later, Dorin has made arrangements for two motorcycles. He does the briefest of introductions: here's the gas, here's the clutch, here's the brake.

We strap on helmets, but I am still not okay with this. The owner of the tour business spends a minute giving Cory instructions, and the bike roars to life. Suddenly, without warning, Cory guns the motorcycle, and it goes up on the rear wheel. While I watch in horror, he goes the length of the long street holding a perfect wheelie and then touches down the front wheel precisely, without a wobble. A gaggle of local kids cheer and wildly hoot their approval. At the end of the street, Cory does a slow turn and comes back to us.

"All set?" he asks, grinning broadly.

"Did you do that on purpose?" I demand.

"Ah, yeah," he says. "Sure. We'll go with that." He pats my helmet.

I climb on the bike. Dorin slides in front of me and starts the motor. The guide leads us out of town and along the coast. The view is spectacular. There is a small belt of palm trees and other tropical foliage between the road and the ocean. Flowers in red, orange, and purple grow wild. We have been told that Americans, Canadians, and Europeans are buying up beach front property at extremely low prices and planning on retiring here.

I sure can see the attraction. It would be easy to move in this direction, and I spend some time thinking about how life would be. We could build a place big enough for a guest room or two, so family could visit. But we have also heard that sometimes, maybe even often, the real estate deal isn't legal. People sell property that doesn't belong to them. We have also heard there is a squatters' law that allows local people to move into any unoccupied home and claim it, so you can never leave the D.R. unless you hire someone to move in and represent you.

The winding road has small houses here and there, each with a second, three-walled, cement block building that appears to be just for cooking with wood heat. It seems like a practical arrangement, keeping heat and smoke out of the living area.

The road widens to a broader macadam, where peanuts dry roast on the shoulders for miles. That might be where the kids get the peanuts that they sell in rolled up paper cones. Or maybe they have their own place to roast them.

It turns out to be a lovely, two-hour, afternoon tour. What a perfect day! Back in town, we down three Coca-Colas from the market, buy a couple of coconuts from a street vendor, and then head back to the boat in a state of extreme wellbeing. Life is so good.

Late in the afternoon, Cory and I are lounging under the awning, reading, when Dorin bolts up the stairs letting out a string of swear words that is uncustomary of him, unless it's a crisis.

"We're dragging anchor! Backwards!"

"Are you sure?" I look around, but everything seems the same, though it's hard to tell, since we swing on the anchor with the tide. Though the tide is only a foot or two at most, we are not in the same place, relative to other boats, as we were even a few hours ago.

"Yes, I'm sure! Cor, let's pull it up and drop it again and see if we can reset it." Dorin yanks on the chain, and it comes up too easily. Obviously, it was no longer buried in the mud. He hauls it hand over hand while Cory lays out the chain on the foredeck so it won't get tangled. When the muddy anchor is up to the bowsprit, Dorin throws it out, away from the boat, and down it goes with the chain clattering across the bow sprit, rapidly playing out.

Dorin visually lines our boat up with others and landmarks.

"Still dragging. And there are boats behind us now."

I notice what I hadn't before: a couple of boats have swung on their anchor lines, so they are more or less in the direction we are dragging. Even if we miss the boats, we'll be aground in the mud flats.

"We'll have to get the sails up and sail it forward. Hurry! We only have a few minutes."

When the awning is up and draped over the boom, the mainsail can't be raised. Cory pulls out his rigging knife, I grab a kitchen cleaver, and we slice all the lines holding the awning. While I pull it together and toss it below, Dorin yells, "Never mind the main now. Cory, raise the jib!" Cory jumps up to the mast and unwinds the halyard. I run toward the bow to see if I can help.

Dorin is at the tiller trying to steer between the boats. We pass them going backwards; at the mast, Cory winches up the jib halyard as fast as he can. When it's halfway up, I can see it's snapped onto the stay all wrong. Cory can also see; in alarm we glance at each other, remembering how he randomly snapped on the bottom of the jib earlier in the day.

Knowing it has to be fixed, Cory releases the halyard, and, on the foredeck, I start pulling the sail down the stay.

"Haul up the jib!" Dorin yells from the cockpit, because he hasn't seen the problem.

"I have to fix the jib. It's all screwed up!"

"We don't have time to fix it. Just get it up!" Dorin, who never yelled once in the stormy Atlantic, is screaming now.

So, Cory rapidly winches it up, and I can tell he's annoyed. When the head of the sail gets halfway to the top, the problem is clear. The jib is bunched together, overlapping itself, and while it's snapping in the wind, it cannot fill. The bottom of the sail doesn't come even close to the bottom of the stay.

Our speed moving backwards seems to be increasing. I know we need some forward power immediately, so I jump on the house and move toward the boom so I can undo the sail cover. "I'll put up the main," I yell. The wind is now screaming, and the jib is flapping and cracking against itself.

"No, we don't have time to put up the main. Take the helm. We've got to get the jib fixed." He runs forward, I jump into the cockpit, and he meets Cory at the forestay, where they pull the sail to the deck and undo and redo the fasteners.

The loosened halyard, no longer cleated off at the mast, is now blowing in the wind from the top of the mast. Dorin sees the line blowing wildly out away from the boat and grabs the boat hook. He reaches out and manages after several attempts to wind the flailing halyard around the pole and pull it in. With the halyard in his hand, he jumps to the top of the house and, winding it around the winch, cranks up the jib with the winch handle. He cleats the halyard off and runs along the starboard side deck to the cockpit so he can steer. He cranks the jib sheet tight and the sail fills.

"It's not going to work on the other tack!" Cory yells. "The port sheet is not attached!"

I see what he means. The only line attached to the clew of the jib is the starboard sheet. I check the port side deck and there it is, lying impotently idle. I grab the forward end and run to the bow.

I hand the sheet to Cory, but he can't reach the clew point of the sail because it's outboard now and under pressure.

"Let the jib go!" I yell to Dorin. He immediately unwinds it from the winch in the cockpit, and I grab at the clew, but the sail is now flapping in the wind and flogs me about the face and head. Cory is holding the end of the sheet between his teeth. He leaps and grabs the corner of the sail with both hands, pulls it in, and we wrestle it into submission enough so he can attach it with a bowline knot faster than I have ever seen him do it. It doesn't look right to me, but what do I know. I still can't tie a bowline without a tutor standing by.

Dorin yells, "Hurry! We don't have any time left."

"Tighten the jib!" I yell back.

I hear the whir of the winch, the starboard sheet tightens, and the jib pulls on the starboard side. We are finally moving forward.

Whew, crisis avoided, I think. Now we can go on the other tack.

Dorin yells, "Goddamnittohell! I won't be able to control the jib on the other tack. The port sheet isn't threaded through the side block."

I run to the cockpit, and he hands me his end of the sheet, the other end of which Cory has just fastened to the jib. Back at the port mid-deck, I thread it through the block.

Dorin screams, "No, the *other* block. No, first, *over* the lifeline. No, *behind* the shroud. No, it goes *over* the lifeline, *behind* the shroud, *under* the lifeline and into the block…yes, that's right…no! This block back here!" I run the end of the sheet back to him. He winds the sheet around the winch and pushes the tiller across. The jib comes over to the other side and Dorin winches it in. The bowline knot, hastily tied, lets go. The jib fails, flapping around, not pulling at all.

"Ke-rist!" Dorin yells.

Cory sprints to the useless jib, picks up the line, and as he pulls on it, Dorin releases the tension. Cory rapidly re-ties it to the clew with a bowline knot, taking an extra second to be sure he's got it right. He swings his arm over his head to let Dorin know he can winch in the jib.

I sense imminent crisis and look up. We are headed at a boat, and if we are lucky, an impact will be a sideswipe, a glancing blow, but possibly damaging. Cory leaps on the house and down to the deck, landing at midships on the starboard side to fend us off. I follow him. The owners of the yacht, looking alarmed, are at mid-ships also and ready to push us off, if necessary.

The only way to avoid this collision is for Dorin to tack immediately. With only one wrap around the winch, he pulls on the sheet hand over hand as fast as he can. We swing around on the other tack in the knick of time.

"Sorry!" he yells to the boaters, who wave cheerfully at us as if this were an ordinary occurrence. The guy pantomimes wiping sweat from his forehead and shakes it off his hand. "Whew!" he yells, but he is smiling.

Now we are headed toward another boat and it's clear, since the wind is coming right at us, we will have to tack back and forth to keep moving and wind a path between boats.

"Put up the main," Dorin yells. Together, Cory and I untie the cover and yank it off. He starts untying the ropes that bundle the mainsail while I dash to the mast, ready to winch up the sail. The main sheet is already wound around the winch and cleated off. I uncleat it, but when I reach for the winch handle, it isn't in the holder. I'm astounded. I unwind the sheet from the winch and try to pull the main up by hand, but it moves sluggishly only about four feet. I'm just not strong enough. Suddenly, Cory is there and grabs the sheet above my hands and pulls as hard as he can, hand over hand until the top of the main is as high as it will go. He wraps the end around the winch a couple of times and cleats it off.

With the extra sail power, after about ten minutes of zig zagging, we are clear of the anchored boats in the harbor.

Dorin keeps going though, and we are silent for a while, waiting for him to process the experience with us. I can tell he is still upset.

"Sorry about not knowing how the sheet comes back to the cockpit," I say. "I didn't really ever notice. It was just there."

"My fault," Dorin says. "I should have taught you...had you thread it through a few times. Sorry about that. And I should have remembered the jib was not fastened correctly. I'm disgusted with myself."

"Oh, man, you can't take all this on yourself," I say.

"Can if I want to," he says.

"We might have lost the winch handle at the mast," I say. "It isn't in the holder. Who was the last one to use it?"

"Ah, that would be me." Dorin shakes his head in disgust. "I think I put it in the air scoop, like we used to before we put a holder on the mast."

Cory strolls forward and pulls the winch handle out of the air scoop and returns it to the winch holder. Dorin winces and nods.

After a while he chuckles. "That was the most embarrassing sailing experience I've ever had. Bar none. It must have looked like a cross between the Keystone Cops and the Three Stooges. If we weren't waiting for parts and the mail, I'd just keep going and head back to Puerto Rico. But..." he says, nodding toward Cory, who is on the deck mid-ships, leaning against the shrouds, "I'm ready to challenge the champ in a bowline tying contest."

Cory looks embarrassed. "I don't know what happened."

"I can tell you what happened. All hell was breaking loose. We tend to drop out details when we are under high stress." Then he talks about one of his favorite psychological principles, the Yerkes-Dodson law about performance under stress, a topic he lectures about in Psych I. Cory comes back to the cockpit to listen; we are all soothed and feel much better.

"Well, I guess we had better return to the scene of the crime," he says. "You know what the worst part is? They will be gossiping among themselves on VHF or ham radio about this."

"But at least it will give them something to say," I reply, referring to Dorin's dislike of the non-conversation chatter. When he first got his ham license, he said all transmissions were about "how high is your tower? How strong is my signal?"

"Professional opinion. Does this reflect the feelings of masculine insecurity of these operators?" I had asked.

He laughed. "This is not my professional opinion, and you are not to share this, but...could be. And that's why I don't indulge. I'm very secure."

We turn around and the wind gives us a nice broad reach on the way back. We anchor without a problem, far from other boats.

"It'll mean a longer trip to shore," Dorin says, "but I'm not taking that chance again."

Through the rest of the day and during the night, Dorin checks the anchor every hour.

The next day, the guys pull the motor and check the cutlass bearing and the prop shaft, and both seem okay. Dorin puts in a new shear pin, and they put it back together.

"We're not out of the woods yet with that shaft," Dorin says. "There's something wrong I can't see."

Because we are so far out, Cory has stepped the *Tinker* mast again, and we sail into the dock in the afternoon. "Let's get this over with," Dorin says. I can tell he's dreading it.

We get to the outdoor bar where, it seems, every one of the harbor's sailing residents is there, including a few new couples we have not met. I recognize the people whose boat we almost banged into. Cory does the first cowardly thing I've seen him do to date: he decides to go for a walk.

"I see you went for an afternoon sail, yesterday," says Jim, drily.

"Was that a tacking drill for your crew?" asks Jake.

"If you wanted to go for a sail," asks Janice, "why didn't you just start your motor?"

"Good job of fending off," says the almost-victim with a grin.

Dorin shifts in his chair in preparation for speaking, but before he can answer, Sebastian says, "That was the finest bit of seamanship I have ever seen."

I snort my reaction and fail to stifle a guffaw.

"It was also the finest stream of colorful language I have ever heard coming from Dorin's mouth," I say.

Everyone laughs. Under the table, Dorin gently squeezes my hand and gives me a quick sideways glance of gratitude.

"I have to manufacture a crisis every once in a while, just to keep the crew on their toes," he says.

"I take it you still can't run your motor?" asks Sebastian. "Bent shaft?"

"Most likely," Dorin says. "I pulled it yesterday and can't see anything. But that's probably the problem. Might have bent it in Bermuda."

"Good thing you got 'er going before you got to the mud flats. I don't know if we could have winched you out," says Jim. "We might have given it a try though."

"Well, that'd be a good way to put down some roots here," I say. "We'd have a permanent home with an ocean view."

"And no mortgage," says Helen.

The subject finally changes to who is going to be moving on to their next port of call and when.

They tell us Chuck and Dottie left for Puerto Rico a day after we did. They ask if we saw them there. We say we didn't, and there is real concern.

"I hope they didn't get into trouble," says Jim. "It can get really rough out there."

"I've been trying to raise them by VHF, but after the first few hours, they didn't respond anymore," says Mac, the person most likely to keep in contact and chat on the VHF. I wonder silently if Chuck and Dottie might feel the same way as Dorin and just turned off their VHF.

"There was no weather while we were gone," Dorin lies. "I'm sure they're fine. We went back and forth between ports, and we could easily have missed them."

Those who have not been to Puerto Rico ask us about the country and details about Mona Passage, and so the afternoon passes pleasantly while we tell stories and pass on tips. Dorin downsizes the four waterspouts to one, and the wind becomes "increased for a few minutes."

I check the post office every day. There are a few letters but no package. We are coming to the conclusion the part for the autohelm will not be arriving. I also go to the market by *motoconcho* a couple of times a week, mostly for fun. We don't need much because we are still eating out. Every couple of days, we try one of the restaurants that other cruisers are enjoying. We dine on excellent cuisine: Chinese, Austrian, and French, as well as *"típico,"* which is traditional food for the area and our favorite.

Now that we are anchored so far from the dock, Dorin says we can snorkel right from the *Fandango*. Cory is enthusiastic and is the first one in the water, choosing to go backwards off the stern of the boat. There is a big splash when he goes under. Then he surfaces and says the mask fits fine. Immediately, he is on his stomach with his face in the water, and he swims out from the boat.

He is quickly back and hangs onto the dinghy. Taking the snorkel out of his mouth, he says, "This is great. You can see everything! There's a huge fish swimming along the bottom. There's seaweed and other great stuff. Awesome!" And then he is off, swimming away from the boat.

Dorin looks at me but doesn't say anything.

"Yeah, okay, I might as well try the mask on." I am not enthusiastic. How is this little cheapo kids' mask going to work for me? Nevertheless, I change into my swimming shorts but stay in my halter top, deciding not to bother with a t-shirt because I'm not going to be out there long. I slip into the dinghy so I can enter the water in a gentler way. On my own, I settle the mask on my face and put the snorkel in my mouth. With a fatalistic point of view, I think *'I might as well get this over with,'* and go backwards off the rubber tube.

The cool, refreshing water envelops me, and I realize the mask is not leaking. Seriously? I lie face down and look into the depth of the bay. Still not leaking and, wow, a whole new world is there in front of me. How had I missed this? It's incredible.

I realize I'm holding my breath. I slowly breathe through the snorkel, and it's fine. I take a few big breaths and then swim away, taking in the world of sea life below us. It's incredibly interesting because the contours of the bottom and vegetation change as I move along. I'm a little nervous regarding the long, thin, serpentine fish that must be four feet in length. It creeps me out, but it stays below and doesn't seem to know I am there. I continue to be entranced and grateful for this opportunity. Then I feel a tap on my arm and turn to see Cory's masked face inches from mine. He points upward so I lift my face out of the water, pull off the mask, and tread water. Cory also goes upright and only removes his snorkel from his mouth.

"Dorin says you have to come back now. You will be getting sunburned." I turn to look behind me and see that the *Fandango* is small and distant. Yikes! Have I swum that far?

"You've been snorkeling for twenty minutes."

"I love this," I say. "I could do this every day!"

"Me too," Cory says. "Well, better get going. You don't want another burn." I swim back to the boat with my face in the water, wishing I had discovered this activity a long time ago.

When I tell Dorin this, he seems really pleased. "If Bob is right and the water in Boquerón Bay clears up, we can snorkel there. But wait until we get to Venezuela. It's supposed to be exceptionally good there."

Later in the week, I go to the market. The *motoconcho* leaves me off, and I spend some time looking at the paintings of a local artist. One, depicting dozens of dark-skinned women with their heads bowed, holding laundry baskets, is powerful, and I buy it. I had promised myself I would not leave this country without a piece of art.

I turn to head back toward my favorite vendor when the mellow sounds of the busy market are interrupted by the roar of motorcycles. Everyone freezes, and a gang of six rolls into the market. The guys are dressed in leather jackets, even in this heat. Two guys set their stands and swing off their bikes. They are clearly threatening, and I can feel the fear of the vendors, who keep their eyes downcast. Shoppers seem to have evaporated into thin air. The thugs swagger through the market, and silently vendors hand them money. I am not nervous for myself. These guys are not interested in tourists, and they seem not to even notice me. They have the local vendors they can shake down.

They make the rounds in a couple of minutes and head back to their bikes. Then the leader spots my favorite vendor, who has not yet paid.

"No!" she says and pulls her apron, which has her cash in it, closer to her. The thug, with his hands in fists, leans aggressively over her and says something in rapid Spanish.

"No!" she says again. Her voice, trembling with fear, is still defiant. Now I'm scared of what will happen next. Will the thug back down in front of all the other victims? In front of his cohorts? I don't think he can, but then he says something with a sneer, and his buddies laugh. He swaggers back to his motorcycle. In half a minute they are gone.

I am breathless with relief, but I am also afraid for our market lady. What will happen the next time these protection racketeers come into town? I head for the lady, and she sees me. Tears are running down her cheeks, and she is embarrassed.

"They no good!" she says to me. "Very bad men. Not from here. From over there," she says waving her hand in a vague direction. She touches the corner of her apron to her eyes and then notices the painting I have tucked under my arm.

"You like?" she asks me.

"Yes, I love it. I will take it back home and hang it up."

"Good artist," she says. "My...how do you say?...my nephew." She smiles shyly but with pride.

"Yes, he is," I say. I buy a few things from her and head back to the boat, still upset and saddened by this revelation of brutish crime in this country that I have been thinking of as paradise. As usual, a *motoconcho* quickly comes by to give me a ride to the docks. I can't wait to get back to tell the guys.

The next day, I sail the *Tinker* into the dock so I can leave off our laundry. I tie up the dinghy and walk down the dock with my basket. I notice a new boat, the *Lone Star*, has backed up to the dock and is, I assume, waiting for Customs and Immigration. A very large, muscular black man I have never seen before is on the dock talking to the captain, who is standing in his cockpit. The Dominican guy is telling him the exchange rate, which is inflated threefold. As I pass behind the Dominican man, I catch the eye of the captain. I barely shake my head no and keep on walking. I hear the captain say, "No, I think I'll wait and go to the bank."

The next day, the captain, whose name is George, and his lady companion, Sue, meet the gang for drinks. He relates the story to our boating friends and thanks me for the tip. He says he's tired of getting ripped off by the cheating, lying locals wherever he goes.

There is silence. The boating community is clearly uncomfortable at this remark, but none of us says anything.

Two days later, I sail in again to pick up our laundry. As I walk along the dock, the big guy appears as if out of nowhere and grabs my upper arm in a vise-grip squeeze. He pulls me up toward him and bends to speak into my ear as he propels me forward.

"If you ever mess with my business on the dock, nobody will ever see you again. Understand?"

I say "yes" and he squeezes harder. "You better believe me. And don't tell your men. They will disappear, too. I will do this." Then he releases me with a shove and walks rapidly away. My heart pounds, and I am weak with fear. I look around for support or sympathy, but there is no one in sight. The dock and the surrounding area are clear of local people.

I had expected to see the laundry lady's husband, but he is not there. In a few minutes, I sail back to the boat, still shaken to my core. As I scramble up onto the *Fandango*, I notice my upper arm is bruised in several places from his finger marks.

My voice shakes when I show the guys my arm and tell them the story.

"It's not like we can go to the local police," Dorin says. "Sounds like it's time to move on."

But it galls me to think of that guy watching our boat go zipping out of the harbor as if we were scared and running.

"No, let's wait a few days. I will not go to the dock alone from now on, you better believe that. And I won't even think of giving any more tips. Just going to mind my business."

"Okay, but one of us will go everywhere with you."

"Both of us," Cory says.

There are other gut punches to my psyche as the next few days go by.

When we meet for drinks, George and Sue are always there. George freely voices his negative opinion of the country and the local people. While we are being waited on by local people, he bad-mouths the intelligence of the general population, and we all freeze.

"And the kids! They send their kids out to work while they lie around. Too lazy to work."

Watching the waiters, I am sure they understand most of what he is saying.

"It's commendable that the kids work hard and add to the family income," Dorin says. "I worked on my family's farm from the age of seven."

"What makes you think the parents aren't also working?" I ask.

"'Cause they're colored. Case you didn't notice," he says with sarcasm.

I am dizzy with anger. Feeling like the air has been forced out my lungs, I push back my chair as Dorin also gets up to leave.

As we walk away, he says, "There's always one or two of 'em, liberal bleeding hearts, in every crowd."

We decide to wait only four more days for the part to arrive, but we also decide to spend most of our time on the boat. We read and snorkel, and Cory drills us on Spanish. Cory and Dorin are back to their timed bowline-tying competition.

On day three, George knocks on our hull. We don't invite him on board, but he is only there to ask us if we saw anyone steal his dinghy motor. We haven't, but from our anchorage, we can hardly see his boat. He tells us it was stolen off his dinghy in the middle of the night.

"I'm going to find it," he says. "No lazy ass native is going to take my motor."

Later that afternoon, Jim rows out to our boat to tell us that George has been going from yard to yard in town, looking for his motor.

"And he finds it, he thinks. But he's been arrested!"

We are confused. "What did he do to get arrested?" I ask, thinking he must have punched someone.

"When he found the motor—it was just lying out in the open in front of someone's house—George said it was his and started calling the homeowner names. He said he would have the guy arrested. Then the police showed up. The homeowner said George was falsely accusing him of a crime...said the motor was his. Then the police arrested George for making false accusations."

I experience a moment of sweet satisfaction. "So what happens now?"

"They are going to have a trial tomorrow. He has to stay in jail. Sue has to take food to him. They don't feed people in jail. Family has to bring them food."

I feel sorry for Sue who has always seemed embarrassed by George.

"Remember that guy Eduardo who's a lawyer and comes by for drinks sometimes?"

I do remember the Dominican gentleman who has stopped by to chat with us a couple of times. He looks Spanish, light skinned and has silver, carefully coiffed hair and is always impeccably dressed in a light-colored suit and tie. His lightly accented English is excellent because he spent six years in the United States in college and getting his law degree.

"Well, we contacted him and asked him to defend George. I don't like George--he's a disgrace to us, but he needs help."

I shrug. I've had enough of bullies, and George is a bully, if only psychologically and verbally.

We decide to miss the drama and stay on the boat. But, instead of leaving, two days later we go ashore for afternoon drinks and to say goodbye to everyone. George is there looking quite the worse for wear—disheveled, grimy and unshaven.

"You can't imagine what it was like after they handcuffed me!" he says. "All of a sudden, there was a mob behind us, and the police were dragging me down the street. The mob was shouting and screaming who knew what! I thought they were going to lynch me. Lynch *me*! Those bastards are the ones should be lynched. So, they throw me in jail and say there will be a trial. Then Eduardo, the lawyer, shows up. Boy, was I glad to see him. He talks to me for a while and asks me questions about the motor. He says he can help me, maybe get my motor back and get me released. I need to tell him how much the boat is worth and how much money I have in cash and in the bank. Well, I lied about how much cash I have, but I figured it couldn't do any harm to tell him about my bank account 'cause there was no way they could get at that! So I tell him $20,000. I can see he is surprised I have that much. I figure he's never seen that much money, being Hispanic and all.

"So I get dragged to court, and, you know, it's like a kangaroo court. Everybody is screaming at me. Eduardo tells me not to worry. He will make a deal with the judge. When he comes back, he says they will let me go, with my boat, if I leave right away and never come back. But the fine is $20,000! That bastard double-crossed me!"

Sebastian stands up from his chair and abruptly turns away, but not before I see he is smiling and trying to stifle a laugh. I also want to laugh and press my mouth closed with my hand. I see similar reactions from other boaters.

"So I gotta go to Puerto Plata. Eduardo will drive me to get my money. Or else they will confiscate my boat." Then he lets loose with a stream of curse words and defamations. "But at least the bastards don't know I have $5000 stashed on the boat."

I surreptitiously glance at the expressionless waiters who appear not to take notice. I'm sure they do. And then a light bulb comes on: this must be how my "mugger" found out it was I who had tipped George about the exchange rate. He had talked about it here.

As we walk to the dock I say, "Sometimes you see justice actually done right here on earth! It's very satisfying."

Dorin nods. "It is. His problem was he didn't keep track of who has the power. This is their country. We all should remember we are guests because they allow us to be. A little gratitude and respect can go a long way."

I nod. "And as far as I can tell, the other cruisers we know here have that attitude. Man, oh man, I am so relieved we won't be seeing him again."

"Don't be so sure of that. He could catch up to us."

"I hope not."

"So, anyway, *now* can we leave?" Dorin asks.

"Okay. But I want to go say goodbye to our market lady." The next day, I buy all three of her dolls. I need these as reminders of this brave woman who befriended us. The dolls are double ended. Two heads, one white and one black, at each end of the body--the skirt hiding the face of whichever doll is down. I press a $20 bill, left over from Puerto Rico, into her hand. It's my present of appreciation for her friendship. She looks up startled, and I close her hand so no one will see how much money she has. I tell her we are leaving, and we hug a goodbye.

I check the post office one last time. By now, the clerk and I are friendly, and he is comfortable enough with me to correct my accent when I attempt Spanish, and he knows we will laugh at my attempts. I tell him goodbye, and I will not be back. He says *"Lo siento, Señora.* Have good trip." These are the first words he has said in English. *"Muchas gracias, Señor,"* I say and find there are tears in my eyes.

It's a sad departure from Samaná Bay, *República Dominicana.*

I feel a loss as we haul anchor, wave goodbye to friends, sail by the Island Connection bridge, past uninhabited Levantado Island, and out of the harbor for the last time.

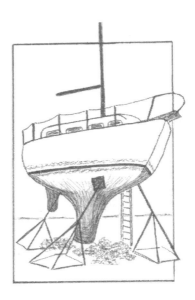

Chapter Sixteen
Getting to the Bottom of Things:
Puerto Real

It's mostly deep overcast, but far out on the horizon, sun shines through weak clouds and turns the ever-changing water to a silvery shimmer. The waves are only three feet high, but the surface, rippled by the wind, looks like hammered metal.

We are barely out into the open ocean, on a heading of eighty to ninety degrees, when the wind diminishes. It's just past noon and a couple of hours underway when we hear on the ham radio there is a weak stationary trough with predicted winds up to twenty knots per hour, southeast.

"Yay! Twenty is good," Dorin says with a grin. "We could be there in twenty-four to thirty-six hours."

Twenty sounds good to me also as it will get us across Mona Passage quickly.

We pass the end of Cape Samaná at 3:20, and suddenly there's enough wind, which has shifted to the west, so that we have to reef the main. At 9:30 p.m. there's a squall. We take down the jib and double reef the main. It blows over in fifteen minutes.

"See?" Dorin says. "I told you squalls only last fifteen minutes." We laugh because, with the one exception in Bermuda, very few "squalls" have lasted "only fifteen minutes."

It's October 17--the 107th day since we left East Boothbay. We have been on the ocean forty-three days and have spent sixty-three days in harbors. In our original plan we would be spending the majority of our time on the water. That seemed like a good-enough plan at the time, but, on reflection, the time we've spent in harbors meeting people, both local and other cruisers, getting a bit of a feel for other cultures, and trying new things, now seems like more the point of the whole trip.

Even as I wax nostalgic, I also think it's been an educational opportunity for Cory that has nothing to do with the books he studies and the samples of marine life he gathers. He has learned about perseverance, problem solving, and how to cope with a little deprivation while maintaining a positive attitude. In fact, now that I think of it, he often is the catalyst for viewing our circumstances with grace and humor.

In our last couple of days at anchor, the guys had fiddled around with some repairs. It was not a big priority since we'd be hauling the boat and overhauling it, so to speak. The depth sounder is working, the VHF has been repaired, and wonder of wonders, the engine is able to run, though we will only use it if we have to because Dorin is worried about the knocking prop shaft. Still not working are the radar and the knot log. We have to conserve kerosene until we can get more in Puerto Rico, but we have enough food that doesn't have to be cooked, so this is not a problem.

The next morning at five a.m. there is barely any wind. We shift and bobble on short, choppy waves that we would cut though if we had more wind.

At 8:30 Cory talks to Janice on the *Kermit D*. They say they are planning to head for Puerto Rico in two weeks. Cory tells them we will see them there.

Off our stern, far into the distance, we can still see the D.R., a thin line on the horizon.

"What the hell," Dorin says. "I'm going to start the motor. Need to charge the batteries anyway." We scoot right along then, about five knots.

At 4:30 he cuts the motor because the prop shaft is making so much noise.

"Maybe it's not bent. Maybe it's the cutlass bearing. Maybe it's gone after all," Dorin says. "We can't run the motor anymore, but at least the batteries are charged. The wind will pick up any time now."

The next day all log entries, in different handwriting, are the same: "Becalmed." At 3 p.m., Cory tries for a little variety. "Becalmed. All day."

Our noon sun sight had told us we were forty miles from Puerto Rico.

By 4 p.m. the wind finally picks up.

After dark we see the glow in the sky that is Puerto Rico, so we can steer in that direction instead of watching the stars. It's much easier on the neck, I think. The guys head for bed. At 10:30 p.m., the wind picks up a little more, not alarmingly so, but enough to really fill the sails. The seas are not high so we slice through the water effortlessly.

Suddenly there's a crack, and I know that sound. I reach up to catch the mainsheet tackle as it goes by, this time not wildly, because the boat is not pitching much. I have it in my grasp and am hanging on when Cory comes bolting into the cockpit.

"You broke it again?" he asks. He leaps on the lazaret locker, grabbing the boom with both arms. Meanwhile, I hang onto the mainsheet tackle with both hands. The boat wallows, but not much, since the waves are low.

Dorin, coming late to the party, says, "What's going on out here? Hey, weren't we supposed to have fixed that? Someone was supposed to fix that."

"Yeah, so, no time like the present," Cory says. "I can hold on another minute or so. Then I'm going back to bed."

"Didn't you buy a cotter pin for this when we were in Mayagüez?" I ask.

"Um, no, the auto parts place didn't have any stainless-steel cotter pins...or I forgot to ask. I'm a little fuzzy on the details of that."

"Let's get our act together, people," Cory says. "And no more safety pin repairs."

"I've got a solution," Dorin says. "I saw it the other day." He goes into the fo'c'sle and rummages around in the repair bin under our mattress.

"Just the thing!" he says as he comes back into the cockpit. "Seizing wire."

"Stainless steel?" Cory asks.

"Well, not exactly. Not really seizing wire either. More like...wire."

There is not much I can do except to climb on the rear deck and sit on the stern pulpit so I can hold the flashlight.

They let some of the sheet through the blocks so there is no tension. Dorin cuts a length of thin wire with his rigging knife, and they thread it back and forth through the hole in the shackle pin to secure the tackle to the traveler.

"There! That should hold it for the night. And stop rolling your eyes, Shirl Jean."

"How do you know I'm rolling my eyes?" I ask.

"I can hear you," he replies as he heads back to bed.

Dorin's notes in the log for the next day:

> By daybreak we could see the island of Puerto Rico. Wind blowing at least 15 to 20 knots. Made hull speed until we were almost in the mouth of the bay at Mayagüez when we were struck by a squall and then immediately becalmed for the next three hours. A very slight breeze (1-2 knots) picked up as it got dark so we ghosted into the harbor and dropped anchor at 0230 hours. Trip uneventful.

I laugh out loud the next day when I read this. I guess that's right. We seem to have become so nonchalant that we are untroubled by wind, too much or too little, squalls, non-functioning equipment, and unreliable safety pins--all part of yacht cruising—at least for us.

Dorin takes care of immigration business in Mayagüez, and the next day we head for Boquerón. Before getting hauled in Puerto Real, we want to check in with Bob and Binnie and tell them our plans. We also hope we see Chuck and Dottie to reassure ourselves they are okay, though Dorin is sure they must be.

"It's not that easy to get in serious trouble," he says.

Cory cocks an eyebrow at me and shakes his head. "Maybe for some people," he mutters, smiling.

By the time we reach the mid-channel marker, the wind is blowing 20 knots.

We skirt the reefs at the mouth of the bay and turn south. Though the wind had been coming from the west, it shifts to the south so we *beat* toward Boquerón. Of course.

The next day we visit with Bob and Binnie on the *Grace*. They tell us they have a water purifier that is supposed to clean seawater and transform it into drinkable water. They haven't been able to use it because they are waiting for a part. I visualize the muddy water of Boquerón Bay in a glass.

I remark that it seems to me that a lot of boats sit for a long time in a harbor waiting for a part for something. They tell us of a cruising couple who wouldn't move out of the harbor because they were waiting for a part for their bow-thruster. None of us can imagine needing a bow thruster on a small yacht. Either you motor away from the dock or, like us, you sail away.

They had seen Chuck and Dottie. The *Seahaven* had been anchored in Boquerón for a week before heading to Mayagüez. They had reported an easy passage from the D.R.

In the morning as we get ready to sail north to Puerto Real, the *Kermit D.* shows up. We row over in the dinghy and chat for a few minutes. Jake says their passage was easy. I don't ask them to define easy, but I quickly realize one benefit they had, as did the *Seahaven*. They motored-sailed the whole way. Janice says they will be leaving soon since they have to be in Ponce in two weeks because their grandchildren are flying in for a month-long visit. We tell them about María's and wish them well on their next leg.

In early afternoon we are in Puerto Real. Dorin rows into the *Villa Pesquera* to make final arrangements with Félix. We talk in the coolness of the bar/café. Félix's office is also here.

Félix is interesting. He's burly and muscular and has what appears to be a perpetual scowl on his broad face. He is commanding--you can feel his "proprietorship," his confidence, that he calls all the shots. He is also respectful and efficient. His English is excellent, and I'd like to ask him where he learned it, but I am a little intimidated by him. I don't think he tends toward idle social chatter.

He tells us we are next in line and can be hauled in two days. Before Dorin gets back, the two little girls have spotted our boat. Outside of the gates of *Villa Pesquera*, from a small dock attached to a house on stilts, they yell, "Cory! We love you!"

"Aarrrrgh!" says Cory. "What am I going to do? I can't ever leave the boat."

"Pretty soon the boat will be on land," I say.

"Okay, so I can never leave the fishermen's co-op."

"Maybe they go to school."

"Yeah, I can hope."

The next day we are excited. Getting hauled is a big event. Cory rows himself and me into the dock at seven a.m., and on the *Fandango* Dorin starts the motor. We hope it will run long enough to maneuver into place. While the travel lift motors on giant wheels toward the water, the *Fandango* does a few tight laps to stay near the shore.

Félix, running the hydraulic travel lift, moves the giant apparatus consisting of steel upright girders joined at the top with steel cross-members, onto the sides of a slip. The giant wheels line up exactly on the little cement "docks." In the middle the water is fairly deep. When the lift is out as far as it can go, Félix motions Dorin in. The *Fandango*, on her best behavior, moves slowly forward into the waiting steel frame. Just as she begins to enter, Dorin reverses the motor for a few seconds to slow the forward movement. She slowly drifts to a stop in exactly the right place. He cuts the motor.

Félix shakes his head, but at the same time looks somewhat impressed. Dorin tries to look nonchalant, like this was an easy maneuver he does every day. Félix had told him the boat could have been moved into place with small "pilot boats" if he didn't get the motor started, but I knew this was a bit of seamanship Dorin wanted to practice in front of a knowledgeable audience.

A couple of men from the yard go into the water to get the sling straps that hang down from the top of the hoist, to take them under the boat and up the other side. When this is done, Félix raises the *Fandango* slowly up out of the water. Water, sparkling in the sunlight, streams off the hull. Then he backs the rig slowly away from the water with the *Fandango* safely cradled in the slings. When he gets our boat where he wants it, the workers adjust five boat stands to keep the boat upright on land and then remove the slings. The Travel-lift moves away, and she stands on "stilts."

We survey the bottom of the boat which has become a crustacean haven, thickly encrusted with living sea life. From the water line to the bottom of the keel, tiny blue mussels and white barnacles cling together, forming a wet, six-inch thick mat decorated with long, grassy-green seaweed.

"I don't know how the prop could even turn," Cory says. And he's right. Even the prop is covered!

"She sure did attract some sea life in three-and-a-half months," Dorin says in awe. "Well, we better get to work."

Dorin's deal with Félix is that *Villa Pesquera* will provide the space and tools, but we will do our own work.

As if to get us into gear, we are handed two long-handled scrapers and a short one that looks like a broad chisel.

I take the chisel and begin scraping the prop, but it's not easy. The smelly stuff is very hard, like brittle cement. I have to wiggle the chisel in between shells and twist. It slips off, my knuckle hits the mass, and a good chunk of skin comes off. I know that barnacles are extremely sharp, but I wasn't paying attention. I wipe the blood on my cutoffs and keep going. Little by little, pieces fall to the ground. It's very satisfying, like peeling sunburned skin. I'm fascinated with clearing the stuff off and seeing metal underneath.

The guys use the long-handled scrapers and have the same difficulty. They lean into it and finally large clumps of crustaceans begin dropping to the ground. By the time I finish the prop, they have one-fourth of the bottom done. Cory hands me his long-handled scraper and goes to get another one for himself. The work is hard but fun. Huge mounds of shelled sea life pile up and begin to die. Water is released and runs down the slope and back into the ocean. Dorin disappears and comes back with a three-foot wide, short-fingered rake to pull the piles away from the boat so we have better footing and safer working space.

By 11 o'clock our t-shirts are soaked with sweat and the bottom of the *Fandango* is fairly clear of growth. But we are not done. The guys who wrapped the slings under the *Fandango* and gave us the tools, now bring us two five-gallon buckets and two flat-blade shovels. We are instructed, by pantomime, to dump our quickly dying bottom guests into the bay a hundred yards away where there is no traffic. Dorin and I shovel while Cory empties the buckets. When we are done, we are handed a pressure washer which cleans off any remaining bits. Dorin chases it all down the ramp and into the bay. At one o'clock we are done.

The two-man yard crew has propped a ladder against the hull. We will be living aboard in the yard until we get dumped back into the water. By now, we are starved, in addition to feeling grimy and smelly. Dorin asks where the showers are. I climb the ladder, something I did a lot of when we were preparing the boat for this trip, to get some soap and towels. We take turns using the two cement block showers, then head out of the yard, and walk the short distance to *Brisas del Mar* for a late lunch.

Dorin's sighs and sits back, satisfied with the martini in front of him, a reward for a hard morning's work.

Cory and I settle for large Coca-Colas. We are feeling good about having done some important work.

"I never expected it to look that bad," I say.

I've helped clean the bottom of the boat before, and it was not remotely like what we just experienced. One time we careened (beached) the boat in

Blue Hill Bay, in Maine, trying to judge the tide so we could clean the bottom by getting off the boat and walking in waist-high water around it while we scraped and brushed. When the tide went out, it was much lower than we had anticipated. The boat was completely over on its side on the beach so that we could walk entirely around it on dry land. We had to sit on a rock and wait for hours for the tide to come back in so the boat would float again. After dark, local people showed up with baskets of food for us. We tried to explain we had done this on purpose, but you could tell they thought it was an accident caused by inexperience.

Now Dorin says, "Yeah, the bottom was much worse than I expected. It does look good now, though. I think it's that super bottom paint concoction we used."

Bottom paint is designed to keep living things from clinging to your boat. Stuff is supposed to just slip right off when it tries to attach. Boat paints used to have properties that were intended to kill marine life that attempted to adopt the bottom of your boat and colonize. But it was eventually acknowledged to be environmentally unsound, and this killer paint can't be bought anymore.

Nevertheless, when we painted the bottom of the *Fandango*, we managed, without originally intending to, to use the outlawed paint.

It came about because we wanted to do two coats. Bottom paint is enormously expensive. We bought one gallon of red, then realized we would not have quite enough for the second coat. Rather than make another trip to Portland and buy a whole gallon that we would only use a portion of, we mixed the new red paint with parts of leftover paint from other years: blue and a metallic bronze. The result was a beautiful shade of lavender with a hint of bronze. We were so taken with it, we wished we could reproduce it for future years. But at least a little bit of the bottom paint was environmentally unsound.

"I never imagined we'd have so many stowaways on the bottom," I say now.

"That's because you've never seen the bottom after it's been sailed in southern waters. The warm water nurtures the little suckers. Plus, we've stayed in harbors too long. You have to keep moving to slough them off.

Once we are back in the water, we will move the boat at least once a week when we are in a port for any length of time."

"But you know what was a surprise to me?" Cory asks. "I didn't see any damage to the hull or keel from bumping around on the reefs in Bermuda."

"I know, Cor!" Dorin says. "I was surprised, too. I thought for sure at least some of the fiberglass would have chipped off the bottom edge of the keel, but it looks fine. And I didn't see any cracks. Good news for us. We would've had to do some damage repair with fiberglass."

Though the little girls were not around when we went to lunch, they appear on the short walk back to the *Villa Pesquera* Co-op.

"Hello," they say in unison.

"Hello," Dorin and I say back.

They seem delighted with our response.

"How are you?" the taller of the girls asks. The girls look tense until we answer, "Fine, how are you?"

They smile with delight. "We are fine. How are you?" the shorter girl says. And then I realize they are practicing English.

By now we are at the co-op. Cory has already gone in. Dorin and I stop at the gate.

"*Hasta mañana,*" I say. The girls look at each other in surprise.

"*Sí, mañana!*" they say. They watch us go into the yard but hang around the gate. Félix is just going by, and he shoos them away.

"You realize you have just promised them you will see them tomorrow?" asks Dorin.

"Uh, yeah, I guess that wasn't a good idea. But they'll probably forget."

"Fat chance. Your son is not going to be happy."

After we return to the boat, the next step is to sand the bottom with our palm sander. It's slow work and we take turns, as we only have one mask. Then I notice one of the fishermen is standing some distance away, watching us. I mention it to Dorin, wondering if we are doing something wrong. When Dorin maintains eye contact with the guy, he turns and walks away. As fishermen return from their daily catch, one by one, we see the same reaction.

Félix is walking by, and I ask him what is going on and he says, "Don't pay attention to them."

Later, Dorin asks him the same question. "Why are these guys staring at us?"

Félix is uncomfortable and doesn't look at me. "Here, women don't work in the yard on the boats. That's men's work. Women don't use power tools. Never. Not here. But don't worry about those guys. They will get used to it."

Later, we shower and change clothes again for supper. As we walk down the street, I notice young teenage girls sitting on their porches, giving each other manicures. They wear dresses that are very feminine. Designed, I muse, to catch a husband. I realize the culture is different here. I am glad I grew up in a setting where I could and did do "boy stuff." Though it wasn't exactly what girls aimed for, I had learned how to climb a tree, shoot a gun, and build things with wood and hand tools. Being the oldest of five children, I had to learn to cook and clean to help my mom, who worked in a manufacturing shop, but I was always the happiest outside, exploring and building. This is why I've enjoyed working on the *Fandango*, helping to maintain her. I'd rather be doing that than any housekeeping chore I can think of.

I get disapproving looks from older women who are out on their stoops and realize they already know who I am—the strange American gringa woman who does men's work. I am sensitive to the fact that I am violating their cultural expectations and standards, but still, they'll have to become accustomed to it. I am not going to sit out the cleaning and repairing of my boat.

In the next nine days, we paint the upper hull with paint we had brought with us and use bottom paint that is available at the *Pescadería*. It might not be the stuff that is environmentally sound, but it's what's available. And with one of the half-dozen, newly purchased, stainless steel cotter pins, also from the *Pescadería*, Dorin replaces the wire that has been holding the pin that has been holding the mainsheet tackle to the traveler.

When Dorin walks down the cobblestone street to the *Pescadería*, I usually go with him. The owner is a good-natured guy who often has a few avocados in a basket on the counter for customers to take. When I offer to pay, he says, "No, I have a tree in my yard. These are free."

While we are out of the water, it's a good time to clean the galley stove soot off the ceiling. Cory and I sand all the bright work on the outside with our electric palm sander and then add two more coats using the varnish we brought with us, on top of the eight coats we started with.

At the beginning of each day, Cory walks down the street to the *panadería* and buys exquisite, delicious pastries. The coffee is ready by the time he returns, and we sit in our lofty cockpit eating breakfast. At lunch time, one of us fixes lunch—canned soup with salad or sandwiches. When the workday ends early, Cory takes the *Tinker* for a spin around the harbor.

"He must be practicing sailing," I say, amused.

Dorin chuckles. "No, I think he's avoiding his admirers."

Dorin stops into the co-op bar for a martini each day while waiting for Cory to get back from sailing and for me to get done with my shower.

Dorin tells me that Félix, who is also the bartender, gets a kick out of how to mix a martini exactly to Dorin's specifications. He always waits until Dorin takes the first sip and watches his reaction. As soon as Dorin pronounces it "perfect!" Félix nods with satisfaction. One day, when I go into the bar and sit beside Dorin, Félix asks if I want a martini. I say no, I don't like them.

"I know the drink for you," he says, *"Cuba Libre...."* He appears to be gauging my reaction.

"Sure, I'll try it."

Cory has just come into the bar and laughs. "That means 'liberate Cuba.' That might be a political issue for North Americans, and he doesn't know how you will take it."

"Not an issue for me," I say.

Cuba Libre turns out to be Coca-Cola, rum and lime juice. I decide it's my new favorite alcohol drink.

For suppers, we return time and again to *Brisas del Mar*. While the menu choices are limited, the service is outstanding. One of the waiters speaks quite good English, so he always waits on us. He also helps us with Spanish, and we learn to say, *"Pollo con arroz y habichuelas,"* chicken with rice and beans. Cory tells us it should be *frijoles* for beans, but the waiter tells us differently, and it's a fun word to say.

On Friday and Saturday nights, Félix keeps the co-op bar open late, and we are invited to join the party. The fishermen and their wives or sweethearts gather for drinks, music and dancing. A couple of guys bring guitars which they pass around during the evening. All of them play and sing. Félix, who has been bartending, brings out a keyboard and plays it. I expect salsa music, but instead, it seems like folk music and romantic ballads. We thoroughly enjoy ourselves and are grateful we've been invited.

The next night, Dorin brings along his guitar. I am surprised because he is very reluctant to play in front of people. I am the one who insisted, over his protests, on bringing it because our summer sailing often included his playing and our singing, me off key, while at anchor after a day of sailing.

When we get inside, he hands his guitar off to one of the fishermen, and it is received with enthusiasm. There are a few more cruising Americans than last night, so all the tables are pushed into one large one, where we can all, locals and visitors, sit together.

As Dorin's guitar gets shared among the fishermen-turned-musicians, we dance to ballads and clap to folk music. At the end of the evening, four musicians play a lovely ballad that has the rapt attention of all Puerto Ricans there. Félix's voice is beautiful as he sings the melody. The others harmonize; by the end, tears are in their eyes, including Félix, who I have thought of as stoic. "They sing about their mothers," a Puerto Rican lady says to me.

The next day, Félix motions me into the bar and unfolds a chart on a table. The fisherman who used Dorin's guitar the most last night has lent me his chart of Puerto Real Bay and the coast nearby, including Desecheo Island. I can keep it for a couple of days to copy it.

I am overwhelmed at this kindness and concern. I can imagine that Félix has regaled the fishermen with the information about our sailing without real charts. I can imagine this being retold among themselves to prove what they already know: Gringos are poor sailors and, evidently, stupid, too. But now, here is this gesture of kindness and friendship.

The chart is old and the paper yellowed, but it has been cared for through the years, perhaps handed down from an earlier generation. There is a barely discernible coffee cup stain in the corner, which gives it character. If I owned this chart, I would frame it.

I thank him and carry it up the ladder to the boat and spend five happy hours copying the chart. The paper is thick enough, but in case it's a little fragile, I don't want to use my usual method of transfer where I draw very light pencil lines forming a grid on the original which I erase when I am done. This time I do a series of measurements and then reduce them to one-fourth on my paper. I feel like I am touching a generation of seafaring history.

I am done by afternoon, return the chart to Félix, and show the results of my chart-drawing efforts. His eyebrows shoot up in surprise as he scans my "chart" carefully.

"Hmm. Very good." He glances sideways at me for a split second and scans the drawing again. Then he nods. "Yes, this will work." For the first time, he smiles just a little bit as he hands it back, and I can tell he approves.

A couple of days later, the yard is abuzz at eight in the morning. The fishermen are still here, which never happens—usually, they are all out on the ocean by now. There is tension as they mingle and talk with the yard workers in small groups. Something's up.

One of the other American cruisers, Carol, speaks some Spanish and is hanging around, listening intently.

"There was a knife fight in a bar last night," she says after a turn around the yard. "One guy works here in the yard, and the other guy is crew on a fishing boat. They didn't come into work, and the police are trying to find them."

It's hard to believe any of these guys, who are so easy going and respectful, would be involved in a knife fight. The men chat quietly among themselves. Carol continues to lurk. She comes back with more information: both guys are young. One has a family of two brothers and one sister to support, and the other is helping to support grandparents. They are all afraid the police will arrest one or both of them.

Shortly after, two policemen do appear, arriving from a rear gated entrance I didn't even know existed. They talk to a few of the men in the yard, but the interviews are short, ending with head shakes and shoulder shrugs. They all say they haven't seen the men the police are looking for. They know nothing. The police do a quick search of the premises, including the freezer and the showers. Then they leave. The tension breaks, and the men chat and laugh.

Within five minutes, one of the young men arrives from the gate we normally use. He's wearing jeans that were once soaked but are now stiff with dried blood. He has a white rag tied around his thigh. He is immediately surrounded by the men, who shake his hand and clap him on the back—a hero's welcome. One of the men walks the young man into the bar. When they return, the jeans have been cut off above the wound, and the wound has a clean bandage on it.

At that moment, another young man appears from behind the building, having used the rear entrance. The two men spot each other and then hold out their arms. The wounded man hobbles forward. The two guys laugh and embrace.

Félix is standing beside us. "They are good friends. Friends have a fight sometimes when they drink too much."

The two young men appear to be retelling the event to the older men surrounding them. There is a lot of laughing, which I think is intensified with relief that the two young men are okay.

"No policía," the wounded man says. "No policía."

"Gracias, mi amigo, gracias," says the perpetrator. They do the handshake embrace thing and both look happy and relieved. The perpetrator takes the arm of the wounded man, wraps it around his shoulder, and helps him limp toward the rear exit.

The drama over, we go into the bar, as Dorin needs to consult with Félix about a needed part.

A couple, who must be from one of the boats at anchor in Puerto Real Bay, follows us in and takes a seat at a table. Félix brings them coffee and then returns to the bar to talk to Dorin.

The woman, whom I've never seen before, says with disgust, "Well, what else can you expect from a violent, machismo culture?"

I stop breathing. I am stunned. Dorin tenses beside me.

Félix roars, "No! No! Get out!"

The woman looks indignant but, with raised eyebrow has the "see what I mean?" expression on her face as she looks pointedly at her husband.

"Not machismo," Félix says, turning toward them. "Is...brotherhood. Leave."

The woman looks surprised and annoyed, but her husband, reading the situation far better than she, stands up, pulls out his wallet, and drops a twenty-dollar bill on the table. He comes around and pulls out her chair, takes her by the elbow, and escorts her outside.

There is silence when they leave. My face burns with embarrassment because, of course, they are Americans. Dorin stares fixedly at his cupped hands. Félix walks to the door and watches them disappear. Minutes go by before any of us moves. Finally, Félix comes back and goes behind the bar.

"Sorry, missus," he says to me.

"No! You are not the one to be sorry. I am sorry. She was awful." He shakes his head then holds out his hand to Dorin. "Sorry, my friend."

At that moment, because he has called Dorin his friend, tears release and run down my face.

In nine days, we finish fixing the boat, and she looks gleaming and new. We are glad to be going back into the water. While the experience in this boatyard has been wonderful, I am tired of using the ladder in the morning to use the bathroom, and we miss the movement of the boat on the water. We also have felt under a magnifying glass, both in the co-op yard and walking through the streets.

Félix reverses the process of getting us out of the water with the lift. It goes smoothly. Out at anchor, we put up the awning and have our privacy once more. But we take it down the next day because Dorin thinks Cory and I should have practice sailing without him.

"Just in case I fall off the boat, and you have to go on without me." He is joking, but this thought has indeed entered my mind a few times during storms, and it is terrifying.

Cory rows Dorin into the dock where he will catch a *público*, first to a bank in Cabo Rojo to get an advance on our credit card because we are nearly out of cash, and then to take another *público* to Boquerón.

When he's back on board, Cory starts the motors and asks if I want to take the tiller, but I do not. He motors out of the harbor and mentions the motor seems sluggish, even after we have cleaned the prop. We put up the sails, and I cut the motor. The wind is right for a close reach, and the time goes quickly. We take turns with the tiller and get a kick out of sailing by ourselves. The trip is quick and without incident. When we sail into the broad harbor, Cory starts the motor. I take the tiller while Cory drops the sails. I notice a large US Coast Guard cutter in the bay. We've haven't seen one here before. We motor over to a familiar place, and I drop the anchor. One of the guys usually does it, but I want to get the experience. Turns out it's way easier than I had thought. The anchor drops and holds, and we are good to row to shore to pick up Dorin.

Also on the dock are a couple of other boaters who Dorin has been talking to. When we climb out of the *Tinker*, they shake Cory's hand and say, "Good job, young man!"

"Shirley also sailed," Dorin says. They don't acknowledge this and continue to chat with Cory about his great handling of the boat. I catch Dorin's eye, smile and shake my head. I'm glad Cory's getting well-deserved accolades, but I have to stifle to keep from saying, "Yeah, if you think that's good, you should see him in a big storm or when the boat is dragging anchor, and we don't have a running motor. Now that's something!"

Cory says he wants to stay in town, so we row back to the *Fandango*.

"I couldn't get any money. Bank was closed for some holiday," Dorin says.

Many of the Puerto Rican holidays are the same as our own, but apparently not this one.

"So we have around $10 in cash. And the larder is getting bare."

I haven't been thinking much about money because we use the credit card for a lot. But one thing we have to have cash for, for sure, is the *público*.

Back on board, Dorin hails the Coast Guard cutter on VHF. The captain asks us about our hailing port. When he finds out we sailed out of Maine, he tells us he's from Falmouth, Maine. When Dorin mentions we live in Waterville, he tells us his sister had attended Thomas College. What a small world.

We eat lunch in the cockpit and discuss the fact that our motor felt sluggish, both leaving Puerto Real and arriving in Boquerón Bay. Up until now, any sluggishness was blamed on having junk on the bottom of our boat.

Dorin notices a new boat in the harbor. "That's a Herreshoff sloop. I think they are flying the South African flag. Wow! Interesting." He picks up the binoculars. "Yes, I'm pretty sure that's a South African flag. They've just done a trans-Atlantic crossing!"

As usual, he tries to be surreptitious with the binocs, but it's nearly impossible. And sure enough, even though we are fifty yards away, a man on board turns and waves toward us.

"Uh oh. Caught!" I say.

While we watch, the man lowers himself into his dinghy, points the bow toward us, and rows in our direction. In spite of his back being toward us, he rows in a straight line directly at our boat.

As he gets closer, I can see he's a white guy, short and stocky, dark brown hair, bushy beard and mustache. A few feet away, with one oar he neatly swings the dinghy so it comes perfectly beside us.

"Good day!" he says cheerfully. He has a delightful accent similar to British and *day* sounds something like *deh*.

"Permission to come aboard?" he asks.

"Yes, of course," Dorin says.

He easily springs out of his dinghy and up on board, and it's obvious he's fit and athletic. He introduces himself as Bast Badenhorst, and his boat is the *Phambili*. We sit in the cockpit while he explains why he is here. He has sailed single-handed from South Africa to Puerto Rico. His destination is Ft. Lauderdale, and it will only take about two weeks. When Dorin raises his eyebrows, Bast says, "Okay, three tops." He has a sister in California whom he wants to join by sailing through the Panama Canal.

I'm so charmed by his accent that I hang on every word. Then he says he is looking for a crew member to help him take the boat the rest of the way, and someone has suggested Cory.

"I've been waiting for you to get back," he says. I'll pay your young man $300 and buy his plane ticket back to San Juan if he's interested."

"Oh, he's just a kid," I say. "Only sixteen." I believe this will end the discussion.

"No, that's very good. I know he has experience. And I just saw him bring this boat into the harbor." The first "r" in harbor is slightly rolled, and the second just sounds like "ah." And there's a lilt to the sentence that is fun to listen to.

Nevertheless, Cory is not going anywhere with a stranger.

Dorin puts an arm around my shoulder and says, "Give us time to think about it?" Bast agrees and asks if he can bring supper to our boat tonight and just meet Cory.

We agree and the South African guy rows toward the dock, waving once.

"Well that's silly," I say. "Cory is just a kid."

"I don't think his age is an issue," Dorin says. "In sailing years, he's an adult."

I think about this. Cory has functioned substantially better than I have as a responsible, helpful crew member. He makes good decisions, isn't reckless, and isn't afraid. He probably has earned this; nevertheless, every fiber of my being tells me he needs to stay where I can see him.

"So, are you going to tell Cory about this?"

"Yeah, I guess I have to. That guy is coming back tonight."

"So. How are you going to handle it?"

"You mean am I going to let him go? Do you think I should?"

"I'm not sure it's your decision to make."

"He probably wouldn't want to go anyway, right? And we have to be heading out to Venezuela."

"We can wait here for a few weeks. I don't have any problem with that."

"I'll think about it." But I already have, and I don't want him to go.

"When you tell him, are you going to let him make the decision?"

He probably wouldn't want to go anyway, I think. Not with a stranger.

"Probably," I say.

"But are you going to say it in a way that lets him know your preference? Or are you going to be neutral?"

"Well, I'm not sure he's old enough to make this decision."

"Tell me something. When you proposed *our* trip to him, did you let him make his own decision without influencing him?"

"Yes. But...this is different."

"Different for you, maybe. But maybe not for him."

The rest of the day I wrangle with this decision until Cory comes back at five o'clock, delivered to the boat by a neighboring yachter.

I tell him about Bast, and I can see he is interested. An hour later, Bast himself knocks on the hull. He has brought us plantain stew. I am not impressed with his choice of meal, but we settle in the cabin with bowls of thick stew that turn out to be delicious.

When I compliment him, he says, "Right! The word starts with an "h" sound like a little puff of air followed by "royt.""

"If Cory sails with me, he won't starve. I can cook."

Bast explains the name of his boat, the *Phambili*, means to move forward or to get going in Zulu. He invites questions and Dorin obliges, and quickly and predictably, the conversation moves into the area of how the boat was designed and built, and eventually what his crossing was like. I decide he really does know what he's doing, but I'm still uncomfortable.

"Do you have anyone you contact regularly in the States?" Bast asks. "Someone who can be a link so Cory can let you know when he'll be landing in San Juan?"

"I've got Bill's number," Cory says. "I'll call him the day before I fly. You'll just have to check with him. Wait for three weeks though."

And with this, Cory has already decided.

After giving us his itinerary, Bast says he would like to depart tomorrow night. I gasp. We need time to think this over. Time to talk Cory out of this.

"Come over to my boat tomorrow for breakfast," Bast says. "See what you think of her."

The next morning, the three of us row over to the *Phambili*. He shows us around, and I can see his stock of food is far better than ours. I'm miserable, but the decision apparently having been made, I try to put a good face on it.

My stomach is in a knot.

Later, Cory goes into town to tell friends he'll be gone for a while. Back on the *Fandango*, he packs his clothes before supper and is ready for us to row him over to the *Phambili*. I have butterflies in my stomach and feel nauseated while I steady the *Tinker* by holding onto the *Phambili's* toe rail so he can climb aboard. He gives me a quick hug, throws his duffle onto the deck, and is up and over the lifelines. We row back to the *Fandango*, and then stand on the deck as we watch the little sloop head for the mouth of the bay.

"It'll only be two weeks, well, maybe three," Dorin says.

"Liar," I say. "The decision has been made, so don't sugar coat it."

"Okay, four is more realistic." He puts his arm around me. "He'll thank you someday for this adventure."

"I don't want thanks. I want him back safely."

Cory waves goodbye just before they turn north out of the bay. I am stunned at the enormity of this event.

"It's going to be an adventure," Dorin says. "It'll be okay."

I nod but can't speak because I'm trying not to cry. He takes a crumbled, oily piece of paper towel out of his pocket and hands it to me. I blow my nose. He engulfs me in a hug. "It'll be okay."

Chapter Seventeen
A Tale of Two Boats

-Cory on the Phambili-

Yesterday I was hanging around Puerto Rico, trying to find stuff to do, and now I'm on a boat with this guy...someone I've barely met...headed for Florida.

I can't believe Mom let me go!

I'm not sure at all that this is a good idea, but I said I wanted to go, and now, here I am. It's not that I'm worried that I'll be ok...after all, it's just another sailing trip. It's just weird to be on a small boat for weeks with someone I don't know.

It was starting to get dark when I got on the *Phambili* about an hour ago. Bast showed me where my bunk was so I could stow my bag. He told me to haul the anchor and that was it. We were off.

Just in time I thought to turn around and wave to Mom and Dorin. And then, moving right along, we head for the channel marker under full sail. And it seems like this little side trip will be fun, right? It seems like it will be an adventure. Of course it will be. Way better, now that I think of it, than being bored in Puerto Rico.

"You play chess?" he asks.

I nod yes, thinking my opponents have mostly been my older brothers and my mother. Mom taught each of us how to play, and then as soon as we could beat her in three games straight, she stopped playing and waited for the next kid to be old enough. She stopped playing me when I was ten. "I might not be very good at it," I say.

"Well, we'll see. We'll see," he says. "You'll get better."

I'm not tired, so we talk. He tells me how he wants the log kept, a few things about how the boat handles, how the motor starts with a hand crank, and how we will share the cooking and cleaning duties. I'm not too bad at accents. I wonder if I could get the hang of his South African accent.

"I'll take the eight to midnight watch," Bast says. "You take midnight to four."

"Yeah, that's the one I'm used to. I like it."

We talk a bit more, then I head to my bunk to get some sleep.

"Your watch," he says at midnight. "Keep the same heading. Wake me at the end of the watch." He goes below and all is quiet.

It seems so abrupt. He just assumes that I know what I'm doing and goes to bed.

Pretty cool, I think. I bet there are not many guys my age who are out on a sailing adventure, taking the midnight watch. They must be sleeping; they'll go to school tomorrow, maybe take a test. I'm steering a boat at night in the Caribbean. It's a good feeling to have people take it for granted that I can handle anything that an experienced adult can.

It's about three in the morning, and we're forty miles offshore when I notice the lights of a boat. As I watch, it seems to be running parallel to us and going our speed. Another sailboat going in our direction at our speed at night? Seems like quite a coincidence.

Twenty minutes go by, and the boat is close enough that I realize it's a powerboat—I can hear it. I'm thinking...that's strange. Why would a powerboat be doing that—going our speed, four knots? And then I realize it's gradually getting closer to us—maybe fifty yards away and now thirty yards. It doesn't make any sense. Could it be pirates?

That seems farfetched...thinking it might be pirates.

All of a sudden, a spotlight comes from the boat and lights up the cockpit.

I duck down. Oh, it's definitely pirates!

I shout to Bast as I run down the companionway stairs. "I think we're being attacked by pirates!" He instantly wakes up, looks out and sees the cockpit lit up, and, as if he had been sleeping with it, he slaps a gun in my hand.

"Start shooting at them. I'm calling in a Mayday."

I'm not sticking my head up into the cockpit, so I reach up from below and shoot in the general direction of the power boat. If they shoot back, the most they can hit is my hand. I squeeze off a couple of shots, and, sure enough, they shoot back.

I hear Bast on the radio. "This is the yacht *Phambili*. We're offshore west of Puerto Rico and are being attacked by pirates. We are armed and prepared to defend ourselves." He repeats it: "We are armed and prepared to defend ourselves." Suddenly the power boat accelerates and moments later, it peels off, flying away from us at top speed.

I bolt into the cockpit and watch them disappear. I hand the revolver to Bast, who has jumped into the cockpit behind me.

"What happened," he says, "is they were monitoring channel 16. So, they knew three things right away. There is more than one of us, we are alert, and we have guns we are ready to use. And, you know, we're a tiny sailboat, which probably now doesn't seem to them to be worth the hassle. Probably we've got nothing, and it's not worth getting shot."

He doesn't go back to sleep. At four, he takes over. I go below and lie down in my bunk, but I don't sleep.

At first light, I hear a chopper approaching. I run up the stairs and into the cockpit. It's the US Coast Guard, and they hover near us.

Using a loud hailer, the voice of the Coast Guard says, "All passengers and crew on deck. Go to channel 16 on your VHF."

From the cockpit, Bast leans into the boat and brings out the VHF mic.

"Go to channel 81, please," the voice instructs.

Bast dials the VHF to 81. "This is the *Phambili*."

"Is there anyone else below?"

"No."

"Are you in any distress?"

"No, we're okay."

"What is your name, the name of your boat, your last port of call, your destination, and the name of your crew member?"

Bast gives the information, spelling out our names.

"Please recount the situation that caused you to call in the Mayday."

Bast tells them briefly what happened.

"Thank you for your cooperation, Captain Badenhorst. Can you say approximately in what direction the boat went?"

I realize, as he tells them, he had had the presence of mind to notice which way the pirates had gone.

"Have a safe trip." They roar off in the direction Bast gave them. I stay at the helm while Bast makes breakfast.

"Well, now, that was interesting," I think, while we eat. What would my Dungeons and Dragons buddies, Chris and Doug, think of this *real* adventure?

Even though it was terrifying for a few minutes, it's already starting to seem cool. I shot at pirates!

Later that day, because we are barefoot, I notice something. Bast has only four toes on each foot—the ones in from the pinky toes are missing. I think about that for a while. I don't think he was born that way. It would be peculiar to have the same toes missing on both feet. He notices me noticing his feet and smiles.

"Funny story, that," he tells me. "I haven't told you that I was a professional soccer player in South Africa. It's how I made a living. It's what I loved to do. I was pretty good. But we were at war with Angola, and the army wanted me to serve. Well, I didn't want to, of course. I wanted to keep playing soccer. I didn't want to get killed. But I had to go anyway. Once I was a soldier, I noticed, rather conveniently, that when I walked in army boots, my toes hurt. The ones in from the little toes. So I complained and complained about the pain. Finally, they sent me to the hospital. When it was my turn to get looked at, the doctor said, 'Oh, I can fix that. I'm going to give you something for the pain.' He gives me an injection. I'm thinking this is going to go well. I'll be out of the army today. He comes back in half an hour and cuts off my toes. 'There,' he says, 'that should be a lot better when you march.' Two days later I was marching in bloody boots. I should have just shut up and served my time. Which I did anyway. I can still play soccer, though."

Bast shows me how to put out a 100-pound-test fishing line off the back of the boat with a jig attached to the end. "We'll trail a line all the time we are moving," he says. "Hope you like fish." He shows me how to fasten a bungee cord to it—when the cord stretches out, there will be a fish on the line.

An hour later, we get a strike. I holler to Bast, and we check it out. It's a six-foot barracuda.

"Nah," he says. "Too big. We can't eat all that. We'll release it."

A couple of hours later, the bungee stretches again. This time I pull in a two-foot fish.

"Yeah, Cory, that'll do us just fine," he says. He takes a winch handle and hits the fish on the head.

"You know how to dress out a fish?" he asks.

"Yeah, I've done it a few times," I say, thinking of the ten-inch fish I've caught and remembering the ones that I had watched Dorin gut out.

"Right," he says. He rolls his 'r's' just a little bit, and the word sounds a little like *roight* with a hard "t" on the end. "The job's yours. Wash down the deck when you're done."

He comes to inspect ten minutes later and says, "Hey! No blood on the boat, *houthoofd!*" It sounds something like *how towft*.

"Dumb?" I ask.

He laughs. "No, Woodhead. In Afrikaans."

"How many languages do you speak?" I ask.

"A few. Not all of them well. I learned some when I was in the South African Army with guys who spoke different languages. A little Zulu, Xhosa, Khoisan, the one with the clicks, Afrikaans, and, of course, English. A little Portuguese because I was in Brazil for a while."

"Spanish?"

"Enough to maybe get us by," he says and laughs. "Maybe."

-Fandango-

On Sunday, the day after Cory leaves, Bob rows over to remind us Thanksgiving is the 26th. María has offered to make Thanksgiving dinner for cruisers at her restaurant for a small fee per head.

"It's going to be great. Turkey is hard to come by in Puerto Rico, but she will get one. There'll be all the fixings. Maybe even cranberry sauce. She knows what to do because she was in the States for a while. It'll be great."

"Okay, we'll probably be there," I say. My heart isn't in it though.

"We'll have to go into town to get some cash tomorrow," Dorin reminds me after Bob leaves. "We're getting short, aren't we?"

"Yeah, we only have $9 left. And, you've probably noticed, we're almost out of food."

We always go together, so on Monday we walk to the *público* curb in the park and pay $2 for both of us to ride into Cabo Rojo, a twenty-minute trip.

The banking experience is always tense for Dorin. The last time we got cash was on our first trip to Puerto Rico, but it was in Mayagüez. The manager there spoke fluent English and there was no problem.

We are directed to talk to the bank manager, who is seated at a large mahogany desk that has nothing on it except a telephone and an in-and-out basket. He's a handsome man, maybe in his thirties, dressed in a suit that fits so well it must have been tailored for him.

"How can I help you?" he asks. His lightly accented English is quite good.

"We need to pull out some cash from our card, if it isn't tapped out," Dorin says and slides it forward. "We might have tapped it out."

I look at Dorin and realize that just in case our card is declined, he wants to be proactive and explain ahead of time that the card might be at its limit, which is far better than for this gentleman to think Dorin doesn't pay his bills.

The manager nods, but he appears to think about what Dorin has said. "Uh, um…." he says, his eyes dart right and left toward his tellers who are listening with rapt attention.

I am pretty sure he does not have a clear grasp of what Dorin has just said, but he doesn't want his staff to know this.

Dorin fills the gap. "Because our agent is supposed to keep it in check, but I'm not sure that we haven't tapped it out."

The manager nods sagely, but he is obviously trying to decipher these words and get something from context.

"We need cash from our card," I say.

He looks relieved and nods. He hands us a form to fill out and sign, and then he takes the card with him to another room.

When he reappears, he is noticeably uncomfortable.

"Um," he clears his throat, "um, your card is decline."

I audibly suck in my breath. The card is Dorin's, and he always takes care of it, but I have been afraid of this. Late last week we paid for the boat hauling, as well as eating out almost every meal. I can tell Dorin is mortified. While I'm used to my credit or debit cards being declined from time to time, including in the grocery store with my purchases already checked out and bagged, he is a stickler for paying bills and not running out of money. For him, this is shameful.

I nod. "Okay, thank you very much. We'll come back soon."

Dorin doesn't speak until we walk back to the station. "We have to call Bill. He has to pay that account. Like today."

We pay $2 to ride back to Boquerón, leaving us $5. From the public phone in the park, we call Bill collect, but there is no answer. We decide that he has probably paid the credit card on the due date last week, and it just hasn't been processed yet.

The next day, Tuesday, Dorin goes into Puerto Real by himself so he will use only $2 to get back and forth. I figure the bank manager will know what's going on this time. Dorin comes back empty handed except for the three remaining one-dollar bills. I call Bill collect again, and this time he answers.

"I'm so sorry," he says. "I haven't been able to take care of it because I've had a plumbing emergency here. I have to get it fixed so we don't have to move in with the in-laws."

"I'm sorry about that, but we need money as soon as possible. We're almost out of food."

"Okay, tomorrow morning I'll be able to take care of it. Promise."

The next afternoon, Dorin goes in again alone and looks discouraged as he leaves the boat. I feel really sorry about this because it's difficult for him. And, Bill is my son. I apologize.

"It can't be helped," he says. "But we have to get money today."

I know it didn't go well as soon as I see him rowing back from the dock an hour later.

"This is so frustrating," he says. "I don't have any control. No way to fix this. There is money in savings. I just can't get to it."

When I row back to shore and call Bill, he says he moved the money from savings to the credit card late yesterday. "It'll probably take another day to process. But then, tomorrow is Thanksgiving. So it might be delayed. Then I think your bank is closed on Friday. You should be able to get money by Monday."

I know Dorin will not allow me to borrow from Bob and Binnie, so before I go back to the boat, I walk to María's and explain the situation.

"Is okay!" she says. "You can pay for Thanksgiving next week. You good customer. No worry."

Dorin is bothered about charging our meal, but he agrees to go. The food is excellent and the camaraderie among boaters is great. It's a good distraction from my worry about Cory. A glass of wine is included with the dinner. When we refuse a second glass, Bob insists on buying a round for everyone.

"I hear your son went off sailing with that South African guy," Fred says. "That will be a great adventure for him. A change from sailing around with the old folks."

Everybody chuckles.

I nod and smile, but I don't speak because I have a lump in my throat.

"Shirley is having a hard time because she thinks he's too young," Dorin says.

"Too young? He must be, what? Eighteen, nineteen?"

"Sixteen," I say.

"What? We thought he must be out of high school. Taking a year off before going off to college."

"This is his junior year," I say. "He's just a kid."

"Shirl, have you really looked at him lately?" Dorin says. "He was taller than you when we left. Now he's taller than me. Got broader shoulders, too."

Everyone laughs again. "The local girls think he's a hunk," Beverly says.

"You mean the little ten-year-olds in Puerto Real?"

"No, I mean the sixteen- to eighteen-year-olds. Here. And probably in Puerto Real, too."

I sit back and wonder, when did this happen? How did I miss this, if it was so apparent to everybody else?

María offers leftovers to me, but I can't take advantage of it because we have no ice in the icebox. In our can cupboard, we have three cans of spam, two cans of tuna, four cans of Vienna sausage and an abundance of rice and beans left for the next ten meals. Worse, we are out of coffee.

-Phambili-

"So, you've been to the D.R.," Bast says the next day. "I wasn't planning on going there, but since you have local knowledge, I think we might stop there for a couple of days."

"Sure," I say. "Sounds good to me." It's not like we're in a hurry, and I don't mind if we extend our trip a little. I'm already having fun.

As we make the entrance to Samaná Bay, I tell him the story of our handmade charts and not understanding the bay on our first approach.

"I don't have charts either because I'm not supposed to stop in the D.R." he says. "White people from South Africa are not allowed to enter many of these countries. You know why, right?"

"Um, apartheid?" I guess.

"Yeah, exactly. The Bahamas are the same."

"But you said we are going to stop in the Bahamas...."

"Yeah, it will be no problem. We'll just drop anchor near some of the outer, uninhabited islands."

"But what about the D.R.?"

"It will be fine, probably."

Probably?

I feel good being able to give him information about the approach and the bay. When we get into Samaná, I tell him to back up to the dock, and he has me tie up his quarantine flag. There's another flag, in addition to the South African flag, that has been flying from the rear stay since I first saw the boat in Puerto Rico, but I don't know what it is.

Pretty soon two customs' guys show up and come on the boat. They don't search, but they do look at our papers, write stuff down, thank us, and prepare to leave. Bast gives them the right amount of money because I have already told him what it should be. They bow and leave.

"Well, that was easy," I say, and I start to untie the stern line.

"Wait!" With his accent it comes out a little like *woit*. "I want to get my camera. I want you to take a picture. Take down the quarantine flag."

He brings a camera from below and hands it to me. He climbs up on the rear deck, leans in close to the stay, and holds up his clearance paper.

"Make sure you get the flag in the picture."

"What's the flag for?" I ask.

"It's my yacht club burgee from South Africa." He grins big while I snap his photo.

"As soon as we anchor, let's go rent some cross-country dirt bikes," he says.

Well, I'm all for that. But when we go to rent them, I realize it's not like the motorcycle I rode the last time I was here. These are for off road. No problem though. I've done this with a friend's dirt bike in the field behind his house.

But I quickly realize these are not like the dirt bikes I have ridden. These are big, heavy and powerful. And brand new, so new looking I think this might be the first time they've rented them out.

"You need *gasolina*," the rental guy says and points down the street. I ride it down the street and put gas in the tank. On the way back I think it would be cool to do a wheelie like I did with the motorcycle the last time I was here. So I gun it, and it goes up way higher than I expect. I try to get it under control, and as I finally come down there's a car right there that I almost crash into. So I lay the bike over, slide down the road and stop. Right in front of the bike rental place. The rental guy looks stunned. Then he helps me stand the bike up. I'm not hurt, so I am sitting on the bike when Bast, who has taken a little test run of his own in the other direction, comes riding up. There is a long scrape and a big dent in the side of my bike.

"What is *this!*" Bast says. "How did *that* happen already? It's only been *five minutes.*"

"This is more powerful than Rusty Bickford's bike back home," I say.

"Hooray for Rusty Bickford," he says, and speeds away.

As soon as we are off road, I know he is good at it, very good.

We go downhill through this long, watery mud trail, almost like a swamp. It's maybe 15-inches deep. Bast goes flying through it, no problem. I'm more cautious; I bog down, and in the middle, my bike dies and falls over in the water. Bast comes back to help me drag it out of the water. "You didn't go fast enough. You need to go faster," he tells me.

At the top of a steeper hill, I see another water hole so I go faster, much faster, down into the mud hole. I hit the bottom, kah-bam! I bury the front wheel in the mud, but I keep on going and fly over the handlebars, landing in the swampy mud.

"Too fast, too fast. Way too fast." Bast says when he comes back to help me drag the bike out of the mud hole.

He takes off, tearing along. I start again and crash again. I'm hitting roots and ruts. The bike flops over several more times.

Bast watches me and shakes his head. My fenders are pretty smashed up. Some of the plastic parts are beat to hell.

We go back on the road for a while, heading east along the coast, and I do much better. We come to a little village, Las Galeras, and buy food from a street vendor who has tin foil packages on a grill. We buy hot meat and rice pies and take them with us, as well as a six-pack of beer.

The road turns to barely a road and then into a swampy, wet trail.

When we get to the end at a point, we are at the top of cliffs above a beach.

"Let's stash the bikes and hike down," Bast says.

Though we haven't come across any people in a long time, we push the bikes pretty far into the jungle, so they can't be seen from the trail, and hike down to the beach. It's not all that easy because I'm carrying the food and Bast is carrying the beer.

We hang out on the deserted beach, eat our rice and meat pies, and drink beer. I have two; he drinks the rest. We carry our trash back up the hill.

"I've been thinking we might need to get some gas on the way back," Bast says as he checks the tanks. "Damn. You still have quite a bit left. I'm almost out."

"Yeah, the guy told me to get gas before we left."

"Well, he didn't tell me."

"He was probably too busy helping me pick my bike up when I crashed."

"Well, we have to even them up to get as far as we can."

He unhitches the gas line on my bike and siphons some gas into an empty beer bottle, then pours it into his tank. "They're about the same," he says after measuring again. "We'll definitely have to stop at the first place we find. It's getting dark, and we have a long way to go."

We start back on the trail, eventually coming to a small dirt road. It's very dark by the time we come to a small village—just a little store and a couple of buildings. The store is closed.

"We've got to find somebody and ask about gas," Bast says. "We're not going to make it back."

"Look down that path," I say. "There's a bonfire in there. Must be people."

We lean the bikes against the store, and side by side, we head down the path, through jungle growth, toward the fire about fifty yards in. A few minutes later, we see about thirty or forty people around the fire, and like a movie about Haiti, they are in full, white-face paint. Their bodies are also painted. I stop and suck in my breath. This is not our place to get gas. It's not our place to be. All that's happening is not good for us.

Without a word we take backward steps for a few yards and then turn around and walk very fast away from there. On the way, we pass a few people going toward the gathering and they take real notice of us. We hustle on by, get to our bikes, jump on, and get the hell out of there.

A little while later, we come to another small village and stop.

"That was weird and scary," I say to Bast. "It might sound funny, but it felt, like, well, kind of evil. I know for sure we were not supposed to be there. At all."

"No, we did not have an invitation to that party. I know a little bit about this stuff from living in Africa. It's not shit you want to mess around with. I think we can get some gas, here," he says. When we are finished filling the tanks and pay, we climb back on and head off.

Still thinking about the voodoo scene only a couple of miles back, we get the heck out of that place, keep riding until we finally get back to Samaná Bay, and climb off the bikes. It's very late and the business is closed.

"We can't leave the bikes," Bast says. He goes into a restaurant nearby, asks if we can put the bikes inside their gates until morning, and gives them $2. They seem very happy to help.

The next morning, when we return our bikes, we both think we are in big trouble. "It's on you," Bast says. "It's your name on the dotted line for your bike." I know he's kidding, but it doesn't help.

The bikes are covered in mud, but I think, "Well, that's okay because the mud covers some of the dents, scratches, and busted parts."

The guy comes out, grabs a hose, and washes the bikes off. Bast's is in perfect condition. Mine is trashed. The owner shakes his head as he looks at it.

Then he turns to us and looks embarrassed.

"*Lo siento.* I am sorry. No deposit back," he says.

"Right you are," says Bast. "Okay."

"But the deposit was only $10," I say. "I did way more damage than that."

He nods, pulls two ten-dollar bills out of his wallet, and hands them to the guy.

"Take it out of my pay," I say.

"Nah, it's okay. I should have known you were a *beginnerling*." It sounds like he's saying, "beh hena lin."

"Stupid?"

"No, beginner. I thought you said you had ridden dirt bikes before."

I think about Rusty's bike. I can pick it up and carry it. Both my feet touch the ground when I'm sitting on it. I have to lift them up so I can ride. I shrug.

Bast shakes his head and waves his hand. We head back to the boat, and he beats me at a couple of games of chess, but he teaches me some moves I didn't know about.

Later that day, we do some grocery shopping before leaving. I ask Bast why he was able to clear Customs with no problem.

"Maybe they hadn't had anyone try to clear from South Africa before, in this port, and they just didn't know it wasn't allowed. It probably would have been different in Puerto Plata or Santo Domingo."

"But you didn't know if we'd be able to clear."

"Sometimes you just have to try and see what happens."

That makes sense, I think. Why not?

-Fandango-

Dorin heads to Puerto Real on Monday by himself with $1 in his pocket, so if there is no money forthcoming, there will be no round trip. He will have to walk back eight-and-a-half miles in the heat.

I am on pins and needles for a couple of hours, waiting to see if he comes back with money. When the dinghy finally comes alongside, I scramble on deck to see Dorin grinning from ear to ear.

"We're good!" he says. "I got extra! I don't want to go through that again! And I bought a few groceries." He hands up four bags of food. "I'm going to be doing a lot of cooking in the next few days. I've been just itching to try out some things." He cooks a delicious supper, and then we sit back and bask in the security of having enough money to survive.

The next day, Dorin suggests we make a quick trip by water to Puerto Real for something to do and to discourage growth on our hull. He asks me to "captain" the boat, and he'll be the deck hand. I know he's doing this to distract me, but I need distracting, so I agree. It's a really easy trip. He nods as we pass through the narrow opening in the right place. "Like a pro," he says.

We have dinner at *Brisas del Mar*. Our favorite waiter, also named Félix, says he'd like to serve us a holiday drink. We take a seat at the bar so we can watch him make it. It's eggnog, incredibly good, and the best we've ever had, we tell him. We sip slowly, savoring it.

He tells us it's a traditional drink for the holidays, especially Christmas. Dorin asks for the recipe, and Félix dictates it to us while Dorin writes it down. When we get back to the boat, Dorin tapes it into our ship's log:

¡El Coquito!

1 large can of condensed milk

1 cup white (blanco) rum

1/3 cup brandy

3 to 4 eggs beaten

¼ teaspoon ginger

1 or 2 teaspoons cinnamon

1 can coconut cream concentrated

Milk to taste

Demonstrated by Sr. Felix Palermo
   Brisas del Mar
   Puerto Real (Calle Principal)
   Puerto Rico

Back in Boquerón the next day, we decide that as long as we are going to be in one place, mostly, while Cory is gone, we should get serious about getting ship-shape again.

There are a few more plumbing and electrical issues that didn't get addressed when we were out of the water, and, quickly, the one-page list becomes three. We work at a leisurely pace, though. We have three weeks, after all, and it's nice to row into the dock and hang out with other boaters, have a drink or two, and trade stories. We take time to read and have exchanged the books for new ones at María's book exchange.

Every couple of days, one of us says, "I wonder where he is now?"

--Phambili-

The Bahamas are different from any other islands I've seen. Small islands, flat, just some scrub brush and low plants. We drop the anchor near an island, barely above water, with just a few palm trees on it. The water is crystal clear. Bast says we'll play a few games of chess, sleep here, and take off in the morning.

After supper I wash the dishes in a bucket, as usual, then dump the bucket over the side, and whoopsie daisy, two forks that were hiding in the bottom of the pail slip into the water. I watch them sink to the bottom. I think, "Eh, that'll just have to be okay." Then the wind changes, and we swing away from there. "So that's good," I think.

The next day, we are getting ready to leave, and we have swung all the way around. Bast is up on deck, and he calls to me.

He says to me, "What do you suppose those are?" He points at the bottom of the bay, and the forks are completely visible.

"It's tough to tell," I say. "Pretty deep here."

He says, "I think that's silverware from this boat. You need to go down there and get them."

It's maybe thirty feet deep. I get my mask and fins on, and I go down there and pick them up off the bottom. I think, "This is about as deep as I can dive holding my breath." On the way back up, I look at the bottom of the sailboat, which I can see as clear as day, and I notice something.

It doesn't make any sense. There're cages attached to the sides near the bottom of the keel. I think, "Huh, what possible purpose could *those* have?" So I swim over for a better look at the cage on the port side. I get a bit of a shock when I realize there are two gold bricks in it. And there's another cage on the other side. As I swim up, I think, "Oh, those are secret...hidden!" When I break the surface, he's there, leaning over the lifeline, looking at me. I can tell by the look on his face, he knows, without a doubt, I saw those gold bricks.

I wonder if he's going to kill me now, because I know for sure he's smuggling.

He puts the ladder down, reaches out a hand, and pulls me up. I watch him as I pull off my mask. He puts out his hand, and I realize I'm still holding the forks. He leans into the galley and tosses them into the sink. I wonder if maybe he didn't think it through when he sent me down to get them. Am I now in big trouble--learning his secret--because I accidentally dumped *Phambili* utensils in the bay?

"Sit down," he says. "I want to tell you something."

Talking is good. I feel a little better about my chances of surviving.

"I don't know how much you know about South Africa, but there is unlimited gold. Gold could be a dollar a pound. The country has all the gold it wants. But they sell only enough to keep the price high. So they limit how much goes out of the country."

I nod that I understand.

"But, if you are resourceful, you can get your hands on some, cheap. I took my life savings, my army money, my professional soccer money, and the money from the sale of my house, and I bought gold. So that $40,000 I invested in gold can support me my whole life for what it's worth in the real world. I just had to get it out of South Africa."

I nod again because I understand what he is saying, but I know what he has done is illegal. Whoever sold him the gold also did something illegal. I wonder what the penalty is if you get caught.

"I earned that money," he continues. "I bought the gold from someone who pulled it out of the ground. I paid him what it was worth to him. So it's mine."

"Got it," I say. He is trusting me, apparently, to keep my mouth shut, and I'm going to, forever. I probably won't even tell Mom and Dorin.

"Okay, let's spear some fish, before we go," he says. "I've got a Hawaiian sling. It's easy." He shows me how to use the fishing spear, and I catch a good-sized fish the first time. This is so cool. As we haul anchor and move on, I feel a little sorry for Mom and Dorin. It must be boring sitting there in the bay.

-Fandango-

One day Bob calls us on the VHF with big news. "The water maker company is sending a repairman here to fix our unit. He's flying in the first of the week."

I had seen their busted system a few weeks ago. I leaned into a cubby, a closet-like space, and saw jam-packed stuff I didn't recognize: hoses of different kinds, electric wires, and tubes that were like cylinders.

"Nice," I said politely and got out of the way so Dorin could lean in. He was entranced and asked questions which resulted in an hour-long discussion regarding types and the benefits of water desalinators. I wasn't remotely interested in thinking about such a thing because, for us, it would take up all our fo'c'sle area.

"And, really...think of it," I said to Dorin later. "Would you trust it to remove the salt from the water, as well as to clean up the dirt and bacteria in, let's say, Boquerón Bay?"

"Well, sure. Only, everything I hear about them is that they are always in need of repair. Would be something to think about though. If we had the space. If we had the money."

Now, after a brief exchange on the VHF, Dorin says, "The repair guy has come and gone. The water maker is working! He wants us to come over. He and Binney are pretty excited."

We climb aboard a few minutes later.

"Look! A glass of water. We just made it from saltwater." Bob is holding up a tall glass of crystal-clear water.

I look overboard at the bay, which is particularly muddy looking today. Bob offers me the glass, but I shake my head.

"No, look." He drinks the entire glass. "Get her a clean glass," he says to Binney. Dorin is nearby, and he coaxes me forward with a hand on the small of my back.

"Go ahead, Shirl Jean. Be brave."

"Yeah, why don't you try it?" I ask.

"Because they're offering it to you." I can tell by his voice, he's happy to have me be the guinea pig.

It's so hard to reach for the glass and slowly bring it to my mouth. It does look as clear as you could hope any water to be. I slowly take the first sip thinking that I'd then hand it to Dorin. But the first sip tastes like real, clean, fresh water. I take a gulp and then drain the entire glass.

"Hard to believe, isn't it?" Dorin says.

"Yeah, I'm amazed. Why don't you try some?" I ask.

"No thanks, I just had a drink of tank water before we came over. I couldn't take another sip."

-Phambili-

The next night we drop anchor near another uninhabited island. Bast isn't sure the anchor is holding, so he tells me to jump in and check. I swim back and down to the anchor and find it's in pretty deep and holding. I surface, take a breath, and then, face in the water, head back to the boat. As I get closer, I can hear him yelling my name. I pick up my head to look at him.

"Swim fast now. Get back in the boat," he says urgently.

"What's that?" I ask.

"I mean it, get out!" He reaches for me, and he pulls me--yanking me up onto the ladder. Before I'm up and into the boat, I look down, and on the sandy bottom, there's a gigantic shadow under the boat. I look around, and there it is. An enormous tiger shark near the surface; it must be 15 feet long! Bast pulls me up as I scramble onto the boat. Whew! I have seen little sharks that eat little fish, but I have never seen a shark this big except on TV.

While we sit there watching it, I think, well, I guess he doesn't think I'm a risk, or he wouldn't have saved me. That's a relief. The shark swims slowly away toward deeper water.

It's nearly dark, and I'm sprucing things up on deck when I notice an animal on the island. No, two. No, a dozen!

I call Bast up to see if he knows what they are.

"Some kind of rodent," he says. "Big though! They look like rabbits with short ears."

We watch for a while. Now that we know what we are looking for we can see they are everywhere.

"I bet they would make good eating," Bast says. "They're pretty big."

"How would we catch them?" I know he has the gun, and I don't like that idea.

"Maybe we can take a basket, put some good food in it, and see if they're interested. No, wait! I have some netting. We can use that."

We row ashore with the netting, walk back to the edge of the beach, and watch. In no time, several of them come investigating. We walk slowly toward them, expecting them to scurry away, but they are not at all afraid of us. They hardly know we're there. Bast throws the net over them and catches two.

He kills them with a winch handle and guts and skins them. He cooks them up as a stew for supper. With good seasoning, they are delicious. I feel like an explorer, and the land is providing for us. And it's a nice change from fish.

The next day, in light breezes, we move on to the next uninhabited island and drop anchor in the late afternoon. We're discussing what to have for supper when I notice something moving on the horizon. Toward us.

"Hey, look at that," I say, pointing to the ship in the distance. "Is that a cruise ship?"

He looks with the binoculars. "No, it's a private yacht." We expect it to go on by, but after a while we can see it's headed for our little secluded harbor. It grows in size until we estimate that it's a hundred and fifty feet long.

"It's probably a 30-million-dollar yacht," Bast says. We watch as the anchor drops. Some of the crew are busy on the yacht, and then they launch their tender with a crane. The tender is bigger than the *Phambili*.

The boat has five men in it, all in dress uniforms. They pull up beside us, and the guy in front stands up. "Good evening, Captain," he says to Bast. "Our Captain cordially invites you to attend dinner aboard our yacht this evening at seven o'clock."

"Yes, we would be happy to come," says Bast.

"Can we pick you up?" the guy asks.

"No, we can come over," Bast says.

"We look forward to your company, Captain," the guy says and salutes.

What will we wear?" I ask when they leave.

"Whatever is clean," he says.

"Nothing. We haven't done laundry."

"Do the best you can."

So a little after six, we row over in our little dinghy, both of us dressed in our cleanest t-shirts and shorts. They have lowered a landing platform with stairs that lead up to the first deck. We fasten the dinghy, head up, and are escorted to the dining room.

The captain, an American, leads the introductions. The first mate is from the Royal Navy. Other officers are from all over the world—Germany, Sweden, Finland, Greece. They all speak quite good English. There are a dozen men and one woman, in addition to us. There are crew there to serve us, and I realize that the whole crew is still not here. There would at least be someone on the bridge. The dinner is very formal, very fancy. I realize they are enjoying putting on a show. The food is fabulous, and the wine, I guess, must be very good. I don't have much experience with wine—just what I've had at dinner at home, once in a while. As soon as I finish a glass, it's refilled.

After dinner, the captain excuses himself and tells us to have a good evening. The first mate is friendly, and everyone relaxes a little.

Bast tells some stories of his sailing adventures and our pirate story. Then he says, "Cory sailed on another boat before the *Phambili*. Tell them some of your Atlantic storm stories," he says. I do and make them funny. Everyone seems to enjoy them. Then there's a general swapping of stories while we work our way through more wine. I start to take a sip of water between each sip of wine, and my water glass is also constantly refilled.

I mention the rodents that populate the island we anchored next to last night.

"Oh, yes," says one of the officers. "That's the Bahamian Hutia. It's an endangered species."

Bast gives me a look from across the table, but it's not necessary. I already know to keep my mouth shut while the guy continues his story.

"They were over-hunted by the Indians and became extinct, or so it was thought. But eventually some were discovered on East Plana Cay, so the government relocated a few on Little Wax Cay and Warderick Wells here in the Bahamas. These three islands are the only places in the world where they exist."

"Is that so?" says Bast.

"Yes, though the population is recovering, they are still considered endangered. It's illegal to harm or capture them," he explains.

"I can imagine," says Bast.

After dinner, three officers give us a tour. This yacht is ship-shape, everything immaculate and gleaming. It's owned by a Colombian guy who only uses the yacht for two weeks a year. "We still work every day," Helen, one of our tour guides, tells us. "We sail all over the place, and all on board have their duties on their shifts. It's not all work though. We have water skiing and scuba diving equipment for whoever has a day off. Everyone gets a couple of days off a week."

"The captain runs a tight ship, whether the owner is here or not," another officer says. "We wear our work uniforms when we are on duty, and we all have our jobs to do every day."

I notice every bit of brass gleams. There is no salt on any railings.

They show us the art gallery, and one of the officers tells us the paintings are by well-known artists in Europe and are worth more than the boat. I don't recognize the artists' names, but then I don't know anything about art.

As we leave, Helen says, "We have to keep the door closed because it's climate controlled in here for the paintings."

We get a tour of the two galleys, which are huge like big kitchens, and find out they have two chefs--one chef on duty around the clock. "If you are on duty at three in the morning, you can order an ice cream sundae just as the owner might."

They show us a walk-in freezer and tell us they can stay at sea for months without going into port. One by one, the officers drop out of the tour, and then one of them offers to show Bast the bridge. It's now only Helen and me.

"Crews' cabins are down this way," she says. In a minute, she opens a door, and we step in. "This one's my room," she says. "Would you like to stay over? There's plenty of room here. I have tomorrow off."

I think, "Yes! Absolutely yes! For sure yes!"

I have already picked up the information that she's twenty-six. I try to say "yes" in my coolest, grown man-voice, hoping it doesn't crack. It squeaks just a little, and I try to cover it with a cough.

When we join up with Bast he says, "Well, time for us to head out."

"Yeah, I think I'll stay," I say.

He looks at me for a second and then says, "All right." He turns away, then turns back and says, "Should I come get you for your watch?" Then he laughs and walks away.

It's not long before I realize she thinks I'm twenty-two-years old.

That'll work.

In the morning, Helen and I are having breakfast in the outdoor dining room. There are a few other crew members milling around, scooping up breakfast, but they don't seem to notice we're there.

Bast rows over to pick me up. He looks like he's in a good mood. In fact, he seems gleeful.

He has a bit of breakfast and suddenly seems very interested in talking about his upcoming birthday. "I'll be thirty-two, which will mean I'll be exactly twice your age!"

It takes a second for Helen to realize what he's saying. I feel her tense beside me, and I want to throttle Bast.

Obviously pleased with himself, he asks, "Have a good night's sleep?"

He chuckles all the way back to the *Phambili*. He continues to ask me this question at least once per day for the next two weeks.

-Fandango-

When we are in Puerto Real one day, Dorin asks Félix about using his phone to stay in touch with Bill so we will know when Cory is flying into San Juan. Félix mentions that a friend of his, Antonio, is planning a trip to San Juan sometime in the next couple of weeks.

"Maybe he could give you a ride to the airport and back."

"Okay, that would be great. I'll let you know when we hear something."

A week before Christmas, we are past the stage of adding two more items every time we cross off one, so the long list of to-do's has been shrinking.

Cory isn't back yet, and I know it's not time to worry, but the tension is there. Dorin, sensitive to my mood, mentions a couple of times a day, that there's no way they could be in Florida yet.

"Listen, Shirl Jean. They are island hopping through the Bahamas. The weather is excellent, and they can't possibly get into trouble! And you can be sure, if they had a problem, Bast would find a way to contact us."

I feel a whole lot better. He's right. What trouble can you get into island hopping in favorable weather?

-Phambili-

We continue on through the Bahamas, stopping near uninhabited islands at night, cooking supper, playing chess, and sailing on good winds during the day. Bast has me start the motor every day to charge the batteries, so I can improve my motor-starting skill. This involves removing the stairs, giving me access to the small motor compartment. I attach a winch handle to the motor and crank hard. The clearance between the handle and the cabinet is just barely room enough to fit my hand.

"When it catches, you want it to catch here and not there," he says. "That's why you smash your wrist or your knuckles against the side of the compartment. One hard rotation should do it."

I crank it several times, and it doesn't start.

"Like this," Bast says for the dozenth time. I step out of the way, and it fires up easily with one rotation.

But he is stronger than I am and whips it around very fast. I crank it as hard as I can, but it still takes a few rotations for me.

"But I'm getting better," I say. "I don't jam my knuckles as much as I used to."

"I should get a shorter winch handle for that," he says.

Still, the motor always runs perfectly, and I find myself wishing the *Fandango's* motor ran like this.

I look at the chart several times a day and keep track of where we are. We are smack dab, I mean, full in the middle of the Bahamas. And we haven't cleared Customs yet because we can't.

One morning, he notices me looking at the chart and says, "Yeah, we are not far from Nassau. Maybe fifteen miles, but we should be okay. We're not going to stop near there."

I'm on watch an hour later, when I notice a ship approaching us. I wait a second to be sure, and, yup, it's heading dead toward us.

"Come look," I say.

"Damn! It's the Bahamian Coast Guard," he says. "It will be okay. Don't worry."

Don't worry? We are smugglers. We haven't cleared Customs. I'm in this as deep as he is.

While I try not to panic, the ship grows really fast, and then, there they are, beside us, the crew looking down at us.

"You will be boarded," a voice says.

They lower a dinghy, and four armed men come aboard.

"Your papers," says the guy in charge. Below, Bast hands him our passports and our clearance papers from Puerto Rico and the D.R. He looks at our passport and compares the photos with our faces. He spends only a few seconds on mine but pauses longer while looking at Bast's. He nods and puts our passports in his folder.

"You will follow us into port," the official tells Bast. Two officers stay on the boat with us while we motor in. I step off and tie up to a dock. Before I turn around to see what's next, one of our escort officers pulls my arms behind my back and handcuffs me.

Okay, now I'm officially scared.

As Bast steps on to the dock, he is also handcuffed. The two officers walk us to the police station where we are pushed into an empty cell. The jailer steps in and shackles us to the wall by our wrists. He leaves us, and we are alone. My heart is pounding, and I wonder if they can just keep us indefinitely, maybe confiscate the boat. I've heard of such things. I've just barely started to live my life. Now what?

"They can't keep you," Bast says. "You're a US citizen. You're only sixteen. You're American. They have to let you go."

Yeah, well, I hope. But then what? If they keep Bast, what do I do? Minutes later, the jailer and an officer come back.

"We're going to let you go," the officer says to me.

While they unlock the cell door, Bast whispers, "There's a secret compartment under my bunk. Bring a thousand dollars back and give it to them, whoever is in charge, to get me out of here." The cell door is open. He leans toward me and whispers, "Look around, you'll find it. Just bring it back and get me out of here."

I'm escorted to the door. No one gives my passport back. I walk back to the boat, and I sit on the bunk for a little while, thinking. I have to do this.

What if I get charged with trying to bribe the police? That's a crime, right?

But, what choice do I have? I have to try. So I hunt around, tap tap tap, and finally this hidden compartment opens up. There's a shit load of money in there. I don't know how much, but a lot. $10,000? $20,000? More?

I count out a thousand dollars in hundreds, put it in an envelope, and slip it into my shorts pocket. I head back to the jail, thinking, "I don't know what to do. I have never bribed anyone before."

I know I can't give it to the first policeman I see at the jail, so I start asking if I can talk to someone about the South African guy in jail. No one seems interested in helping me, but I keep asking, and eventually I am directed to an office.

Behind the desk is the guy who must be in charge. My passport is in front of him on his otherwise clear desk.

"Did you know a South African boat cannot land in the Bahamas?" he asks me.

"No," I lie. He asks why I am sailing with this South African man, and I can see he's disgusted and angry. I tell him about being recruited in Puerto Rico and that I'm really sailing with my parents. They expect me back soon.

"Apartheid!" he says. We talk about it for a while, and he lectures me about the injustices. I tell him I agree, and I do. At the same time, I'm thinking, how do you tell someone you want to bribe him? Can you do it without getting into more trouble?

"Okay," he says after a while. "I don't know what I can do. There's this very big fine. Very big. You have to pay the fine, or your friend can't leave. His boat can't leave either. You are free to go."

"Well, I can *pay* the fine," I say. There is a short silence.

He glances at me with a message in his eyes. Then he looks at a place on his desk and casually looks away, waiting. I pull the envelope from my pocket, lean forward, and put it on his desk. He looks at it a second, then takes a book from a shelf, and puts it on top of the envelope.

He pushes my passport toward me. "You can go now. You can leave."

A police officer takes me out of the police station, and I realize it's nighttime. He doesn't say anything, so I still don't know what's going on. He leaves me there without a word and goes back in.

I wait outside the jail. Twenty minutes go by, then half an hour…long enough that I don't know if Bast is coming out or not.

I wait. What else can I do?

I am so relieved when he finally comes out, walking fast toward me. He's got papers in his hand.

"We have to go. Right now," he says.

We work our way rapidly down the long dock past many boats that are tied up. We can see down at the end of the dock, where the *Phambili* is tied up, there are a lot of people milling around. As we walk down the dock, I can see there are at least thirty guys, all Bahamians, and they are tough looking customers. They are clustered around, throwing beer cans and bottles down onto the boat and shouting.

"They know," I say to Bast. "They know it's a South African boat."

Bast nods and pulls the keys out of his pocket. "Follow me," he says.

We approach from behind the crowd, and Bast pushes through the guys. They don't seem to realize we are there. Maybe they think they are being jostled by others in the crowd. We just thread our way through and then jump onto the boat. He unlocks it, throws back the hatch, and we scramble below and close the hatch.

"You have to show them your passport," he says. "Tell them we are both Americans. I can't talk to them. I have an accent."

I'm thinking they are going to murder me right now, because as soon as we hopped on the boat, they really started shouting and smashing bottles on the boat. They are about to drag us out of here and kill us, I think. They are going to murder us. If they don't kill us, at the very least, they are going to beat us hard.

"Go!" says Bast.

I step outside and yell, "Hey! Hey! What is going on? Wait! Wait! We're Americans. We're not South Africans!" I wave my passport, and finally someone grabs it.

Bast whispers, "Tell them the South Africans are someplace else. Some other boat. Tell them to go down the dock. The South Africans are down that way."

"If you're looking for South Africans," I yell, "they are down the dock." I point. "Down that way."

The guy with my passport says, "They *are* Americans!" He hands back my passport. The crowd seems confused. A few drift in the direction I had pointed.

From below Bast says, "Here, cut the lines. Cut the lines." I look down. He has a knife in one hand and the gun in the other. The stairs are already up and out, giving access to the motor. He slips me the knife. As the crowd starts wandering off, I slice the dock lines as fast as I can. As soon as the second line is cut, he fires up the boat, and we go full speed in the dead of dark, right out of the harbor. We lay offshore that night. I'm dead tired, but I don't fall asleep. I replay everything in my mind, what happened, what could have happened, and how much or how little I will tell Mom and Dorin. By morning I decide that at the very least I will tell this story to Doug and Chris. Oh, you played Dungeons and Dragons last night? Well, ha! How do you like my adventure?

The next day we sail on to the next harbor in the Bahamas. But it's okay. We've cleared Customs--that was the deal Bast struck with the Bahamian official. And now we're legal.

-Fandango-

The day before Christmas, we sail up to Mayagüez to give us both something to do. Around noon we drop anchor in pretty much an empty harbor.

Dorin says he wants to make *El Coquito* for Christmas Day. "But I need rum and brandy, and we are fresh out of...well, any alcohol. Why don't I just row into shore. Maybe I can find a little store open."

"Good idea. I want to work on the weather cloths." The weather cloths are a project that never got done before we left, so we brought the material with us and then forgot about it. When finished, they will be long panels of canvas that we'll tie onto the top and bottom lifelines. In theory, they will deflect water blowing into the cockpit. I've been folding and stitching around the edges. Eventually we'll put in grommets.

"That sounds good. I should be back in less than an hour," he says.

When one hour passes, I'm a little nervous. But I know how he likes to talk, and a lot of people in Mayagüez speak English. He might not be back for a couple of hours. But when three hours go by, I'm a nervous wreck. What if something has happened to him?

What if he got mugged?

What if he never comes back?

Maybe I could hail somebody. But from this vantage point I can't see the dock or the dinghy. Another hour goes by and I'm trying, unsuccessfully, not to think of the reality of my situation. What am I going to do? I can't get anywhere because Dorin took the dinghy. I'm marooned on the *Fandango*. No one knows where we are.

Another hour goes by, and I'm nauseated with worry.

Then I hear a motor.

As I clear the companion way, I see a wooden dinghy with three men in it motoring toward the boat. Dorin raises his hand and waves. The *Tinker* trails behind the wooden boat.

Dorin looks sheepish as he climbs back on board.

"Do you want to come aboard?" he asks the men.

"No, no. You have good Christmas. *Feliz Navidad!* Here is your food."

One of the men hands him a baking sheet mounded up and covered with aluminum foil. Dorin hands it to me and then turns back as the second man hands him a brown paper bag with two bottles in it.

"This is my wife," Dorin says, turning to me. "This is Juan and Carlos."

The men stand in the dinghy and bend forward in an exaggerated but dignified bow. *"Buenas tardes, Señora. Feliz Navidad!"*

They untie the *Tinker* from behind their boat, retie it to our stern cleat, and moments later, they motor away.

"Am I in big trouble?" Dorin asks. "I'm so sorry. They were trying to help, and it got out of hand." He never slurs his words when he has an extra drink or three, but I can tell he is feeling no pain.

Now that he's back, I start to tremble all over.

I draw in a ragged breath.

Then relief washes through me, leaving me weak.

But he's okay. My breath whooshes out.

I'm okay.

I peel back the foil. There is a small mountain of pulled pork that smells out of this world. I am hungry and grab a couple of plates.

"No, not for me," Dorin says. "I've had too much to eat. I am so sorry. I didn't mean for this to happen."

"No, I'm sure you didn't. But I was so worried. Worried sick!"

He groaned. "What time did I leave? How long was I gone?"

"Only five hours." I pile some of the meat on my plate. There are also some sweet potatoes and fried plantains. It looks deli...

No.

I drop the plate on the table and turn toward him. "Do you know how scared I was?"

"I was concerned about that, but I couldn't seem to get control of the situation."

This has a complete ring of truth to it. How many times has he been shanghaied after work by friends or coworkers and, with the best of intentions, tried to get free but failed? If we'd been at home, I wouldn't have given it a thought. But here, where he doesn't have cronies...?

I sigh and nod. "Okay. Tell me about it." I pick up my plate and nibble at the meat.

Dorin is already stretched out, leaning back on the dinette seat. He yawns.

"Well, when I got to the beach, a couple of guys were there pulling their boat up on shore. I asked them if they knew where I could buy some rum. They said yes, and I got in the car with them. I thought they were going to take me to a store. The next thing I knew, we were at Juan's house, and I am meeting all his family. I had to take the drink Juan offered me, to be polite. They were all watching to see if I would. So I did, and they all relaxed. We started having a heck of a good time. They offered me some appetizers, and I was really hungry, so I ate a few. I don't know what they were, but they were delicious. I washed them down with another drink.

"Finally, I said, 'I have to get back to my wife on the boat,' and said I would walk. I didn't have any idea, by then, where we were or how to get back, but I figured out I would just head for the ocean and try to keep it in sight. But Carlos insisted on driving me back to the boat. Instead of going back the way we came, we, all three of us, went up a mountain and further inland.

"Finally, we stopped at another house, and we went in. Carlos' family was celebrating, so they welcomed us in and insisted we have another drink. And then another. Then they wanted me to have supper with them. I said I have to get back to my wife.

"'*Esposa*,' Carlos explained to his family.

"'*Ah, sí*,' Carlos' wife said.

"Then she starts piling food on the baking pan. I keep telling her 'enough, enough,' but I don't think she understood. She just kept piling it on. Maybe she thought I was saying, 'more!'

"We were just leaving when Carlos says, 'Wait!' He goes into another room and comes out with two bottles, one rum and one brandy. I say 'no, I can't take this,' but I could see they were going to be hurt if I didn't, so, finally I did. I said I would pay for it when we got back to the boat, but they said no, '*No problema. No pay. Feliz Navidad!*'"

Dorin yawns deeply and leans further back onto the dinette cushion. "And that's my story, and I'm going to stick to it! I'm so sorry. I knew you'd be worried. But I thought I was only gone for a couple of hours, tops. Boy, these people are so nice and so helpful and so hospitable! I don't think I thanked them enough."

Dorin yawns again, closes his eyes, and drops off to sleep, leaving me with my thoughts. I am glad he had a good time. He deserves it. He often gets this reaction from people, but, I think, maybe even more here in Puerto Rico.

My guy, Mr. Congeniality.

After I eat, I put the rest of the dinner on ice for tomorrow. I wake Dorin up, and we decide to head back to Boquerón, even though the sun is setting. We don't want to be away from the phone in the park, in case Cory has called Bill. We know the coastline so well, we can waft along in a light breeze and watch the terrain slide by, enjoying the lights that climb the ridges of the hills and dot the jungle growth. We drop anchor at midnight, nibble on some more pork, and feel we've had a pretty adventurous Christmas Eve.

On Christmas Day, Dorin is clear-eyed and chipper and, as usual, none the worse for wear. We sail out of the bay to shallow but clear water and go over the side to scrape the crud off the bottom of the *Fandango*. Back at anchor, we dig out all of the caulking from every crack and crevice so we can put in fresh stuff when we get a chance.

From the pay phone in the park, we talk to my folks and then Bill and wish them a Merry Christmas.

"So, you haven't heard from Cory?" I ask.

"No, and both Tina and I are trying to tend the phone day and night. Is he overdue?"

"Depends on who you talk to. Maybe not."

"Tina will be here all day this week. Maybe you should call us every day."

Later, back in the *Fandango*, we celebrate the day with seriously delicious El Coquito. The talk, as it does every day, turns to Cory's journey.

"It's going to be okay, Shirl," Dorin says. "I bet he can't wait to get back so he'll have something to do. And he's only been gone about four weeks. Way too early to worry. Things are probably going so smoothly he's completely bored."

-Phambili-

The next day, we tie up at another harbor on another island. Bast says he's going in for some groceries and some parts. It's my job to clean up the boat. There is broken glass everywhere from the bottles those guys smashed on the boat. I don't want to go ashore in the Bahamas again, anyway, so I am happy with this deal. A couple of hours go by. In the beginning, I don't think much of it. But then I begin to wonder. Did he get into trouble again? Did he take the clearance papers with him? I look in the folder, and they are still there. But his passport is not, so he must have taken that. By now, every shard of glass and trash has been swept and mopped away. I fix some lunch and then find some cleaning chores to do.

Finally, he comes back in a good mood, with groceries and a fuel filter for the boat.

He tells me the Bahamian National Soccer team was practicing, and he scrimmaged with them for a couple of hours. The coach offered him Bahamian citizenship if he would join the team.

"Guess I can still do okay," he says. "Listen, I got an idea back there. A cruise ship stopped for a while and tourists got off, looking to spend money as fast as they could. So that gave me the idea. When I stopped in the islands, they were selling t-shirts that said *St. Maarten* on them, and they were splattered with paint. Tourists were crazy about them. So I'm going back and buy t-shirts that say *The Bahamas* on them, and we are going into business. Look around and dig out any old paint you can find."

He comes back with 50 t-shirts with The Bahamas logo on them. We spread them out, take sticks, dip them in paint, and splatter it on the shirts. Three colors on each shirt. Every shirt is different, and they look great.

"There's another cruise ship coming in tomorrow, and we'll be there," he says.

And we are. We take a spot close to the other venders and put down our box of shirts. I put one on and I hold up another one.

"Get your souvenir t-shirts," Bast yells. I think his accent stands out, and quickly a mob of people gathers around shoving, handing Bast ten-dollar bills. We sell them all, except the one I'm wearing, in half an hour.

Bast is shaking my hand when I look over his shoulder and see a tall, angry Bahamian man walking toward us. There are two guys with him, a few steps behind.

"This is our place to sell," he says to Bast. "You don't come here and sell in our place! In our country. You leave now!" He leans over Bast and points in the direction of the ocean.

The guys behind him nod and look pretty threatening.

Bast nods. "Okay, sorry, man. I didn't know." He backs away and motions me to follow him.

"Man, he was bonkers," Bast says.

"And don't come back!" the man yells.

"You know we just took $500 in sales away from them," I say.

"Yeah. I guess we should untie and leave," he says. "A bit richer than when we came."

A day later, we approach Florida. I am happy, but also disappointed. This trip has been fun, and I'm not ready for it to end.

As if reading my mind, he says, "You know, you could continue on with me. Go through the Panama Canal, up the Pacific Coast, on to California. Or, hey, we could just decide to sail around the world. Think about it."

I do think about it. I kind of want to do that. I know Bast can get into all kinds of trouble, but he also gets out of it. It would be never be boring.

But I'm not quite seventeen. And it seems like I should go back. Don't I need to graduate from high school? Isn't that what people do? But if I don't do this sailing thing now, will I get another chance?

We tie up and clear Customs in Fort Lauderdale. At the dock, we are right beside this huge private yacht that has also just cleared Customs. The owner starts a conversation with Bast, and he tells us he owns a big corporation that deals with diesel engines. He invites us aboard to have drinks. The yacht's not as big as the yacht in the Bahamas, but it's still big and really nice. We hang out for a day, and then he tells us he has a mansion very close by on the water. He is flying somewhere on business, so he invites us to stay at his guest house and gives us the keys to an Alfa Romeo Spider that he keeps on hand for guests.

I have my driver's license—got it just before we left on the trip. It was my idea to time it so that I'd spend my probation period at sea. I figure, even if I get stopped for anything in Florida, it won't hurt my license in Maine. Bast makes me the driver, and I drive us all around Miami in this classic Spider.

So, this is the way we could live? From yacht to yacht to mansion?

One day, we stop near a beach and see a dozen people coming ashore. We walk onto the beach and realize they have swum from their raft the last hundred yards to shore. People help them out of the water, and they walk away from the beach and disappear.

Shortly after, immigration shows up, looking for them. A guy is standing beside me and, in accented English says, "It's okay. Once Cubans are on shore, they are fine. Political asylum. They'll be okay."

Bast is ready to continue his trip.

I had a tough decision to make. I'm going back to Puerto Rico after all.

We go to the airport to buy my ticket and then call brother Bill to tell him when I will land in San Juan.

The night before I leave, I am just cutting through to the docks when five drunk college guys come out of a bar. They surround me, and two guys pull my arms behind my back. Another guy takes my wallet and pulls the money out. "Hey! Look at this!" he says. "Would you believe he has $300 on him? Let's go!" They run down the street and around a corner. I tell Bast when I get back to the boat. He just paid me, and now I have no dollars. He gives me another fifty to travel with. The next morning, he brings me to the airport and stays until I board the plane. Part of me wishes I were staying. Life would never be boring sailing with Bast.

-Fandango-

On Sunday, Bill has Cory's travel information for us. He will arrive in San Juan on Tuesday. Bill gives us the flight number and ETA. We take the *público* to Puerto Real to talk to Félix about arranging for his friend Antonio to give us a ride to San Juan. The friend will be in Boquerón visiting his mother on Monday, so he would like to pick us up there.

Antonio shows up in a new, red Honda Civic. By private car it's an easy three-hour ride to the airport, and Dorin and Antonio chat all the way. It seems like every Puerto Rican man we talk to has some connection with fishing, so they trade ocean stories, but I'm not really listening. I can't wait to get there, see my youngest child, and see for myself that he's okay. Though it's only been six weeks, it seems like months since we last saw him.

From the terminal we watch the runway.

"That's him," Dorin says about the plane on final approach. He squeezes my hand.

The plane touches down smoothly. I wasn't aware I have been holding my breath until I exhale.

The twin-engine plane empties its passengers out onto the tarmac, and just when I think he must not be on it, there he is bounding down the mobile stairway, jogging toward the terminal. He sees us, waves, and heads for Customs. Then he comes swashbuckling toward us, duffle over his shoulder, looking taller and fitter than ever, and grinning from ear to ear.

He engulfs me in a hug, kisses me on the top of my head and says, "Aw. I missed you." Tears run down my cheeks. Out pops a sob.

"Hey, hey, I'm back. It's okay."

I nod and release him. He turns to Dorin, who puts out his hand. Cory grabs his hand to shake it, and then pulls Dorin into a hug.

"Man, it's good to have you back," Dorin says.

"I've got so much to tell you," Cory says. "And I'm starved."

"I will bring you to the restaurant, and then I will go visit a friend," says Antonio. "I will pick you up later. In two hours?"

He leaves us off at a very nice restaurant. We order food and settle in to hear all about Cory's trip.

My eyes keep popping open as he regales us with his adventures.

"Pirates? *Pirates!*" I say. He nods.

"Gold? *Smuggled!*" He nods and smiles.

"A shark? *While you were in the water? A shark?*" He shrugs and smiles.

"Endangered? *Endangered!*"

"Yeah, that was kind of too bad," he says. "Tasty, though." He pantomimes picking his teeth.

"Arrested! You mean arrested, as in *arrested?*"

I look at Dorin, wanting to get my message across: "I knew he was in danger," but he is leaning forward, nodding, smiling, hanging on Cory's every word.

And then I can see Cory is having a blast telling us about his adventures. And, after all, he's safe, right here in front of me, and looking well. Is he looking older? Or am I just now noticing how full his beard and mustache have become, how broad his shoulders are. He'll be seventeen in a month.

"But what else is wrong?" I ask as we finish our meal. "There's something you haven't told us."

He nods. "I don't have the money," he says. "The three hundred-dollars. I was mugged by a bunch of college kids in Fort Lauderdale night before last. I wasn't in danger. They weren't going to do anything. Disgusting though. When I got back to the boat, Bast gave me another fifty dollars so I'd have money with me for the flight. But it's okay. I had a great time. I loved it!"

On the way home, Cory and I sit in the back, my arm through his. I feel like I won't ever let him out of my sight again.

I ask Antonio if we could stop at a post office before going back to the boat. I have brought some letters to mail, and I need more stamps.

"Yes, there is one in the next town. I will take you there."

He parks on the street about thirty yards down from the front of the building.

I enter the small post office and get in line behind three other people. There are two windows, but only one is open for business. I sense the people in front of me are uneasy; they seem stiff and look off into the distance. This is not a tourist town, so maybe they are unused to Americans standing in line in their post office.

Passing the time, I read the sign at the head of the line: *Próximo*. I have seen this word before, and I think it means "next." Then I scan the Wanted posters on the bulletin and try to pick out a few words that I know.

I grow bored and after a while, I realize the line has not moved since I arrived.

I glance over at the clerk's window, and after a heartbeat, it registers: a customer at the window is reaching into a large satchel that is wide open on the counter beside him. He pulls out four bundles of hundred-dollar bills. The clerk pushes a money order toward him. He consults a list and then fills in the money order. He hands it to the clerk and dips in the bag to pull out more. The bag is still more than half full of bundled money. I try not to react while I process what's happening. Yikes! Can this be drug money being laundered through the United States Post Office? At this point, I'm aware that tension among the other customers has increased. They know I have caught on. I take a slow breath and go back to scanning the bulletin board, my eyes averted as much possible, trying to look casually oblivious. I feel their relief.

Out of the corner of my eye, I take occasional notice and see slow progress. The clerk seems to be stiff with nerves. Finally, the man takes his stack of money orders, puts them in the bag, tips his baseball cap to the clerk, and leaves. It takes the clerk a few seconds to allow herself to sag in relief. As she closes her window, the second window opens, and another clerk nods at the first customer in line. The rest of the customers remain stiff, and I decide it's because I'm there. Perhaps they are embarrassed. Maybe they think I'm going to cause trouble. Now that it's over, I'm shaking inside. I want to run outside and back to the car, but it now feels safer in here. I stick it out until I get my stamps and mail my letters.

Once outside, I run down the sidewalk, despite my high heels, and back to the car. I jump in and sink back in relief. "Can we get out of here fast?"

"What took you so long?" asks Dorin.

"Let's just go, go, go, and I'll tell you on the way."

I don't really think the guy is hanging around outside, but I want to put some distance between us and the post office.

Antonio speeds up as he listens to my story and says, "I am sorry, missus. Sometimes these things happen. Is very bad. Can be very dangerous. But what can you do?"

Finally, we get back to the *Fandango*. Back to the three of us.

The next day on a light breeze, we waft into Puerto Real Bay. We are barely inside when we hear the long, low note of a conch shell horn...and then a second, haunting blast that can be heard across the harbor.

We see the two little girls on a dock, waving to us. "Welcome, welcome home, Cory," they shout.

"No." Cory hangs his head. "I forgot about this stuff."

Dorin laughs. "They must have heard you were back and have been watching for you."

Another long bass note. "Cory, we love you!" they shout.

"They can't be blowing that conch," Dorin says. "It's too difficult." Sure enough, standing in the shadow of a building, one of the guys from the fishing co-op laughs like hell. He's holding the conch shell.

"Absence makes the heart grow even fonder," Dorin says. "Welcome home, Cor."

Chapter Eighteen

Putting Down Roots

"You know you are walking in time to the music, don't you?" Cory says.

"What? No. I'm just walking. Carrying grocery bags."

"You are. You are almost dancing down the sidewalk."

We are in Cabo Rojo doing the weekly shopping at a grocery store that has great produce, fresh meat, and fish. We always go in together to carry the heavy bags across town to the *público* station. Though private cars have their A/C on and the windows closed, taxis drive around with popular salsa music blaring from their open windows. It's exhilarating to walk along the sidewalks and under flowering trees, being on vacation. The next thing I know, I'm nodding my head to the music but trying to control the rhythm of walking so it isn't in time with the music.

"Good try." Cory laughs out loud.

When Dorin goes on these shopping forays, we always make a stop at the hardware store, or *ferretería*, a word we have been unable to master. Then we walk the extra few blocks to the ice cream store. There I have discovered *uva* (grape) ice cream that is the most delicious flavor I've ever eaten. The ice cream, the same as in the D.R., is also very creamy— noticeably better than ice cream in the States.

Since we have found a really decent supermarket, we indulge in good food and take turns cooking up meals to surprise each other. Steak, pork chops, a variety of rice dishes, many kinds of fish, fresh vegetables. We gradually create a store of spices and herbs.

Every few days, I empty the icebox of food then bail and siphon out the melted ice water. By the time I'm done, one of the guys is back with a block of ice wrapped in a towel sling Dorin made. The ice is handed up to someone on deck and then lowered into the icebox. We are grateful for easy access to ice, which so improves our menus and diets.

The only cloud on our culinary horizon is that the stove, which has been a pain right along, is getting worse—increasingly difficult to start and keep running. It's also creating more sooty smoke. But we manage, and the uptick in the quality of our meals makes up for it.

One day, the three of us arrive at the *público* stand in Cabo Rojo, and Cory says, "I want to walk back, just for the heck of it." He hands the driver our groceries to be stowed in the trunk.

"Yeah, I'd like to, also. I could use the exercise," I say.

"It'll take a couple of hours," Cory says.

"That's okay. It'll be a nice walk, shady. I can do it."

"Sure, sounds good to me," says Dorin. "You don't mind if I accompany the groceries in the taxi back to Boquerón?" Almost immediately, the *público* leaves the station, and Dorin leans out the window to wave.

"Good luck!" he yells. It's easy to see from his Cheshire-cat grin, he's gotten the best of the deal.

"You know the way, right?" I ask Cory.

"Yeah, pretty much a straight shot," he says. "We've done it a hundred times by car."

On that positive note we start our little hike, enjoying seeing the landscape and foliage up close instead of from a car window.

After a while I say, "I don't remember the road rising like this."

"Yeah, I was just thinking that."

"But we're heading in the right direction," Cory says. "It parallels the road we usually take. Let's just keep going. Be quicker than going back and starting again."

We trek on as the road, bare of shade trees, continues to rise sharply, so much so, the ocean comes into view. "See I told you we were heading in the right direction," Cory says. "It's hot though. We probably should have brought water."

We continue to wind upwards on the blistering road. On our left, toward inland, the ground rises up from the road. On the right the land slopes downward toward the ocean. On both sides of the road, there are architecturally gorgeous homes on spacious, landscaped grounds, surrounded by tall, wrought-iron fences, gracefully positioned here and there—none too close to the other. But there are very few trees near the road, and the sun beats down on the scorching pavement.

"We're lost. You know that, don't you?" Cory asks.

"Do you think it's much farther? We've been walking for over two hours."

"We're on top of one of those mountains where the lights run along the ridge at night. Yeah, a lot farther. Still going in the right direction, though. As long as the ocean is on our right, we're okay. Man, I wish we had water."

Sweat runs into my eyes. This is the hottest environment I have ever experienced. "If only there were shade," I say. "Maybe we should head back and find out where we went wrong."

"Look," Cory says. Ahead we spot a palm tree barely leaning over the road. We cross diagonally and stand for a minute in the sparse shade it provides. Suddenly, across the road a large dog gallops up the manicured lawn of a mansion and throws himself at the gate, snarling.

"Let's go," Cory says grabbing my arm and propelling me in giant steps farther along the road. "He probably can't get out, but let's not wait around and find out. I think that answers the question. I don't think we should head back," Cory says. "I don't want to tempt that guard dog."

We are soaked with sweat. My feet are burning from the heat through my shoes.

"We have to have something to drink soon," I say. "We've been walking almost three hours in this heat."

"Look, another tree." We slog to the other side to stand in the small shade of the palm, which gives a bit of respite.

"You okay?" Cory asks. "This has to come out somewhere."

"Nothing we can do but keep going."

We continue to crisscross the road to rest in the weak shade of occasional palm trees.

But where, I wonder, will we come out? How much longer do we have to keep going? I look down at the road and see spots in my vision.

"Well, at least it's scenic," Cory says. "We never would have known about this part of Puerto Rico. Could have been worse."

"How?"

"We could be walking in jungle."

And suddenly we are. The road curves inland, and we lose sight of the ocean. It's now noticeably cooler, but there are no houses, no electricity poles. Just a shady road through jungle. Relief provided by the jungle foliage is welcomed, but I am no less thirsty. I wonder how much I would be willing to pay for a glass of water.

"I'd give a hundred-dollars for a glass of water," Cory says, as if reading my mind. I nod in agreement.

The road changes to dirt and curves further inland. As we come around a corner, there, almost like a mirage, is a hut with a large, red, chest-type Coca-Cola cooler outside, in front of the house. We both stop for a second in disbelief.

A man sits behind the cooler. He lifts the lid and holds up a bottle. "Coca-Cola?"

As we run, Cory and I go through our pockets to find money. We come up with two dollars and hand them to the man. Using a bottle opener he snaps the caps off the bottles and hands them to us. Cory lifts his and downs the Coke without stopping. Before I can drink half of mine, he hands the bottle back to the owner, who puts the empty into a sectioned wooden crate.

"¿*Una más?*" Cory asks.

"*Sí.*" The man seems curious about us. He glances at the road we have come down. "¿*Americanos?*" he asks as he hands Cory another opened Coke.

Cory drains half of it before he says, "*Sí.*"

The gentleman asks a question I can't understand except for "*casa.*"

"*Barco,*" Cory says as he holds the cold, condensation-covered bottle to his forehead.

"Aah," the man says, as if this makes sense, but I can see it doesn't. He glances back up the road that goes over the ridge of a mountain that is populated with grand houses with great security.

"¿*Dónde está la Bahía de Boquerón?*" Cory asks.

"*Ah. La bahía. Un barco. Ah, sí!*" He has put it together, a boat and a bay, and it makes a little more sense to him, but not entirely. You can see he still has questions about why we are on this road.

"*Aquí, Señora,*" he says and hands me a second bottle. I exchange it for my empty.

Then he begins a description that I can't follow, but Cory nods, asks a question, and nods again. "*Muchas gracias,*" he says to the man.

The gentleman bows and says, "*De nada. Buenas tardes.*"

I hand back my half-empty bottle, and he shakes his head, motioning me to go and take the bottle with me.

"*Muchas gracias, Señor,*" I say with gratitude. I'm too full to finish the bottle, but I am still thirsty.

"*De nada, Señora.*"

Refreshed and encouraged, we eventually come to a small village and then, five hours after we left Cabo Rojo, a recognizable Boquerón.

Our dinghy is tied to the dock, so we guess that Dorin left it for us and had Bob take him back to the boat.

When we row out and approach the *Fandango*, Dorin appears in the cockpit.

"Hey, what took you so long? Did you take the scenic route?"

* * *

We begin to notice the tubes of the *Tinker* need to be pumped up about once a week. One of the guys gets into the little boat and foot-pumps air to inflate the tubes. This is not easy because, though the floor of the *Tinker* has small plywood reinforcement sections held in place by rubber, there is flexible space between them.

"Seems not to be holding air the way it used to," Dorin says. "We need to check for leaks. We have a patching kit."

We pull the dinghy onto the deck and spend an hour brushing a mixture of liquid soap and water over every inch of tubing, watching for any bubble to appear to indicate a leak. Nothing. A week later, as I am sitting on the side tube on the way into the dock, I notice I'm lower, relative to the rest of the tubing. That afternoon Cory and Dorin try again to locate a leak. Still nothing. Dorin, on his hands and knees, puts first his ear close to the tubing and then his face to see if he can hear or feel a leak. Nothing.

"That is peculiar," he says. "I don't get it. This dinghy got great reviews. Well, we'll just have to pump a little air in every week or so." Dorin's lack of concern allows us to ignore the problem. It doesn't even make the list.

The good life goes on. One day, Dorin is serving us lunch, one of our favorites, Nasi Goreng, a Southeast Asian dish. "Have you guys noticed the bay is clearing up?"

Cory glances over the side and laughs. Then he looks at Dorin's face. "Oh, you're serious."

"Not as good as the Bahamas, you're right," Dorin says. "But you've got some visibility. Better than it was…maybe better than Maine lake water, and I've been scuba diving in that. Not bad."

"So you're saying we should go snorkeling," I say.

"Yeah, it's good enough that you can see for several yards, I think. I understand there's a reef of sorts in the middle of the bay. You could check that out."

"I'll do it," Cory says.

As soon as we finish lunch, Cory rows the *Tinker* around the bay, pausing to peer into the water. Finally, he gives us a thumbs up, dons the mask and snorkel and is over the side into the barely-less-than-murky bay.

I watch the snorkel intently as he swims in circles. Then it disappears. I gasp, but Dorin says, "Don't worry. He's just diving down. He'll be up in a moment." He's right. But when Cory surfaces, he stands up in chest-deep water with both hands in the air.

Dorin laughs. "He's standing on the reef."

Cory rows back a few minutes later. "Come on in you guys. It's not bad. I can see almost as good as when we were in Samaná."

"I have an idea," Dorin says. "Why don't I row you guys over to the reef and leave you there so you can snorkel your way back here. But Cory, no standing on reefs. They are fragile, and you can damage them."

"Yeah, I know. Bast told me about it. This seemed more like a rock. But I won't stand on anything, just to be on the safe side."

I rummage around until I find my trusty mask and snorkel. A few minutes later, Dorin rows us to the spot where Cory had been standing in the water. I slip into the water, and Dorin hands me the mask.

Dorin rows back to the boat, and Cory and I snorkel around for a while. It's still cloudy, and the bottom is not at all interesting--not nearly the experience of discovery I had in Samaná Bay. In a little while I touch Cory's arm and raise my head. He does too and drops the snorkel out of his mouth.

"Kind of cool," he says, "but it's not the Bahamas...."

"Yeah, not as good as Samaná either."

We agree we are done for today and turn to snorkel back to the boat.

In a minute, I see jellyfish ahead of us—at first three or four, but in less than a minute a swarm surrounds us. I am alarmed because, as we have read and heard, jellyfish can sting. Cory signals me to surface.

"There's nothing we can do," he says. "We just have to swim through them."

"We can signal Dorin, and he can pick us up."

"No, he isn't looking this way. And it would take too long for him to get here. We'll get stung anyway. We have to swim."

"Okay, you lead." We put our heads in the water and swim as fast as we can. Light filters weakly through the water, highlighting the translucent, floating blobs. I think about all we've heard about jellyfish—those whose stings can kill you, those that can merely maim, and those that will just make you miserable with painful stings that can last for days. These must be the good guys, I think. Just painful. Already I feel the stinging on my legs, even as I flutter kick as fast as I can. Meat tenderizer, I remember. That's what's recommended to reduce the pain of stings.

I'm sure we have no meat tenderizer on board.

If I were watching these through a marine museum glass wall, they'd be interesting and quite pretty. But damn! This hurts. Do I remember someone telling us the stings can paralyze for hours? I lose sight of Cory and lift my head. I see his snorkel 20 feet away, headed directly for the boat. I realize I am off course and turn to follow him. Is there nothing in this bay but pulsing jellyfish?

Cory turns to look back at me and then continues. In what seems like an hour, he turns and grabs my arm. I look up and see we are at the dinghy. As I wrap my arm around the tube, he pushes me upward, and I'm over the side. In the next second, he boosts himself over and into the dinghy.

"Done already?" Dorin asks.

"I bet we don't have meat tenderizer," Cory says.

"No. What? Jellyfish stings?"

"Dozens," I say.

Dorin leans over to give us a hand up.

Now that we are safe from the attacking jellyfish, the pain really kicks in. Dorin hands us towels. "Scrub as hard as you can to get any tentacle pieces off," he says. "I'm going to pull up a bucket of seawater. I read you should wash with seawater. Baking soda. Do we have any?"

"Yes. I have a box for cleaning the head. In a pocket on the door."

Dorin mixes the powder with fresh water, and we dab it on our welts.

"Oh, oh, ouch, ouch," I yell.

Cory doesn't say anything, but he is gritting his teeth and rocking. Dorin brings prescription strength Tylenol from our med box and hands us a glass of water. We share the water and down the pills.

"Are we in any trouble?" I ask.

"No, I don't think so. If you were sensitive or allergic to the stings, it would already be apparent. I don't know if you would have made it back to the boat. I can tell you one thing. We are getting fins for you guys. You would have made it back here in half the time."

"I think I'm done in this bay," I say.

"Me too. I'm cured," Cory says.

"I don't blame you. It'll be better in Venezuela," Dorin says. "All the literature says it's great snorkeling and scuba diving."

We keep reapplying the baking soda paste when it dries out, and the pain is less in a few hours. But my joints and muscles are sore the next day, and it takes four days before the welts disappear.

During this time, Dorin cooks all the meals, and we are treated to eggs Benedict, stir fry with sausage, onions and sweet peppers, spicy chicken breast, crispy pan-fried fish, fish tacos, and Moroccan chicken with carrots and artichoke hearts.

"Do you think we should tell him we are feeling better?" Cory asks me.

"To tell you the truth, and in case you haven't noticed, he likes to cook. This gives him an excuse."

Sure enough, later in the day, Dorin apologizes. "I am just using your injuries as an excuse to monopolize the cooking. If you guys are chomping at the bit to cut loose in the galley, feel free."

"I'll do some cooking," Cory says. "I want to try a recipe that the del Toros showed me."

"I'm passing the baton," Dorin says and hands Cory a spatula.

"Mom?" Cory asks.

"I'm good," I say. "Go for it."

I'm thinking life couldn't get any better.

One morning, we are sitting in the cockpit eating breakfast when a boat enters the harbor.

"Oh no," Dorin says. "It's the *Lone Star*."

"George," I groan.

We watch the boat make progress into the bay and then anchor far away. I'm glad the bay is so big.

That night we go to María's. As people switch tables to chat with one another, I find myself beside Sue.

"I admire you," she said. "You seem to know a lot about sailing."

"Only a little."

"I wish I knew more. I think that if something were to happen to George while we're out on the ocean, I wouldn't know a single thing to do."

"Hey, I could teach you a little. We could take my rubber-ducky, my sailing dinghy, around the bay someday, and you could learn how to use the wind and sails to make the boat move. That part is easy."

"I don't know. I don't know if George would let me."

I raise my eyebrows.

"Well, okay," she says. "How about Saturday morning?"

"Sure, no problem. I'll sail over to your boat and pick you up."

"No, how about you pick me up at the dock? George is going somewhere. I'll go into the dock with him and wait for you there."

"Okay. We're going to Puerto Real for a few days, but I'll be back by Saturday."

The next morning, we chug out of the bay and by lunch time cozy into the place that feels the most like home. On Friday, we head back to Boquerón so I will be there for Sue's sailing lesson.

"Okay, Shirl Jean, maybe it's time for you to single-hand the *Fandango*. How about today? Cory and I can take the *público* and you can sail'er on down to Boquerón. We couldn't have better weather, and you are so ready."

"Actually," Cory says, "the del Toro family has asked me to hang out with them this weekend, so I'll stay right here."

Though I have been adamant I wouldn't solo, because why do I need to, I think of Sue who doesn't even get an offer. Dorin is giving me this opportunity.

I take it.

Dorin uses the VHF to tell Bob and Binney he'll be coming in by taxi, and Bob says he'll pick Dorin up at the dock so they can hang out on the *Grace* until I get there.

Cory puts his hands on my shoulders and looks like he's thinking of and discarding important things he wants to say. Finally, he just nods and says, "Okay. Do good."

He rows us into the dock, and when Dorin gets out he says, "I'll be waiting for you, on deck, sipping my martini."

Seeming confident and worry-free, they wave casual goodbyes as they head toward town. It feels a little strange being alone as I row back to an unoccupied boat. Well, nothing to do but get at doing this. I take the sail ties off but leave the sail drooping from the boom.

The motor starts easily. Leaving it in neutral, I go forward and begin ratcheting up the anchor. When it's almost to the bowsprit, I pull it the rest of the way by hand and secure it temporarily on deck. Back in the cockpit, I push the lever forward and experience a little thrill when the boat obeys by moving forward. With the tiller, I turn the *Fandango* around and head toward the opening of the bay. I glance toward the *Villa Pesquera* and see Félix standing in the yard with his fists on his hips, watching me. He gives a nod and barely a smile that I interpret as approval. Nice!

Out on the ocean, I experience a few butterflies, but Dorin was right, the breezes are light and perfect for an easy reach. I crank up the main and decide to go with just the one sail. After an hour of the wind coming from the same direction, I am bored so I start the motor to cover the distance more quickly and leave the sail up. Finally, I see the opening of Boquerón Bay. Rather than fuss with the main in front of an audience, I lower the sail and put on the sail ties while the boat chugs on in. When I get closer, I see quite a number of people milling around on the dock and wonder what is going on. I go through the same routine that I did when Cory and I came in, dropping the anchor and backing off, waiting for the boat to swing on the anchor, making sure it's set. I feel a lift in spirits. I can set an anchor!

Dorin is on the *Grace* waving both arms and then giving me the thumbs up. "Yahoo! Good job!" he yells. Bob and Binney are also waving excitedly.

I am a little pleased and a little embarrassed. What I just did was a minimal accomplishment worthy of acknowledgement, maybe, but not worthy of a fuss. Bob signals he is going to come pick me up.

"That was great!" Dorin says when they come alongside. "I knew you could do it. I didn't doubt it for a minute."

"It was not a big deal," I say, wanting to downplay it, but a little pleased nevertheless. Then I notice a couple of dinghies headed our way filled with some of the cruising guys from the boats anchored in the bay.

Bob looks over his shoulder and then back at me. "Um, this is probably my fault. I happened to mention to a couple of the guys that you were soloing from Puerto Real."

"I told them it was not a big deal when I got here," Dorin says. "But by then they were all in a lather...."

The first of the dinghies drifts to a stop near the stern. Fred stands up and hangs onto the stern pulpit.

"Wow, glad you are safe. Whew! We were really worried!"

My eyes are wide open, and my eyebrows are nearly to my hairline.

I look at Dorin. He nods but avoids eye contact.

A second boat stops nearby and Sam, another guy I remember from María's, throttles back the motor. "Glad to see you are okay. We were just deciding to call the Coast Guard."

"What?!" I look again at Dorin, who is clearly embarrassed. He stares at the bottom of Bob's dinghy.

"Yeah," the guy continues, "George was reminding us that there are reefs out there, and you can get into real bad trouble if you don't know what you are doing. It takes a lot of experience and some local knowledge."

I can feel my head snap back toward Dorin. He finally looks up and says, "I'm sorry. But I didn't have anything to do with this. They started chattering on the VHF, and it took on a life of its own. When I heard 'Coast Guard,' I intervened and told them to knock it off. Come on, let's go over to the *Grace* and visit for a while."

"No, I don't think I'm in the mood. I'm going to hang out here." I nod to the seven men in the two dinghies. "Thanks for your concern. I'm okay now." I turn and go down the stairs.

Dorin climbs aboard and says goodbye to Bob. I hear the three dinghies motor away. I am so angry I cannot talk.

Dorin intuits this. "When you're ready, can we talk about it?"

"What the hell?" I blurt. "That was a milk run. That was sailing-by-number. I wasn't even overdue. The Coast Guard?"

"I know, I know. I heard them talking about it on the VHF and got on there and nixed it. I am so sorry." He presses a glass of wine into my hand. I hadn't even noticed him uncorking and pouring.

"I'm pretty sure George started it. He got them all wound up."

"I bet they didn't take much winding."

"Probably. For all the talk of their wives being 'first mates,' men consider sailing as a gender-based, male-only activity."

"Even in the face of women circumnavigators?"

"You'll never hear them acknowledge it. I've tried it. I might as well have been speaking a foreign language."

"You know what this is about, don't you? George doesn't want Sue to go sailing with me tomorrow."

"Yeah, I thought of that. Look, being a man, I have never experienced what you have your whole life...dealing with men who need to be rude or need to denigrate women or put them down in some way so they will feel superior.

"I can't help the fragile ego of some men, and I'm so sorry this happened. I was the one who encouraged you to do this. I was so proud of you when I saw the *Fandango* round into the bay, and you just looked so calm and so in control. You set the anchor like you've been doing it your whole life. I was thinking, 'There, that will show them.'"

"But they had already tasted blood."

"So, what do you want to do? Sail out of here?"

"No! That will make it so worse. And I want to take Sue sailing tomorrow in the dinghy. Let's just pretend it didn't happen. Let's go for a drink tonight. I don't think they will bring it up again. They got what they wanted. Listen, I just need to brood for a while and feel some righteous indignation. Can I have some alone time?"

"You got it," Dorin says, and refills my glass with wine. "Want me to go back to the *Grace*?"

"Yeah, that would be good. I need to get my balance."

He kisses my forehead. "I'll come back and make supper. Will that give you enough time?"

"Perfect. You don't think I'm overreacting, do you?"

"God, no! That was the height of ridiculousness."

When he pulls away from the *Fandango,* I sit cross-legged on the bed in the fo'c'sle with my glass and the bottle and think about the many attempts men have made to keep me in my place. A few years ago, when I was working on a wooden boat that was fiberglassed over, I went into an auto parts store and asked for sixty grit sandpaper. I could get it by ordering it from a catalog, but I needed it that day.

"Sixty?" The clerk said in disbelief. Then in a challenging voice he asked, "What are you going to use it for?"

Annoyed at his attitude, I said, "I don't see why you need to know that."

"I don't think you want sixty grit, lady. Why don't you tell me what you need it for, and I'll tell you what grit you need."

"Will you sell me sixty grit paper?"

"Why don't you go ask somebody what grit you need, if you don't believe me."

"What I'm going to ask somebody is who owns this business and tell him or her how you treated me."

"Okay, okay! I'll sell you the paper, but I'm telling you, you'll be back."

And then there was the time....

And then....

And then....

I spend a couple of hours reviewing and licking my wounds until Dorin comes back and cooks supper.

After supper, we row ashore and, hand in hand, walk to María's. We chat with the usual crowd, and mercifully no one says anything stupid. Then Sue pulls a chair up to our table.

"Hi," she says. "I just want to say I think you were so brave today when you were in trouble. I'm glad you're okay." She glances over her shoulder toward the closed men's room door. "I can't go sailing with you tomorrow."

"Why?"

She looks over her shoulder again. "George says no. And, well...it sounded really, really bad today. Everyone was talking about it. We all thought your boat would go down, and you would die. That's when he said women don't belong at the helm. And really, I am scared when I think of going sailing tomorrow."

A surge of anger surfaces again. "Sue, there was never any danger, and it wasn't difficult. We've been sailing up and down that little piece of coast for months. If it hadn't been great weather, I wouldn't have done it. Tomorrow we'd be in the bay in a little boat. Even if, worst case scenario, we capsize, someone would come help us out. If you can swim. You can swim, can't you?"

"I can, but I can't go," she almost whispers.

I look across Sue's shoulder to see George, still several feet away, striding toward us with a scowl.

Then it hits me. Dorin has given me so many opportunities to step out of the mold and explore. He has always been supportive when I try new things that are outside of my "gender role." He has trusted me with jobs that provided learning experiences, and he never shadowed me to make sure it was done right. He celebrates my explorations and accomplishments. I am so lucky to have Dorin as my partner. What do I care what anyone else thinks?

As George closes in, I smile at Sue and wink. "And that's where you can buy really great coffee. Check it out."

* * *

It's our practice to listen to BBC news on the ham radio almost every morning, but then the rule is we shut it off as soon as we're done so we aren't vulnerable targets for chit-chatting. And of course, the VHF is always off when we're hanging around. One day, though, someone, not saying who, but it wasn't me or Cory, leaves the ham radio on. Dorin and I took off, so we missed it when we were hailed by Mac of the *Fancy Dancer*. When we got back, Cory said Mac just wanted us to know they were on their way to Puerto Rico and would see us soon. About 48 hours later they arrived, and Dorin rowed over to welcome them and to invite them to join the crowd at María's. Mac agreed but asked him to monitor VHF so we could keep in touch while we shared the same harbor.

"Sounds like a plan," Dorin had said. When he reported it to us, he said, "Okay, absolutely no VHF radio on. If anybody wants us, they can motor over or see us at María's."

That night at María's, Dorin says to Fred, "Since you're heading north, I was wondering if you have any charts you want to sell."

I do a double take because we haven't talked about going anywhere. I had begun to accept we would spend the rest of our time here in Puerto Rico. I've wanted to raise the question, but what if I pushed for us to move on, and then it didn't turn out so well?

"Yeah, I do," Fred says. "The whole island chain—the Leewards, the Windwards, all the way to Grenada. I'll let 'em go cheap."

"What about the coast of Venezuela?"

"Nope. Never got that far."

"We're probably going offshore. Quicker. We're behind schedule."

"I didn't know we still had a schedule," I say.

Then I notice a silence from the surrounding tables.

'Um, have you given this thought?" Fred asks. "Everyone island hops to Venezuela."

"I've been telling him," Bob says.

"I'm exploring our options," Dorin says.

"Do you have your visas to get into Venezuela?" Fred asks.

"No, we were planning to stop in Grenada."

"That makes sense. But I don't think I've ever heard of anyone going offshore," Fred says.

"That's because it's not recommended," another boater says. "The wind direction and ocean current...."

The spirited discussion continues, but it's clear all those in favor of sailing to Venezuela down the island chain want to make their positions known.

Even while the discussion continues, I know this is not making an impression on Dorin. We have sailed in adverse winds and currents, and while it might slow us down a little, we get where we're going just fine. Right?

Dorin nods. "I'll take that under advisement, but I'll buy the charts. If we don't use them going down, we can use them coming back."

As we row back to the *Fandango*, Dorin says, "No damn way, right?"

"Well, I don't know. Are we throwing caution to the winds? So to speak?"

"If our goal is to get to Venezuela, we have a finite amount of time—I have to teach in the fall, and Cory has to go to school. Offshore will save us a lot of time and give us more time to enjoy South America. Supposed to be incredible snorkeling."

"Yeah, I keep hearing. If we're going to go, taking a shortcut...that makes sense. If we were retired like everybody else, we wouldn't care how long it might take."

"Exactly. We could leisurely drift down through the islands. So, we're agreed, offshore, right?"

The next day Fred brings the chart books over, and Dorin pays him. The three of us sit at the dinette and pore over the glossy pages. Looking at charts and planning sailing trips always gives me a lift. The lure of the unknown beckons.

More so when I am safe and dry at home, or in this case, floating in a calm bay. "We still have enough time. Why don't we get Bill to order a chart kit for the coast of Venezuela?" I ask. "Have it shipped to *Villa Pesquera*."

"Sounds like a plan," he says.

The next morning, someone leaves the ham radio on. I'm not saying who, but it wasn't me and it wasn't Cory. When Mac hails us, Dorin heads out into the cockpit and says to Cory, "Get that, will you?"

Cory groans but picks up the microphone. "This is the *Fandango*. Dorin is busy right now. He'll get back to you. Over and out." And he hangs up.

"Well, that was a little bit rude, wasn't it?" Dorin asks.

"Says the man who won't respond," Cory says with a raised eyebrow.

During the past weeks, the boat has continued to slow down when under motor. I don't pay a lot of attention since we travel almost exclusively by sail, mostly running it once a week to charge batteries. It does worry Dorin though, and he mentions it to Bob.

"You have to run them wide open every once in a while," Bob says. "Or at least three-quarters power. That burns the carbon out." So every couple of days, especially when Cory and I go shopping, Dorin rams up and down the bay at full throttle.

"Is it helping?" I ask.

"I don't think so," he says. "If anything, it seems like it's more sluggish. Trouble is, 3600 RPMs is max for this engine, but I can't get that much out of it. When we got this motor, the propeller that should have come with it didn't get shipped. I ordered it from the Netherlands, remember? It was going to take too long to get it, so I just installed the old prop. Trouble is, the prop I had for the old Grey Marine engine was bigger than the one that is supposed to come with this motor. I'm guessing that's why I can't get more than 1900 out of it."

"Is that a problem?"

"Could be. Bob says to run it at least three-quarter power. That would be 2700. So, it's really running at about half the RPMs. Maybe it will need a motor job."

"What should we do?"

"It's got to be cheaper to get it done in Venezuela. The rate of exchange is very favorable. And we'll have more money in the bank by then. I vote we wait and get it done there."

The rest of us don't bother to cast our votes. Decision made.

I finish sewing the weather cloths, which has been a slow, tedious and half-hearted effort. I dig out the grommet kit and set large grommets so we can tie the cloths to the lifelines. Then I pack them away since we don't need them while at anchor or on our milk runs up and down the west coast.

The chart book arrives. Dorin glances at it but doesn't seem particularly interested. I stow it in a dry locker to keep it safe.

He probably doesn't take an interest because he's preoccupied with the motor and some lingering electrical problems.

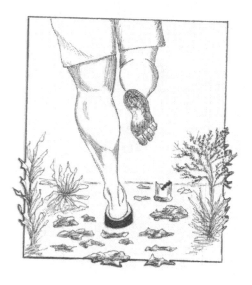

Cory's Story

This morning I was thinking we could sail the *Fandango* up to Puerto Real so I could stop in and say hi to the del Toros, but Dorin is planning on working on electrical stuff.

"I want to go to Puerto Real. Okay if I sail the *Tinker*?" I ask him.

"Yeah, sure, Cor. Fine with me. Just ask your mother."

Since I got back from the trip with Bast, Mom pretty much says yes to everything I want to do.

"Sure. We are not planning to go into Boquerón today, so we don't need the dinghy. When will you be back?"

"Before dark, for sure. Two hours each way, a little more, maybe. I might hang around for a while. A couple of hours."

Maybe they will ask me to stay for supper, I think.

"So, as long as I'm home before dark, that's okay?"

"Sure. Don't forget to take a lifejacket."

I throw my flip flops, a gallon jug of water that is half full, and a life jacket into the dinghy. I grab my favorite pair of sunglasses, and I'm wearing my hat.

I'm in a great mood as I sail out of the harbor in a brisk wind. This is the life!

It's not until I round out of the bay that I really think about the wind. It's an offshore breeze, which is unusual for daytime. Because of the cooling and heating of the land, it's usually steady offshore at night and hard onshore during the day, maybe 95% of the time.

I'm sailing along, and it's getting windier and windier, so much so it's hard to hold the tiller. I try to let the boom out to take pressure off the sail, but the line that goes through the block on the boom snags, so with the sail in too tight, the *Tinker* starts to tip. I quickly crank hard on the tiller to turn the boat completely down wind, when the tiller comes off on my hand! I can't believe it. The entire tiller just breaks off in my hand. And over the boat rolls...capsized.

I'm in the water, and the *Tinker* is upside down, but, okay, it's not the end of the world. I'm outside of the reefs and only half a mile out, no big deal. So now what do I do?

The center board sticks up from the bottom of the boat. Well great, I can use that to flip the boat over. I scramble onto the overturned boat, grab the center board with one hand, lean across to grab the tube on the far side of the *Tinker*, and pull. The thick marine plywood centerboard breaks, and I fall into the water. The ragged edged centerboard pops up beside me.

Man, how did this happen? The centerboard seemed really solid. I just leaned hard on it—I didn't throw my weight against it. And it just breaks.

I think about it, and suddenly, it's obvious to me. I was never going to pull the boat over that way, even if the center board hadn't broken, because the mast and sail are still down in the water. What was I thinking? I can't do it that way, flip it over with the center board—it's just silliness.

I climb back on the overturned boat to think about it for a minute. I realize now I have been moving farther out to sea in the offshore wind-- maybe a mile offshore!

Then I see a pleasure boat approaching from Puerto Rico. Whew! This will be okay. I'm going to be rescued. They're four people, two couples, in their runabout. What a relief!

I can stand up on the dinghy because even upside down it's very stable. I wave the broken piece of the center board. I'm almost smiling with relief because I'm going to be talking to them in a few minutes.

They are so close I can see the expressions on their faces. They look confused. I wave harder and yell. "Hey, I need some help! ¡Pueden ayudarme! They just watch me, and the expression on their faces looks like they're thinking, "I've never seen anything like this before."

And they just keep going.

"Hey!" I scream. "Hey, I need some help!"

And they just keep going.

I am one person standing on an overturned boat waving a board and yelling, and they just keep going. I am outraged. Incensed. "You idiots!" I scream, but they already too far away to hear.

Well, now. No one is going to rescue me. I have to figure this out myself. It's time to make a plan. What I need to do is swim under the boat, untangle and pull the sail loose, and then try to flip the boat over.

I swim under the boat and realize there is no air pocket at the point where I have to untangle the lines. I dive many times, staying under for maybe a minute each time while I work on the lines. Little by little, I get all of the sail and rigging separated so I will be able to flip the boat over.

When I get it done, I figure half an hour has gone by. When I come up for air the last time, I realize the wind has picked up and is now howling. I look back at Puerto Rico and it's much, much smaller. Crap! Am I a mile and a half away, maybe two?

I take a line, tie it on the side of the dinghy, and pull it toward me. It starts to come up out of the water, but then it slips back. I try again with the same result, but it feels like I'm so close to getting it back over. I try again and again and again, but it comes part way up and slips back onto its overturned position.

I'm getting really tired, but I give it everything I have. I lean on it, and it almost comes all the way up, but then the stay breaks on the near side, and the mast falls down into the water. Without the drag of the rigging holding it down, the boat slips over and upright. I hoist myself into the dinghy and feel much better. I've been in the water for quite a while and being in a disabled but floating boat seems like a big improvement. I can start problem solving now.

I see my flip flops floating one way and the half-full gallon of water moving fast away in the other direction. The life jacket, now free from the boat, bobs nearby. I think about it for a minute. What I need the most, right now—is the water. But what if I swim after it and can't swim fast enough to get back to the rapidly moving boat? The bobbing jug is quickly drifting away, so I slip off the boat, grab the life jacket, slip one arm through, and swim.

Holding the water jug in one hand, I side stroke back to the boat and toss it in. I slip my other arm into the life jacket and snap it closed. One flip flop floats beside me, but not the other. I toss it into the bottom of the boat and climb in. I take a small gulp of water and think about it. I never could have swum back. I'd have been fighting the current and wind, going nowhere, exhausted, with no water and no boat. I'm much happier and safer here in the boat. Now I just have to fix it before I drift all the way to the Dominican Republic!

I look around, and it's a mass of wreckage. I don't have a center board or tiller—just broken pieces, and the stay for the mast is broken. The mast is lying in the water, floating, but it's tied on with one of the lines.

I pull the mast and all the rigging into the boat, and I get the oars out. I need to row ashore. I look at Puerto Rico, still shrinking as I drift away. I must be at least three or four miles offshore. And the wind is still howling, driving me away. I realize I'm actually drifting faster now with the boat upright. The rigging had been acting like a sea anchor, slowing me down, keeping the wind from blowing me as fast across the surface. It seems like it's blowing thirty knots!

I dig the oars in and pull; the boat briefly slows down, but when I lift the oars to take another stroke, I am just flying away from land. The oars are short with plastic oar locks. If you pull too hard on them, they pop out and have to be reset. Every time that happens the dinghy goes in reverse at a high speed, until I can start rowing again. I row like that for a long time, but I can't come close to breaking even—can't even stay in one spot, much less get closer.

Rowing as hard as I can, I am ripping away from the land, and I'm getting really exhausted. I take a small sip of water every once in a while. I save as much as I can because I am thinking it might be tomorrow, at least, before anybody sees me. If nobody sees me in two days, and I have no water out here, what have I got? If I drift for three or four days before they find me, I'm dead.

Okay, so rowing is not working. I need a different plan. What do I have that I can use? I still have the broken piece of center board, about 24 inches long. I still have a mast and sail.

I untangle the rigging and get the mast up and stepped. Though the bottom of it is crinkled, the stays hold it. But now, with the sail up, it's acting like a parachute, and I'm flying faster than ever out to sea. Puerto Rico looks a lot smaller than the last time I looked.

I have to figure out how this is going to work. Fast.

I look at the 24-inch piece of centerboard. It's jagged, broken plywood. I have to have a center board to beat into the wind, but I realize it will disappear into the ocean if I put it in the slot.

I have to steer, but I don't have a tiller. I slowly insert the plywood into the slot, careful to keep a grip on it. I lean back so I can hold the back of the rudder behind the pivot point with my other hand. The wind is still blowing hard offshore, so I have no choice but to beat into the wind.

The boat starts to move toward land, but I quickly realize I have to steer in reverse. The opposite of how I'm used to, how I've done it for over a thousand hours.

I have to keep thinking about it: normally, if I want to go to starboard, I would push the tiller in the opposite direction, to the left, but now, to turn the boat to starboard, I actually have to pull the back of the rudder right. It feels so wrong. I just get moving along and then, aargh! I turn it the wrong way. I finally get on the right tack and, duh! Wrong again. Grrr! I did it again!

I finally get into the rhythm. And so I beat back and forth, back and forth. But I hold pretty even. At least I'm not flying away from Puerto Rico. Maybe I'm even making a little progress. Yeah, I'm pretty sure the land is getting a little larger.

The sun continues to beat down. Now I miss my hat. That and my sunglasses are at the bottom of the ocean.

When I think I have about two miles to go, the wind lets up, and the sailing is much easier. It's late in the day, and the wind dies down. I cover the distance faster now. I can actually tell I'm making progress.

A mile out, the wind totally dies. I stow the center board piece in the bottom of the boat and pull out the oars. I row in, but there's a reef and breaking surf. I row south for a little bit until I see a beach where I can land. But it's not a beach that people use, and there probably isn't a road nearby. I pull the *Tinker* up as high from the water as I can and tie it to a tree.

It's the wilderness. Of course. The fact that I had retrieved only one flip flop now seems like it matters.

But, I'm on solid ground and am going to survive. I put the flip flop on my left foot, grab the water jug, which still has a little in the bottom, and push my way through the dense growth. It's briars and thickets, stones and roots. My right foot takes some punishment.

I walk through thickets for a long, long time until finally I come to a path at a sugar plantation, but I can't tell where it goes. I wander around there for a long time. Eventually, I come out on a tarred road. The road is still extremely hot. The edge is broken tar and glass shards, and plants and rocks. I hop-walk on the road so my right foot is in contact with the surface for only a split second.

I've lost track of time, but it seems like I've been on this road for a really, really long time. I drink all but the last few sips of water, not even a cup full remains. I am determined to save some until the very end.

It's getting dark when I finally I see a sign.

Boquerón to the right.

What a relief.

At least I know where to head and how far I have to go. I'm only half a mile away, when someone stops and asks me if I want a ride. I'm thinking I'm going to finish this now, myself. Do I really want a ride? I know where I am, and I'm going to go ahead and finish on my own.

"No, gracias."

He must think I'm crazy! I'm hopping along half barefoot, sunburned, and very ragged looking, carrying a nearly empty gallon jug. He slowly drives away, looking concerned. If only the idiots in the power boat had been so nice!

It's completely dark when I get back.

There's a bar near the beach, and I go in. I'm really, really thirsty, but I don't have any money. One of the local guys recognizes me and asks if he can help me.

"Can I get a ride out to my boat?" I ask.

He nods, and quickly we skim over the water toward the *Fandango*.

Mom is out in the cockpit watching as we approach.

She looks relieved to see me. "What happened?" she asks, looking at the guy who brought me out. He shrugs his shoulders and smiles.

"Thirsty!" I say as I climb on board. "Thirsty!"

"Muchas gracias," I say to the guy who has already pointed his dinghy toward shore.

Dorin hands me a glass of water and directs me to sit. I drink all of the water, and Mom hands me a second glass, which I down immediately. When I catch my breath, I try to tell them my story. Mom is horrified, and Dorin looks concerned.

"I have some food for you," Mom says. "We saved your supper."

"No, tired. Just sleep."

When I wake up in the morning, I realize I don't even remember lying down. Dorin has asked Bob if he can help us retrieve the dinghy. Dorin hands me one of his spare hats that I've been coveting. "Yours now, Cor."

It doesn't take long at all to motor up the coast and find the *Tinker*. Bob beaches his runabout, and we walk over to the boat.

"Impressive," says Dorin as he looks over the tangle of rigging, sail and mast. He picks up the broken piece of the center board and shakes his head.

"You are a lucky young man," Bob says.

"I don't think it was luck," Dorin says. "He saved himself. Most adults would not have been able to do that."

"What do you think about the boat?" I ask.

"Oh, we can fix her. And now we know she can double as an emergency vessel. She stayed afloat, right?" Dorin says, laughing.

We tow the *Tinker* back, going more slowly than we did on the way to get her. There is a tendency for water to slosh into that rubber dinghy.

Back in Boquerón Bay, we look over the damage. The bottom of the metal mast is crinkled because it bent over while still in the fitting on the bottom of the boat. We cut off the bottom two inches with a hacksaw.

"I don't think we can shorten it anymore, or the sail won't fit," Dorin says.

But I am worried. There is still a crease at the new bottom of the mast.

With the *Tinker* tied on behind us, we sail the *Fandango* up to Puerto Real to get some plywood to make a new centerboard and a piece of mahogany for the tiller. We work on the dock in Puerto Real Bay, using shore power and a couple of power tools Dorin had tucked away in fo'c'sle storage. When that's done, we replace the stays, and then slip the *Tinker* into the water.

"You do the honors, Cor," says Dorin. I jump in and sail her around the harbor with no problem. From the dock he gives me a thumbs down and then a thumbs up. It's a question: how's it handling?

I give him a thumbs up.

Maybe this is the end of our problems with the damn *Tinker*. I can see her continuing to be a decent enough tender to go to and from the dock.

But I've been thinking--as a lifeboat? I don't see it. I can't imagine the three of us fitting in it with a canopy over it.

Not going to matter probably.

I don't think we're going anywhere besides up and down the coast of Puerto Rico.

Chapter Nineteen
Current Affairs

It's January 21, and almost three weeks have passed since Cory's ordeal off the coast. "What are we doing today?" he asks as he finishes off his fifth pancake. Dorin turns off the stove and joins us in the cockpit. "Have you noticed nobody ever leaves Puerto Rico to head south?" he asks.

Cory, suddenly alert and somewhat suspicious, pauses mid-bite. "Yeaah," he draws it out. "Aaand?"

"I'm not suggesting we should take the same course of action, Cor."

"You mean course of non-action?"

Dorin ignores the sarcasm and nods. "What's today? Thursday, right? How about we leave today? Are we ready?"

This is so sudden. I stifle a gasp and glance at my clipboard list. There are maybe ten items on it, but most of them have been crossed off. The remaining jobs are small, busy work. Sounds like we'll be busy at something else. I push butterflies away. "Sure, I guess so. I don't see why not. We just got ice for the fridge yesterday. We have fresh food on board. The diesel tank is almost full."

"I'm *so* ready," Cory says. "You can't *believe* how ready I am. I am so sick of sitting here doing nothing!"

We both look at him in surprise. He has seemed so serene and adaptable.

"You haven't said anything," I reply.

Dorin shrugs. "Maybe he's developed a taste for adventure somehow? Look, he's almost seventeen. Of course he's sick of sitting around. So, agree? Let's head out now."

I'm nervous probably because I've been lulled into a false sense of security, but I'm also a little excited. The frying pan and dishes go into the sink unwashed. Anything that can move while underway, I quickly stow. Cory is on deck taking the sail covers off. Dorin pulls out the chart we will need and slides it into the plastic chart protector. Ten minutes later, at nine o'clock, we motor out of Puerto Real Bay and into the ocean. The guys raise all sails into a decent wind and kill the motor.

We slow down dramatically. "Whoa," Dorin says. "You know what we should have done? Scraped the junk off the bottom. By now, there must be a ton of barnacles and seaweed attached. We should go over the side and scrape off the crud under the water line. Let's stop in at Boquerón and get it done."

Cory groans, but he stands ready to drop the anchor near Sandy Beach inside the bay.

Dorin, wearing his crusty shorts, is the first one over and does a show-off, perfect dive off the bow sprit.

"At least his shorts will get clean," Cory says and grabs the hat Dorin has left on the deck. As he prepares to throw it, I say, "No!" but too late. The hat sails in after Dorin. "I think this needs a bath, too," Cory yells to him. A second later he cannonballs into the water, coming up a few feet beside Dorin. He grabs the floating hat and hands it to Dorin who grins, shakes off the water, and puts it on his head.

I hand them scrapers, then jump into the warm, clear water and help out. Mats of living crustacea and marine algae in the form of waving grass peel off and gently float downward to the floor of the bay.

In an hour we are done. Using the dinghy as a step-up, we are back on the boat. We change into dry clothes, and at 11:30 we haul anchor and sail south out of the harbor, down the coast, in a direction we've never been before.

"Kind of feels like we might sail off the edge of the earth, doesn't it?" Dorin asks. "Maybe anything south of the corner of Puerto Rico is mythical."

In a couple of hours, the swells are seven-feet high and steep. Both Cory and I feel a little nauseated. We also realize we haven't remembered to tie the new weather cloths along the lifelines, so every wave that hits the side of the boat results in our being doused by gallons of warm seawater.

"We need to head back for tonight," Dorin says with a big yawn. "It's just too uncomfortable right now for you two. We can head out tomorrow."

I know when Dorin yawns it's an early warning signal of seasickness. I look at Cory, expecting him to object, but he just nods, and I realize he must not be feeling well either. "We've been at anchor too long," he says.

"I promise, no matter what, we will leave tomorrow," Dorin says.

It looks like Cory is about to say something, but he nods again.

On Friday morning, Cory and I take prescription motion-sickness pills. After breakfast, I tie the weather cloths on the portside while Cor does starboard, and we head out.

We are underway only an hour when Dorin chuckles and says, "We did it again. It's Friday, isn't it?"

"I was hoping you guys wouldn't notice," Cory says.

"It's hard to say if Friday is good luck or bad," I reply. "We've had a few sketchy experiences, but then again, we've survived them. Maybe Friday is good luck."

"Yeah, hard to say," Dorin says, looking amused. "We need more data."

When we get beyond the headland, the swells are eight to ten feet, but the motion-sickness pills apparently work because we feel much better than yesterday. The weather cloths do well in that we only get smacked in the head with water instead of a whole-body soaking.

That night the wind is fifteen to twenty-five knots, and the swells are still steep so Dorin heaves-to for five hours during the night so we can all get some sleep.

During breakfast Saturday, we rise and fall on the large swells and see, when we are at the top, there are no other boats visible.

"No wonder people don't use Puerto Rico as a jumping off point," Dorin says, "if the seas are always this bad."

"And," I say with emphasis, "*no wonder* it's advised to go down the island chain." No reaction from Dorin.

"Instead of going offshore...."

Still no reaction.

We spend the whole day reefing the mainsail and, hour by hour, taking down the jib when the winds build, and then, when we slow down, unreefing the main and putting the jib back up.

The wind is from the east, and we are trying to sail southeast so, of course, we are on a beat again.

"Really?" I ask Dorin. "Is there any other point of sail?"

"I just checked the pilot chart, again," he says. "This wind direction is pretty normal for this time of year."

"I thought you said, many months ago, that this leg would be 'an easy reach.'"

"Well, I guess that was when I expected we would do this leg a lot earlier. Or I misread the chart. Or something."

But the autopilot is once again a working member of the crew, and that is worth a lot right there. While Dorin takes a catnap, I run the motor for an hour to keep the batteries charged. I notice it slows down, losing power for a few seconds, and then comes back to normal. I make a mental note to mention this.

Sunday morning, the fifteen- to twenty-five knot wind is still from the east, drat it all; the swells are ten feet. We triple reef the main and go without a jib at all, but we keep the stays'l, which seems to steady the boat so it doesn't hobby horse as much. Still, the swells are steep and close together, so it's a bumpy ride. Cory and I no longer suffer from seasickness, and we are all feeling great on our fourth day out.

Dorin's calculations from sun sights and the RDF [Radio Direction Finder] tell us we've averaged ninety miles a day since we left. Later in the day, I notice with surprise the dinette cushions are a little damp. Not that we use them to sit on to eat, because we usually eat in the cockpit, but I have been accustomed to using the dinette seating next to the ice box for resting or reading ever since the big storm at the beginning of the trip. It's close to the cockpit, sheltered from water, and near fresh air. Since no water has splashed in, I am puzzled. Later in the day, Dorin mentions the fo'c'sle cushions are damp.

"And the bilge pump has been working a lot more," he says. We join Cory in the cockpit.

"My bunk cushions are dry," Cory says. "But you're right. The bilge pump has been going on every few minutes. I should have said something."

"We'll have to do some checking," Dorin says. "I'm sure it's nothing major. Meanwhile, let's run the motor to top off the batteries."

For an hour, the motor runs, but sluggishly, sometimes even sounding like it will stop. Then it winds back up again.

"Good thing we are going to get a motor job done. I've been thinking we should check on getting it done in Grenada. Sounds like sooner would be better."

He cooks well-seasoned corned beef stew that is delicious, with canned corn beef, real potatoes, onions and carrots.

"Well, so far so good," Dorin says during supper.

"What about the dampness?" I ask.

"Yeah, we should look into that soon."

None of us do though.

On Friday, we started off with two dozen eggs and two pounds of bacon, and now on Monday, I use the last six eggs for veggie omelets, served with the last half pound of bacon. Our fresh provisions are dwindling, but we have plenty of canned and packaged stuff for the last little bit of this voyage. We'll be able to restock fresh produce as soon as we get to Grenada.

Dorin gets a noon sun sight, and, after he reduces it, he comes out in the cockpit.

"Well, I've good news and so-so news. Which do you want first?"

We both say, "So-so."

"We've only made fifty miles in the past twenty-four hours. But...the good news is I was able to confirm my dead reckoning within thirteen miles. So, damn, I'm good. And it looks like we're halfway!"

We give him air high fives.

"But, if the wind stays from the same direction, and it's coming steadily from the east, the last half may take a little longer, because...um. We'll have to tack in."

I groan. "That's the good news?"

"Well, maybe that's also so-so news. Actually, it's not all that bad. I'm planning, when we get closer to Grenada, just to motor on in. We have plenty of fuel, and we can go on a direct heading."

At three o'clock we have to put the jib back up to keep our speed up to four-and-a-half knots. But the swells are long now and only three and four feet, so it's a smoother ride.

Finally, we see a few freighters and cruise ships in the distance. It's always nice to have some company out here.

At four o'clock, Dorin tries to start the motor to charge the batteries, but it doesn't start.

"Oh, damn, I forgot to mention...." I say. "Yesterday it kept slowing down while I was charging the batteries."

"Probably not much I could have done about it. This could put a damper on our plans," Dorin says. "I had reconciled to the idea of motoring in."

I wonder if he is secretly pleased that we can't motor in. He pulls up and removes the motor cover and works on it for a couple of hours.

"I don't think it's going to start. I think it does need a valve job. And each time I try to start it, it drains the battery, which is a bigger concern.

We're still on the first one, and the other two are fully charged, but I want to keep it that way. We'll need them to run the bilge pump."

Cory says, "And the autopilot. Well, we've got plenty of wind. We can do it, right?"

"Yeah, but it's a little disheartening that we can't just power in if the wind and current remain adverse."

We don't look at each other or discuss turning back.

"I'll make supper," Cory announces, and minutes later, he's chopping onions and humming.

Tuesday morning, Dorin makes pancakes for breakfast, and as we eat in the cockpit, we talk over our situation.

"I told Bob we'd contact him by ham radio every day to report our progress. It takes a lot of battery to transmit," Dorin says, "so I'll just radio him once more to let him know the situation." He sits at the dinette and tries for ten minutes but doesn't get any response.

"May not be enough power left in the battery," Dorin says. "We ran the radar and running lights all night because we were in traffic lanes. I also used the interior lights for a while."

"And we used the autopilot all night, too," I say. "How about we steer during the day and just use the autopilot at night?"

The guys agree.

When Dorin takes his afternoon sun sights, he is concerned. Though we have been sailing hard as close to the wind as we can, we are drifting southwest of our intended course.

"If we keep slipping off course like this," Dorin says, "we'll definitely have to tack before we can make the approach to Grenada. I don't want to do it for another twenty-four hours though. Aves Island is out there, and it would be impossible to see it at night. I don't want to be heading over that way until I'm sure we're well south of it. Maybe before that, the wind will shift, and we'll be able to make more headway toward the east tomorrow."

The wind drops to ten knots so we put up the jib and are quickly flying along on a calm sea at six knots. According to Dorin's calculations, we have only 150 miles to go. We have been on the same tack since leaving Puerto Rico. The wind builds to twenty-five knots, and now we move along at seven knots. Since the hull speed is six and a half, we are actually hydroplaning a little. Dorin takes down the jib, and we drop to 3 knots, which is not acceptable. Then he remembers he has an old "storm jib" somewhere that might work.

"I haven't seen it in years, but I know it's here somewhere."

"Where do we have enough space to store a sail that we haven't seen?" I ask.

"Oh, ye of little faith," Dorin says, when ten minutes later he finds it and tosses it into the foot well. "This sail is three quarters the size of the one we are replacing."

"And you are just thinking of it now?"

"I was probably keeping it for a surprise. Or something."

The white sail is very dirty with rust stains all over it.

"Come on, Cor, let's bend it on." They remove the jib and hank on the storm jib. Our speed booms to six knots, but the wind and seas are building. The problem is that without some sort of jib, it won't sail as close into the wind as we need to, to maintain the course we want. So, when we've had to go without the jib because of too much speed and heel, we've pointed too far off the wind, around one hundred and seventy degrees. Every time we've had the jib up, we've tried to compensate by tucking it in at one hundred and thirty degrees, which makes for a steep heel. The main is already triple reefed, so we take a reef in the stays'l. In two minutes, we boom along at a reckless six-and-a-half knots. We take the stays'l down and our speed drops to five knots.

The wind stays at twenty to twenty-five knots from the same direction. We sail with double-reefed main and both heads'ls. Our speed holds constant at four-and-a-half knots. During the night, we are able to maintain the heading of 140 degrees that Dorin is looking for.

In the morning, I hand out bowls of peanut butter and banana oatmeal, which is a crowd pleaser.

"So, what's happening today?" Cory asks.

"Time to change tack and head northeast for a day," Dorin says. "We're much more south than we should be for the speed we're going. The current is really sweeping us southwest. Probably add an extra day or two," he adds. "But we're in pretty good shape. Do we have any ice left?"

"Doesn't matter. We don't have any fresh food."

"That's okay," Cory says. "Gotta love those rice and beans."

"Yeah, and we have spaghetti, meat sauce, veggies, and canned meat. We'll be fine," I say.

For lunch I decide to make toasted cheese sandwiches and heat some canned soup, but the kerosene stove stops working. Dorin fiddles with it for half an hour before announcing, "Ah, I have sort of bad news. It's really and truly dead."

"And it shouldn't be resuscitated," Cory says. "It's a piece of junk. I hate cooking on it."

"Yeah, buying that was a mistake. I thought it would be great because kerosene is cheap," Dorin says.

"Better than the alcohol stove we used to have, though," I say.

"So how much trouble are we in?" Dorin asks.

"Not bad." We have a lot of cold provisions like saltines, spam, tuna, canned vegetables, and fruit. "We've done it before in the storm. Lunch will be ready in a minute. Literally." A minute later I hand them paper plates of food.

"Cold lima beans?" Cory says. He eats the tuna and saltines.

"Hey, don't disrespect the lima bean. I love lima beans." Dorin scoops our undisturbed lima beans onto his plate and offers us some of his tuna, which we are happy to accept.

For supper I use the last of the bread for sandwiches.

"You make one helluva peanut butter and jelly sandwich," Dorin says. "You'll have to save that recipe."

As usual, the wind increases during the night. When we douse the jib, our speed drops to four knots, and we continue to sail northeast all night long using the autopilot.

At 4:00 a.m. Cory wakes us. "Hey, just want to tell you the running lights have dimmed. I'm still using the autopilot. I just switched to the second battery."

Later Wednesday morning, after a breakfast of cold cereal and warm, carton milk, Dorin says, "If we're careful with this battery, it should get us to Grenada. We'll still use the running lights at night...and the bilge pump. We will save power by tying the tiller and let her self-steer during the day. She'll do that pretty well on a beat, but we'll still use the autopilot at night."

In the afternoon, I'm on watch, and Cory is doing schoolwork in the cockpit. Dorin is below, reducing the noon sun sight.

"What the *hell?*' he asks.

Cory and I look at each other. This can't be good.

"We can't possibly be where this indicates we are."

Minutes later, he joins us in the cockpit. "I don't want to believe it," he says. "I checked it twice. I'd ask you to come check my figures," he says to me, "but I confirmed the position with the RDF."

"What's the problem?" Cory asks.

"This noon sun sight puts us at sixty miles off the coast, northeast of Caracas...way too far west. That would mean we haven't made any northeast progress at all. In fact, it looks as if we've been pushed back, westward, by the current for at least a day, I'd guess. Let me check a few things."

After fifteen minutes fiddling with the RDF and checking the chart, he realizes he has picked up radio stations in Carenero and Caracas, giving him a positive fix.

"So how far are we from Grenada?"

He looks at the cockpit floor and then at the horizon, as if stalling.

"We are west of Grenada by two hundred and ten miles," he says.

Cory and I gasp.

"A combination of not being able to point close enough, and then, well, the pilot chart says there can be a vicious current here sometimes. We can't make it into Grenada. Be different if the motor were running."

I am dumbfounded. Cory steps out of the cockpit and walks stiffly to the forward deck. Hanging onto the forestay, he steps out onto the bowsprit. His body language says he's frustrated and angry.

"It's a humbling experience, Shirl Jean," Dorin says. "I assumed sailors didn't do this trip offshore because of fear of being out of sight of land for more than a day."

"I know."

"I'm sorry. Give me a few more hours to see if I can get closer. There's a chance the wind will change direction."

The twenty-knot east wind continues, and at 4:00 p.m., we have again confirmed our position by RDF. Not only are we way too far west, between the noon sight and a subsequent sight, we confirm our southern position.

This is a bitter pill to swallow. Seven days of offshore sailing, and Venezuela is nearly in sight. We could be there by tonight.

"Don't even think about it," Dorin says. "The Venezuelan laws are very clear. You must have a visa before entering the country. They will ask us to leave immediately, and that would be the best scenario. They can confiscate our boat and put us in jail if they want to."

"First time for everything," Cory says. "Except for me."

For supper, I offer Vienna sausage and cold green beans.

"No thanks," says Cory. "I'm all set."

"Yeah, sounds good," Dorin says, "but I really filled up on PB & J sandwiches."

We continue to try to sail to the northeast all night. On Thursday, we have not improved our position much at all. Dorin brings the chart out into the cockpit.

"Okay, crew. Let's take stock of our situation. The motor needs, at the very least, a valve job. We need a new stove."

We look at the chart and discuss the possibility of heading toward one of the islands north of Grenada.

"We'll make very slow progress, if any," Dorin says. "Even if we can make the American Virgins, it would be farther to travel and probably more expensive to repair the motor, buy a stove, and re-provision than it would be in Puerto Rico. In Puerto Rico we know the resources, the transportation system, the people."

"It's taken us, what, six days to get to where we are now?" Cory says. "How long would it take us to get back to Puerto Rico?"

"Well, the way back would be a close reach instead of a close beat, so it should be a fast, easy trip—maybe four days," Dorin says.

"We're still using our second battery," I say, "but it must be getting low."

"Yeah, we'd have to conserve even more."

By noon, all sun sights and the RDF confirm, once more, our position. My mind rebels at the idea of turning around. We've come so far...we are so close.

"We'd be on a more comfortable point of sail if we return to Puerto Rico," Dorin says. "We can't do anything about the stove now, so we'll have to tough out the food situation, but the trip back should be relatively comfortable."

I can see his reasoning is practical and sound, but it still takes a few minutes before I nod.

I look at Cory and see he is trying to process this idea, too. But an hour after we have confirmed our position, we turn north to Puerto Rico.

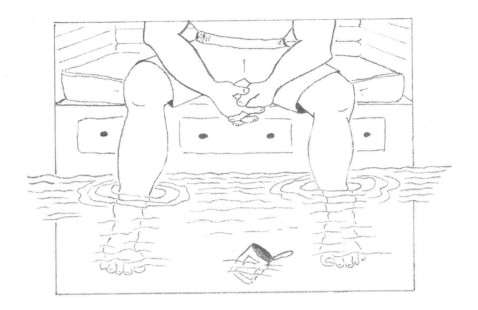

Chapter Twenty
Where Did All This Water Come From?

On a heading of 340 degrees, all sails up, no reefs, we boom along at five or six knots on a comfortable broad reach. A couple of rain squalls come through and are nothing, lasting only fifteen minutes, but Cory takes advantage of them to hang a couple pairs of his denim shorts on the lifeline to rinse out any saltwater.

Dorin tells us he's going to set a course for Ponce, a city in the middle of the south coast of Puerto Rico.

"It's now particularly important to consider the current," he says. "As you know, Puerto Rico is only one hundred miles wide and forty miles long. If we miss it to the west, we could sail up Mona Passage right by Puerto Rico and never see it."

After an hour of sailing on a reach and a comfortable five-degree heel, the wind shifts toward the north, putting us back on a close beat and more than a fifteen-degree heel. "Of course," I think. "What else did I expect?"

At 4:00 p.m., winds increase to thirty knots, and the seas build to twenty feet. In spite of being concerned about the batteries, we listen to the high seas weather report. A low has settled over Hispaniola and is expected to move out of that area and move into ours in the next twenty-four hours. I open cans of Spam, peas, and peaches and distribute them to the guys.

"Hmm. It just keeps on getting better," Dorin says.

"Love the peaches," Cory says.

The next morning, Dorin and I discover we have saltwater boils on our butts and backs.

"Probably from sitting on the wet lockers while we steer or keep watch," Dorin says.

"What are saltwater boils?" Cory asks.

"They are boils that fill with pus and are very painful. And then they break and drain. But they leave open sores, which sting like a son-of-a-gun because the saltwater continues to aggravate them. Just keep changing into dry clothes and try to stay dry."

"No way to do that," I reply. "Everywhere we sit or lie down is damp."

"I don't have any boils," Cory says.

"That's because you *stand* in the cockpit. And if your shorts get wet, you change into dry ones."

Cory nods. "Yeah, what else would I do? Also, my bunk isn't wet," he says with some satisfaction.

The boils make it very painful to do anything. Sit, lie down, stand up, walk, use the head.

Brisk winds keep us moving at six knots all day Friday and Saturday. We are making better than a hundred miles a day. The cold front arrives late in the day, and the wind increases to thirty knots as the last of the light fades. As night comes on, waves break over the bow and surge back to the cockpit. We reef the main at 10:00 p.m. and take down the jib, leaving the stays'l still up and full.

"My turn for the watch," I say.

"No, I think I better stay here for a while," Dorin says. "But thanks."

He hand steers with the tiller. When I ask him about it, he says we need to conserve the battery, and besides, it's too rough for the autopilot. "And I guess I'm antsy. I need to be doing something."

I know he is tired, so I stand in the companionway to keep him company.

At 1:00 a.m., the running lights go out. I check the interior lights to confirm. The second battery is dead.

At 2:00 a.m., Cory comes on deck to take his watch. We break the news of the battery and talk about what we will use the final battery for: to listen to the High Seas weather report twice a day. Listening doesn't take much power. We will not use our running lights at night, unless we spot a ship. The radar is on the "no" list, as it has been since the first battery died. We will not use the autopilot for even nighttime steering but will rely on hand steering or rigging the tiller when we can.

Dorin says, "I already took the bilge pump off automatic. We'll only switch it on momentarily if we really need to. So, this last battery is to be used primarily to listen to the ham radio and emergency transmitting, if it becomes necessary."

Dorin asks a groggy Cory to reef the stays'l. He steps out of the cockpit and onto the side deck.

"Put your harness on," I yell as he stumbles. I grab it from below. He appears to be half asleep as he grabs and slips into it and attaches it to the lifeline. As soon as the stays'l is reefed, Dorin sends him back to bed. Dorin mans the tiller, standing, and I stand on the stairs, leaning against the companionway opening because it's way too painful to sit. The waves are closer together now, one rapidly following another, not only crashing over the bow but also over the cabin. Water rushes along the deck and back to the cockpit.

"Do you want me to take the watch so you can rest?" I ask. Thinking of being the only one on watch in these conditions makes me nervous, but Dorin must be exhausted.

"No, it's getting pretty rough. I'll stay out here for a while. Why don't you rest so you can take over later? Or maybe I'll heave-to. Right now, I'm going to try to tie the tiller for self-steering."

I back down the stairs and lower myself carefully onto the dinette cushion, trying to minimize the pain from boils that cover my back from neck to tailbone.

Dorin has tied the tiller, and I watch him now standing in the companionway keeping watch and am comforted by his calm stoicism. I realize I have great faith in his ability to take care of us. At some point, I fall asleep.

On Sunday, at 5:00 a.m., I hear him on the foredeck and know he is heaving-to. I peel myself slowly, inch by inch, off the settee cushions, head for the fo'c'sle, and climb into bed.

"Now we can get a little sleep," he says and climbs in beside me. "Wow, it's really getting wet in here, isn't it?" And he immediately falls asleep.

The waves are coming in almost on top of each other, but still we are level and mushing. I'm used to trusting this, so I also fall asleep quickly.

At 7:00 a.m., I awake with the intent of using the head. I'd rather get this done while we are relatively comfortable, instead of on a heel that I know we'll be doing shortly. I slide my bare feet to the floor and gasp as I pull them back. "The floor is wet!"

"We must have more water coming in somewhere," he says. "How much is on the salon floor?"

I stand up and look out into the salon. "A couple of inches, maybe three."

"Give me an hour more, okay? And I'll check it. It's nothing major."

He goes back to sleep.

When I slosh through the cabin, I can see huge swells behind us. Cory is already in the cockpit preparing the boat to get moving again.

He notices me gaping at the rolling ocean behind us and grins. "Yeah, I think they're probably up to twelve feet. And we're taking on more water now. In case you didn't notice."

Dorin, having cat-napped for only fifteen minutes, crawls out of the bunk and staggers to the bilge pump switch. The water immediately pumps out of the back of the boat. "We have to be careful about this," he says. "I have to see if we can use the manual bilge pump today."

"Do you want something to eat?" I ask.

"No, just another hour of sleep."

"Cor?"

"Definitely not hungry."

The waves continue to slam hundreds of gallons of seawater over the boat. Cory manages to sidestep the surging water and keeps dry.

"Want some company out there?" I ask.

He smiles and shakes his head. "No, you can't sit. You'll get doused. And there isn't room for both of us to stand."

I prop the wet dinette cushions higher against the backrest so I can at least see outside.

When Dorin gets up an hour later, we pull up the floorboards in the cabin, but there is nothing to see in our very shallow bilge except sloshing sea water. He tells me to hit the switch, and it pumps the bilge nearly dry, which takes only a few minutes. I use a towel to mop up the shallow puddles on the uneven surface. We watch as water seeps steadily back in. In the cockpit, he looks into the depths of the sail lockers, and there is little to no water.

"It's a real puzzle, guys. Where the hell is the water coming from?" Dorin scratches his beard in thought, then steps into the fo'c'sle.

"I know it's not the hatch." He reaches up to twist hard on the hatch wingnut. He sits on the bed cushions and then springs up, lifting the front edge of a cushion that is our mattress.

"This is much wetter than I thought." He motions me forward and steps aside. I turn sideways and lean in to see. The plywood bed surface has a quarter inch of standing water.

"Yikes!"

"What the hell?" he says. Dropping the cushion in place, he crawls forward to the chain locker doors. "Hand me a flashlight, would you?"

On his hands and knees, he looks into the chain locker. "Okay, okay! I think I've got it figured out. The water is coming in through the hawse pipe. Every time a wave hits the foredeck...." At that moment a wave pounds over the boat, and from the cockpit I hear Cory say in disgust, "Crap!" He's just been doused and is annoyed because his shorts are wet.

"Yup, this is it," Dorin says. "The water drains down into the bilge like it's supposed to, but some runs across the ceiling, drops down off a ridge, continues into the fo'c'sle and onto the head of our bed. Can you find me a rag from your stash? I'm going to block the hole around the chain from the outside. Might slow it down a little."

I produce the rag and, from the companionway, watch him attach his harness to the lifelines and, stanchion by stanchion, go forward. He kneels on the deck and, using two hands, pushes the cloth into the hawse pipe.

The *Fandango* suddenly slides down off a wave and noses deep into the next wave, engulfing Dorin in a wall of green water. My heart slams in my chest as he goes out of sight. Then the bow surges up, and he is still there, hanging onto the lifeline. He kneels and stuffs the rag into the hole above the chain locker.

Minutes later, in the cockpit, Cory says, "I knew he had his harness on, but I was sure he'd been knocked off. I looked over the side for him, thinking I'll throw the buoy to him, but how are we going to get him back on board? Then, when I looked at the bow again, there he was!"

I'm speechless as Dorin makes his way down the bobbing deck using the lifelines and the shrouds to hang on. He unhitches from the lifeline and comes back into the cockpit.

"There, that should slow it down a lot." With a satisfied smile he runs a hand over his face and beard to clear water off.

We remark on the huge green water that swept over the boat, and he laughs.

"Yeah, that was interesting for a minute. So, now let's try to maintain a course of twenty degrees, Cor, to compensate for the current. But it won't be easy the way the wind is coming from."

He goes below to check our position with the radio direction finder.

"Uh oh," he says a few minutes later. "The RDF isn't working. The batteries must be dead. We have more batteries, right?"

I find the batteries in the companionway locker. He replaces them and tries again.

"Nope, it's still not picking anything up yet, and it's too rough to take morning sight. We'll have to keep watch from inside," Dorin says.

Waves crash over the cabin with such regularity we can time our getting into the cockpit to look around and then duck back in. We split the horizon into fourths and wait until we are at the top of a wave to look for boats. Then, we duck back down as the wave washes over the boat and dash back out to look at the next quadrant.

Before noon, the water is well above the floorboards once more, and there is visible water dripping from the cabin wall, port side, onto the cushions.

"Well, the hawse pipe might not be the only culprit," Dorin says mildly.

"So," I ask, "what is different from the storms we've sailed in before? Not counting when water came in through the open hatch in buckets."

"Nothing I can think of," Dorin says. "This has always been a pretty tight boat. We've always had it well caulked."

"Right," I say. "And we just redid it days before we left Puerto Rico. In fact, Cor did it, and he does a better job than either of us. So that can't be it."

"Whoa, whoa, wait!" Cory says. "Whaddaya mean I caulked it?"

"Yeah," I say. "I saw you with the caulking gun one day, maybe last week. The job was on the list, so I crossed it off when I saw you do it."

"No, you never saw me do it because I didn't. I didn't even know it needed to be done."

"Well, yeah, of course. I removed as much of the old caulking as I could while you were gone with Bast. So I put 'recaulking' on the list."

"Nope," says Cory. "Didn't happen. Yes, I did use the caulking gun one day for a little job I was doing...I think around the hole where the antenna comes through. Just something I wanted to do."

We are dumbstruck for a minute. And then Dorin throws back his head and laughs.

"So," he finally says, "there's no caulking around the portholes? Or the cabin top handrails? Or...anywhere? Well, that certainly answers why we're taking on a little water. Hmmm. Well, it's a good thing we're not taking on much." He works hard to suppress a smile, but there's a twinkle in his eyes. "We can live with a little dampness."

I look inside. Dampness *rains* on everything except Cory's bunk.

"So, we'll wait for a dry day and caulk the holes," Dorin says.

I do not hold out for the possibility of a dry day before we get to Puerto Rico.

The High Seas weather report at noon sounds better. The front is weakening, and winds are predicted to be fifteen to twenty knots today and tomorrow.

"I hope it turns out that way," Dorin says. "Dead reckoning gives us one hundred and twenty miles to go. But of course that doesn't mean much with what might be an adverse current. It's too cloudy to get a sun sight."

I decide to change into what I know is the last of my dry clothes. I lean carefully across the soaked bed cushion to open my clothing cubby and am dismayed to see everything is wet. I look in Dorin's locker and find the same thing.

"So much for dry clothes preventing more boils," I tell Dorin. "We have none."

"I don't know what's the matter with you guys. I don't have any boils," Cory says.

"No, and you probably won't either," Dorin says. "You don't wear a shirt, and your shorts always seem to be dry. I don't know how you do it. Your bunk is not even damp."

"Right. And you guys can't sit on it. You'll get it wet. I think it's the only dry place on the boat."

There is no danger of sitting on Cory's bunk. As a bed it's fine, but it's too deep, and there are no cushions for the back, so it's uncomfortable seating.

"No worries. We won't," I say. "But it must be nice to have a dry bunk."

There are maybe five inches of water on the floor. The bookshelves are also dripping wet.

Dorin sees me looking at the bookshelf. "I moved the ship's log over by the ham radio to keep it dry. I noticed it this morning. Luckily the ham radio is also dry. Good thing it's located on the starboard side."

"Maybe I should go shirtless for a while," Dorin says. "Works for Cory." Standing in the companionway, he slips off his shirt.

I gasp, "Oh, no!" There is almost no skin on his back that doesn't have boils in some form--either new ones with pus centers or open ones that look like raw meat or a few that are healing and have scabs on them.

"Oh, my God!" I say.

"I bet yours looks as bad," he says. I raise my shirt in the back.

"Yeah, it looks like raw hamburger," he says. "Smarts, doesn't it?"

As the morning wears on, I think of my culpability: the discomfort and suffering I have caused Dorin and me. How could I have been so incompetent, so stupid, so ridiculously impulsive, so...so.... And then I realize I am saying this out loud.

"Hey, I think we should consider this a no-fault accident," Cory says.

"Yes, I'd say this was a blameless incident and not look around for someone to point fingers at," Dorin says with a chuckle.

My eyes fill with tears. They are being so nice in the face of our shared misery.

"Oh, come on, Shirl Jean. This is something to celebrate. We know what the problem is, where the water is coming from...."

"Yeah, everywhere!" I say.

"But now that we don't have to look for leaks, we can just cope with the problem. I'll probably get a good night's sleep tonight just because I won't worry."

"Yeah, fat chance," I say. "It's all my fault."

"Don't go grabbing blame," he says. "We'd still have turned around. We'd still be fighting our way back to Puerto Rico." He pauses and grins.

"With or without tons of saltwater raining into our boat. Getting our stuff wet...."

Cory laughs. "Mostly, the worst thing that's happened is you guys getting gross boily things all over you. So, not to worry. I don't have a problem with sloshing water in the boat."

"Well, the first thing to do now is to get the manual bilge pump working. I haven't heard great things about them, but we cannot be choosy. But first, if you're okay out here," Dorin says to Cory, "we'll go below and bail." He ruffles my hair. "It'll be penance for your mother."

Dorin has an idea that we can bail more easily if we bail out of the locker under the rear dinette seat because it's lower than the cabin floor. He kneels in the water that sloshes as the boat pitches and swoops. He dips the bucket into the locker and hands it to me. I swoosh to the sink and dump it.

"Hey, I got a better idea," I say. "Get up for a minute."

He looks puzzled as he stands up. I push him aside, take the bucket, and sit on the floor. The water comes almost to my waist. I dip the bucket and hand it to him.

"No, Shirl Jean. No fair. I do that part. Don't take the penance thing seriously."

"This will be easier for me," I tell him. "It's heavy, so it will be easier if you lift the bucket and dump it into the sink."

"Okay, you might be right." He dumps the bucket and brings it back.

He keeps count, and as we're wrapping it up, he says, "Sixty-two gallons. Are you sure this is the best way for you to do this?"

"Oh, for sure," I say. "And I have to do penance...."

"Next stop, the port sail locker," he says.

Cory hand steers in the cockpit. Dorin lifts the locker cover and eases himself into the locker, which is a tight fit. "The handle must be in here somewhere," he says. "Probably in the bottom." His head and shoulders disappear from sight.

Suddenly a large wave hits the port side, and gallons of water pour down the deck, over the coaming and into the sail locker. Before much gets in, Cory slaps the cover closed, and the rest of the water whooshes into the footwell and drains out of the scuppers.

"You all right?" Cory asks Dorin as he lifts the cover.

"Yeah, I'm all right. I can see the handle. Thanks for keeping my back dry." He hauls himself out of the locker and fits the handle into a slot. Sitting beside the open locker seat, he swings the handle back and forth. We hear water coming out of the stern of the boat. But it doesn't sound like nearly as much water as the electric pump manages.

For the rest of the day, Cory and Dorin take turns sitting in the cockpit, pumping constantly, while I steer.

At one point, a squall comes through. Cory and I take cover below, but Dorin sits in the rain and continues to pump.

"Yeah, I know. I look ridiculous, right?" he says with a comical look on his face as rainwater cascades off his hat.

But even with their best efforts the water level on the floor drops very slowly, hardly noticeable.

"Not very efficient, is it?" Dorin asks after four hours of the two of them constantly pumping. "I think we'd be better off to bail. Or, maybe a combination? Cuz this is just too damn slow."

We bail again from the same port side every four hours, usually with a three-person bucket team, which turns out to be quite fast and effective. We keep count and bail sixty to eighty gallons every four hours.

To conserve the battery, we decide not to use the radio anymore to listen to the weather.

"Nothing we can do about it anyway," Dorin says.

We are all thinking what we don't bother to say: we need to keep the battery in case of emergency communications.

The wind increases during night. Dorin had pulled the stays'l over to backwind at 10:00 p.m. because the boat was hobby horsing and the bowsprit was smacking on the water. Our ride smoothed out, and we are still moving at three to three-and-a-half knots.

At 7:00 a.m. on day twelve, we break our resolve and listen to the High Seas report. We hear the wind is thirty knots, gusting to forty, but predicted to drop to between fifteen and twenty today.

"I don't know about you, Shirl Jean, but I am a tired bunny," Dorin says. He is sitting on the ice box, the only dry sitting area, besides Cory's bunk. We are looking out at the undulating horizon as we rise and fall on the waves.

Cory ties the tiller in the middle and comes down into the salon, grabs his toothbrush, and goes outside to brush his teeth.

"He still does that every day, doesn't he?" Dorin asks.

"Yeah, I don't think he's missed a day."

"I heard that," Cory says. "Don't think I endured braces for two years just to let my teeth rot. You guys should do the same. Have some pride, old people. Oh, yeah, never mind. Doesn't matter."

"Wise ass," Dorin says.

At 10:00 a.m., Dorin says he believes his calculations give us 65 miles to go. He pumps with the manual pump for an hour, but only small squirts come out of the back and into the ocean. "I have to tear into this pump," he says. "Something's wrong. First, I'm going to snug up the mainsheet for you, Cor." He lays the pump handle on the end of the locker cover and grabs the winch handle. Before he can get the handle into the winch, another monster wave washes over the boat and surges down the port deck. Dorin slams the locker shut to try to prevent water from going inside, but some does. We are so concerned about how much might have gone in that it takes a few minutes before we realize the manual pump handle is no longer on the boat. It's the first thing of any significance, unless we count the approach chart to Bermuda, we've lost overboard.

We bail by hand for a half an hour before we reduce the water to almost floorboard level.

"Sun sights indicate we are at fifteen degrees latitude, but I'm getting concerned," Dorin says. "We've been maintaining our compass heading, pointing at Ponce, but we still might not make even the corner of Puerto Rico, forty miles to the west because of the current. Let me take over for a while."

He stands in the cockpit making small adjustments to the sails, trying to keep it as close into the wind as possible. We are moving almost directly north.

"By yesterday's calculations, we should see Puerto Rico now," he says at 5:00 p.m. "Maybe we'll see the lights by tonight."

But we don't.

At 11:00 p.m., Cory spots a barge heading west. Dorin tries to hail it, but it doesn't respond.

"I hope this doesn't mean there isn't enough power left in our battery to reach anyone," Dorin says.

He takes the presence of the other boat as an indication that we must be near the southern coast of Puerto Rico, in the shipping lanes, so a constant watch for traffic will be needed. No more checking every fifteen minutes.

At 2:00 a.m., I hear Cory bailing, so I get up, and we bail ninety-six gallons.

"All set," Cory says. "You can go back to sleep. I'm going to hang out in the cockpit with Dorin." But no land shows up, and at four, Dorin comes below to get a couple of hours of sleep.

At dawn Tuesday morning, Cory yells, "Lay-und ho!" We come tumbling outside to see the sun's first rays touching land on the horizon.

"Yahoo!" Cory whoops, and we laugh joyfully with him. But two hours later, our excitement ends because it's not Puerto Rico that is getting gradually closer and more distinct. Dorin and Cory recognize it as uninhabited Mona Island, 35 miles west of Puerto Rico. We have missed Ponce by 70 miles!

Still, it's good to see land of any kind because it tells us where we are.

We chatter, making predictions that we might actually be in Puerto Rico by 5:00 p.m., if we sail hard all day. We talk about food—which restaurant we will eat at tonight.

The northeast wind drops to ten knots, and we realize we have been drifting perilously close to Mona Island. Cory shakes one reef out of the main, puts the jib up, and we head east toward Boquerón on a close beat, but, alarmingly, we continue to get closer to the steep cliffs of Mona Island.

Cory takes out the last reef in the main.

"This will probably set us over on our ear," Dorin says, "but we have to do it. This current is treacherous."

We do heel steeply, and I have to brace my feet against the other side of the cockpit. Heading southeast for an hour, we make slow progress away from the island, then east again, aiming once more for Boquerón Bay, the southernmost bay on the west coast.

Dorin tells Cory to go get some sleep because we will need him later. Cory jumps down the companionway, sloshes through water, and rolls into his bunk.

I bring Dorin some food, but he refuses.

"Remember the days when we thought the dangers of Mona Passage were overblown?" he asks.

"We were just innocents then," I reply.

"And maybe just a touch arrogant."

"Nah," I say and grin.

Water continues to accumulate on the cabin floor, but it doesn't alarm me much. I know with some combined effort, we will be able to bail it out. I want to let Cory rest a few hours.

At noon, I wake him and tell him we need to bail. He swings into a sitting position and sits on his bunk with calf-high water swirling around his legs. His elbows are on his knees, and his chin in his hands. His eyes close. "Okay, just give me a minute."

In five minutes, I call his name and he wakes up, startled. "Sorry. I'm okay now."

We begin to bail but quickly realize the sink won't drain.

"I'll tear into it later," Dorin says. "Meanwhile, how about dumping it into the ocean. I'll help."

So I sit on the floor and hand a bucket to Cory. He walks to the stairs and hands it up to Dorin, who dumps it overboard. This takes a lot longer than usual, and we are exhausted when we finish. Cory sits on his bunk again, seemingly too tired to lie down. Then I notice a brown ring around his calves.

"What's that?" I ask, pointing.

Cory looks at the front of his bunk. There is a brown line like a watermark across the front of it. He runs his finger along it. "Huh. It's sticky." He smells the gunk and says, "Varnish!"

"Look at your legs. You have varnish rings around them."

He examines the front and back of both calves. Smiling, he shakes his head and shrugs his shoulders. "I'll shave."

I open a dinette locker we haven't been into in a couple of months. My stomach sinks. There's a gallon can of varnish, rusted and now empty. I lift out the can and show Cory.

"Crap!" he says. "All the water we just bailed had varnish in it!"

"What's up?" Dorin asks as he comes below.

We explain and Cory adds, "There are dolphins down there. And turtles, octopus, jellyfish!"

"Yeah, that's regrettable, Cor, but, think about it. Even if we had known before we started bailing, what else could we do? We have to bail to stay afloat."

"We shouldn't have brought the varnish!" Cory says. "It was almost half a gallon we just dumped."

"In all the years I've owned this boat, that locker has never been wet," Dorin replies. "I've stored paint in it for months. It should have been okay. I'm as sorry as I can be, Cor, but I can't fix it after the fact. We need to focus on getting to Puerto Rico."

I nod and think that this trip has been a series of things for Dorin to fix, sometimes repeatedly, sometimes under extreme conditions. I know this is a gut punch for him, and he will internalize his guilt regarding this spill.

"You're right," I say. "Let's get back to Puerto Rico. How's the wind?"

"Well, I shouldn't be surprised that it's coming right out of Boquerón Bay," he says. "We've been on a beat since we started back."

When our speed drops to three knots, Dorin says the current must be at least that strong, so we will not make headway.

"I am so frustrated I could smash something," Cory says. He goes forward to put up the jib, and our speed increases to four and sometimes five knots. At 2:00 p.m., he tells Dorin to go to bed because he can take the watch for a while.

We drop to two knots.

"Aaaargh! It's from the worst possible direction," Cory says, "and it can't even keep that up. I need more sail, but I don't want to wake Dorin up to ask him. I want to put up the original jib. We've got to get more speed."

"Do what you need to do," I tell him. "I'll take the tiller."

In ten minutes, the larger jib is up, and all sails are unreefed.

"Don't know what will happen if we get hit with a gust," he says.

The speed goes up to five, then back to three, then back to five. "That's the best we can do," he says.

At 5:00 p.m., Dorin comes out and walks forward to the bow. Hanging onto the forestay, he stares ahead for a while.

"Nothing?" Cory asks, when he joins us in the cockpit. Not only do we not see Puerto Rico by 5:00 p.m., we also don't see lights by dark. Dorin thinks the wind and notorious southwest current must have carried us far enough south that we can't see Puerto Rico.

No one wants to eat.

At 7:00 p.m., Dorin turns north and watches for lights. For the next eight hours he stays at the tiller, and we sail north most of the time, occasionally tacking to the east, then back toward the north, averaging just under four knots. We sail until 3:00 a.m. Wednesday morning, when we heave-to and take turns napping off and on and taking watch in the cockpit.

At 7:30 a.m., Dorin takes a sun sight that puts us west of Mona Island. "I'll have to disregard this one," he says. "It's gotta be wrong." He is rechecking his calculations when Cory says he can see Puerto Rico to the east.

"Whew, am I glad I was wrong on this one!" Dorin says. With Puerto Rico in sight, we celebrate and once again plan what we will be doing, when, in five or six hours from now, we will be in the harbor.

From the rear stay, Cory takes down the Puerto Rican flag, which is in tatters.

"No way we're going into port with the flag like this." Below, I tuck it away with the other flags we have collected.

An hour later we recognize the land mass; it's the west side of Mona Island all over again. We had sailed hard away from the island to the northeast for 21 hours, and now we are 20 miles west of where we had started.

"Just in case you want to know," Cory says, "this is one of those times when I say, 'why in the hell didn't I keep my feet on land?'"

"I'm sorry, Cor," I say.

"Also, as you will soon discover, the Stripeeze Paint Remover busted out. There's more sludge, and the paint is coming off the floor. So, if you were really sorry, you'd go stick your feet in the sludge and walk around for a while." Then Cory looks at my face and says, "Just kidding. About walking around. There really is paint remover on the floor."

"But, could be worse," Dorin says.

"How?" Cory asks.

"We could be in a leaky boat."

Cory checks the chart and says we need a heading of 104 to make Boquerón.

"We can't quite make that," Dorin says. "It'll have to be 120, so we'll have to tack when we get closer." Aside, to me, he quietly says, "You know, with these winds and the current, it could still be two more days."

At noon we have crackers and peanut butter and jelly.

The three of us bail forty gallons, dumping the water overboard. We are beyond caring, much more than a flinch, at dumping our chemical-infused water into the sea.

We put all sails up and head as close into the wind as possible, but an hour later, heavy winds force us to single reef. Our speed drops to three-and-a-half knots. Heading east toward mainland Puerto Rico, we pass Mona Island at 9:30 in the morning. Steep waves continue to wash over us. I take an hour's rest. As usual, I pull a wool blanket over my head so the saltwater doesn't drip on my face. The blanket is wet, but it does the job.

At 4:00 p.m., Mona is still very much in sight, though finally behind us. Puerto Rico, of course, is not visible because we are thirty-five miles away. We try to adjust to the idea that we aren't going to be in port even on the following day, though we wonder if we will at least see the radio tower light after nightfall. Dorin takes a nap lying on his stomach because his boils are so painful.

At 5:00 p.m., the wind moderates and shifts to the north. We are still sailing with just the stays'l and single reef main.

The three of us share a small can of chicken for supper. There is still plenty of canned food, but we are not hungry.

We discuss our options. If we don't see Puerto Rico in the morning, we could head for Samaná in the D.R., which would be easy to do, and it isn't that far away.

"But," says Cory, "then we'd still have to deal with Mona Passage again to get to Puerto Rico."

"Or we can still keep trying for Puerto Rico," I say.

"Or, we can call the Coast Guard," Dorin says.

This is a big surprise because Dorin doesn't give in to solutions that depend on being rescued.

After half an hour of discussion, during which I've made a case of how tired Dorin and Cory are, we decide to call the Coast Guard. Dorin calls them on the VHF, but they don't respond.

"Oh, well, it was worth a try," Dorin says, appearing massively relieved.

But he looks gray with exhaustion, so we send him to bed.

At 10:00 p.m., when he comes on watch, we are on a fifteen to twenty-degree heel. "I'm glad you have the big jib up," he says. "I feel like we're finally making distance and in the right direction. Do you want to go get some sleep?" he asks me.

"No. I'm sitting up with you. I don't want you to fall asleep behind the wheel."

"Thanks, the company would be welcomed."

On Thursday, just past midnight, we see a freighter overtaking us from behind, traveling in the same direction.

Dorin switches on our position lights, hoping there is still enough juice in the battery. It's difficult to tell if we are on a collision course or not. When it appears to be within four miles of us, Dorin hails them on the VHF.

"General cargo vessel. I am on your starboard side. Do you read me?"

A cultured voice within a Swedish accent identifies himself as the captain and gives his ship's name.

"Just a moment, please," he says. In a minute he is back. "Yes, are you a sailboat? You are two miles away. Yes, I have you."

"I'm calling to say I'm trying to sail a disabled boat under adverse conditions into Boquerón. It would be difficult to change tack. Is that a problem?"

"What's your heading?"

"One hundred ten."

"I'll change to 145 and pass you on your starboard side."

"Thank you very much, Captain. While I have you, can you give me a position fix?"

"Be glad to. Just a moment."

Cory, having been awakened by this activity, is near the table so he can check the chart.

"Keep in mind I'm two miles away." He gives the position in longitude and latitude.

"That's going to be very helpful. Thank you very much."

"Have a good cruise, Captain."

I stay on deck while Cory and Dorin check the chart by flashlight. "Cor, we are so close to Boquerón Bay," I hear him say. When they come back to the cockpit and look up, there is the red light of the radio tower with which we are so familiar.

We realize that, from the height of his bridge, the captain must have been able to see the light.

"He must have thought I was an idiot, asking for position when he could see a navigation light that close," Dorin says.

He radios back to the ship. "You must have been able to see the Cabo Rojo light. We couldn't."

"Yes," the captain says, sounding amused. "I have a little height on you. Good sailing, Captain."

We still have fifteen or eighteen miles to go. We sit in the cockpit the rest of the night, watching the sky gradually lighten on our fifteenth day at sea. The wind drops steadily, so Dorin shakes out the reefs, and Cory puts up the jib. At dawn, just as we can see the broad entrance to the harbor a couple of miles away, the sails droop. We watch as each little puff of wind fills them out for a minute and then is gone. Just as we get to the mouth, the sails go completely limp, and the boat barely moves.

Dorin is almost asleep on his feet. "I'm going to shut my eyes for a few minutes," he says. "You know, we could drop the anchor so we could all sleep."

Cory laughs. "No, I don't think so."

A light breeze comes up.

"See?" I say. "We are still moving."

"Okay. You can use the last of the battery to pump out the boat here. We can't do it in the bay." It feels so good to flip the switch and hear the water blast out of the stern—something we had always taken for granted. In an hour we are barely moving again, and I talk Cory into getting some sleep.

"See?" he mumbles as he falls into bed. "I told you that Friday stuff was BS." And he's asleep.

The boat is barely ghosting along but still making progress. Just past daylight, Dorin's muffled voice comes from the fo'c'sle.

"Are you sure you're heading into the wind as much as you can?"

"Yes."

"You should turn it until the jib barely starts to luff and then back off a little."

I move the tiller two inches, and the jib gently luffs, so I move it back.

"Your jib is luffing," he says.

I smile. "Shut up and go to sleep."

Three hours later, we are still moving on an even keel on a flat bay, undisturbed even by a ripple, and are quite a way into the bay.

Cory comes up on deck with a spring and a smile. "You know, three days ago, I thought if we didn't make it in the next day, I'd fly apart."

We laugh and shake our heads. Cory stands at the tiller steering, and we spend the next hour watching the sun rise in the sky. We're almost giddy with feelings of joy and well-being as the *Fandango* continues to drift into the harbor.

Suddenly, Cory says, "Oh, no!"

He's looking forward to the anchorage we are heading toward. "Bob is headed this way."

I stand on tiptoe, and there is Bob, motoring in our direction, holding up a tow rope for us to see.

"No." says Cory through clenched teeth. "We did not come all this way on our own to get towed in. We only have a hundred yards to go!"

Dorin is suddenly in the cockpit with us. "He's just being neighborly."

"I have a plan," says Cory. "I know where I want to anchor. I want to bring her in myself. When she is drifting almost to a stop, I will go forward and drop the anchor. Myself!"

I see fire and rebellion in his eyes.

"He has a point," I say to Dorin. "He's earned it."

By then Bob is drawing close, grinning and excitedly waving the tow rope. "I'll tow you in!" he shouts. "Welcome back!"

"Don't let him do it," Cory says.

I'm with Cory, but I can see his pleas are not going to keep Dorin from doing what he sees is the polite boating-thing to do. He goes forward to take the tow rope from Bob and winds it around the cleat.

Cory looks to me for help, and I can only nod in sympathy.

Dorin comes back to the cockpit. "What was I going to say? Back off. We don't want your help?"

Cory takes a deep breath and then goes forward to prepare to drop the anchor. I can only imagine his frustration.

Bob gives us the only news that happened while we were gone: Mac and Cindy of the *Fancy Dancer* have left for the island chain south of Puerto Rico. Then he invites us over for breakfast, but Dorin explains we have to get some rest and then take care of the boat. He says we will talk to them later in the day and thanks him for his help.

We each collapse in a dry, sunny spot on the deck. Dorin and I lie on our stomachs and sleep a couple of hours. When we awake, we haul all the cushions on deck to dry. Dorin and I don't have any dry clothes, so we row ashore in our damp, salt encrusted shorts and t-shirts. Cory, of course, wears clean, dry clothes. We walk to our favorite outdoor restaurant near the beach and order one of the best meals we've ever had. While we watch the egrets fish for bugs in a quiet pool behind the restaurant and the palm fronds sway gently in the breeze, we down, between us, a dozen eggs, a pound of bacon, and a gallon of orange juice.

Before we head back, Dorin calls Customs from the phone booth, while Cory and I talk about how unusually vivid and sharply defined everything is, from the purple flowers to the white feathers on the egret. I feel somehow like I'm seeing these things for the first time.

Dorin comes back with a half-gallon of ice cream; we row to the *Fandango* and pig out.

Life is sweet.

Chapter Twenty-one
Taking Care of Business

After napping on deck for a couple more hours, we haul everything out on the deck to dry. We decide that rowing wet laundry to the dock and then carrying it to the laundromat would be too difficult, so we dry it first. With clothespins and string and safety pins, we attach our clothes to the halyards. Dorin hauls them up the mast and forestay, where our clothes flap and snap in the wind. We attach the blankets and towels to the lifelines. We lay the books on the deck, open in the middle, the breeze randomly turning the pages.

A couple of hours later, Dorin and I go ashore to pick up a few groceries—fruit and other things we don't need to cook. Standing on the dock, we look at the *Fandango,* decked out from stem to stern and deck to masthead, with a colorful display of our breeze-blown laundry.

"Talk about a ragtag outfit...." Dorin says.

"Looks kind of festive to me. Like when boats get decorated with flags for special events. I think we should parade around the bay. Maybe set a new tradition."

He laughs and shakes his head. "Always looking on the bright side."

We decide to take the laundry in today, so we haul everything down from the halyards and lifelines. Cory takes our stash of quarters and rows in to do the laundry.

February 6th is Cory's seventeenth birthday. We talk about how to celebrate, but he says some guy on the beach has asked him to help crew for a race with his catamaran, and he'd like to do it. We go out for supper though, and he tells us the boat he was on spent more time capsized than sailing. "Didn't bother me though," he laughs. "Capsizing isn't so bad, and anyone could tell it wasn't the crew's fault."

I phone home the next day, as I've done periodically, to let my folks know where we are. My father tells me my mother has been very sick. She's in the hospital and facing hernia surgery.

"You have to fly home," Dorin says. "We'll hang in here and get some stuff done. Maybe we'll do a little caulking...."

Calling from the public phone in the park, I buy a plane ticket from San Juan to Boston and a return from Boston to Mayagüez. María tells me where to catch a van in Mayagüez that goes to San Juan.

I pack a few clothes, realizing I am flying north in the winter and have nothing but summer clothes. I call my father and ask him to find someone to pick me up at Logan Airport and to send a winter coat for me.

In Mayagüez, the *público* leaves me off at the place where I catch the van. My seatmate introduces himself as Julian. He speaks excellent, only lightly accented, English, and says he's happy to have someone he can practice his English with. He gives me some Spanish lessons, and I find out our attempts to pronounce the words *ferretería* (hardware store), *panadería* (bakery) and *farmacia* (pharmacy) are all wrong. We laugh when I tell him how we have been pronouncing the words. He helps me switch from '**fer**ah *terah* **ee**ah' to my best attempt of 'ferre teh **ree** ah,' with the emphasis on the next to last syllable, the E sound in '**rí**a.' Then we work on farmacia, which I have been pronouncing 'farma **cee** ah' but is really 'far **mah** cia.' I am nearly in tears from laughter by the time we are done.

Julian is into Eastern philosophy and says our paths did not cross by accident. Random or not, I am grateful for his company on the long 4 ½ hour trip to San Juan.

Approaching Boston in the air at night is enchanting, as I knew it would be. The landing is fun because I can see the engine out of my window and watch it pass over the tiny buildings below…sort of like watching the Starship Enterprise pass over a planet. As we lower toward the runway, we can see there is hard packed, bumpy snow. The passengers applaud when we touch down for a very smooth landing.

When my sister Donna and her husband pick me up at the airport, she also has gloves and winter boots to lend me. I arrive at Mom's by 11:15 p.m. and find the thirty-degree outdoor temperature not too bad.

My mother recovers quickly and comes home, and we enjoy a satisfying visit. Although she tires easily, she wants to sit up as much as possible so we can visit. Soon we almost have to hold her down so she rests. She says she hopes to go shopping with me before I leave. She wants to buy me clothes in my new size. Dad and I convince her to hold off until I come back from the voyage, to see what my final weight might be.

Dad, who thinks I need fattening up, does the cooking, and we have one wonderful meal after another. The bathroom scale tells me I have lost thirty pounds since beginning the trip. Mom and Dad ask a lot of questions about our trip, right up to the present, and I give them a watered-down version and promise that the rest of the trip will be quite safe. My son Michael drives in from Rome, New York, with his eight-month-old daughter Laura, to visit for a couple of days. I am delighted to meet my newest granddaughter.

While I am in Massachusetts, I find land-based living is both strange and a welcomed respite: hot and cold running water, a shower, a four-burner stove, and an oven! I am so happy to use a toilet that flushes, instead of the *Fandango's* head, which has to be pumped two dozen times. I marvel at these things almost as if they are new inventions, but I long to be back with Dorin and Cory on the *Fandango*.

As I anticipate the return trip, I am anxious about money. I had withdrawn what I thought I would need for the trip, but facing the return trip to Puerto Rico, I realize I might have miscalculated. My father has already scheduled the local limo to get me to Boston. My flight schedule requires me to leave my folks' house at 3:00 a.m. I'm nervous about the expense of the transportation to Boston, but there are no alternatives…not at three in the morning. While I contemplate asking Dad for a loan, Aunt Edith drops by to say hi and goodbye and hands me an envelope with $50 in it! I am so relieved. I put aside $30 for the limo—the charge with no tip.

Ten days after arriving in Massachusetts, I am on a flight from Boston to Atlanta and then on to Mayagüez, Puerto Rico. I have a window seat so I watch as we pass over water in a few hours that took us over a month to cross.

When we land in Mayagüez, it is so hot on the tarmac it feels like the air is being sucked out of my lungs. But as I walk to the terminal, I notice the clean air is rich with the aroma of flowers and damp soil. I feel giddy with happiness to be here in this tropical setting and to see the guys again. I fantasize about going out to dinner tonight here in Mayagüez — someplace special. We'll have a glass of wine and get caught up on news from home and from the boat.

I look around for the guys and am surprised they are not there. Maybe they are late?

Do I dare wait? I have barely enough money left to take the last van to Cabo Rojo, which leaves in a few minutes.

I decide to take it and hope the guys aren't here in Mayagüez, stuck in traffic. When we arrive in Cabo Rojo, I realize we have parked on the other side of town from the *público* station.

I panic a little because the last run of the day to Boquerón leaves in ten minutes. Fearing I will be stranded in Puerto Real with no resources, I run, with a suitcase in each hand, block after block to the station. I am out of breath but very relieved to see one taxi still sitting at the terminal. I have just enough money for the fare.

The driver puts my bags in the trunk, and I slide into the back, where three other overheated passengers are ready to roll. When our sweaty arms touch, the woman beside me gives me a dirty look. At that hour, she must have thought she was home free, until a perspiring American showed up.

I settle in, and on the ride to Boquerón, I fantasize about regaling the guys with the story of this part of my adventure: getting home from Mayagüez on my own. I feel kind of heroic. I can imagine our laughing over a glass of wine.

Though the *público* normally doesn't go to the beach area, the driver kindly delivers me to the dock at dusk and hands me my bags from the trunk. I hand him my last dollar, regretting I have no money for a tip.

I look around for Dorin, who will be able to provide the tip, but no one is there to meet me. I know he knows when I am returning. I wrote down the return date when we purchased the tickets. I can make out the *Fandango* at anchor; the lights are on. I know they can't hear a shout from here, so I am flummoxed. What to do?

One of the fishermen I recognize is walking toward me. "You need ride?"

"*Sí.* Yes. *Por favor.*"

He pulls his dinghy up to the dock, and I climb in. He hands down my suitcases. I am tired from traveling since 3:00 a.m., and my nerves are a little frayed from worrying that I might have been stranded overnight in Cabo Rojo with no money.

He starts the motor and doesn't have to be told which boat to deliver me to.

"*Muchas gracias.*" I tear up.

When we reach the boat, I step up on the dinghy seat, grab the *Fandango*'s lifelines to pull myself up, and, one at a time, swing my legs over. He hands up a suitcase. I say, "I, ah, don't have money. No *tengo dinero.* Wait, please."

"*No, no es necesario,*" he says firmly as he hands the second suitcase up to me.

"*Muchas gracias,*" I say. He nods, turns his boat, and motors toward shore. When I appear in the companionway, Dorin and Cory are stunned to see me. "I thought you were coming in tomorrow!" Dorin says.

"I was wondering who was trying to board our boat. Why are you here early? Is everything okay? How did you get here from Mayagüez? We were going to meet you there. Tomorrow. What happened? Why are you a day early?"

Testily I say, "No, this is the day. I wrote it down for you." I pick up the logbook and find the sticky note I had left for him with the flight schedule. I hand him the note.

"Oh." He shakes his head and doesn't take the note. I can see he feels really terrible, but he doesn't say anything.

Thoughts of a restaurant with a white tablecloth, stemware, the clink of glasses, and delicious food fade. I consider for a moment suggesting that we go out for supper, maybe still salvage the day and get reconnected, but I see that Cory is just finishing up cooking a one-dish meal.

"Okay, we should eat in." I try to cover my disappointment. He scoops rice, peas, onions and spam on my plate.

I decide this is not the time to regale them with stories of my Dad's fabulous cooking and other tales of civilization. We catch up on news about my mom, and they give me *Fandango* news.

The boat has been caulked within an inch of its life. They have installed a new propane gas stove on a gimbal that Dorin rigged so we can cook even when the boat heels.

"We installed two propane tanks on the stern, so we'll be good for quite a while," Dorin says. "And it should be easy to get them refilled."

"You won't believe how much easier it is to cook," Cory says. "You don't have to fight with this one. And we can cook when we're heeling." He demonstrates the pivot feature that allows the stove and the pan on the stove to stay level, even when the boat is tipped.

"You made this?" I ask Dorin.

"Well, I didn't invent it. You can buy them. But I did put it together from the steel strapping Cory got at the hardware store. So, does this get me off the hook for not picking you up at the airport?"

"I don't know," I reply. "I'll have to use it first. Underway. And then we'll see."

"Ah, you're a hard-hearted woman, Shirl Jean."

He tells me they have also researched getting a valve job done locally, but the news was discouraging. One mechanic wouldn't touch it because it was a marine motor, even though Dorin told him it was a Mitsubishi block. Another said it would be four months before he could begin.

"So, I have decided...I have the manual, and we only need to pick up a few things. We are going to do the job ourselves. We'll just pull the motor, I'll take the head off, and we'll do a valve job right here."

I'm quite taken aback, but then Dorin has pulled off so many things, I have no reason to doubt it.

The next day, we go into town, and with our dictionary in hand, we take a taxi to a section of Cabo Rojo we've never seen. The few words I picked from the dictionary prove to be good enough for the driver. He gets us to an auto parts store.

We are anxious about being able to describe what we want, but the guy behind the counter figures us for Americans right away and says, "Welcome to my store. How can I help you?"

Dorin comments on a photo of an antique car that is taped to the cash register. He and the clerk chat for twenty minutes about the merits of the car and entertain each other with anecdotes.

"Of course," I think. In the States, Dorin never goes anywhere without striking up a long conversation that neither of the participants wants to bring to an end.

One time, in our early sailing relationship, we drove to the boatyard, and barely out of the car a minute, Dorin struck up a conversation with a guy about the merits of his boat. Dorin is a great admirer of other people's boats. I carried six bags of groceries down to the dock, two bags at a time, and then I brought our individual duffle bags and a box of miscellaneous stuff that looked like boat parts.

The men were well into storytelling. The car keys were still dangling in his hand, so I eased them out, parked the car, then unlocked the boat and began to move the assembled stuff from the dock to the cockpit. The men were just winding things up, and as I lifted the last bag of groceries from the dock, Dorin said, "Here, let me help you with that."

Today's conversation doesn't surprise me one bit. Dorin finally gets around to telling the shopkeeper the history of our motor.

"Yes, you are right, Captain. This would foul up the valve seats, so you wouldn't get good compression. You have to have good compression to get diesel engines to run. The diesel fuel won't burn completely, and you'd get oily carbon on the valve seats."

Dorin asks about replacing the rings and bearings, but one ring would cost $200, so he decides to just do the valve job.

We buy the necessary stuff, but the guy refuses payment at this point. "You may need more parts. Pay me when the job is done."

We are flabbergasted. Can the guy who we had assumed was an employee make this kind of decision? Then he insists he give us a ride back to Boquerón. He turns out the lights, locks the door, and ushers us to his truck. "Then you own this business?" asks Dorin.

"With my brother, yes."

The next day Dorin and Cory pull the engine forward and then out onto the salon floor, leaving us no access to the outside except by hoisting ourselves up through the front hatch with only arm strength, which, I realize, is no longer difficult for me. Not only am I stronger, but I have less weight to haul up.

We go to work. Cory and I stand by with emery strips and some compound goop. One of Dorin's purchases yesterday was a spring compressor tool. When he takes the head off, he tries to keep the head gasket intact, but it tears. The valve stem edges are pitted enough for Dorin to believe this is what has caused the problem. The valve seats appear to be good. He is concerned about the head gasket, however, and goes back to the auto parts store to buy some head gasket material. And to pay the guy, I know. He was impressed by the parts guy trusting us, but it's been bugging him that he owed the money.

When he gets back, we scrape most of the stuff off the valve seats and valves. Then, he puts coarse compound around the valve seat and valve. Taking the valve stems between our palms, Cory and I rotate the valves against the seats. When they seem smooth and no pitting shows, we finish with fine grit compound until the valves look shiny.

Dorin cuts the new head gasket and reassembles the motor, using instructions to apply the correct torque.

Once the motor is securely back on the motor mounts, we are on pins and needles to see if it will work. Dorin primes the engine, and it starts! He runs it for a while, charging the batteries, and then we take it for a spin in the harbor. It purrs like a kitten, with sufficient power, though it still only runs at 1900 RPM tops.

We motor to the dock to fill the water tanks. Everything we touch on the exterior is salt-scaled and grimy so, gloriously, we wash the boat with fresh water from a hose. Now that we have fresh water in our tanks, we can also wash down the interior. What a luxury.

The next day we taxi into Cabo Rojo to buy a few clothes. We estimate we have lost 50 pounds between us—more than half of it by me.

We are hanging out in the cabin one morning and realize *someone* has, yet again, left the ham radio on when we hear:

"This is Mac of the *Fancy Dancer* calling the *Fandango*. Calling the *Fandango*. Come in, *Fandango*?"

Dorin, who is reading a book, nods briefly to Cory and continues to read.

Annoyed, Cory picks up the mic. "Yup. This is the *Fandango*."

"This is Mac of the *Fancy Dancer* calling Dorin. Over?" Dorin waves a hand and shakes his head no and continues to read.

"Yeah, *Fancy Dancer*. He's right here." Cory hands Dorin the mic.

Dorin's eyes open in surprise then slowly takes the mic. He inhales big, clears his throat, and then pushes the button on the mic. "Ah, hi there, Mac. This is Dorin of the *Fandango*. Ah...over?"

"How you doin' this morning? How you doin' this morning? Over?" says Mac, who wants to sound like a ham operator handling an emergency situation--repeating everything for clarification.

"Oh, we're just fine. We're just fine. Over?" Dorin looks helplessly at us and shrugs his shoulders.

"Roger, Roger, that sounds good. What have you got there for weather? What have you got there for weather? Over."

"It's hot here, about 85. It's hot here. There's a little breeze. There's a little breeze. Over?"

"Roger, Roger," Mac says. "It's hot there. It's hot there. You have a little breeze. Over?"

Dorin looks at us, raising his shoulders as if to say, "What am I *supposed to say*?" He takes a breath and pushes the button.

"Well, how are you doing? How are you doing? Where are you? Over?"

"We're fine. We're fine. We're in the American Virgins. We're in the American Virgins."

"Oh, that's good. That's good. How's the weather there? How's the weather there?"

"Had a little shower yesterday. Had a little shower yesterday. Over?"

Beads of anxiety sweat have broken out on Dorin's forehead. "Roger. That sounds fine. That sounds fine. You had a shower. Ah, um, ah, how are you reading me? How are you reading me? Over?"

"You are coming in good, *Fandango*. You are coming in good. Over?"

Cory who is now sitting on the top stair puts his cupped hands to his mouth. In a low voice he says, "Breaker, Breaker, one nine? Come in. Do you copy?"

Dorin waves his arm at Cory to indicate he should shut up and then plugs his free ear with his finger. "Roger, Roger, copy that. I'm coming in good. I'm coming in good. Ah, over?"

"Are you reading me good? Are you reading me good? Over?"

Dorin wipes the sweat from his forehead. "Roger, Roger. You are coming in clear. You are coming in clear. Ah...over?"

"Well that sounds good. That sounds good. Over?"

Dorin looks around the cabin as if to find a way to escape. "Roger, Roger, That's good. That's good." He pauses. "Well, talk to you tomorrow? Talk to you tomorrow? Over."

Cory looks a big "What?" at Dorin and lifts his hands in disbelief.

"Roger, Roger, Roger, copy that! That sounds fine. That sounds really fine! Over?"

"Roger. Ah, have a good day. Have a good day. Over?" Dorin says.

"Roger, Roger, we'll have a good day. We'll have a good day. Over?"

Dorin pauses and shakes his head, looking at us for help. Then he says, "Oh…kee doh kee. Ah, over and *clear*."

"Roger, Roger. This is Mac of the *Fancy Dancer*. Um, over and *standing by!*"

"Wow, that was exhausting. I have to rest." He heads for the fo'c'sle. "If anybody ever calls again, and it's not Glenn…I am not here!"

"You gotta admit," Cory says, looking at me. "That was fun."

The days pass while we make improvements on the boat, including sanding and applying varnish to the bright work during the day. In the evenings, we enjoy the company of other cruisers. Eventually the conversation drifts around to questions about why we, or anyone else for that matter, would ever head out again, when everything we could want is right here.

When forced to focus on the question, it hits us: without being aware of it, we have, once more, gotten sucked into the easy life and safety of Puerto Rico.

It's the beginning of April, and we realize with shock our time is rapidly running out. We get serious about provisioning and making final preparations, and in a week, we say our final goodbyes and start out again. We take it for granted, without discussion, this time we will sail down the island chain to Venezuela.

And this time we do not leave on a Friday.

Chapter Twenty-two
Deep Six

When I come on watch at midnight, Dorin says, "Get Cory up. I want to show you two something."

When we climb into the cockpit, Dorin grabs the boat hook and says, "Let's go forward."

He leans over the lifelines and stirs the water with the boat hook. Thousands of stars swirl around the hook as he moves it in a figure eight.

"Phosphorous," he says.

"It's beautiful," I say. "Look! The bow wave is sparkling! Whew, this is gorgeous."

"This area is known for it," he says.

"It's like the bibbidi-bobbidi boo wand of Cinderella's Fairy Godmother," Cory says. Mesmerized, we hand the boat hook off to each other and play with the water.

"Go flush the head," he says. As the seawater swirls around in the toilet, it sparkles.

"This trip is already going better," I say. We continue to pass the boat hook from one to the other and play with the phosphorous. "Enchanting."

At the cape called Cabo Rojo, we turn eastward to follow the coast.

Cory and Dorin go to bed, and I sit in the cockpit for my watch. I am feeling secure and happy with this easy-sailing life. I nod off.

I awake, suddenly alarmed. A little off our bow and only about a hundred feet away, going in the opposite direction, is a black, moving wall.

A ship.

"Dorin, come here!" I yell.

Cory is the first one into the cockpit, followed a second later by Dorin. My heart thumps as the huge wall passes quickly, but silently, past us.

"How can it be so close?" I ask.

"I doubt they even saw us," Dorin says. "I'm really questioning the effectiveness of our radar reflector. No one seems to pick it up."

"But what kind of ship is that? Not a cruise ship! Not even a cargo ship. There are no lights."

"I saw a position light as I was coming out here…green on starboard. See there's white on the back. Probably a US Naval ship out of Vieques," Dorin says.

"But no lights except for navigation lights! And it's silent! That's creepy."

"Maybe a stealth ship," he says with a laugh. "It's past us, so let's not worry about it. You want to head back to bed? I can take over."

"No, I'm wide awake now!" I think of my early fears about being run down by a "killer ship" that doesn't pick us up on radar. "How can we keep safe from ships that don't see us on radar, and we can't hear them and can't see them until they are on top of us?"

"If our radar were still working, that would help. So, just watch for navigation lights. Don't forget to look up. High."

"Got it." For the rest of my watch, I stand in the cockpit and scan the darkness on all sides, looking for navigation lights. I don't wake Cory at four, since I am still wide awake.

The next day there is no wind, so we start the motor. A few hours later, we are off soundings. "Probably more than 600 feet of depth," Dorin says.

"You know what I've been longing to do?" he asks. "Wouldn't it be satisfying to bury the old stove at sea?"

Cory, instantly alert, barks, "Ha ha! Awesome idea!"

"If you don't want it, why didn't you let us get rid of it in Puerto Rico?" I ask Dorin.

"Well, I didn't want other cruisers thinking it would be a good idea to install it in their boats. It should never be used again. So, what do you say? Overboard? It's plenty deep here. No one will ever recover it."

We decide to make an occasion out of it. I write a eulogy. Cory puts on his "dress uniform," which is his white duck pants and a white t-shirt. Dorin lends him his well-worn captain's hat. They lash together the *Tinker* oars to make a platform, and Cory places the edge of it on the lifelines on the foredeck. Dorin lays the stove on it and covers it with our American flag. Cory holds on to the end of it so the flag won't blow away.

I deliver the eulogy:

> *This stove came from simple beginnings, manufactured in 1986. Purchased shortly after, it was much anticipated as a working, dedicated member of the* Fandango *galley. With high hopes, we specifically purchased it to replace an out-of-favor alcohol stove.*
>
> *We made an effort to bond with our new stove, so highly recommended by other cruisers. With excitement we poured alcohol into the warming cup under the burner and lit it with a match. When we guessed the burner was warm enough, we pumped the valve to force kerosene into the stove. Then we used a second match to light the burner. We soon learned using a clicker would better preserve the hair on our fingers.*
>
> *Still, we were enamored with our new stove, and by trial and error, we learned that during cooking we had to pump air into the tank to keep pressure up. And, as the fuel depleted, we had to pump more often and for a greater period of time to keep*

the flame alive. We learned to use the vent screw to adjust the height of the flame and became proficient at it. Before ever leaving on the trip, however, it was clear the stove would need a lot of maintenance on the burners, and we'd have to bring a lot of spare parts...like extra burners.

But still, we had confidence this was the best choice. According to many sources, kerosene was super cheap, and more importantly, more available than alcohol or propane.

Our new stove rewarded us for our knuckleheaded dedication by emitting noxious fumes, spewing black soot upon the ceiling, and requiring constant attendance.

In summary, I am sure we are all united in our heartfelt sentiments: Never in sailing history has a manufactured crew member done so little for so few."

"Here, here!" says Dorin.

"Amen," says Cory.

While Dorin plays the "taps" on his rolled-up paper trumpet, Cory lifts the platform and the stove slides off into the sea. The three of us rush to the lifelines to watch the stove glide gracefully from side to side like an autumn leaf, slowly, slowly down into the deeps. We watch for a long time because the sun strikes off the stainless steel making it visible in the clear water. We make guesses as to how long it will take for it to arrive at its final resting place. A couple of hours, we finally decide, and whether or not it's accurate, this is a satisfying thought, as we slowly sail on.

That night, the motor runs slower and slower and finally quits.

"Fact is," Dorin says, "my knowledge of diesel engines might be somewhat superficial. I read about them. I listened to Bob and the parts guy. Maybe the head gasket didn't seat right. Maybe the valve seats? Maybe it's the fuel filter? I talked to Fred, and he was leaning in that direction."

"But we're not going back, right?" Cory says.

"No reason to. We can conserve the batteries...we'll be dry. We'll look at getting a professional engine job done in Venezuela."

It's pleasant sailing by day, and we enjoy our new propane stove. After the guys teach me how to use it, we take turns cooking and become accustomed to decent home cooked meals.

Unburned and highly explosive propane gathering in the bottom of our boat is unlikely because we always have the front hatch open for ventilation, except in high seas weather. To be safe though, we turn off the gas in the cockpit rather than relying solely on the valve on the stove.

"Just think...we could have started this way instead of fighting with that disgusting stove that required a Herculean effort just to get it to run for twenty minutes," I say.

"At low heat," Cory adds.

"So we done good," Dorin says with satisfaction.

We decide to stop in at St. Croix, one of the US Virgins Islands, because we won't need to clear Immigration or Customs.

The wind dies early in the afternoon, and we realize we cannot make port at Christiansted before nightfall.

"This is not a harbor we can sail into at night," Dorin says. "I don't want to drop anchor out here. We still have enough wind to maintain steerage. Let's just mush along and tack back and forth during the night. I want to move gradually farther back from the harbor, but we'll be careful not to get too far away. Snap on the running lights."

Dorin is on watch at midnight when he calls us. "Shirley, Cory, get up here now!"

As we burst into the cockpit, he points out to sea. "There's a fishing trawler coming right at us. I don't think he can see us. We're right in his path. I think he can't see our lights because of the lights from the city. Cory, get on the radio and try to hail him."

Cory jumps down to the sole of the salon and grabs the VHF.

"This is a disabled sailing ship. We are in your path to..."

"Christiansted," yells Dorin.

"Christiansted," says Cory. His voice is tense.

"Repeat it," yells Dorin. "Keep repeating it."

The boat continues toward us without deviation. I can now hear the drumming engine of the oncoming boat, and it gets louder by the minute.

Dorin pushes me out of the way, and from a cockpit locker, he pulls a search light with a cord on it that ends in soldered-on terminals. He jumps below and pulls the battery cover off, connecting the search light terminals to the battery posts.

"Keep it up!" he says to Cory.

From the cockpit, I watch as the huge trawler grows steadily larger and is aimed directly at us. Dorin leaps back into the cockpit, turns the light on, and flashes it off and on into the window of the wheelhouse. Nothing happens. Cory is still trying to get the trawler on the radio.

The boat continues without deviation.

"Life jackets!" shouts Dorin.

I can feel the throb of the ship's motor in my chest. I open the locker and pull out our life jackets. I toss one to Dorin, but he's focused on the oncoming boat. As he shines the light directly and steadily into the pilot house, we can see the back wall. There is no one at the helm.

I scream, "Cory, get up here!"

As he bolts into the cockpit, I shove the jacket at him.

Dorin continues to flash the light steadily into the cockpit. I wonder if we'll survive the crash or, if we do, the ship's large propellers.

The boat looms high above us.

Still coming.

Suddenly it changes course to port. I count, and seven seconds after the ship turns, it slides by our bow, missing us by a few feet.

We sit in the cockpit, and it's several minutes before Dorin says, "Dodged another bullet."

We laugh.

But we don't talk for a while.

"Okay, where is the goddamn horn blast can? I couldn't find it," Dorin says.

"I don't know," I admit. "We've never used it. I don't remember seeing it for a long time. But I've seen that spotlight hanging in the sail locker. I didn't know what it was for."

"Illegal fishing. I just soldered the connection ends to it last week."

"I'll find the blast horn tomorrow," I say.

"Well, for tonight, we are going to do our best to tack away from the island and stay well away from lining up with the entrance. I'll take the watch for the rest of the night," he says.

"I'm not moving," I say.

"Me neither," says Cory.

The next morning, still shaken by our close call, we see the island far in the distance. We take advantage of a stiff breeze and sail on a reach into the harbor. The island is lush and very green. The water, sparkling in the sunshine, shows us various shades of blues and lavenders. A cruise ship, looking immense in this harbor, is at anchor. Near the long and deep sandy beach, the turquoise water is clear to the bottom. The harbor is full of cruising sailboats, dozens of them at anchor. The beach is crowded with sunbathing tourists.

In spite of the overwhelming touristy feeling of the place, I am excited to drop anchor and explore a little.

"The *Tinker* tubes might be a little soft," Dorin says.

"I'll fill them," Cory replies. They haul it up onto the deck and Cory uses the foot pump. Then, while Cory rows us to shore, Dorin points out various interesting boats in the harbor.

We find a supermarket but are disappointed at the lack of fresh produce. There is some, but not much. It doesn't look in great condition, and it's pricey. On the way back to the dock, Dorin strikes up a conversation with a fellow cruiser who tells him that much of the produce is imported. We are shocked that vegetables and fruits are not grown locally.

"Well, there are mountains, and part of the island is arid. Some of the real estate is too valuable for gardening," he says. "Maybe over at Frederiksted they have vegetables."

"What's interesting to see here?" Dorin asks.

"The fort is really worth checking out. You'll learn a lot of history." He tells us how to get there.

On the way back to the boat we have to avoid a jet skier and then bob in its wake. Water laps over the side of the dinghy.

"I don't think this is fully inflated," I say. No one answers.

"Hmm," Dorin says thoughtfully. "I didn't survive the rigors of offshore sailing to come to a place I could get to by cruise ship. My God. The place is infested with tourists!"

"You are a sailing snob," I say.

"Yes, I am," he says with satisfaction.

"But, you gotta admit," says Cory, "it has all the charm and appeal of a travel brochure."

The next day, Dorin encourages Cory and me to go check out the fort. "I want to hang in here and do a few things," he says. "Take plenty of time. Be tourists."

We walk to the fort; it's an impressive yellow structure on lovely park grounds. We wander through the interior and read the information. Back outside, we buy lunch from a vendor and sit at a picnic table, enjoying the view.

Since we are not in a hurry, we wander around the charming town and shop at a couple of stores before we finally head back to the dock.

I step onto the rubber side of the *Tinker*, and it buckles a little. "Didn't you just put more air in this thing?" I ask Cory.

"Yes, filled it to the max. Well, as max as I could get with the foot pump."

"We'll talk to Dorin about it."

As we approach, Dorin sticks his head up out of the companionway.

"Hey, did you have a good time?"

"Yes, it was nice. The fort was like a museum. You would have loved it."

"I'm sure. Come aboard, I have a surprise."

He has us sit in the cockpit and then hits the starter button. The engine starts!

"What? Did you find out what was wrong?"

"Well, I took it apart and cut a new gasket. Since I had it open, I also worked on the valve stems and seats a little more."

He looks so pleased. "I didn't know if it would work, so I thought I'd send you away for the day."

"But didn't you need our help?"

"Now that I know a little more what I'm doing, it was pretty quick."

"This will make the rest of the trip easier," I say. "Batteries charged?"

"Yep. I also have supper ready," he says. "I hope you haven't eaten."

Over supper, we agree we should move on. Next stop, St. Martin.

In the morning I mention that the *Tinker* seemed low again yesterday.

"We'll have to check it out later. Let's trail it the rest of the way, as long as we have relatively calm seas," Dorin says.

Soon Cory hauls the anchor, and in a 20-knot wind, we tack east toward St. Martin. It's a smooth and easy passage, and we arrive at the port of Marigot the next day in gray waters under a cloudy sky. We'd heard that it was difficult clearing immigration in French-held St. Martin—that the officials were rude and obstructionistic. Dorin and I go ashore to check in, Cory electing to stay behind and do some cleaning up. Dorin and I are surprised and delighted to find officials courteous, helpful, and professional. Encouraged, we go back and get Cory so we can go into town to do some grocery shopping. Cory rows and Dorin points out the interesting sailboats in the harbor—their make, their type, if their rigging has been modified, and where they are from. "He appreciates beautiful boats and boats that have been rigged for offshore cruising," I say to Cory.

"Really? I hadn't noticed," Cory says.

"Look, there's an impressive schooner, four-masted, steel hull...the *Polynesian* out of England. Four-masted! What a beauty!"

"This one is very interesting. A good designer, built in France...."

"Uh-oh," he says as we glide past a sleek, black-hulled boat. "Um...ah, close your eyes, Cory."

Cory laughs and keeps rowing.

"What?" I ask. "Why?"

"Um, ah...."

"What!" I ask again.

Then I see what. On the deck, a fair maiden, taking advantage of the first ray of sunshine poking from under a cloud, is sunbathing. In the nude.

Not topless. Nude.

"Um, look the other way, Cor," Dorin says. "Um, I guess it's too late."

The *au naturel* sun bather, perhaps sensing an audience, sits up and applies sunscreen to her legs.

"That's a prop," I say. "She has such a golden tan, she doesn't need sunscreen."

"Anywhere," says Cory, laughing at Dorin's discomfort.

"Um, yeah, I heard that the, ah, French boats, I mean boaters, I mean the females on the boats, well, maybe the males too, have a more natural, more or less, more outgoing, well, you know, take more freedoms, you know, in ports and so forth."

By now, both Cory and I are laughing out loud at Dorin's discomfort.

"Not that we should censor them, or, you know, criticize, or complain."

"And we're in a French port," I say.

Cory nods. "Yeah. *Vive la France!*"

We wander around until we find a small grocery store. I pick up a few items, but again there's no produce. At the checkout, the clerk seems arrogant or aloof. When I hand her my American money, she takes it, looks at it with disdain, and then makes change. She deliberately lays the money well away from me, where I have to lean and reach for it. She looks past me as if I'm invisible.

We are not used to rudeness, and I wonder what message she is trying to give me. Walking back to the boat in the gray day, we feel a chill from passers-by--either a glare or an obvious frozen countenance on averted faces.

There is a sign in both French and English in a store window that announces a van travels to the Dutch side of Sint Maarten every day. The double "a," Dorin tells us, is in keeping with how the Dutch spell it. We stop in and Dorin buys tickets for us. Soon we are squeezed into a 10-passenger van and enjoy the ride over the mountain to Sint Maarten. Dorin is particularly happy. He spent a year in the Netherlands that he often recalls fondly.

When we arrive in the port of Philipsburg, it's as if we have arrived in a different country...as if a black and white movie has turned into vivid Technicolor. The sun is now out, and there's not a cloud in the sky. An atmosphere of conviviality and high spirits welcomes us. A jazz band is warming up, and as we watch, the musicians put on a short concert and then parade through the street where locals and tourists alike dance to the beat. There is color, color everywhere—in the clothing, in the profusion of flowers, in the paint on the shop fronts.

"Wow, this is my kind of place!" I say. "Can we live here?"

"Would you like to?" Dorin asks, obviously pleased.

"I'd sure consider it someday!"

We quickly find a grocery store and are overwhelmed. There is more richly colored, fresh produce than we have seen since we started—maybe ever, I think.

We gape and speak in awed whispers.

"Well, let's load up," Cory says, and we fall to, with a grocery cart.

"We can't take too much, though," Dorin warns. "We have to get it back in the van and then the dinghy. Hey, do you want to anchor here? We can sail around and check in here for a while."

Cory and I beam with enthusiasm. We select a small amount of what we would like to buy, then walk around town with our grocery bags, finding the atmosphere high-spirited. When we finally board the van, we can't wait to get back and move the boat to Sint Maarten.

"And! We will get another stamp on our passports!" Dorin says.

We arrive at the *Fandango*, still excited about what we'd just experienced. As dusk approaches, we hear a knock on our hull. I stick my head up out of the companionway and see a guy in a dinghy bobbing beside us.

"Good day, mate," he says with a charming Australian accent. "Do you have any good books to trade?"

Dorin comes out and chats with him, and they talk about the boat the gentleman has sailed from Australia, before we get down to the business of trading.

"I have two Stephen Kings," the Aussie says. "Do you happen to have any Tom Clancy?"

We do and we spend a few minutes comparing titles. When we are done, he rows away with four of our books. We have three of his, but two of them are Stephen Kings, so we are happy with the exchange.

"Wasn't that neat?" Dorin asks.

We haul anchor the next morning in a twelve-knot wind that blows from the east as always, and as always, we beat most of the way.

We spend three glorious days in Sint Maarten. Dorin hears Dutch spoken at times, but he is too uncertain of his rusty Dutch to try it out, so he sticks to English. We enjoy the beach, browse the shops, and have great lunches out. I discover coconut soda in a bottle, and I buy six bottles in case we don't find any to buy anywhere else.

Only the need to reach our goal of getting to Venezuela and back before the end of the season allows us to detach from Sint Maarten and head out once more—this time with a bunch of fresh veggies and fruit and three new books.

Dorin naps off and on during the day, telling us what to watch out for, but he stays at the tiller all night using the chart and flashlight, the knot log and the binoculars, watching for lights that would indicate what islands we pass by.

On Saturday, the 30th of April, we are eating breakfast and Dorin says, "I'm sorry we didn't leave enough time to island hop and enjoy this area. So I'd like to compensate a little for rushing us through the islands, by stopping in at Dominica. They say it's beautiful, and we'll be there in a few hours. Good opportunity to get some fresh produce."

He's been at the tiller almost around the clock, so when at 8 p.m. we approach Prince Rupert Harbor of Portsmouth, Dominica, we heave-to so Dorin can catch up on sleep.

At first light, we motor into the harbor. We are surprised to see there is nothing to see but the thick, green jungle surrounding the bay. No houses, no village, no other yachts.

Dorin gathers our passports, and because there is no wind, rows ashore and disappears from sight.

"Get a look at this!" Cory says a little later.

Three children are swimming our way. I am surprised because we are quite far from shore. As they get closer I see, first, they are grinning from ear to ear, and second, they are outstandingly good-looking children with perfect teeth. They are maybe between eight and ten years old.

Cory and I bend over the lifelines as the kids come close. They have string bags over their arms with fruit in them.

"You buy some bananas?" asks the oldest boy, his eyes sparkling.

Cory looks from the child to the shore and back. It's a long way.

"Yes!" I say. "But I only have American money." The currency here is ECs (Eastern Caribbean currency), and I have a ballpark idea of the exchange rate.

The girl nods, still grinning. "Yes, that is good. We can take it."

The expressions on all three faces say that this is a fun adventure for them. They tread water while I get some money. Meanwhile the children lift two bunches of bananas and four mangos up to Cory. "Thank you. Thank you very much!" Cory says. I can see by his frequent glances toward the shore he is very impressed.

He squats down on the deck and hands the money to the girl, who puts it in a little bag on a string around her neck. "Thank you," she says. Though she is a little smaller than the biggest boy, she seems to be in charge.

Then the high-spirited kids wave and, not appearing tired, swim toward shore.

"If Dorin were here, he'd say, 'Isn't that neat?'" Cory says.

"Yeah, and he'd be right. Oh my, those kids can swim well. And they are so handsome!"

"Yeah. Maybe everyone here is good looking."

We peel the bananas, and I take a bite. "Oh, wow. This is the best banana I have ever eaten. I can't believe it. I didn't know they could taste this good."

"These are probably the freshest bananas we've ever had. They might have been picked this morning."

"Yeah, ripened on the tree. Tastes like a whole different fruit."

We each peel and eat a juicy mango with the same result. Lunch comes and goes, and we are content that it consists of fabulous tropical fruit.

When Dorin returns, he says he cleared immigration. It only cost five ECs, but he didn't have the currency, and there was no place to change his money, so he gave the official $2. Customs was closed. He was told to come back in the afternoon.

"Everything was closed. Almost no one around. There doesn't seem to be anything to do. I don't think it's even worth your time to go into town," he says.

We tell him about the kids, and he's sorry he missed them. He finishes off the fruit.

"I'm going to check in and out at the same time when I go back," he says. "We might as well move out today. I guess I didn't pick the right place to stop."

"Or, maybe the right time?" I ask.

After a rest, he rows back to the shore in the afternoon.

While he is gone, a small, motored dugout canoe approaches from shore. A young man shyly introduces himself as David and asks if we want to take a trip up the Indian River. We tell him we can't because we will be leaving soon, but we had been hoping to get fresh vegetables and fruit here. "You should be able to," he says.

When Dorin returns, he says Customs is still closed. He will go back tomorrow. I ask if we might just leave without clearing, and he says, "I want another stamp on our passports." He drops into bed and sleeps almost through the night, waking only briefly for supper.

On Monday, he makes the trip again.

While he is gone, David motors toward us. He asks if we have been able to buy any food, and we tell him no.

He offers to go from house to house and buy food for us. We talk about prices and quantities.

Dorin returns, saying it's a holiday and everything is still closed, including Customs, but a very polite and helpful immigration official clears us out and stamps our passports.

A few minutes later, David is headed back our way with a couple of teenage boys paddling a long, narrow dugout canoe.

Smiling, they drift toward our boat. The young boy's eyes sparkle with interest and apparent delight at being included in this adventure. In the bottom of the dugout, there are grapefruit, melons, mangos, bananas, papayas, limes and oranges. David says we owe $10 EC, so Dorin gives him $10 and a $5 tip, which, as far as we can calculate, is about four times what he asked for. But it's worth it to us, and they really went out of their way to help us. The boys hand us our fruit as fast as Cory and I can grab it and say repeated thank yous. Then David and the boys wave goodbye and paddle back to shore.

Cory hauls the anchor, and we are off again.

When, four days later, Grenada is in sight, I notice Dorin is working the sails with intensity, tweaking minute by minute. I look around to see who he is racing, because this is his racing mode. Then I see a beautiful, sleek, dark green yacht off our port side, just a little ahead of us.

Dorin says, "They've got length on the water line, but I'm gaining on them."

"Do they know you are racing?"

"Oh, yeah," he says with delight. "It's been a race for the past half hour." He's in his element and loving it. In all the summers we have sailed, I have noticed that when two boats are more or less lined up and going in the same direction, it becomes a good-natured race.

"Oh no!" Dorin says. "They started their motor! Well, that's not fair."

The yacht pulls ahead and beats us into the harbor. Just inside there is an abandoned, dilapidated wharf that we tie up to so Dorin can check out the harbor.

"I'm going to step the mast for the *Tinker* and find a good place to anchor."

The green yacht that entered the harbor before us is just getting anchored much farther in. Dorin sails over to it, and when he boards, I know he has engaged the owners in a conversation about how extraordinary their boat is.

He comes back an hour later, and we sail on a gentle breeze to an anchorage not far from the yacht.

"They're from Great Britain, young people, really nice, name of Meg and Doug. They've invited us over for supper tonight."

"We won't complain about the *Tinker*, right?"

"No, of course not." But he frowns.

"You were going to, weren't you?"

"Yeah," he admitted sheepishly "Well, they're Brits, you know. They should be aware so they don't make the same mistake."

"No, you just want them to take responsibility for an inferior product made by their countrymen."

"Yeah, I guess so. Okay, I'll be good."

They serve an elegant meal with great wine. During the conversation, they joke about the impromptu race.

"You turned your motor on," Dorin says. "You probably could have won without it."

"We started the motor so we could enter the harbor and maneuver safely," Doug says.

"Oh," Dorin says. "That's makes sense."

"Well, didn't you?" asks Doug.

"Um, we came on in under sail."

"In *this* harbor?" Doug asks incredulously. "This harbor is really tricky!"

"Yeah, I wasn't thinking, I guess," Dorin says. Cory and I exchange glances and suppress a smile. It's a matter of principle, we know. We're sailors, not motor-sailors.

The next day, Cory un-steps the mast, pulls the *Tinker* on deck, pumps it up, and lowers it into the water. The guys re-step the mast, and the three of us load into the dinghy, excited to go into town. I wear my pink skirt, as I have done before in a new country, until I see what the accepted dress code is. I sit on the tube, and Dorin takes the tiller. Soon I notice the tube buckling under me. I look around in alarm.

"Hey! I'm getting wet. The tube is collapsing," I yell.

"Oh, wow, can you hold on until we get to the dock?" Dorin asks and grabs the oars out from under the seat.

"I don't know if we'll make it," I say, moving off the tube and onto the wooden seat. I hug our documentation, protected from water in a plastic bag, to my chest. The port is long and narrow, but still, getting to the closest side would be a long swim. Cory grabs the foot pump, attaches the hose to the tube filler, and begins to pump but it's not very effective because the bottom of the dinghy is softer than usual...nothing solid to push against. I wonder if we go into the water, will I be able to keep our documents safe and dry?

Dorin rows like he's in a race, pulling as rapidly as he can. We slowly sink deeper. When we are thirty feet from the dock, the *Tinker* is barely above water, and rowing is difficult. Dorin strains at the oars. "How much farther?" he asks, out of breath.

Before I can answer, a voice from the dock yells, "You're almost here." A small group of people are crowded together at the closest dock. As we nudge among the floating dinghies, several men are on their knees, reaching forward to grab the bow. We come to rest against pilings, and someone grabs our bow line. Other hands reach down and pull us up onto the dock. My skirt is soaked to the waist in the back.

"That was close," someone says. "We thought you were going to be swimming the last hundred feet!"

Dorin shakes hands and thanks everyone. I can see he's embarrassed though. "Do you need a ride to your ship?" a local man says. "I can take you, cheap, Captain. I have a water taxi."

"I'd like to take you up on that," Dorin says. "How about in a couple of hours? We need to find Customs and get some money."

"Sure. I will be right here, Captain.'"

I really, really want to return to the boat and change, but I can see it's more practical to walk around and let my skirt dry in the heat of the day. It feels awful though, as it sags and drags against my legs.

"Cory, walk behind me."

"Sure. Why?"

"My skirt is wet in the back."

He slips in behind me. "Yeah, no doubt about that." Then he walks about a stride behind me, and I feel protected.

We consult our SSCA map for directions to the Venezuelan embassy and hike uphill for what seems like a couple of miles until we reach our destination. Dorin tells the officer we need visas for Venezuela. I hand our documents over, and we fill out papers. Then the officer tells us we have to leave our passports with him, which makes me uncomfortable. We can come collect them, he tells us, when we are ready to leave. Also, we have to deposit $126 EC in the customs' account in a bank in town and come back Monday, after 12, to clear out. We had hoped to take care of the Customs and Immigration stuff all in one day and leave Sunday. As we walk back down the hill, I notice my skirt is now dry.

"Okay, you're off duty, now," I say to Cory. "But I kind of like the idea of your following in my footsteps."

The next couple of hours are fun. After clearing Customs and getting some cash from our card, we stroll through markets and stores. In a gift shop, I buy postcards that say, "Welcome USA" and "Yanqui Go Home."

In the fresh air market, we are interested in picking up some vegetables. I pick up a bunch of carrots and ask the merchant, a tall, handsome man, "How much?"

I don't understand his reply and say, "I'm sorry, but I only speak English."

I simultaneously see the man's stunned look and feel Cory and Dorin's horrified reaction.

"What?" I ask them.

Cory leans toward me and says quietly, "He *is* speaking English."

I am mortified. "Oh, I am so sorry," I say to the gentleman, but he looks ferociously at me and does not appear in the least appeased. Cory puts a hand under my elbow and leads me away. He whispers in my ear, "I just can't take you anywhere."

The water taxi, trailing our limp and barely floating dinghy behind, takes us back to the boat. I cook supper while the guys haul the dinghy on board, pump it as full as they can, and examine every inch. The oar locks are held on with rubber patches which have loosened and might be leaking air. Under the wooden seats, which are also attached with rubber patches, they find more places, including the strips of plywood, where air might be leaking out. They do the soap bubble test and find other possible culprits. We have patches that came with the *Tinker*, as well as goop. We also have liquid rubber in a can. Together, the guys rough the raft's rubber surface and plaster on the goop and patches. Now the waiting, because we can't test the boat until the goop sets...at least 12 hours.

Early the next day, we are on pins and needles while Cory foot-pumps the *Tinker* until the tubes are hard. They lower it in the water, and Dorin climbs down into it. "I want to be the one to test it out," he says. He steps the mast and sails it all over the harbor. We watch anxiously, but after fifteen minutes, he thumps on the tubes with his fist and then gives us a thumbs up.

Feeling pretty good about the dinghy, we sail to the dock and then walk to the packed open-air market. We find a break in the crowd and sidle up to a woman holding two grapefruit, one large and one small.

"I want to sell you a grapefruit," she says. I asked her how much.

"Fifty cents."

"For what size?"

"For any size."

"I'll take ten," Dorin says.

She looks surprised but rummages around in her supply and picks out the biggest she has. She fills a plastic bag full.

"Um, maybe this was a mistake," Dorin says as we walk away. "Now we have to carry ten grapefruit around for the rest of the day."

Most of the time the prices are reasonable, except for the carrots! A vendor holds up a bunch of ten, tiny carrots.

"How much?" I ask.

"Ten dollars EC," she says. One dollar for each little carrot? We keep shopping around and every vendor gives that price.

"We don't need carrots that much," Dorin says.

"I bet you can't buy carrots reasonably here because you insulted the carrot vender." Cory rolls his eyes and shakes his head. "Carrot deprivation because Mom is rude to the natives."

We continue to push and be pushed by the crowd through the market and buy cabbage and lemons. Back at the dinghy, we lower our produce into it, and then notice a grocery store near the seawall.

"Let's check out the store and see what they've got," Dorin says. "We'll have to hurry. The sign says it closes at 12:45, and it's now 11:15."

We hurry around and pick up many items, including half a gallon of ice cream, but the checkout line is long.

"We done good, crew. It's 11:45," Dorin says as the clerk starts to check out our groceries.

At 11:50 she tells us the total: $82 EC.

"Uh-oh," Dorin says. "I only have 58 dollars. You guys wait here," he says. "I'll go back to the boat and get more money."

The clerk is disgusted. We watch from the door of the store while Dorin jumps into the dinghy and untangles it from the crunch of dozens of dinghies.

"It'll be okay," Cory says. "He's got almost an hour." But I can hear the tension in his voice and remember the times he's been with me in the checkout line when I realize I don't have my checkbook with me. He's been mortified when I've left him at the store with the groceries while I run home to get my checkbook.

"Grrrrr!" he says now through clenched teeth. I look out, thinking Dorin must be almost to the boat, but he is just barely past the dock and adjusting the sail to get some speed going.

While we watch, the mast falls over.

"Arrrrgh!" says Cory, smacking his head with his palm.

Dorin scrambles to pull the sail into the boat and rolls the mast across the dinghy. He pulls out the oars and rows. Cory is pacing now.

By the time Dorin gets to the *Fandango*, moves the mast and sail to the deck, and rows back, there are four minutes to spare.

"Don't want to talk about it," he says when he strides toward us. We load the groceries in the *Tinker* and start the long row back. It's crowded, so I lean against the tiller.

It comes loose from the rudder.

It's very quiet as Dorin rows the rest of the way to the boat.

Cory climbs out first, and I follow.

While Dorin hands him the bags, Cory says, "Quick, get bowls and spoons and start chowing down on the ice cream. It must be half melted."

As it turns out, it is less than half melted, and we slurp the ice cream with our spoons.

"Whew, close one!" Dorin says.

"The damn *Tinker*?" I ask.

"No, the ice cream. It's still edible."

Cory turns in early, and Dorin and I sit in the cockpit and talk about the *Tinker*.

"That is such a piece of junk," he says. "I thought I was being smart and buying an exceptional lifeboat. Damn good thing we haven't had to use it to save our lives."

"Will we have to stop sailing it?"

"No. I can still rig it to sail. But it's embarrassing."

"We don't care what other people think, do we?"

He chuckles. "I care what you think. I'm really sorry."

"Can we baby it along to finish the trip?"

"Yeah, everything has been fixable, but what a fiasco. Humiliating."

"As long as it keeps us afloat as a tender, I don't care. And I won't tell anyone about your disastrous lapse in judgement, if you don't," I say.

The next morning, Cory and Dorin again rig the *Tinker* for sailing and repair the tiller. We spend another day in Grenada, sightseeing and visiting with Meg and Doug, with whom we exchange contact information.

On Monday, early in the morning, we prepare the boat for departure and then go into town. Once again, we hike up to the embassy, but the embassy has lost its power and can't use the Telex. We have to come back tomorrow. After 12....

"This is trying my patience," Dorin says. Usually sunny in disposition, he isolates himself as much as possible for the rest of the day and broods.

The next morning, he makes coffee and sits in the cockpit staring at the shore, still not into conversation. At 11 a.m., he lowers himself into the dinghy and sails toward shore, no wave, no thumbs up.

"Looks like the *Tinker* is holding up," Cory says. And, indeed, it sits high in the water and skims across the water as fast as we've ever seen it move.

When he returns a couple of hours later, he just nods and asks if we are ready to haul anchor, and we are.

We are on our final leg to Margarita Island in Venezuela, at last. The wind varies from fifteen knots to five, so it's slow progress.

"But at least the current is fer us instead of ag'in us," Cory says. "And we thought it couldn't happen."

Chapter Twenty-three
Venezuela

"Well, I'll be damned," Dorin says. "If I am correct, that just might be Margarita Island up ahead." His mood is light for the first time since the *Tinker* almost sunk in Grenada.

"Yeah, sure, like there's any doubt." Cory laughs. "Like you haven't been plotting every step of the way since Puerto Rico."

I glance at the chart in the cockpit. There's a pencil line from island to island, including the ones we didn't stop at and the ones we passed in the night.

Fascinated, I watch the small spit of mountainous land gradually increase in size. All over the world, I muse, in the history of ocean crossings, all hands must feel compelled to come out on deck to watch the land unfold, to wonder what mysteries it holds.

"So, what do you think, guys? Will Venezuela be the most exotic landfall we've made?" I ask.

"More exotic than the D.R.?" Cory mimics awe.

"Maybe more intense," Dorin says. "Economic and political tensions. Not too long ago, it was the richest country in South and Central America because it is sitting on a lot of oil. Probably the biggest oil reserves in this hemisphere, maybe the world, but now the economy is crapping out."

"Why's that?" Cory asks.

"The production of oil is all Venezuela has going for it, and now that the demand for oil has dropped, it doesn't have a fall back economy."

"So that's why oil is so cheap here?"

"Yeah, unbelievably cheap. Big yachts plan their itineraries so they can fill up in Venezuela."

"Hmmm. So what do you mean, 'political tensions?'" I ask.

"There've been some demonstrations. I think the government is nervous."

"But it's a democracy, right?"

"Sure. But there've been some coup attempts."

"And we're coming here, why?"

Dorin looks amused. "You want to turn back? We did it before. We can do it again."

"No! Well, maybe no. Let me think about it. Ah, will it be safe?"

"Hey, hey, hey!" Cory says. "What are you saying? Of course we are not turning back. After all we've done to get here? Get that mutinous thought right out of your head." And he gently bops me on the forehead.

Dorin laughs out loud. "Don't worry. Cruisers haven't reported any problems. Besides, we have to drop in and get some cheap diesel."

I think back to our last attempt to reach Venezuela and how upset I was that we had to turn back. I would have given a lot to accomplish a legal landfall. And, now, here we are, safely in sight of our goal.

I turn my attention back to the horizon, and to my surprise, city buildings are appearing. I realize I've been absurdly picturing tropical jungle with oil wells sticking up from the canopy.

Instead, here's a modern city, just back from the sandy beach.

The harbor is crowded with sailing yachts, which is comforting. They wouldn't be here if it weren't safe, right? We anchor far out, then change into going-ashore clothes, and head out. When we're settled in the dinghy, Cory thumps the tubes with his fist. They are really hard. Finally!

On the beach, a dozen or more brightly painted, wooden fishing dories are perfectly lined up, side by side. They are long and thin, and the bow comes up to a high point. I bet, unlike the *Tinker, they* don't take in any water over those bows. I've never seen boats painted in shiny crayon colors--red, orange, bright blue, yellow and purple.

When we are close to the beach, a guy that the SSCA bulletin mentioned is wading chest deep in the water. He is very large and bald, looking like a black Mr. Clean.

"Hi, I am Jimmy," he says. "I help you." He takes our bow line and pulls us toward shore. He motions Dorin and Cory to stay put. Then he scoops me from my seat and carries me to the beach. *"Señora,"* he says and bows. Then he goes back and pulls the dinghy closer. When it bottoms out, Dorin and Cory, holding their shoes, step out into a few inches of water. Jimmy walks the *Tinker* away from shore, and then, with the bow line in his teeth, he swims out to deeper water and ties it to the buoyed circle of rope that has more than a dozen other dinghies tied to it.

"Hey, that was fun," I say.

"Yeah, cool," Cory says. "Don't we have to pay him?"

"We will when we get bolivars," says Dorin.

We quickly go from deep, sandy beach to the city, and the city is amazing—very modern looking. Shoppers and business people are all dressed up: men in suits and ties, women in high heels and dresses. We step out of the way so they can pass, and they swarm around us, seemingly without noticing us. But they must see us, and I wonder what they think of us straggly boaters invading their beautiful, sparkling clean city.

"I've been to Hamilton, Ft. Lauderdale, and San Juan on this trip, and this is the first city where I've truly felt out of place," Cory says.

"Look," I say, trying to nod surreptitiously toward the wide street. There, beside a sleek, modern, luxury bus is a guy in a worn-out straw hat walking his sugarcane-laden donkey.

"Isn't that neat?" Dorin says. "And look there," he says under his breath. A woman dressed in traditional clothing and worn out sandals expertly carries a bundle on her head as she passes by fashionably dressed, sophisticated women. I wonder how they view each other.

I wonder how they view me.

Or if they view me at all.

My head swivels as I try to take in all the exotic sights in this impressive city. Then, in the heat of the day, a welcome sight--a large, shady park with trees, flowers and paved paths.

"Wow, look down," I say in awe as we step into the park. The walkways are made of colored mosaic tiles in intricate, beautiful designs.

"Look up," Dorin replies softly and puts a hand on my shoulder.

I see three heavily armed soldiers wearing bulletproof vests walking around the park with automatic rifles in their hands. I suck in my breath.

"Shhh," Dorin says near my ear.

Does political tension equate to armed soldiers in the streets? Passersby appear to ignore them, but I'm sure they are very aware of them. How could they not be?

With one hand on my back and the other on Cory's shoulder, Dorin propels us through the park and out the other side.

I have a small, hand-drawn street map that I tore out of an SSCA bulletin. For a while we wander around trying to make sense of the map, but we are confused. On a side street there is an armed soldier with bandoliers crisscrossed on his chest. He is facing somewhat away from us, and I don't think he's seen us.

"You want me to ask for directions?" Cory asks.

"No. Let your mother go, if she's willing. She's less threatening."

"Tell me again how to say 'immigration?'" I ask Cory.

"*Inmigración,*" he says.

"Oh, yeah. Right." Duh.

"Wait, are you sure you want to do this?" Cory asks. "You have suddenly gotten brave."

"Yeah, he's not going to shoot me in the street for talking to him. Okay, here I go."

I walk forward, as though approaching a soldier with his gun at the ready is a normal thing.

"Excuse me, *Señor. ¿Usted la policía?*" The soldier spins toward us, and the rifle he's been holding diagonally across his body, swings down toward, but not quite at, me. He scowls and my heart skips a beat.

"*Perdón,*" I say. "*¿Usted la policía?*"

He nods slowly but doesn't move the rifle away.

"*¿Dónde está la inmigración?*" I ask.

He looks blankly at Dorin and Cory and then back to me. I can see he still doesn't know what is going on. I can also see he's not much older than Cory.

I repeat the question and this time add, "*Por favor.*"

I take a step toward him and hold out my piece of paper. Cautiously he lowers the rifle and takes the piece of paper, but he glances at Dorin and Cory to be sure they are not moving.

He reads the words. "*Ah, inmigración!*" He looks relieved and motions for Cory to come forward. This is not new. Everywhere we go, local people assume he speaks more Spanish than we old folks. And they are right. The soldier hands the paper back to me and but gives Cory the information, using his unarmed hand to emphasize the directions.

Cory and I thank him in Spanish, and Dorin joins us as we walk the way the soldier had told us to go.

"Seems like he overreacted just a tad," Dorin says when we are out of earshot.

"Guess their training doesn't include giving directions to out-of-towners," Cory answers.

We finally find Customs and Immigration, but, even though we are the only ones waiting, we are held up for a couple of hours, as we sit in the waiting room under a slowly turning ceiling fan.

After an hour, Cory stands up. "I'm going outside because it's cooler. And the scenery is better."

When we are finally called into the office, it only takes about fifteen minutes to take care of business, and we are out of there.

Our next stop is a bank, which is large and very impressive with marble floors and columns. Cory's father has been depositing money for him in my account, but Cory had not wanted to take any until we got to Venezuela because we'd read the exchange rate here would be the best on the whole trip.

We find out from the teller that today's exchange rate is 29.25 to one. The teller slides a bundle of colorful cash toward me. I sort it out and hand a stack to Cory.

"Will that hold you for a while? You have a whole lot more coming, but you don't have enough pockets to carry it."

"Whew! This seems like a lot of money," he says. "I think maybe I'm rich in Venezuela."

"Not only is the exchange rate good," Dorin says, "but they say the prices are also low. Far as I can figure, that money's going to go a long way."

"What are you going to do with your money?" I ask as we walk toward the stores.

"I'll probably buy all my school clothes and shoes here, maybe three pairs of really good sneakers--one just for the basketball court, never to be worn outside. Maybe some electronics? I'll shop around and see what there is."

Dorin buys some huaraches, which surprises me. I didn't figure him for a sandal kind of guy, but then he also owns wooden shoes from his year in the Netherlands. I wouldn't have predicted that either. And the huaraches look really cool on him. I buy a few things in my smaller size. Cory buys sneakers, shoes, jeans, shorts, and shirts.

"And I still have so much money left," he says.

We find our way back to Jimmy. He spots us, holds up a finger, and then swims out to get the *Tinker*. I wonder how he remembers which boat goes to which people. While he's getting the boat, I walk over to the painted, wooden fishing dories and see that each boat has three or four different brilliant colors, including the insides, and they appear freshly painted. I look inside. They are immaculate. Not a speck of dirt. I wonder if they are really used for fishing, or are they there because they look like a postcard picture.

Jimmy taps me on the shoulder, and when I turn around, he picks me up, walks into the water and puts me in the boat. He motions for Dorin and Cory to come get in the boat. Dorin hands him ninety bolivars, and Jimmy thanks him and pushes us off.

On the way back, Dorin says, "Let's get slicked up. I want to take you guys out to supper tonight. There is a restaurant recommended in the Seven Seas bulletin."

Back at the boat, we heat water so we can shampoo and wash. Dorin trims his beard closely for the first time in months and looks totally different--more like his professional image.

"You need a haircut to match," Cory says and picks up the scissors. When he's done, Dorin looks quite spiffy.

"Your turn," I say. "Sit down." I've been cutting my kids' hair since the 70's when long hair was in, so it looks pretty good. Cory trims his own beard. We dress up in our new clothes.

"Hey, we can probably pass for regular tourists," Dorin says. "Let's go knock 'em dead!"

It's almost dark when we reach the shore. It's quiet because the daytime beach people are gone. We tie the dinghy to a tree and take a taxi to the restaurant. I'm glad we dressed up because this is a swanky restaurant. Tablecloths and cloth napkins, flowers on the table. The diners are all dressed up, and the waiters are wearing white shirts, black pants, vests and black ties. The waiter escorts us to a table near an open window, and Dorin seats me.

Dorin orders drinks for us, and then we order from the menu: lobster for me, prime rib for Dorin and Cory. When our meals arrive, the waiter begins to grind pepper on our food.

I catch something out of the corner of my eye and gasp. I kick Dorin's foot under the table, but he has noticed, at the same time, an enormous cockroach on the white wall beside us, about eye level, not fifteen inches from my shoulder. The waiter sees the problem right away. He takes the folded, white towel from his forearm, winds it up, snaps it, and nails the cockroach. He picks up the bug and tosses it out of the open window.

"Lo siento," he says. And goes back to peppering Dorin's steak.

After we finish our meals, the waiter brings the dessert cart to our table. Dorin picks flan, Cory picks coconut cake, and I pick *dulce de leche,* a really moist cake with caramel sauce.

"Looks really, really good," Dorin says of my dessert.

"Yeah. Yours is the best," Cory says.

"I get the hint," I say and give them each a big bite, since mine *is* clearly the best.

When the very handsome waiter delivers the bill, I say with a lot of feeling, *"Muchas gracias, Señor."*

He bows slightly toward me and says warmly, *"Es un placer servirle,"* instead of the *"de nada"* I am expecting.

I catch my breath because, though I don't know what he has said, I can tell from his smile and manner, it's good.

"It's a pleasure to serve you," Cory translates.

"Sí," the waiter says, smiling and nodding at Cory.

Well, now. "I like that so much better than *"de nada,"* I say.

We look over the bill which seems, on first glance, too high--390 *bolívares,* so we do the math and realize the total is $13. What? Drinks, expensive meal (in the States), and dessert.

"Wow, this will take some getting used to," Dorin says.

We decide to walk back to the beach. We've read about the dangers of walking at night and the possibility of muggings in Venezuela.

"But maybe that's exaggerated," I say. "It's a beautiful night, and there's no one around. And it seems like a nice part of the city."

Dorin and I walk in front, holding hands, with Cory right behind us. We are talking about the great evening we just had, and I don't notice Cory has dropped back. As we stroll through the park, Cory suddenly comes up beside us.

"I'm pretty sure we almost got mugged," he says. "I noticed when we came out of the restaurant and crossed the street, two guys dropped a few yards behind us. When we turned left, they turned left. We turned right, they turned right. We crossed the street and went into the park. *They* entered the park. When they started to close in, I peeled off to the side and stepped in behind them. They split right up and speed-walked in opposite directions. I'm pretty sure we were potential mugging targets. I guess they didn't like one of us behind them."

"Are you taller than they were?" I ask.

"Yeah, quite a bit."

"And younger and stronger, probably," Dorin says.

"Probably."

"Good job, Cory," Dorin says. "I knew we brought you for a reason."

At the beach, Cory says he's rowing us back. "I'm not saying you are blitzed. But I'm not saying you're not, either."

The next day, we sail north for a few hours and anchor a little way off the coast in twenty feet of water. Now we can finally try a little of the famous Venezuelan snorkeling that Dorin's been promising us.

He stays on the *Fandango* to be our support crew, tethering the *Tinker* on a fifty-foot line so we can use it to jump off from. I'm still adjusting my mask when Cory goes over the side and dives to the bottom.

After almost a minute, he breaks the surface. "Look, you won't believe this. It's a sand dollar!"

"It's as big as a dinner plate!" I say. "That's amazing. The biggest I've seen is about four inches across. This one must be nine or ten."

"Yeah, the bottom is sandy and just littered with all kinds of shells. This one is alive. You can tell because it's covered with brown velvet, but I had to show it to you. No one will believe me if I don't have a witness. I have to put it back, but I'll bring some other stuff up. Are you coming?"

I shake my head, thinking about how long he was under water. "No. I just realized I don't think I can hold my breath long enough to get to the bottom and back. You go ahead."

He brings back a conch shell that is also huge.

"It's dead and empty," he says as he hands it to me. I put it under my seat in the bottom of the dinghy.

"There's a few more things I can bring up." And he's gone again.

When he surfaces again, he has a few white sand dollars and a seahorse skeleton.

"Listen," he says as I place the items on the seat next to me. "I think this can't be fun for you, so we need to move to a shallower place so you can snorkel."

He hoists himself up and climbs back into the dinghy. There's a couple of inches of water sloshing in the bottom, as usual, from trailing it behind the *Fandango*. I'm sitting on the rear seat when something shoots out of the conch shell.

It's alive!

I scream and jump out of the *Tinker*.

Cory follows me a split second later. "What's wrong?" he asks as we hang onto the tubes. "Why did we jump?"

"This thing was in the conch shell, and it just shot out. It's in the bottom of the boat."

"What does it look like?"

"Brown, slimy, or at least shiny, moves like lightning."

We half hoist ourselves up onto the tubing and look in, but we don't see anything.

"Well, guess what?" he says. "Whatever it is, I bet there are more here in the water than the one in our boat. Let's get back in."

"Nope. Unh-uh. Not on your life. You can row back. I'll push you from behind with my flutter kick."

"Hey, I see it! Nope, it's gone again. Under the seat. I can't tell what it is. Okay, let's go."

Back at the *Fandango*, Dorin says, laughing, "So what's up? Did you spot a needle fish?"

I hoist myself onto the dinghy tube. Dorin takes my hand and pulls me up.

"Hand me something, something like a jar," Cory says.

I rummage around and come up with a large, empty, clean mayo jar. Holding the jar, Cory stands in the bottom of the *Tinker* and rocks it from side to side.

"Hmm. Nothing." He jumps up and down a little to make the water slosh back and forth.

"There it is!" He scoops it up with some water.

"I got it!" He hands the jar to Dorin.

"Hey! You know what you've got here?" he asks.

"If it's an eel, it's going back into the water," I say.

"It's an octopus. A baby octopus."

Cory climbs into the cockpit, and we take turns looking at our ocean-life acquisition, an eight-tentacled baby octopus.

"Cute little guy," Dorin says. "Too bad we can't keep him."

"Can't we? For a little while?" I ask. The miniature octopus has attached a couple of tentacles to the inside of the jar.

"We don't know what it eats," Dorin says.

"How about we just keep it overnight," Cory says.

We sit in the salon and examine our new pet as we pass the jar around. We can see tiny individual suction cups that Oscar, the name Cory has given him, uses to maneuver around the jar.

Dorin drops in tiny pieces of cooked meat that Oscar ignores.

We sail on and anchor in shallow water near a small island that appears uninhabited.

This time I'm the first one in the water because there are reef formations near the surface, and Dorin says there should be good snorkeling. We can see in the shallows that it looks interesting. And it is! The reefs have little growths attached that look like puff-ball flowers in red, yellow and purple.

When I lift my head to tell Dorin, he hands me the boat hook. "They are sea anemones. Tap once on a rock and see what happens."

I do and the "flowers" immediately disappear, pulled back into little mollusk-like growths attached to the rock.

"Leave them alone for a while, and they'll come back out," Dorin says.

I turn away, and Cory and I flutter kick into deeper water, swimming through schools of tiny fish that flash silver, purple, and blue when the sunlight hits them. They separate and swim around us. I look at Cory, and he gives me the "okay" gesture and nods. He's also enjoying this.

After a while, Cory signals me. When our heads come out of the water, he tells me he's done for now.

I nod. "Okay, I want to keep going for a few more minutes."

After what seems like a few minutes, there's a tap on my foot.

I lift my head, and Cory is there without a mask. "So, um, Dorin says you have to come out of the water, or you will burn."

"I've only been in the water for ten or fifteen minutes," I say.

"Try an hour and a half!"

I look around and sure enough, the *Fandango* is a far distance back.

"Are you having fun yet?" Dorin asks when we get back to the boat.

"Hey, is there any way I can earn a living doing this?" I ask Dorin when we climb back into the boat. "I'd do this every day if I could."

"So, it's true what they say about snorkeling in Venezuela? I didn't oversell it?"

"Oh, my goodness, no! I love it, love it. I didn't know it could be this beautiful. And there is so much variety of sea life that just keeps changing as I go."

We eat supper inside, and Cory keeps Oscar's jar by him so he can watch him move around.

"What if he's a she?" Dorin asks as he drops a piece of fish in Oscar's jar. "She's kind of cute."

"Then I'd call her Oscarita," Cory says.

When Dorin and I get up the next morning, Cory is already at the dinette. "You won't believe Oscar. Come and see."

They sit and look at the octopus moving around. "Wow," says Dorin.

"So, it's not my imagination," Cory says. "He grew overnight."

"Oh, yeah," Dorin says. "Half again as big. Look, she is on the bottom and her tentacles can almost reach the top of the jar. We'll have to let her go."

"Wait, we have a bigger jar. I'll fill it with water."

Cory finds a half-gallon jug and is back in a moment, having filled it with seawater three quarters of the way to the brim. He pours the water slowly from the smaller jar into the new, larger one. Oscar is not having any of it, though. Even as the water drains, he clings to the sides of the jar he's in. Cory pours water back into the small jar and then upends it quickly before our octopus is able to get good suction going. Oscar slips into his new vacation home.

In the afternoon, Cory and I snorkel near shore, and then we wade in a shallow pool and harvest empty seashells to bring home. We find dozens of sea urchins of different shades of green and purple. They don't have spines on them, but I turn each one over to be sure it's empty. Cory also finds a tiny, tiny live crab, and back on the boat, he drops it into Oscar's aquarium.

That night Dorin says, "Uh-oh. I think Oscarita grew during the day."

I'm shocked because he is taking up much more room in the jug than he did in the morning. We sit and watch the actions of the suction cups as he moves around the glass.

"There's a small section on octopus in my book, but not much," Cory says. "The mother dies as soon as the eggs are hatched, and they raise themselves. When they are really young, they are vulnerable prey to larger fish, so they hide in shells and crevices in rocks."

The next morning, Oscar can reach one tentacle out of the jug.

"She's going to climb out of there soon," Dorin says. "You know what that means."

"Okay," Cory says. "I guess you're right."

"I'll do it if you don't want to," Dorin says.

After breakfast, Dorin enters the water in the shallows where I discovered the sea anemones. I hand him the jug. He lowers it fully into the water and waits for Oscar to swim out. He doesn't. Dorin yanks the jug backwards, trying to force eviction, but the octopus holds fast to the inside. Dorin walks in water up to his chest and tries to release Oscar again. No dice. Oscar is holding on for all he's worth. Finally, Dorin asks for his mask. He snorkels further out along the reef. He holds the jug very close to a crevice in the reef, and Oscar shoots out, slides into a narrow crack, and almost disappears from sight.

"I guess octopuses are smarter than I thought they were," Dorin says when he climbs back onto the *Fandango*. "She didn't want to be exposed to predators until she could find a safe place to hide."

The next morning, we decide to keep moving to see as much as possible before having to head home.

"If you guys are still interested in snorkeling, there's what appears to be a deserted island that looks interesting, not too far away. Of course, if you're tired of it, Shirl Jean...." Dorin says.

"Hah!" Cory says. "We run a bigger risk of her jumping ship so she can stay here and snorkel for the rest of her life."

We approach and notice part of an old wreck sticking up out of the water. Cory drops the anchor, and we see right away the island is not completely uninhabited. A large fishing boat is anchored just a little offshore, and there are four men on the beach, their long dinghy pulled up on the sand. We talk about it...should we go ashore?

"It feels like maybe we'd be trespassing," I say. "Plus, I don't know...maybe they don't like North Americans."

Dorin tries surreptitiously to view the situation with binoculars, but that usually doesn't work. People always know when he's looking at them. And sure enough--they look our way.

"They have a campfire going on the beach. They are cooking over an open fire," Dorin reports.

"There is a makeshift shelter further back on the beach," Cory says. "And I don't need binoculars to see it."

"Yeah, their boat isn't big enough for sleeping quarters," Dorin says. "Not if they are putting fish in their hold. What do you say? Do we go ashore?"

"Sure. The worst that can happen is...." We could be dead. I shrug.

"The worst that can happen is they are territorial," says Dorin.

"We were in more danger in the park in Porlamar," Cory says. "These are working guys, not criminals. Let's *go*, people! Time's a-wastin'. I'm not getting any younger, and I need an adventure fix." He takes the binocs out of Dorin's hand and puts them away.

I grab the camera, and we load into the dinghy. Cory rows while Dorin watches the reaction of the men as we slowly make our way ashore. They watch us but don't seem upset.

"Look!" I say. The face of a cliff off to our left, which had not been visible from the boat, can now be seen. In four-foot, red letters someone has painted ELVIS.

"How the heck...?" I say. We all laugh in wonderment.

"How the heck can anyone have been able to do that?" Dorin says. "Too high off the ground and too far down from the top of the cliff. Neat though."

We are wearing flip flops so it's easy to get out of the *Tinker* in a couple of feet of water. Dorin and Cory pull the *Tinker* up high on the beach.

I look over at the fishermen. They have long black hair and scruffy, short beards. They are standing around a cauldron over the fire. They smile, wave cheerfully, and motion us over. As we walk toward them, they point to their enormous cooking pot and pantomime eating from a bowl. And then they point to us.

"They are inviting us to eat!" Dorin sounds pleased. "What do you think?"

"Bast used to make fish stew for us. This could be a really good idea," Cory says.

"No, I don't think so," I say.

"*Gracias, pero no,*" Cory says.

They smile and shrug and wave as we head inland to explore.

"Sorry, all I could picture was floating fish heads and bones," I say.

"Could have been a good photo op," Cory says.

"And could have been an adventure," Dorin says. "You'll be sorry someday that you didn't try the local island cuisine."

"Yeah, but it could take a while," I say.

This is an arid island covered with cactus. Dorin spots a giant cactus far inland, so we decide to head toward it so we can keep oriented on our hike.

Cory, in the lead, stops suddenly and points to the path. "Watch out! See those little pointy, brown things here? They are caltrops, and the spears of one of those can penetrate right through your flip flops."

We look down as much as up, frequently sidestepping caltrops as we pick our way toward the small rise on the island. While we're looking down, we also spot seashells scattered around on the sandy ground. How the heck did they get way up here, so far from the water? Did birds drop them? Sometimes we see bleached bones of small animals scattered around.

I stop to take photos of the different types of blooming cacti. When we finally get to a giant cactus, we realize it's about eight feet tall. We click photos of each other beside it.

"Let's keep going," Cory says. "You guys can use the exercise, right?"

Eventually, we come to the other side of the island. From our height, we look down on what might be a salt flat. The huge area is level and looks hard. There is not a single bit of visible growth on it.

"Bet you could use that for racing cars," Cory says.

"Bet you could land a plane on it," Dorin replies.

We walk down part way onto the hard flat, and I take Dorin's picture.

"I hate to break up this exploration," I finally say, "but we've been hiking for a couple of hours without water and still have to get back to the boat."

Though the makeshift shelters are still there, the fishermen and the large fishing boat are gone when we get back to the beach. Cory and I spend the rest of the day enjoying incredible snorkeling on reefs, collecting shells. I did not expect this activity could be so rewarding.

We spend a few more days checking out good snorkeling places until we decide we should get some groceries.

Cory's Story

We drop anchor in Porlamar again because Mom and Dorin want to hang out here for a few days. Every day, while the old folks do boat stuff like laundry and electrical repairs, I offer to do the grocery shopping so I can row into the city to do some exploring.

I discover a Tropi-burger stand where the burgers and fries are so cheap, I can't believe it. And there is always the same really cute girl who smiles when she takes my order. Sometimes I go twice in the same day.

She's really cute.

At another place, I buy a huge ice cream cone for what I calculate is a nickel. Venezuela is the best place we've been. I love this place.

Eventually, Dorin decides we should go to the mainland, so we set sail to Cumaná.

The next day, we are out of sight of land. I'm on watch, and I see a disturbance in the water on the horizon far behind us. There are no clouds, and the wind is light. I call to Dorin as the disturbance gets closer. Before he can even get to the cockpit, I realize what it is, and I can't believe it. As far as the eye can see, dolphins are leaping and swimming all in the same direction. The water boils with them.

"Look, a mega-pod of dolphins," I say to Dorin. "Have you ever heard of such a thing?"

"No, the most I've seen is a dozen or two. Amazing! Shirl?"

Mom comes up into the cockpit. "Oh, my gosh! This is incredible!"

As they pass around us, the ones close to the boat leap high in the air, slip under the surface and then back in the air. Water flies off their bodies and streams off their flippers. They just keep coming, leaping, and moving rapidly through the water.

"What? Thousands?" I ask.

"Uh, yeah. I would say so," Dorin says.

We watch for a while, until the giant migration moves past us.

"I didn't even think to take a picture," Mom says. "But I wouldn't have left the cockpit to get the camera. What an incredible experience."

"I didn't know there were that many dolphins in one ocean," I say. I think the whole trip was worth it, just to see this.

We are almost out of diesel and want to get one of the propane tanks refilled. When we arrive in Cumaná, there doesn't seem to be any place to dock—all the docks and slips are full.

I row in with a five-gallon can for diesel, the empty propane tank, and find a place to tie up. I ask directions and come to a fueling place. There are a couple of really big yachts tied up there—one as big as the one Bast and I had dinner on in the Bahamas. I get the propane tank filled for fifty cents and the five-gallon can for thirty cents. The six-pack of Coke costs more than the fuel--$1.50. I get back to the dinghy and put the stuff into it. I stand there a few minutes admiring the yacht, comparing it to the one I was familiar with.

"Where are you from?" a voice asks me. I turn around, and there's a ship's officer behind me.

I tell him I'm American, and he asks where I've sailed, what experience I have. I tell him I've crewed on two different sailing yachts. He asks if I speak any other languages. I tell him just a little Spanish.

"We are short one hand," he says. "We're leaving tomorrow. We have a crew of fifteen from various countries. Would you be interested? We spend a lot of time at sea, but we're heading for Europe. You get some time in every port. Pay's good. And the food's good."

I am really surprised. "Ah, I'd have to think about it. Can I get back to you in a couple of hours? And I've got to take this stuff back to our yacht," I say, waving toward the couple of dozen boats anchored in the bay.

"Sure. Come by and ask for me. I'll give you a tour." He shakes my hand.

I think hard about this as I row back. Is this how life could be? You sail around, get to see the world, and get paid for it? It's very tempting. I could do it. Just go.

But what about finishing high school? I wonder. Shouldn't I at least finish high school? It's always been taken for granted I'd go to college. But isn't sailing around the world a great and unique education?

I don't share this opportunity with Mom and Dorin. I don't know yet what I want to do, so I have to decide that first, before I bounce it off them. After I drop off the diesel, propane and six-pack of Coke, I tell them I want to row around and look at boats. Dorin waves that it's fine.

While I'm rowing and drifting, I think chances like this don't just come along, and I've had two in a few months. I might not get this lucky again. But then I think that I have brothers, two of whom still live in Maine, Dad, Mom and Dorin, as well as friends. And something else...I can't name what it is, tells me this is not the path for me right now.

Having decided this, I row back to the *Fandango* to bounce it off the folks. Dorin's looking over a brochure that was slipped into the six-pack of Coke.

"I think you guys should think about doing this," he says. "It's an ad for a place in the interior called Camp Canaima. You have to fly in...there are no roads. It looks interesting."

"What about you?" Mom asks.

"I wouldn't for a minute go off and leave the *Fandango* unattended for more than an hour. But it would be fun for you guys. We can sail to Puerto La Cruz, and you can fly from there to Caracas and then take a plane into the jungle!"

"Can we afford it?" Mom asks.

"Yes, it's really a bargain. Think about it. The two of you could go."

"Heck, I'll pay for my own," I say. "I'm loaded."

So, without even mentioning the world-traveling yacht opportunity, I make the final decision. I hope I decide someday that it was the right one.

The next afternoon, we row into Cumaná and phone the company to book the Camp Canaima trip. The yacht is gone, as I knew it would be. I feel a little sad, like I've lost something I might like to get back.

We find out our trip will be a week from now, and we'll leave from the Puerto La Cruz airport, fly onto Caracas, and then into Canaima.

We are sailing off the coast toward Puerto la Cruz, when, one morning, I notice a bunch of iguanas on shore. I look at them with the binoculars. These guys are big, four or five feet long, maybe six, nose to tail. As we move along, I see hundreds of them, and they cover the shore. The rocks at the edge of the water are coated with them. Then I see a hundred or more in the water. I don't know how this is possible. There are no sea iguanas in Venezuela. When our original plan was to get to the Galápagos in the Pacific, I read about iguanas, and I think the only sea iguanas are there. I call Dorin and Mom and hand the binoculars to Dorin.

"Big suckers!" he says. "I didn't know they traveled in herds."

I tell him the only iguanas that should be here are land iguanas. "They don't go into the water."

"Maybe something disturbed them," he says. "Well, that's some place you can't go ashore."

"Yeah, I was just thinking that." They move slowly, but they keep a-comin' down onto the rocks and then into the ocean. There are still hundreds on the rocks and land. I'm glad we are moving along slowly, so I get a chance to watch them for a while.

The next day, we arrive in Puerto La Cruz. We pack our new clothes in two duffles. Dorin rows us to the dock and waits until we get a taxi to the airport. From there we board a plane to Caracas. The airport in Caracas is large and busy—a lot of hustle and bustle. We follow the signs to get us to the right gate. When we walk out onto the tarmac, I can't believe we are about to get on that plane. It looks like something out of an old, black and white Tarzan movie. The small, silver plane has a clumsy looking fuselage. An antenna cable runs from front to back, which I have never seen except in old movies. The first thing I notice when we get inside is that the seats are all different: the backs are different heights and the upholstery material is different, some faded red, some faded blue, and a couple are patched. This is the plane we are taking into the jungle? I look at Mom, but she seems kind of oblivious and only becomes concerned when I point out the seats. As we get settled, I see a man holding a kitchen sink, with faucets and handles, on his lap. A baby goat sits on a woman's lap.

Once we take off it seems okay. Very soon we are flying over the jungle, and then we are just socked in with fog. The pilot says, "If the clouds part, on your right you will see Angel Falls." And there it is, far away but still impressive. Then we are immediately back into thick fog. I am not too thrilled with this situation.

Suddenly the plane banks very hard to port, and we can see out the starboard side, extremely close to us, a huge mountain! The fog must have cleared just in time for the pilots to see it and turn.

Mom and I look at each other.

"Dodged another bullet," she mutters. Usually Dorin says that, but he is usually joking. This was no joke.

By way of interesting information, the co-pilot tells us there are no roads into Canaima. The only way to get there is by plane. That explains the sink and the goat. That's what you do, I guess. If you need something, you bring it on the passenger plane.

I am relieved when we touch down. We get out on the starboard side of the plane and are directed to go around to the other side to get our luggage. We walk under the port wing and around the tail. On the other side, I am so surprised when I have to duck under the starboard wing. It's about six inches lower than the port side. What? I look at the tires. The tire on this side is a lot less inflated than on the other side.

If we had another way out of here, even if it's by donkey and would take a week, I'd pick it over going back on this plane.

I scan the area for donkeys. Just in case.

At the resort, I see we are on the edge of a wide river fed by broad waterfalls that look strange because they are a funny color, sort of a weak orange, like brewed tea. It can't be pollution. Not out here in the middle of a continent that is mostly jungle.

Mom looks around. "This is wonderful! Look, all the buildings have thatched roofs. How fun!"

The staff herds us to a large, covered pavilion and offers us water and refreshments. I'm starving, so I fill my plate, and it's really good food.

People with clipboards sort us out and gather the English-speaking tourists into one group and other-language speaking tourists into different groups. They give us maps of the camp and a schedule of mealtimes and available activities.

"Let's do this one," Mom says and points to "Half-hour helicopter ride, $150." She laughs. I know she's joking. We are not going to spend that kind of money.

"You couldn't *pay* me $150 to get back in the air," I say. Then I remember we have to get back on a plane to fly out of here. Maybe it will be a different plane. With matching seats.

Newer than four decades old.

We carry our luggage to our bungalow, which is nice looking: cement and stucco with a thatched roof. Inside it's really, really nice, and there are red tiled floors, two large beds and a shower in the bathroom. The hand-crafted exterior door is thick, heavy wood, but I notice there is an inch gap at the bottom.

Supper that night is in a large, elegant dining area also covered with a thatched roof. The walls only come halfway up so it's open-air dining.

There is an incredible buffet, and I pig out, making three trips to fill up my plate.

They ask us to sign up for whatever activities we are interested in during the next few days. We pick a canoeing river trip and a trip to the waterfalls. The rest of the time we will be on our own to wander wherever we choose. That night I fall asleep listening to sounds I've never heard before: different birds, maybe monkeys?

In the morning, I wake up when Mom yells, "Oh, no!"

"What's the matter?"

"Oh, no! Gross! I got up to go to the bathroom during the night, and there were crunchy leaves on the floor that must have blown in under the door, so I just walked over them. I didn't want to turn on the light and wake you up."

"Yeah. And?"

"Look on the floor."

Littered across the tile floor are a couple of dozen large, black beetles that look like June bugs. Some of them are squished flat.

"Blah! Yuk." Mom says, wiping the bottoms of her feet on the blanket.

"It's the Jungle Package. It comes with the room." I laugh. I can't help it.

"Wait a minute." I unlock the door, and sure enough, the broom I saw leaning against the patio wall is still there so I sweep the bugs out of the door and off the patio.

"Ready for breakfast?" I ask.

Today we are doing the river trip. After breakfast about forty of us gather near the shore of the river. There are five very large dugout canoes resting on the beach. They are the real deal, made from trees. You can see the marks of hand woodworking tools that shaped the insides. I try to imagine the size of the trees that were used to make these boats.

Our guides are all Indian and wearing loin cloths, which I figure is for the tourists. I bet they wear jeans and t-shirts when they're not working. They have clipboards and are calling off names and directing people to the boats. I realize that we are all English-speaking in our group, though for some people, English is not their first language. Our guide speaks excellent

English. Something about that feels right. When going on a trip down a river in the jungle, you hope you will understand what your guide tells you.

We are asked to lift and carry our canoe into the water, and all of us guys rush forward to do the he-man thing. We wade in the water, get in the canoe, and settle two by two on the wooden seats. At the back, an Indian guy fires up an outboard motor. Our guide stands in the front of the boat and asks if everyone is all set.

"Are there any snakes?" someone asks. I tense because Mom has a phobia-level fear of snakes. I mean freaking-out fear.

The guide says, "Oh, yes. Beware. Anacondas in the river, boas in the trees."

Mom's head whips around to look at me. I grin and shake my head a little. It's a joke for the tourists, I try to relay.

As we go along, I notice there is water on the floor of the boat that wasn't there when we started. But maybe that's the way dugouts are. A little seepage.

Our guide tells us the legend of why the rivers and falls are red. It has something to do with a feud between brother kings and bloodshed. I'm not paying that much attention because I notice the water is a little higher. Hmm.

The broad river soon narrows through thick jungle. Mom looks up at the overhanging trees. Our guide, whose back is toward us, tells us about the history and culture of his people. He tells us that his culture is very quickly disappearing and that only a few people speak their language now. Someone asks if he speaks the language. He says yes and Spanish also.

The water has risen to ankle level, and we put our feet up on the seat in front of us.

"We have water on the bottom," a Brit says.

Without turning around our guide says, "Yes, a little water will come in but don't worry. Only a little." And he continues his guide-talk.

A few minutes later, the Brit says, "We have more water on the bottom."

Our guide reaches down into the bow, brings up two coffee cans and, without turning around, hands them to the people on the first seat.

"Bail," he says. "It will be no problem."

The people in the front hand the cans back, and passengers start to bail fast. I know how long it takes to bail, and this is not going to do it.

"See here. I do insist. We have a problem," the Brit says.

And he is right. The water is almost up to our seats, and the boat is low in the water. Mom looks into the river. She is on anaconda watch.

The guy at the motor in the back says something in an Indian language, and our guide turns around to look. He does a big double-take. His eyes open in alarm.

"Crap!" he says. He gives the motor guy instructions, hands us two more coffee cans, and we angle toward the riverbank.

"Just like the *Tinker* in Grenada," I say to Mom.

"Yeah, except there were no thingies in the water there."

She can't even say the word "snake."

The gunnel is just inches above water when, a few minutes later, the guides pull the canoe up on a small strip of sandy beach. The Brit and I step out to help.

"Don't worry," the guide says, looking worried. "We have a plan."

Soon a second canoe comes up the river, and our guide waves the boat over. And then a third boat and a fourth and finally a fifth. The guides confer and then break us into groups to get into the other canoes. Mom and I, just the two of us, are directed toward a canoe.

"You speak Spanish," he says. Mom vigorously shakes her head no.

"You do," he says to me. The only way anyone could think that, is because I ordered my breakfast food in Spanish. "You go. It's okay." He waves his arm toward the canoe and walks away to help others.

People pull their children on their laps to make room for us in their canoe. The remaining three canoes take on our other ten passengers. They must not have been filled to capacity. Bet they are now!

As we continue down the river, our guide speaks to us in Spanish, but it's pretty rapid-fire, and I catch only a word here and there. At some point, the current picks up and our speed increases. I realize the guide has become excited and speaks more rapidly than before. I don't understand a word. He waves his arms and the passengers lean forward, listening intently.

I lean toward Mom so I can speak into her ear. "I feel like he must be saying, 'We are coming to dangerous rapids so you must do exactly what I say. Then we will come to a waterfall. But if you follow my instructions perfectly, you will all survive.'"

"You be sure to translate for me as we go over the falls," Mom says.

We eventually motor to the side of the river, where the other canoes are already beached on the sand. A lunch has been set up for us under a canopy. We congregate with the passengers we were with originally, and they say they are having a good time. The passengers are mostly Spanish speaking people, but each boat has at least one bilingual passenger who can translate for them.

"You've heard the joke, right?" one American guy says. "What do you call someone who speaks two languages?" he asks Mom.

"Bilingual," she says.

"What do you call someone who speaks three languages?"

"Trilingual?" I ask.

He nods. "Right. And what do you call someone who speaks one language?"

While I think this over, he delivers the punch line. "An American!"

You gotta laugh. It's true.

After lunch, we motor back to the camp and take a walk along the paths near the beach and through the jungle.

"Tomorrow, we do the waterfall trip," Mom says. "That should be fun. And maybe a little less adventurous."

"Don't want no more adventure?" I ask.

"Nope, I'm all 'ventured out."

That night I roll up a bath towel and put it on the floor in front of the door. In the morning there are no beetles on the floor.

After breakfast, we find there is one dugout canoe on the beach, because only eight of us will go on this trip. We have two Indian guides, different ones from yesterday. These guys are dressed in jean shorts and t-shirts that say Camp Canaima on them.

We motor out past the huge waterfalls that crash into the river, sending up massive turbulence. As we pass there's a rainbow near the foot of the falls. We come to another waterfall and beach the canoe beyond it. They offer a plastic bag for us to put anything in we don't want to get wet. Mom puts her camera in it.

"We walk behind the falls," the guide says in Spanish and repeats it in English.

We climb on rocks until we are beside the falls. Tons of water crash down, throwing off a spray that gets us a little wet. I can't see any way we can get under the falls without walking through the cascade, and that's impossible. The guide tells us to hold hands, and he leads us along the rocks and then, yes, there is a small opening. We step in behind the falls. There is a rock shelf that we walk single file on. The iron-colored water thunders like a constantly changing thick wall, just in front of us. Awesome. Then our guide moves us along the wet rock, and we come out on the other side.

"That was great!" Mom says. "I wonder how many years, how many centuries, ago it was that the Indians discovered you could walk behind the falls." The guide hears her and says, "Long, long time ago."

We hike up wet boulders and rocks until we get to the top of the falls. The guides look at the river and then walk away from us and talk quietly. Both look worried.

"Roll up your pants," the head guide says to two of the guys who've worn slacks. "We will cross. Hold hands." He leads us out into the river at the head of the falls. The river bottom is mostly large flat rocks; the warm water flows really fast. We are halfway across, and the river is running so fast, I can feel my leg being pushed forward every time I pick up my foot. I realize if anyone slips, they will go over the falls immediately, maybe pulling others off balance too. The guide looks anxiously at us, going tiny sidestep by tiny sidestep. He says something to the other guide in their native language, and I can tell he's very worried. Are they wondering if they should go back the way we came? As we get to the middle of the falls,

I grip Mom's hand hard. She looks up and nods. She knows this is dangerous. Slowly we progress with the guide looking sideways at us, watching us closely. Finally, we are on the other side, and both guides look very relieved.

"Was it deeper than usual?" Mom asks the guide.

He nods. "Sometimes it is to the ankle. Sometimes up to here." He indicates a couple of inches above the ankle. "But this was almost to the knees. Not usual this time of year."

When we get back to the canoe, lunch has been set up by other Canaima staff. After that adventure, everyone is starved.

"This is really fun, but I'm glad we only signed up for two activities," Mom says. "I prefer spacing my adventures out a little."

The next two days, we hang around the camp. Mom reads a book while lounging on a deck chair on the beach. I paddle a small canoe around the bay, do a little swimming, and hike the trails. The last night, we all hang out at the dining pavilion enjoying native music and singing provided by the staff.

Great.

In the back of my mind, I'm concerned about the plane ride back to Caracas.

The next day we board a similar plane for the return trip, but it looks two decades newer than the one we came in on. The sky is overcast, but we encounter no fog on the flight back.

In the Caracas airport we have to wait two hours for our connecting flight, so we wander around and check out the gift shop.

Mom notices a cassette for sale. "Look!"

It's Paul Simon's *Graceland*. We need to buy this," she says.

Before we left on the trip, we had been listening to "You Can Call Me Al" and "Diamonds on the Soles of Her Shoes" on the radio and loved them. Once we started the trip, when we listened to BBC, we heard these favorites and others from the album.

We are astonished at this find in a Spanish-speaking country.

"It's 600 *bolívares!*" I say. "Did you do the math?"

Mom hands her credit card to the clerk. "Yup," is all she says. We are owners of this cool cassette.

"Dorin is going to be happy about this," I say. "He really likes this music."

"Yeah, me too," she says. She wears her smile all the way to the Puerto La Cruz airport.

Dorin is waiting for us when we arrive. "Let's get right back to the boat," he says. "I have supper waiting for you."

We are full of stories, but he has two of his own. He brought the *Fandango* into a dock to refuel, and the attendant said the price would be $4 a gallon instead of twelve cents because Dorin was an American.

"I said, 'Never mind.' And I sailed up the coast and found a place I could get gas at the same price everyone else was paying. I hate to be gouged."

On another day, he went into a bank to get enough cash to last a couple more weeks because we would be heading to Puerto Rico soon. He was back on the *Fandango* only a few minutes when an official boat with armed, uniformed, military men came aboard to "inspect." After a cursory glance around, they told Dorin he had to pay them. He emptied his wallet of 2,500 *bolívares* and they left.

I dive for my bunk, and out of the foot well, I pull out my sleeping bag. Tucked in the bottom is my remaining wad of almost 5,000 *bolívares*.

"I thought we'd go out to a restaurant to celebrate," Dorin says. "But we'll have to wait until we get back to Margarita Island. I'm not leaving the boat unattended here even for a few hours. I think the island is much friendlier and safer than the mainland."

I'm happy to be back in Porlamar. Late in the afternoon, I row to the beach to check things out, and I see right away something's going on. There's music not far away. A couple of blocks in, there's a parade with floats. Some people dance in traditional costumes. Others are decorated with huge, brightly colored feathers and sparkling gems. The people watching the parade are dancing to the music, and there's a major party atmosphere. I think about going back to get Mom and Dorin, but they had both said they were tired and needed to rest. So I'm on my own. This is really fun, watching everyone have a great time. I stroll around and buy street food and just enjoy the excitement and atmosphere.

Time goes by, it gets dark, and I'm in no hurry to leave. I'm really enjoying this. Suddenly, I think of the dinghy that I had left pulled up on the beach. Though I pulled it pretty far in, a lot of time has gone by, and there is a tide here. Not much, but enough. I start running through the crowd. I can just picture the *Tinker* floating away.

I zigzag around people while I envision the boat far enough out that I will have to swim to get it. What if it isn't even in sight? Then what will I do?

I pick up my pace and dodge through the crowd. Suddenly, in front of me a guy steps backward into my path. I lean left to avoid him and plow right into someone else. I see before he even hits the ground it's an armed soldier. His hat flies off as he goes down hard.

Oh, no.

The crowd is shocked into silence. My first thought is to apologize, but before I can think of the words in Spanish, the machine gun comes up, pointed at me. A jolt of fear goes through me. I think, this is it. This is how I'm going to die.

I put my hands up and try to back away. "I'm sorry, I'm sorry," I say. I still can't think of the words in Spanish.

He springs to his feet and starts toward me, jabbing the rifle toward my chest while he yells at me. I turn and run, and the crowd parts for me. I run as fast as I ever have and don't look back until I get to the beach, but I know he's not behind me. I realize now, if he were going to shoot me, I'd already be dead in the street.

The *Tinker* is still there, though the ocean's water is lapping at the sand only a couple of feet away. I yank it into the water and jump in. I'm so full of adrenalin I row around for half an hour. I know I will not tell Mom and Dorin about this. Someday, maybe, but not now. Mom still has safety concerns, and I don't want my freedom cut back.

When I get back to the *Fandango*, Mom and Dorin are in the cockpit with glasses of wine that Dorin picked up in Sint Maarten for a special occasion. Dorin pours a glass for me.

"What's up?" I ask.

"Well, we've been talking, and we want to get your thoughts," Dorin says.

"What if we just head back to Puerto Rico?" Mom says. "And then head home?"

"Yeah," Dorin adds. "I might be done with Venezuela. Getting boarded was disheartening."

I take the glass of wine and sip. And take a breath and think about this.

"Yeah, okay, that would be fine with me," I say. "I love Venezuela. It's the best place we've been. But, you know, I might be getting a little bored."

They nod, sympathetically.

"And I wouldn't mind getting back home in time to have a little summer left with my friends."

"I feel like I'm short-changing you guys, heading back," Dorin says. "We worked so hard to get here, and now we're cutting it short."

"I don't feel short-changed at all," Mom says. "Remember, in the beginning Venezuela wasn't even in the picture."

"Right. We were going to circumnavigate," I remind them.

"Yeah. About that. You guys disappointed?" Dorin asks.

"No! I think we have had about as much adventure at sea as I would like," Mom says, laughing. "But, how about you? Would have been nice for you to be on the short list of circumnavigators."

"We would all be on the list."

"No, it would say Dorin Zohner and a crew of two," Mom laughs.

"Hey, as far as I'm concerned, I figure I have enough bragging rights to last for quite a few years," I say, thinking they don't even know about the last one.

"Do you think we would have made it? Survived it?" Mom asks.

"Well, I believe the *Fandango* could have made it. Not sure my navigation and seamanship skills would have been up to it."

"Whaddya mean? You sailed the heck out of every situation. You saved us so many times! You're our hero," Mom says.

"Ha!" he says. "To begin with, look at who got you into those situations where you had to be saved?"

Mom raises her glass. "Nevertheless, to our fearless captain!"

We clink our plastic stemware in toast.

"I agree about the boat," Mom says. "I thought I had confidence in her, but I have much more now. She's strong, sails into the wind like nobody's business, and can withstand a lot of pounding."

"We really tested her, didn't we?" Dorin says with satisfaction. "So, are you guys feeling up to sailing offshore since it seems like we all are ready to head home? I can make the necessary adjustments, now that I have experience in these currents."

"Sure," Mom says. "I'm game."

"Sounds good to me," I say. "Course we have to steer by hand."

"What else is new?" Dorin says.

Mom and I reprovision, row the bags of groceries to the *Fandango* and put the stuff away while Dorin clears us out. The next morning, we head for Puerto Rico. I have mixed feelings because I am leaving behind any further opportunities to be asked to travel the world by sea. But I think I'm ready to hang out with friends and get ready for high school. I have a lot of schoolwork to get to teachers before the end of the summer so I can join my class in September. I realize I really don't want to miss my senior year. But I wouldn't have missed this trip for anything in the world.

Chapter Twenty-four
Home on the Horizon

The next morning, Cory hauls the anchor; we put up the sails and head for Puerto Rico. The seas are kind and the wind steady, and sometimes we are even on a reach. Often, we tie the tiller and go about our business. The motor gives us no problems, the batteries stay charged, and the bilge pump works.

As we make steady progress, indicated by Dorin's sun sights, I wonder what it would have been like if the whole trip had been this easy. Boring, maybe.

One day, the three of us lounge in the cockpit after Dorin reduces the daily sun sight. "I figure we are a day out of Puerto Rico. I don't want to get your hopes up, so let's say two to be safe."

"This sure is different from our last trip back from Venezuela," I say. There are no clouds in the sky, and the sun lights up the swells and choppy water; there's glitter, glitter everywhere. We are dry, the *boat* is dry, life is good.

The guys nod and smile, but Cory holds a shushing finger to his mouth. "It's better if you don't say it out loud."

Dorin is at the tiller. "Yeah, let's not tempt the sea gods."

I stretch deliciously and tip my face to the sun. "I should go below and clean up. It's a disaster down there. Stuff everywhere. But I just don't feel like it. It's good to be sitting out, just enjoying...."

Cory holds a finger to his lips and gives me a warning look.

".... the weather," I finish in a whisper.

"Give yourself a break," Dorin says. "We'll give you a hand with it later."

No problem. I lean back against the bulkhead, hands behind my head.

We skip right along under sail power at five knots. There isn't anything in sight, no boats, not even birds.

Cory suddenly jumps to his feet. "Look, a plane." Sure enough, a small fighter jet is skimming unbelievably low over the water, heading toward us.

Dorin reaches for the binoculars, but before he can raise them to his eyes, the plane is upon us and then passes, so close we can see the pilot looking at us as he flies by.

"Military," Dorin says as the plane disappears from sight. "United States."

"Well, that's kind of exciting," I say. "I've never seen a jet that low. Training maneuvers maybe?"

Dorin smiles and shakes his head. "I don't think it's a coincidence he's out in the same spot in the ocean we are. I think he was checking us out."

"Why?" Cory asks.

"This morning's calculations put us pretty close to leaving international waters. Let's hope getting buzzed is all that happens. I'm going below and look at the chart. Take the tiller, Cor?"

Ten minutes later Dorin's back. "Yeah, if I'm not mistaken, we've crossed into US waters, but we may also have skimmed too close to the restricted area around the naval air base on Vieques."

"So, we're three miles from Puerto Rico," Cory says.

"Give or take." Dorin puts his arm around me and gives a little squeeze. "How does it feel to be home, lady?"

I laugh. Ocean is ocean, and there is no land in sight. "Gee, no welcoming party."

"Be careful what you wish for."

"There's a ship behind us," Cory says a few minutes later. "Maybe a tanker?"

We look where Cor is pointing, and there a tiny ship is silhouetted on the horizon. Dorin looks through the binoculars. "It's pretty big but not a tanker. Not a cruise ship, either. Hmm. It's heading directly toward us." He hands the binoculars to Cory.

"Wow, she's coming fast…really moving," Cory says. He watches for a minute. "I think it's a Coast Guard cutter."

"That means I'm right. We're in Puerto Rico's territorial waters."

"They are coming right at us," Cor says. "Wow, I've never seen a big ship move that fast."

We can see the bow waves as the ship slices steadily through the water without any bobbing or weaving. In ten minutes, we can see details of the ship that gleams white in the sunlight. It's sleek and tall, and the many-windowed bridge is high. There's a radar tower and a multitude of antennas bristling up. In spite of the red diagonal US Coast Guard stripe on the hull, all of the communication antennas give the massive ship a threatening feel. The boat slows just fifty yards off our stern on the port side. Now I can see men in dark blue uniforms lining the deck.

"I think they'll board us," Dorin says.

"What? Why?" I ask.

"What do we do?" Cory asks.

"They can't go below," I object. "It's a mess down there."

"I don't think we'll have a say in the matter. They won't be asking permission." Dorin sounds relaxed, almost amused about this.

"How much time do I have? I have to see how much stuff I can pick up." I turn to go below.

"No! Stop. Stay on deck. Don't make any sudden moves. Keep your hands visible." His voice is firm. He's not kidding.

"What? Why?" I ask.

"They'll be looking for drugs, right?" Cory asks.

"What! Why?"

Dorin nods. "I expect so. Try to relax. It'll be okay."

"It's huge!" I say.

"Yeah, I estimate upwards of four hundred feet," Dorin says.

As it closes in, I crane my neck to see the bridge so high above us. Now I see that the six men lined up along the deck are holding rifles pointing upwards, across their chests. My heart thuds hard.

A loudspeaker barks out, "This is the US Coast Guard. Maintain your course and speed. You are going to be boarded. Do you have firearms on board?"

"No," Dorin yells out. "Well, just the flare gun."

"How many hands and passengers on board?"

"Three."

"Is there anyone below deck?"

"No. Do you want me to lower my sail?" Dorin calls out.

"No. Maintain your course and speed, Captain."

By electric winch, an orange, rigid-hulled, inflatable boat is slowly lowered toward the water. Four men wearing orange floatation devices are in it.

"They will have a rough time of it getting onto the *Fandango*," Dorin says. "The water has a real chop to it."

In less than a minute the dinghy comes alongside, but Dorin is right. As our boat rises on the choppy water, the Coast Guard dinghy drops and bobs. An officer stands up and attempts to grab the lifeline, but the boats separate, rise and fall, out of rhythm. The officer tries again and again, and I realize I'm holding my breath, trying to wish him safely onto our boat. Finally, he grabs the toerail. He has a line in his hand which he attempts to tie off to the stanchion base. A second officer grabs a stanchion base as the dinghy rises, and he manages to hang on. The first guy ties off to a cleat, and the second officer ties off to a stanchion. Though the boats will not separate now, they toss and heave, as if uncoordinated, in a separate dance. In an amazing feat of strength and agility, the young man grabs a stay, and taking advantage of a momentary rise of his dinghy, heaves himself aboard to stand on the toe rail. I hear Cory release his breath in relief.

The young officer starts to step over the lifeline, hesitates, balancing, and says, "Permission to come aboard, sir." It's a polite question, but his voice says it's perfunctory only.

"Permission granted," Dorin says.

I realize this young officer who emanates authority can't be much older than college age. He steps into the cockpit as the second officer also manages to get aboard. He is barely past teenage years. They both wear sidearms.

"Sorry to inconvenience you, sir," the first officer says. "When the boarding is done, you will be provided with a copy of the report. Do you have any weapons on board?"

"Ah, no, just the flare gun, but I'm not sure it works."

The officer jots down the answer.

"What is your last port of call? Where are you coming from?"

"Ah, Pampatar, Venezuela."

"Next port of call?"

"We hope to make landfall in Boquerón Bay, Puerto Rico."

"How many people in your party?" He glances toward the companionway opening to see if there are any more people.

"Three."

"What is the purpose of your voyage?"

"Just cruising for a year...we've been down among the islands and...."

"Thank you, sir." The officer cuts him short.

I am surprised to see the orange rubber dinghy with two officers still in it has dropped back fifteen yards or so and the "mother ship" even further. It feels less threatening, but they still have guns.

The senior officer says, "I need to see your documentation."

"It's below," I try to reply. My voice comes out hoarse, and I clear my throat. "It's below."

He nods and indicates I should go below.

"Stay in the cockpit," he says to Dorin and Cory. "This officer will search your lockers."

Below, I get out our packet of documents. He examines them and continues to fill out his paperwork.

"Okay, ma'am. Please stand here. I'm going to search your ship."

I am still tense, and my mouth is dry so I just nod. He starts in the salon lifting cushions, opening lockers and emptying them. He piles stuff on the table and floor. Every locker is emptied. He discovers the diesel tank under Cory's bunk and asks, "What is this for?"

"Um," I clear my throat, "it was diesel, but it's empty now."

He nods and thumps the tank, unscrews the cap, and looks inside with a flashlight. He shines a light into the foot of Cory's bunk.

"Stay here," he says. "I'm going to search the head and the fo'c'sle."

Outside, things are tossed onto the cockpit floor. I'm trembling and try to stop. We're Americans, and these young men are American protectors. I try to take a deep breath, but it hurts under my ribs.

I peek into the fo'c'sle and see he is on his knees on the mattress, looking into the chain locker with a flashlight. Then, while still on the bed, he pulls up the mattress, backing toward the salon as he pulls it toward him. Then, standing in front of the bed, he pulls the sheet off and examines the underside of the mattress. Pushing it aside, he removes the lids of our tool lockers and then tests to see if there is a false bottom. He lets the mattress fall back into place and pulls our clothing out of the lockers, leaving them in heaps. He must sense I'm watching him because he glances back. For a second there is an agonized look of apology on his young face, but it quickly turns neutral and professional.

Back in the salon, the galley locker gets emptied, as well as the ice box. Then he opens the dish cupboard behind the sink.

"Oh, oh," I think. Our hidden stash of baking supplies is finally going to be discovered. I breathe a slow sigh of relief when he doesn't take the dishes out and so doesn't see the hole in the surface that allows us to remove the false bottom. He kneels in front of the open can cupboard and looks up inside with his flashlight. From this angle he can probably see the hanging net bags. I'm afraid he will sense my fear and get more curious, so

I try to relax, but I have a hard time breathing. He shuts off the flashlight and stands up. "Please go into the cockpit," he says. Then he follows me out.

Now that they are done, their demeanor is different, more relaxed, respectful. "Sorry for the inconvenience ma'am, sirs." He nods to include Cory. "Have a good trip."

I realize the mothership has closed in again, and the inflatable dinghy has pulled alongside. In seconds, the two officers are over the side and drop into their boat. They untie and depart.

"They didn't even bother to check our safety equipment," Dorin says. "That's what they are supposed to do. So they were looking for drugs."

"You think?" says Cory.

In less than a minute, their dinghy is raised onto the deck, but the ship maintains its proximity to us for a few minutes. Perhaps the officers are reporting to the captain. Then over the loudspeaker we hear, "Thank you, *Fandango*, for your cooperation. Have a safe passage to Puerto Rico."

The ship reverses, turns and rapidly heads back the way it came.

"Makes you proud, doesn't it?" Cory says.

"Oh?" I say.

"In the United States, we know how to search!" he says, smiling.

"Were you worried?" Dorin asks me.

"No, not really. I mean, when you think about it, there was nothing to be worried about."

Cory looks sideways at me, raises an eyebrow, and shakes his head. He's not buying it.

We stand in silence and awe for a few minutes as we watch the ship quickly get smaller in the distance. Then Dorin says, "Aren't you glad you didn't clean up first?"

Cory starts putting stuff back into the lockers and straightens, smiling. "Hey! We just successfully smuggled five pounds of Domino's pure into Puerto Rico. We might have something going here!"

A few hours later, Cory is the first to spot the dot of land on the horizon. We are a little tense. Are we looking at Puerto Rico or Mona Island? The guys pass the binoculars back and forth for a while. "Nailed it!" Dorin finally says. "That's Puerto Rico right out there. I must be getting the hang of this."

"Or...everybody gets lucky once in a while," Cory says.

Dorin laughs and then says, "It's kind of sad, though. I don't know about you, but I'm going to miss Puerto Rico." We nod. In many ways it seems like we are coming home.

"I've been thinking," Dorin says. "What if we don't sail back to Maine. What if we leave the boat in Puerto Rico and fly home? Then we can come back every summer and use her for a vacation home."

We sit in silence for a moment while we contemplate this.

"So, for this trip, we are basically done. That'll take a little getting used to," Cory says.

For me also. I feel quite reluctant to reenter so quickly the high-speed hassle of life in the US. I'll have to get a job, find an apartment. Go back to the daily grind of alarm clocks, schedules, and deadlines.

"You just want to get back to daily showers in your own home," Cory accuses him.

"You got me," Dorin says, laughing. "And I like a little structure in my life."

"We're going to have to drag her back kicking and screaming, though," Cory says with a nod toward me.

"You're right about that," I say. "Don't want no structure. I like to wing it."

"You are a born nomad, Shirl Jean," he says. "Would you just keep traveling if it were possible?"

"Yeah, just as long as I could see family from time to time."

But by the time we sail gently into Boquerón Bay after dark, I have agreed this is a good plan. The idea of coming back to Puerto Rico every summer helps a lot.

The next morning, I go to the public phone and buy airline tickets for Boston. Then I call my parents.

We visit with Bob and Binnie and tell them about our adventures. In the afternoon, a couple of the other cruisers row over and sit in our cockpit, and they ask questions about sailing down the islands—something they are poised and nearly ready to do. We give them our charts.

Having said our goodbyes and promises to keep in touch, the next day we sail to Puerto Real, our true home away from home. We tie up at the dock outside of *Pescadería* and have our last lunch at *Brisas Del Mar*. Félix, the waiter, is working so we are able to say goodbye. Nearby, we stop in at the *Pescadería* to thank the owner for all his help and, on the other side of the street, to thank the folks who own the little grocery store.

Back in the boatyard I say a cheerful goodbye to Félix, though I am sad. As Cory and I prepare to leave, Dorin says to go ahead, he'll be right along. He and Félix are deep in conversation as we leave.

On the dock, the two little girls, one in a school uniform, wait with their bikes. They look sad, and one wipes her eyes. Below in the *Fandango*, I look up the Spanish word for address and find a piece of paper and pencil. They are still outside on the dock.

"*¿Puedes escribir tu dirección?*" I ask. I am prepared to have them look confused, because *dirección* must mean direction, not address, right? But they are gleefully happy as they put the paper on the dock and write down their information.

When Dorin returns, he says Félix has recommended one of his *Villa Pesquera* workers who would do a good job of looking after the *Fandango*. An hour later, the guy, whom we recognize as the guy who blew the conch for the little girls and who we know doesn't speak English, shows up. Dorin writes an amount of money on a piece of paper that he will send each month. The man writes his *dirección* on the paper, and they shake hands.

The trip home is bittersweet for me. Leaving the boat behind, in spite of the lure of future vacations, is hard. The *Fandango*, which we put in harm's way so often, valiantly provided us with a home in calm conditions and protection from the elements that could have left our bodies at the bottom of the sea.

And, I realize, I was not kidding about preferring a cruising life to the demands of a life at home. But that could be partially due to the frantic life I had been living before Dorin invited us to come along. I look forward to seeing my family, Mom, Dad and my kids who live in Maine, again. Cory is excited to rejoin his social group. I can tell.

So instead of regret, I choose to bask in gratitude to Dorin, who thought I would weather well, this adventure.

Epilogue

When we first got home, I spent a couple of months beginning this book of our travels. I got as far as arriving in Bermuda, but work prevented me from continuing.

We did go back to Puerto Rico for three or four weeks during Dorin's summer vacations each year. The first time was a big surprise to us. When we took the padlock off and pulled out the companionway boards, we heard a scuttling sound and quickly found that *las cucarachas* (cockroaches) had discovered what other searchers had not: our secret stash of flour, pancake mix, and sugar that we had forgotten to empty. This food had allowed hundreds of them to flourish. Dorin and I slept in the cockpit for a few days while we attempted to eradicate them. After we returned home that first summer, Hurricane Hugo, a category 3-4, came through in September, slamming Puerto Rico's east coast. In the west, gusts of 130 to 140 were experienced. We learned the *Fandango* was one of the few sail boats to survive without damage.

Dorin and I returned to Puerto Rico each summer for the next five years to do maintenance on the *Fandango* and to enjoy Puerto Rico. We used the *Tinker* solely to get back and forth to the dock, pumping her up for each little trip. When we decided it was time to bring the *Fandango* home, we bought a used fiberglass dinghy to trail behind. But, what to do with our rubber ducky?

I was on the deck of the *Fandango* when Dorin rowed our new, rigid dinghy to the dock, trailing the *Tinker* behind. I watched as he communicated, using hand gestures and a few words like *gratis* and *muchas gracias*, with the man who had been taking care of the *Fandango* for the other 48 weeks of the year. I wondered how it was going, but it was quickly evident the gentleman *had* caught on. He grabbed Dorin's hand and pumped his arm up and down enthusiastically. We had wondered if he would think of the rubber inflatable as a liability, but it was clear from his joyful reaction that he was happy to be a boat owner in Puerto Real Harbor. He tied the dinghy to a dock cleat, and smiling, he strode off—a man on a mission with things to do to get his boat ready to sail. I'm sure he was able to fix the damn *Tinker* and make good use of it.

In 1993, Cory, now a 21-year-old college student, offered to sail the *Fandango* home. He and college buddy Scott sailed her from Puerto Rico to Florida. They had enough exciting adventures to fill another book. Dorin and I took over in Florida and sailed only as far as North Carolina, so he could be back in time to teach. He pressed me into the role of captain and navigator. This offshore leg was not without excitement and narrow escape adventures.

Ultimately, the prop shaft that plagued us during the voyage described in this book, finally failed. We limped into Beaufort, North Carolina, under sail, and then, because it was late in the summer, we left her in a boatyard there.

The following summer, we had the boat hauled overland from North Carolina to Maine. Dorin and I spent weekends repairing damaged bulkheads and rebuilding the interior. I took out the can cupboard and replaced it with the original drawers. When we finished, we agreed that we probably enjoyed working on the boat as much as we enjoyed sailing her.

Meanwhile, Cory, always on a quest for adventure, became a whitewater rafting guide. During these years, he met and married Jessica, a kindred spirit. Their honeymoon was a whitewater rafting trip. They bought a boat and sailed for a year but then settled down to have a family. They have two fearless, high-achieving daughters.

Though Dorin and I embraced a dream of returning to cruising in our retirement years, life had other plans for us. In 1995, twin grandchildren were born whom we ended up raising—an experience that was rewarding and gratifying. We did get the *Fandango* back in the water when the children were five, and we took them sailing a few times. As you would expect with this precious cargo, these trips were fun but uneventful. When we hauled her for the last time, we surely didn't know it was the last time.

For a while, Dorin and I faithfully covered the *Fandango* with a tarp every fall, though often it was November and sometimes during an early snowstorm. One year, I remember, it was blizzard conditions, and halfway through, we went for warmth and food to Sonny's Pizza. The TV was on and the Patriots were playing the Bills. We warmed up, watched a quarter, and then returned to finish the job in the snowstorm.

Dorin was diagnosed with lymphoma in 2004 and entered ten years of successful chemo treatment. We continued to have a happy and productive life and did some traveling, not by boat, however, to Costa Rica a few times and later lived in Honduras with the twins for a year when they were twelve.

The *Fandango* was on the back burner for most of that time, and we missed covering her a year here and there. After Dorin passed away in 2014, care of our boat became more haphazard. Often, I would forget I owned a boat until I caught a Patriots and Bills game and then would have an "oh, shit" moment. So some years she got covered for the winter months and some years she did not, exposing her to the harsh elements of wind, sun, snow, and rain.

Near the time of Dorin's passing away, he encouraged me to pick up writing this book. It was tricky because I had written the first five chapters on my beloved Mac. However, during the intervening 25 years, I had switched to a PC. The story was stored somewhere on three-inch "floppy" disks. A friend researched the problem and found a program that might, just might, be able to retrieve the files for my PC.

It seemed a miracle when Tomasz was successful. I read the chapters to Dorin, who became quite enthusiastic about my continuing.

My problem was that I didn't have enough information and memories of the details of what followed next. Dorin, with his incredible memory, dictated a lot of information to me while I typed as fast as I could.

After his passing, I experienced various health problems and wasn't able to continue, though I still felt pressure to write. I had the notes Dorin had dictated, but there were not enough details to trigger memories of stories of day-to-day living.

After I recovered, my next-to-youngest son, Drew, was helping me clear out a rental storage unit. He discovered a milk carton-style, hanging folder box. Assuming it was ancient financial stuff a decade or more old, I told him to chuck it.

"Are you sure?" he asked as he always does when he thinks I'm rushing to judgement and being irresponsibly rash. He pulled files out and discovered the *Fandango's* ship's log as well as an abundance of notebooks and journals giving day by day details of our year sailing to Venezuela. I was overjoyed.

And so began the writing of this book.

I found, as I pored over the handwritten material, often in soft pencil on lined paper, memories surfaced, and I felt, at times, as if I were still sailing in the Caribbean. The names of parts of the boat came back as well as how things operated—stuff that I had believed was gone from my memory forever.

When I was well into the storm in Mona Passage (Chapter Nineteen, Current Affairs) my grandson Dustin, one of the twins and now 21, drove out to check on the boat and came back with sad news. The hull was dented where it had leaned heavily into one of the jack stands, and topsides, much of the wood trim was rotted. The varnish hung in shreds, fluttering in the wind.

I went out with Drew one day and saw the tarp hanging in tatters. Though I longed to believe we could still restore her to her former self and use her for a vacation home in the Carolinas, the reality was clear.

Not at my age.

Not by myself.

So I turned to Craig's List.

I didn't go out to the boatyard the day she was hauled. I thought it would be pushy and uncomfortable for the new owner and, also, too painful for me.

However, there is still one last postscript to the story. On the day the *Fandango* was being hauled to Belfast, my friend Pam, who had never seen the boat, but who had helped me with a lot of editing and critiquing of this book, had an appointment in Belfast. As she pulled out to pass the boat hauler, she recognized the name on the stern of the boat. She turned around and followed the *Fandango* all the way into Belfast.

And so, our beloved *Fandango* had a friendly escort on what was probably her last trip.

I lost contact with the new owner who thought he would have to part her out (and I was in agreement with this fate), but he held out a little hope that he would be able to convince someone to take her on as a project.

I don't suppose I'll ever know. Maybe it's best that way.

Maybe I'm meant to remember her as she was in her glory days: with her sails full, on a beam reach, with the Caribbean sun beaming down, Cory laughing, and with Dorin forever at the helm.

-Acknowledgments-

I am so blessed to have friends and family who pitched in as readers/editors/critiquers and advisors. It did take a team to build this book, which, over time, developed from the idea of a memoir for family members to, dare I think it? a real book.

In order of appearance:

My friend **Pam Ames**, a first-class critiquer who spent many hours on *Never Leave on a Friday*, was the first to encourage me, over several glasses of wine, to think of this book as more than a memoir. Her suggestions and editing skills gave my writing ability a big boost.

My granddaughter, **Miranda Shepherd**, provided early assistance in the direction and tone of this book, thus saving me from myself. She also added much-needed support when I twisted her arm to critique my early attempts at sketching.

My friend **Don Reiter**, an educator and a talented writer, also edited, encouraged, and suggested I think of the manuscript as a publishable book. His comments and encouragement were the turning points for building confidence in my writing.

Brenda Zohner, Dorin's daughter-in-law, devoted many, many hours to this project, reading the manuscript, twice! She provided a great deal of encouragement and made excellent suggestions for improvements.

Brian Zohner, an educator and Dorin's grandson, lent a hand and taught me the valuable use of Google Docs for editing and sharing my work with my volunteer helpers. From him I also learned an accepted way to spell "fo'c'sle," that boat names should be italicized, and that I am very inconsistent with punctuation.

My dear brother, **Bruce Koch**, volunteered to read the book, and like Brenda, he read it twice. His feel for storytelling and knowing when an anecdote has gone on far too long has made *Never Leave on a Friday* a so much better and mercifully shorter book. He knew when to cut chapters into two and showed me where this could happen, when I couldn't see it myself. His constant support was an energizing boost throughout this process.

I went to my first and only high school class reunion (60th) not long ago and got reacquainted with classmate and former Navy man, **Dave Bennett**, (Captain, US Navy Retired) who, I discovered, had spent a lot of time sailing with his wife, Carol. He graciously agreed to read the manuscript with an eye toward checking out sailing details. His suggestions and corrections regarding sailboats, sailing, and more were invaluable. His approval of *Never Leave* was a shot in the arm that kept me going.

Cory Shepherd, whom you will recognize as one of the characters in the book, added so much to this narrative by being willing to share the details of his memories of that 1987/88 trip when he was a teenager. Thank you, Cory, for being a brave and caring crew member. In truth, you were a better crew member and a better cook! than I was. We depended on you to help us stay alive and afloat in rough weather and critical times. It was a far, far better, safer, and more fun trip for your presence.

My fourth son, (Andrew) **Drew Shepherd**, contributed by reading for continuity, which was sorely needed. Because I made up boat names and kept changing the owners' names, he had to keep the couples together and always on the correct boat. His other big contribution was to come up with many of the chapter titles when I was stumped. Some of these titles were the inspiration for the chapter sketches.

My second son, **Mike Shepherd**, himself a published author, contributed critical moral support throughout the process of writing this book. Lending me his energy, cheering me on, he kept me focused and urged me onward. The next to last reader, he found hundreds of places for corrections and improvements. I am so grateful for this.

Carol Sturtevant, an educator in Spanish and English, began by doing some much needed correcting of the Spanish in this book. In the process, she agreed also to check the English. Thank goodness. Carol's excellent eye and very fine attention to detail rescued *Never Leave*, after I thought it was pretty good to go. She worked tirelessly, and I will be forever grateful.

BOSN3, **James C. Bridges**, U.S. Coast Guard, graciously checked out the scenes that involve the Coast Guard and gave me some additional information. He also provided the photo that I used for the chapter title sketch. Thank you, Jim.

My grandson **Dustin Shepherd**, Miranda's twin brother, lent his hand when it was critically needed: when it was time to upload and format the book on Amazon. Though Dustin has lived with me most of his life, I had no idea he has such a grasp of how to use a formatting program. He rescued my sketches when I was ready to give up and leave them out. He did in days what would have taken me weeks to accomplish, and the end result is far superior to what I would have settled for.

My middle son, of five, if you're counting, **Garrett Shepherd**, did the proof reading after the book was formatted. An incredibly busy man with a demanding job and a large family, he found the time, and I don't know how. But thank goodness for his efforts!

I am particularly fortunate to have friend **Tomasz Wachowski**, who is a computer genius. Through all my trials and tribulations with electronics, he always came to my rescue and kept my computers and printers running. He got me out of trouble every time I messed things up. So many times. Certainly, without him, I could never have completed this book. He also designed my website.

Janet Norton, a talented Maine artist, produced the cover art. With only my scribbled sketch on a piece of notebook paper to go by, she understood my idea and did a superb job.

The only one of my sons who was not involved in the writing/editing/proofreading of the manuscript is my oldest son **Bill Shepherd**, who appears in the pages of this book. He was our constant, trustworthy contact, reliably handling so many business and personal details for us, including our finances. He was also our link with everybody back home, and he always had our backs.

Hey, guys. I hope you all enjoyed this journey that we took together in writing *Never Leave on a Friday*. You are in my heart, and I'm forever in your debt.

Made in the USA
Lexington, KY
28 October 2019

56125152R00247